Books by Tony Scaduto

BOB DYLAN: AN INTIMATE BIOGRAPHY
HANDLING YOUR MONEY
GETTING THE MOST FOR YOUR MONEY

MICK JAGGER

MICK JAGGER
Everybody's Lucifer

Tony Scaduto

David McKay Company, Inc.

NEW YORK

MICK JAGGER

LIBRARY OF CONGRESS CATALOG CARD NUMBER: 74–81264

ISBN 0–679–50452–4

MANUFACTURED IN THE UNITED STATES OF AMERICA

For Stevie, whose voice fills all
the silences, like the wind's soft
loving:
And for Lillian Roxon, whom I miss
very much, and who has left us all
feeling so empty because we'll
never see her again.

What is evil? I don't know how much people think of Mick as the Devil or as just a good rock performer. There are black magicians who think we are acting as unknown agents of Lucifer and others who think we are Lucifer. Everybody's Lucifer.—KEITH RICHARD

BOOK ONE

BRIAN JONES WAS still alive back then. But just barely so. His drugged and wounded and forlorn figure hung like a ghost over everyone connected with the Rolling Stones. Even Mick Jagger had finally become concerned about Brian's deterioration, and his concern seemed rather remarkable: The one trait noticed by all who know Jagger is his ability to sidestep personal problems and postpone facing up to them by pretending the unpleasant will go away if ignored long enough; of being able to "abstract" himself, as he's put it, from emotional situations. But the problem of Brian Jones refused to go away.

The public Jagger was submerged now, Marianne Faithfull later recalled. Here in his town house in Cheyne Walk, near the Thames, he appeared worried about Brian. Jagger. Head Stone. The great rock Father. The androgynous yin/yang totem who figures in the sexual fantasies of little girls and big men. The jagger (Old English for knifer, he once said), whose enormous talents as a performer rest at rock bottom on his ability to portray both raper and raped and to insinuate himself into the psyches of all who desire to ravish or be ravished.

This was another kind of Jagger, she felt, in one of his rare moments of sensitivity. He was concerned about Brian because of the drama that Marianne was enacting before him in their kitchen. Marianne had asked the *I Ching* a question about Brian and was tossing the coins for the answer. Jagger had often told friends that religion and the occult were meaningless, despite the superstitious streak in him that made him often believe in astrology, the Tarot cards, handwriting analysis, and the *I Ching*. Apparently he believed, but he didn't want to believe because the superstitious nature clashed too violently with the other Jagger.

That other Jagger is composed of an irrepressible energy that forces him to constantly be on the move, and that is not satisfied unless he is camping it up on stage or working in a studio with his band. And, most of all, a driving ambition that appears to totally dominate him. Jagger is the man John Lennon has said is still "king of the scene" after ten years because he has a power lust and because he has never lost that adolescent need for ego-gratification that more mature pop stars eventually turn their backs on. In the beginning of the fantasy called the Rolling Stones, when the group was formed and she would go to watch them play in small clubs, and grew close to Jagger, Chrissie Shrimpton understood that he appeared soft and vulnerable on the surface, but that he was hard and tough deep inside. Others caught a feeling of cruelty and ruthlessness (their words to describe him). That contrast between the hard and the soft was one of the things that made Jagger so appealing, Chrissie remembers; if he had been totally hard he wouldn't have been a sympathetic person. Chrissie, and other women and men in Jagger's life, recognized something else about him: that he had a strong ambition, was unscrupulous, didn't want anyone to stand in his way, and actually got rid of those who did get in the way of his need to dominate his group and the pop music scene.

But the hard, ambitious and urbane Londoner that most of his closest friends knew seemed to Marianne now transformed as he somehow became open and receptive to the *I Ching*, let its subtleties and vibrations flow over him. Marianne tossed the last three coins, seeking an answer to the question that had nagged at them all for months. What was going to happen to Brian now that he had been formally, but not yet publicly, fired from the Stones, the group he had helped create?

Marianne interpreted the coins, drew the final line to complete the hexagram. She leafed through her worn copy of the Book of Changes and found the hexagram that corresponded to the one she had drawn. Hexagram 29, the Chan Hexagram. She read aloud in the cultured voice that she knew had enraptured Jagger through the three years they'd been living together.

"It's about the nature of water." Looking sad and a little frightened, almost like Ophelia, she said Brian was a *Pisces*. The water sign. And it said Brian was going into a dangerous defile. Where the water was. A pit, a perilous cavity. There would be *evil*, it said. And the second line warned that he was in *all* the peril of the defile, but soon he'd get a little of the deliverance he sought. *What* deliverance? Water closing over him?

Jagger seemed annoyed to Marianne, possibly because he thought she was acting. But she wasn't acting. She was quite horrified by what she was reading. She read on now, more quickly.

She saw that the third line said *everything* is peril for Brian, and unrest, *any*thing he tried would lead him deeper into the cavern. The fourth and fifth lines were a little better, they said the water hadn't completely filled up the cavern yet. "And there will be no error."

Marianne took a deep swallow from her glass of red wine and quoted the book's interpretation of the last line of the Hexagram:

3

"The topmost line, divided, shows its subject bound with cords of three strands or two strands, and placed in a thicket of thorns. But in three years he still does not learn the course for him to pursue. There will be evil." She told Jagger that the book stressed evil and that Brian would die. And there was one part she hadn't read. It said that if someone didn't teach him about the seasons of peril Brian would never come out of it. "The book's telling us to go to him," she said.

"Let's drive down there." Jagger's Yardley-red lips, almost a caricature of the Jean Shrimpton ads in the pages of *Vogue*, seemed to her to have suddenly been brushed with chalk. Within minutes they were in his white Bentley driving across the Albert Bridge and into the country. It was one of those early spring days in England that makes the dismal, rain-sodden winter worth living through, the warm March sun intensifying the gold of the daffodils that bloom everywhere to announce the arrival of the season, daffodils in sooty window boxes, the borders of suburban tract homes, and the formal gardens of the aristocracy. Jagger drove fast. His driving usually frightened Marianne, and almost everyone who was forced to suffer through it, but Marianne's fear for Brian made her forget to worry about the always-real possibility that they would smash against a tree or a wall.

"Mick, do you think he's going to die?"

Jagger pulled round a Morgan, almost the precise copy of the custom car he had owned and loved and finally stopped using because he had ordered one of his aides to get a new paint job done on it and, after the original paint had been stripped away, couldn't make up his mind about the new color for almost a year. He was like that in so many things, postponing decisions almost as if he hoped they'd resolve themselves. Women of whom he'd grown tired would be especially hurt when they realized Jagger had mentally ended the relationship long before the actual break, but had been unable to inform them it was over.

4

"I wish Brian wasn't staying at Redlands."

Jagger didn't respond. There was no need to. Redlands is the thatched mansion south of London in which Brian was temporarily living while the home he had just bought was being renovated and made ready for him. Redlands, with the moat all around filled with water. *The "perilous cavern" of the I Ching?* Marianne wondered. Keith Richard's mansion, and Anita Pallenberg's. She had once been Brian's woman and now was Keith's, was expecting Keith's baby in August. *Keith and Anita—the thicket of thorns?* Marianne shuddered, trying to concentrate on how to save Brian from the fate so delicately and cruelly etched by the *I Ching.* Save him, really, from his own death wish, so obvious to all who knew him.

From the very beginning, even before the group came together and before Brian had suggested the name Rolling Stones, from the title of a Muddy Waters song, Brian would deliberately drive himself into situations which would get out of hand. Violent situations with which he couldn't cope. Brian was completely uncertain of himself, since the earliest days. He was always telling other members of the group, "I don't know whether I should continue trying to be a musician," and he was easily the best musician among them. Sometimes, during the early months, when the group couldn't get club dates, Brian would break down and cry and say, "I think I'll give it up 'cause we're never going to get anywhere." His insecurity made it necessary for him to prove something. He would pick an argument with a customer in a club, knowing he was certain to get beaten up, knowing he was physically weak and emotionally fragile, and he would take a terrible beating. He was the most aggressive of them without being built for it physically, and it seemed to friends that he was asking for destruction; a slightly built 145-pounder, he always picked on 200-pound giants. All the needling of the audience that went on when the Stones were first beginning to excite crowds was done by Brian, jumping to the edge of the stage

5

and snapping a tambourine in their faces, leering at them, daring them to attack him, and then dancing back out of reach. His performances made his friends wonder about Brian's balance. And for every beating he took, and every hurt he inflicted on others, the insecurity he was trying to fight seemed to grow deeper.

But it was more than Brian's self-destructive nature that made his friends feel strongly, this early spring of 1969, that Brian would soon die. It was, also, the neglect of friends. The cruelty and revenge they inflicted on him. It was incidents that seemed small, almost hilarious, at the time. Such as sneaking him out of the hospital after he became ill from a drug overdose, and immediately feeding him the acid that was destroying him. And the major incidents: Keith Richard taking from Brian Anita Pallenberg, whose constant presence with the group as almost a sixth Stone was a reminder of what Brian had lost, acting like a corrosive that ate away his self-respect. Even Brian's parents knew how deeply he felt about Anita and realized that little pieces had begun flaking off Brian's soul when she left him for Keith.

And Brian's feeling, not far off the mark despite his extreme paranoia, that Jagger was jealous of his musical ability. Brian played a special role in the band, a musician's musician who seemed to be everywhere at once, whose function within the band was to use all the instruments he had mastered to create the ringing harmonics that gave to the Stones' music the texture and embroidery that made them the so-called "greatest rock-and-roll band in the world." Brian's music was the strength and the weight that brought the Stones together in the beginning and held it like glue through the trip to super-stardom. Brian had always felt he started the group, and was its leader. During those early years he was the only real competition to Jagger, the only other member of the group with a real identity of his own. In Germany and the Scandinavian countries Brian was the star of the group, its raunchy public

6

image. All the others, even Jagger, were part of the pale background color. At the start it didn't matter very much, and no one disputed Brian's leadership. Only when the fame and adulation and wealth overtook them, and it became worthwhile for someone to dispute his leadership, did Jagger, Keith, and the Stones' manager, Andrew Oldham, ease Brian into a secondary role.

The entire time that she lived with Jagger and knew the Stones at close hand, Chrissie Shrimpton realized that none of them liked Brian. It was difficult to like him because he was frustrated in so many things. Although he was a fine musician, he couldn't play as well as he wanted to play and was unable to get into his music the sounds he heard in his head. He was almost strong enough to control the group, but not quite strong enough, and often compensated with a flash of ego. At one time Brian used to travel in a Rolls with his girl friend during concert tours, while everyone else jammed into a mini. Jagger,
Keith, and Andrew reacted by criticizing him constantly, criticizing his stage performance and his personal life. And the other members of the band would go along because they didn't know how to stop the flow of bad feelings. Several times Chrissie saw Brian try very hard to get back into Jagger's favor, as she puts it, but Jagger had grown suspicious of him. And eventually Brian believed Jagger was trying to destroy him, out of jealousy, hoping to remove the only real competition.

Actually, by the time Brian was dismissed from the band there no longer was a place in it for him, because his musicianship had deteriorated so appallingly that he couldn't play even passably well. The drugs contributed to that, of course. And the police, who seemed to sense that Brian was weak and couldn't take harassment, and who frequently raided his home and arrested him for possession. On at least one occasion the drugs appeared to have been planted in his flat; Brian

7

swore to closest friends to whom he had no reason to lie that the cannabis found in his place had been brought there by police, who promptly threw him in the nick as a public menace. And everyone who knew what was happening understood that the authorities were trying to break Brian, one of the symbols of those dirty Rolling Stones, as the American police broke Lenny Bruce.

Yet even more critical than the drugs, in Brian's deterioration, was the way Jagger and Keith continued to undermine his shaky confidence even after there was no longer any question about Jagger's leadership of the group. *It's time for Mick to stop torturing Brian*, Marianne had thought after reading the *I Ching*. Perhaps it wasn't conscious, or deliberate, but it seemed a form of torture. Jagger and Keith would call the Stones into the studio for a recording session without letting Brian know, and later would instruct him to go in alone and lay down his own track, of tambourines, sitar, flute, dulcimer, or guitar. At other times, if Jagger did tell Brian of a studio date, he would be forced to sit in a corner or a small room, alone, while the other band members worked in the main studio hall. Brian wouldn't be able to play. He'd sit on a hard folding chair, his head in his hands, crying softly, and no one would go to help him. "It's us and *him*," Jagger on one occasion said to the other band members, which now included studio musicians playing horns and piano to fill the void left by Brian. And once Jagger told Brian: "You're not a good musician, man. You're just not good enough to play in the band." Brian didn't play more than a few bars on the last two albums that bear his name in the credits, because he wasn't wanted. Until all the strength had been sapped out of him, and he was fired from the greatest rock-and-roll band in the world.

"We must help Brian," Marianne said as Jagger slowed the Bentley and pulled into the entrance to the long driveway that led to Redlands. "At least stop the evil flow between you."

8

Jagger said that's why they had driven down.

"It's gone far enough. It's time for you and Brian to be friends."

Tom Keylock, Brian's chauffeur, opened the front door and smiled quickly to hide the frown that flickered across his face. He had originally been Keith's chauffeur but Keith had become annoyed at some of his habits and let him go. Now he was Brian's man: fifty quid a week and all the fringe benefits that come with working for a superstar. Keylock led Marianne and Jagger into the drawing room, where Brian was sitting before the fire with his girl friend, Suki Potier. Marianne went to Brian, kissed him, held him close. Tried to examine him without appearing to do so. He wore a gold brocade Arab caftan down to the floor. His gold-blond hair, cut in bangs, almost covered his eyes, as if he were trying to hide those drug-dimmed eyes that had once sparked with mischief.

Marianne chattered a bit, nervous, trying to put Brian at ease. She had, after all, come to save his life, and how do you tell someone like Brian that he's going to die soon if he's not careful? The first rush of words from Marianne trailed off, and Jagger picked it up. "Just wanna see how you're doing," he said.

"I'm okay. Off drugs and getting back to drinking, like in the old days." He waved a bottle of Guinness.

Jagger laughed and said he was pleased. The four of them laughed. But Brian's laughter was cut short, and what he was feeling and wrestling with poured over Marianne, for she knew him intimately enough to understand, without a word passing between them. Brian had always been as paranoiac as any man can be, but in the last year or so his suspicions of everyone and everything around him had grown worse. Brian's emotional and psychological balance rested on such a precarious fulcrum that he trusted no one, nor what they said to him. It was almost impossible to make a straight statement to Brian and have him believe it because he was always working out what was really meant, what the motivations behind the statement were. Much of the time he decided that what was said actually meant something else. Something nasty and vicious.

But he let Jagger's remark pass this time and asked his chauffeur to open some wine and cook lunch. Jagger said they couldn't stay that long. They had just dropped in to see how he was doing. Brian insisted that they eat with him. Jagger didn't argue the point. He seldom knows how to say a firm "no" when he wants to turn something down, because he's never certain that he should. And by not refusing from the outset he makes it appear he is agreeing. When the refusal does finally come it often leaves wounded feelings.

They talked for a long while, about drugs and musicians who had become junkies, and then backed away from that subject because it was too close to what Brian had gone through. He had been on pills, acid, heroin, every form of narcotic a man can screw into his brain, and at least a small part of him blamed Jagger, Keith, Anita. Blamed them for robbing something from his soul, destroying his ego, turning him into a drugged-out vegetable. A man who no longer believed he was a musician, or even a human being. Yet Brian never understood what it was all about—that everyone was carving slices out of everyone else and because he was the most fragile and the most breakable he would be the one to die. And it was strange, because Brian had seemed to be the strong one in the beginning. When he began to weaken, to disintegrate, Jagger had been too busy with career and the business side of pop music, and was not sensitive enough to understand that enough slices had been carved out of Brian to feed all the flashing egos in the pop industry.

Marianne deftly turned the conversation away from drugs because she herself had just been hooked on heroin, four jacks a day and "friends" to shoot her up because she couldn't stand to shove the needle into her arm, and though she was certain

10

Jagger had not yet become aware of her addiction she didn't want to risk his discovering it now through some offhand remark in her talk with Brian. Jagger doesn't take drugs, except for occasionally snorting coke, because he has an excess of energy anyway and because he's afraid drugs will spoil his complexion and his figure. Marianne began talking about her acting, to get out of the dangerous waters they'd been treading. She was excited about her role as Ophelia in Tony Richardson's production, a role that won her good critical notices. "Tony's going to film it soon, at the Roundhouse. It was so weird, playing Ophelia. Because after a while I wasn't just playing a part. I *was* Ophelia."

"Yeah, me ducky," Brian said. "And I'm Hamlet: 'Get thee to a nunnery.' "

"Methinks all me years in a fuckin' nunnery were enough, methinks."

Brian laughed, skipping about for a few steps, his eyes almost beginning to light up that brilliant blue they once had been. He seemed to be coming alive. "You've been out of that convent school for five years and you're still bitchin' about the nuns!" he shouted, holding his arms out to her with a feeling of joy. But just then Tom Keylock came into the room carrying a large Moroccan tray with a roast and several steaming casseroles on it, said that dinner was ready, and Jagger rose from his cushion in front of the fire. He pulled Brian aside and asked him not to let Tom know, but that he couldn't eat his cooking. He said that everything Tom cooked always looked so grimy to him, and everyone knew how he was about food.

Brian's translucent skin flared into a pale pink. "You just don't want to eat with me," he whined. "You really can't stand to be around me."

Jagger denied it, and it wasn't true; he simply would not have been able to get down the meal because he is as fastidious about his food as he is about his clothing and makeup, and he didn't consider the chauffeur a proper sort of cook.

11

"Look, we'll come back later," Jagger said. "I really want to talk with you." He turned to Marianne: "Let's go. We'll come back a little later."

"Oh, Mick, please let's stay."

"I really can't. Must run a few errands."

Marianne couldn't tell Jagger what she was feeling. Not in front of Brian, and not to a man she'd been living with for years but was still unable to communicate her real feelings to because, she had always felt, he didn't really want to hear them. She wanted to say it now, but she couldn't get it out: *If you refuse to eat with Brian you'll destroy all the good you've been trying to do. Why can't you see that?*

Jagger said they would be back in a couple of hours. He took Marianne's arm and propelled her toward the door. Brian simply stared at him.

They returned about two hours later, after eating and drinking in a local pub. As Jagger walked across the drawing room toward the table on which lay the remains of the roast he had spurned, Brian picked up a steak knife and waved it in front of him. His voice was shrill and painful to hear: "I'm going to kill you. You don't deserve to live." Jagger smiled, uncertainly, but the smile was quickly erased as Brian lunged at him. Jagger sidestepped the knife thrust. Marianne cried out; Suki buried her face in the divan as Jagger skipped around it, trying to put distance and furniture between himself and Brian. But Brian continued to press after him, and Jagger stepped quickly to the table and picked up a carving knife, to defend himself. Brian came at him again, unsteadily, dancing at Jagger with the knife held low, and Jagger parried the attack. With only grunts from Brian punctuating each thrust, they fought wordlessly across the drawing room, Brian attacking and Jagger on the defensive, slipping out of reach each time Brian swung the knife at him. *It could be an Errol*

Flynn B picture if it wasn't so damned serious, Marianne thought. She was too frightened to do anything but call out for Tom Keylock, who didn't respond and apparently had vanished somewhere within the huge home. Brian was actually trying to stab Jagger, trying to drive his knife into the body he'd come to hate, Marianne saw clearly now. Once more, as he had always done, Brian was forcing a confrontation that could only lead to disaster. For Jagger was faster, in better condition, and he could have stabbed Brian any time he wanted to. But he wouldn't think of stabbing Brian, of course, any more than he'd ever be able to understand, or admit, that his driving competitive spirit, his need to dominate, and all his equivocations had contributed to Brian's deterioration and had led to this insane fight.

The knife fight carried through French doors out to the terrace at the back of the house, Brian trying even harder in the fading sunlight to drive his knife into Jagger's body and Jagger dancing away, among the rhododendrons, leaping and twirling as he does on stage, gracefully awkward. His teeth worried against his huge and extraordinary red lips that usually hung off his face like chunks of beef liver but now were sucked into his mouth as he concentrated on avoiding Brian's knife. They danced and stumbled to the edge of the moat. Brian's legs suddenly locked tight. He stood there, panting, his hair almost floating as he shook his head, no, no, repeatedly shaking his head. "I don't want to live," he said, his voice husky and knotted. He threw his knife down at his feet, walked slowly and deliberately to the moat, jumped in feet first, and sank beneath the sun-flecked water. Jagger hesated only a moment and jumped in after him. He wrestled Brian to the edge of the moat and shoved him up and onto the grass.

Spitting out water, Brian said, "I don't want to live on the same earth with you." He struggled to his feet and shoved Jagger aside. "I can't kill you, so I'll die instead." He jumped into the moat again. Three times Brian tried to slip beneath the waters of the moat, and each time Jagger rescued him. After pulling him out the third time, Jagger put his arm around Brian's shoulders and gently, almost lovingly, led him back to the drawing room, past Marianne and Suki at the French doors where they had been watching, unable to speak. Jagger and Brian gulped down some sherry and went upstairs together to change out of their wet clothes. When they came down again they seemed to have been transformed from violent enemies into close friends.

It didn't last long. When Jagger and Marianne were ready to return to London later that night the drawing room was filled with the leaden air of a doom that had been simply delayed. Brian had been forced into the insufferable position of being grateful to Jagger for saving his life and, Marianne realized, that kind of debt, piled upon hatred, made Brian's hatred grow stronger. Jagger's one attempt, his only attempt as far as Marianne knew, to personally reach out to Brian and save him, had failed miserably. They didn't speak much on the way back to London. Marianne wasn't certain whether Jagger understood that he'd failed, and she couldn't bring herself to try and explore his feelings. Jagger, as usual, didn't volunteer.

About a month after the fight, Jagger called Alexis Korner. "You know Brian's out of the band?" Alex said he had heard it. "Alex, will you see if you can do anything with Brian? He's in bad shape. Maybe you can talk to him." Alex promised to help, if it was at all possible.

After the phone call from Jagger Alex couldn't help flashing back on those early days, his first contacts with Jagger and the birth of the Rolling Stones.

He had been responsible for bringing the Rolling Stones together. He'd been playing black American blues since long before any members of the Stones were born, although he was only about a dozen years older than any of them. By the late 1950s, in the days when jazz groups dominated the popular music club scene, Alex for the first time had been able to get a hearing for his blues in a London club. In March 1962, Alexis' group, Blues Incorporated, opened at the Ealing Club as the steady Saturday night band. It was a breakthrough, of sorts, for the blues: Alex had to fight the purists who insisted that white men couldn't play black blues, and he had to contend with the knowledge that only about 100 people in the entire British Isles would pay to hear the blues. But as the word spread about this strange thing happening up at the Ealing Club, Alex gradually discovered that little pockets of young musicians in every part of the country were also listening to and playing the music of Elmore James and Big Bill Broonzy and Slim Harpo, had actually formed bands of their own, and were coming to Ealing to hear Blues Incorporated.

Among those playing that music were Jagger, Keith, Dick Taylor, and several other nineteen-year-olds from suburban country down around Dartford. Jagger's group called itself Little Boy Blue and the Blue Boys. Jagger was Little Boy Blue, the lead singer who couldn't read music and didn't play an instrument. The name was Jagger's idea: "I like the sound of it, man, it tells them we're playin' the blues." They never thought of playing professionally, Dick Taylor remembers, because they also didn't think there was anyone else in the entire country who was interested in American black music. Especially not the black, urban rhythm and blues, with electric amplification, that the Blue Boys had begun to play.

"We knew we were maybe among thirty or forty people who listened to and played that kind of music," Dick Taylor says. "And then one day Keith and I were at art school and we picked up *Melody Maker* and saw an advert announcing that this jazz club in Ealing had started one night a week with Alexis and his group, and there was a picture of the group. We showed it to Mick as fast as we could and his reaction, all our reactions, was: 'What! This can't be happening. This can't be true. Let's go and see what it's all about.' "

Jagger borrowed his father's car, and they drove up to the Ealing Club the following Saturday to listen to Alex and his group. From then on they'd drive or take the train into London every Saturday to watch Blues Incorporated, which included Brian Jones playing some Elmore James and Muddy Waters numbers, including "Rolling Stone."

Little Boy Blue and the Blue Boys had made a tape of their very limited repertoire some months earlier. Although the tape has long since been lost, Dick still remembers the songs they recorded: "One of them is still very clear in my head, Mick singing 'La Bamba' of all things. That was a favorite record of his, 'La Bamba' by Richie Valens. He got all the words off the record, in pseudo-Spanish, words that sounded like Spanish but weren't real words at all. And we also re-corded a couple of Chuck Berry songs— 'Around and Around' and 'Reeling and Rocking,' our favorite rhythm and blues number. And the Jimmy Reed thing, 'Bright Lights, Big City.' And Mick sent the tape off to Alexis in the post."

Alexis hadn't realized the boys had been coming to the club to see his band until he got the tape from Jagger, and a follow-up phone call a few days later. Jagger talked about the blues for a while, and Alex told him to come by the club so they could talk further. "Mick was completely interested in the music, totally committed to the blues. But he was mostly into the *image* of the music, the image of the performance, which no one else was into yet. He had an enormous amount of energy. I also sensed at the time that he had a lot of ruth-lessness, which he didn't really show in those first few months we were together. It was something I just sensed. I think at the time Mick was quite soft, really, on the surface. But there was some physical thing about him that made me feel a ruthless-ness, a certain cruelty in Mick which I couldn't pinpoint at the time. Just the vibes I got from him, a certain feeling. I didn't get that from Brian as immediately as I got it from Mick. Yet in a matter of months it was Brian who was aggressing and being violent on stage. The violent image of the Stones was much more centered on Brian than on Mick. Only later did Mick begin to get strong, but even from the beginning I always felt that Mick had the ultimate strength and the little streak of cruelty and ruthlessness. It may very easily have been Mick's defense mechanisms operating, making himself seem more cruel than he was and thus less likely to suffer attack. But the feeling of cruelty and ruthlessness was definitely there. And also his sullenness, which is what I thought it was at the time. But he wasn't sullen so much as he was shy. He was just shy and didn't talk very much. Yet it came across as sullen. And that was a part of the attraction of Mick."

He called Brian now, in 1969, in an attempt to save his life. While Alex didn't think of his mission that starkly, there was a definite feeling among most people who were familiar with the conflict between Brian and Jagger that Brian was racing toward his death.

Brian was pleased at Alex's call, and apologetic: "I'm sorry that I haven't been in touch with you in so many years, Alex. But a lot of strange things have happened since the old days."

"That's fine, I understand," Alex said. And Brian never mentioned the missing years again. He invited Alex down to Cotchford Farm near Hartfield, in Sussex, the home he had bought the year before from the estate of A.A. Milne and had recently moved into. Brian left Redlands behind, hopefully along with all its bad vibes. Alex had never been there before and he had difficulty finding the road to the house at the edge of the Ashdown Forest, until he finally decided to drive into a leafy tunnel that led off a small bank. Almost immediately, he felt he'd entered another kind of world. Huddled under a bank was a delightful old steep-roofed farmhouse, and as he came down the wide sweep of gravel drive toward the house he could see garden and meadow, with a wood of small trees and bushes beyond it. Further off he could see the hills of the forest. Brian came out to the terrace as Alex was getting out of his car, and he insisted on showing his guest around the garden, which was filled with stone images of Pooh and Piglet and Christopher Robin.

"It's great living out here," Brian said. "Gives me a feeling of peace." They strolled through the garden, and then into the house, and Brian began to talk about the massive hurts he had felt in his final years as a Rolling Stone. He had been deliberately isolated from the group by Jagger and Keith, he said, and had not even been told about recording sessions until Jagger felt he was ready to have Brian come into the studio to put his little bits on after the main track had been laid down. And Brian felt that Jagger and Keith had been engineering his isolation from the group in an attempt to drive him out by making him feel he was not a member of the Stones and was only in there for old time's sake and a few legal complications. He was very upset as he talked to Alex, and very vicious in the things he said about Jagger. But Alex wasn't surprised at the viciousness: "Brian had always been very vicious, he always overstated everything whenever he wanted to make a point."

"The thing that hurts the most," Brian said, "is that there's never been any Rolling Stone hits written by Brian Jones. I don't want to say anything, man, but it's all Jagger/Richard, all Jagger/Richard. What about *my* songs? They never used any of my songs. They wanted it all for themselves, the publishing money, the royalties, the ego-thing about writing songs. They wouldn't let me into it. They wouldn't ever give me a chance to do the things I want to do. My kind of music. That's why I stopped digging the Stones and what they stand for."

He rose suddenly and poked angrily at a few logs in the unlighted fireplace. The drawing room was of a strange shape, with unexpected nooks and crannies, possibly enlarged from several smaller rooms. The mantel ran completely across the breadth of the huge chimney, then unexpectedly turned a corner to run at right angles along the edge of the chimney. The fireplace itself was a very tiny opening for such an enormous chimney. Above the opening, half circles of brick rose in ever-widening radii to repeat the half-moon shape of the fireplace opening. Brian traced a forefinger along the grouting of the brick face, trying hard to control himself.

"I don't know what the hell they thought they were doing with the *Satanic Majesties* album. I don't understand it or dig it, musically. That's not Rolling Stone music. That's not any kind of real music. I don't like that kind of playing, I don't like the way the Stones have gone in the last year. I didn't get any kicks out of it anymore. No kicks from the music in a long, long time. And the personal relationships, with Mick and Keith, they've been very bad. Just dreadful, really. So I didn't see any reason to stay there. I just couldn't stay in the Stones and survive."

Brian paused, as if to catch his breath after speeding on with such anger. Then he continued, sounding very confused, slightly drunk from wine, and so angry that he could barely talk about his future in any logical way: "Think there's room for me in your new group, Alex? Like to get right out touring and playing again. Back to the old days, Elmore James and Muddy stuff." But before Alex could respond, Brian plunged on in his bitterness: "You know what they did to me? They put a nurse in the house to look after me, and she wouldn't even let me ring up friends. I got to the phone once when she wasn't looking, and she found me out and disconnected the call. They're keeping me prisoner. They're trying to destroy my ego. They're keeping me quiet. And on top of all that, they keep moving furniture out on me, stealing my furniture. Odd chauffeurs and people like that keep showing up and stealing things. I'm being robbed by everyone. They're overcharging me for the building work, and I'm certain the people who're stealing my furniture are getting a percentage of the overcharge."

He seemed almost out of control, and Alex was stunned and began to roll a joint. When Brian saw Alex lick the glue on the edge of a Zig-Zag paper and line it up carefully with another Zig-Zag and press them together, Brian halted his tirade in mid-sentence. "I wish you wouldn't smoke, Alex," he pleaded. "Can't afford another bust. They're still out to bust me, you know, and I have to stay clean now. Besides," he smiled broadly, "I'm off drugs and back into some great drinking, like in the old days. Alcohol can't hurt you much, but drugs will destroy your brain. I know, I've been through it all, through everything. Drink's a thousand percent better than dope."

Alex scrunched the papers into a ball and threw it into the fireplace, and couldn't help remembering what Brian had been like when he last saw him about a year earlier. It was in that *Satanic Majesties* period when Brian was taking a great amount of acid, and Alex was horrified at what had happened to him physically. Brian became at that time almost repulsive—Alex could understand people saying he was repulsive at one time, when he became so heavily involved in drugs. Had he not felt for Brian the way he did feel, he would have experienced the same repulsion. For Brian was, Alex remembered, like a stupid glob of jelly in that period, acting almost like one of those ga-ga French kings of 400 years ago—Alex smiled now at the thought—when they grew too old to know what they were doing, when they would sit and dodder and smile vacuously at all sorts of things. Brian was like that when he was on acid. He couldn't play, and Alex didn't like what was happening to him. But now, since being fired from the Stones, he seemed to be much improved. Alex sat there, fascinated as Brian sped on about the social scene at the village pub he'd been getting into, drinking with the locals who liked him so very much that they protected him against the local constabulary:

"Man, I got pissed in the pub one night with all the men of the village and when I got back on my Triumph I couldn't even get the damned thing started, I was so blind. I took off—vroom—and went right through a plate glass window of some shop. Got cut up and smashed hell out of the place, and I was laying there thinking it's the Scrubs for me, they'll probably plant dope on me again and put me in the Scrubs. And all the boys came rushing out of the pub and got me and my bike home and hushed up the whole thing. The coppers never came into it at all, the whole village protected me. It's a great feeling, you know."

It must be, Alex thought. Insecurity was the most obvious feature of Brian's personality, an insecurity so overwhelming that you wanted to comfort him because of it. Which is what he wants you to do. And the idea of being protected by an entire village was just the kind of ego-boost Brian so desperately needs at this point. He's pro-alcohol and down on drugs, Alex felt, because pubs are a special kind of social setting, and the type of friendships one makes there are vastly different than among heads. And Alex realized something else as Brian continued to speak against drugs and in favor of alcohol—that alcohol is a cross between a legal and a manly drug, and Brian was into alcohol because he was pulling back from the androgynous pop music scene of which Jagger was the campiest figure. A scene where the distinctions between man and woman are often blurred, where homosexuality is accepted and encouraged. Brian was now seeking another kind of image. Back to the old-time drinking and womanizing, virility and manliness, with none of the fuzzy confusions that exist in the pop world. Back to those basics because he wanted to return to the hard black blues that had originally brought him together with the other Stones, and that had vanished in the bisexual image that Jagger had created for himself. If Brian was going to return to his musical roots, he would have to remodel his entire personality. Alex felt that strongly as he listened to Brian that first day, and he felt also that even if Brian wasn't being completely realistic at least he had made a marked improvement since the last time he'd seen him.

Over the next week or so Brian and Alex talked over the phone almost daily, trying to work out ways in which Alex could help him get back into the kind of music he so desperately wanted to play. In the first conversations Brian continued to be full of hatred and paranoia.

"I want to come to town and see you, and talk," Brian said one time when Alex rang him up. "But I can't get away."

"I've got plenty of time for you."

"I just can't get to London. They won't let me. The office. They're keeping me prisoner, not letting me move around at all."

"Brian . . ."

"No, listen. The office is trying to convince me that I'm mad. I know I'm not mad. I mean, I'm *not* mad, am I? Maybe a little paranoid, acid does that to you, and the busts, that's why I'm so against drugs. Paranoid, sure. But not *mad* . . ."

Brian ran on for about ten minutes, incredibly bitter at the things he believed were being done to him. Through all his accusations he implied strongly that "the office" was acting against him through pure malice and evil. As he listened to Brian, Alex tried hard to sort fact from fiction but it was so difficult to do. What Brian was trying to get Alex to understand was that the Rolling Stones organization—employees controlled by Jagger—was deliberately trying to drive Brian over the edge. But Alex couldn't believe that, no matter how sincere Brian sounded. He didn't want to believe, but he wasn't certain whether he should believe. *I believe some things,* he thought as Brian continued his long series of complaints, *I can believe Brian is being ripped off around his house, I can believe that. But would the office restrict his freedom of movement in any way except certain occasions when it's very much to Brian's disadvantage to be free to move? Because he isn't in very good shape. But Brian certainly believes the office is doing things out of evil.*

When Brian had run out of steam and rung off, Alex put down the phone, inhaled deeply, and let it all out: "Ooooooph!" He had to sit down for a few minutes because Brian's soliloquy had been so intense and devastating.

During those couple of weeks, as Brian continued to use Alex as an unofficial psychiatrist, getting much of the anger out of his soul, Alex realized that Brian was unable to talk about something that was obviously weighing quite heavily on him: his loss of Anita Pallenberg. They had been living together since 1965 and had created what friends call an evil court scene, Brian as flaked-out king and Anita as queen and some kind of witch who seemed almost beyond human dimensions and who had an almost magical control over her consort and the entire court. Even back then Marianne Faithfull and so many others realized that Keith wanted Anita desperately. But she was with Brian, and the antagonism began to grow and the sores to fester. In 1966, with Brian going under because of the drugs and his dissatisfaction with the music—they were planning the *Satanic Majesties* album then—Anita went off with Keith while Brian was in a Swiss hospital being treated for what was officially called "pneumonia." Anita returned to Brian after he was released from the hospital. But weeks later, during a brief vacation trip to Morocco, Brian was completely out of his skull on acid and kif. While listening to a group of Arab musicians playing music that had induced in True Believers trances, visions of gods, and primeval forces, Brian believed he had undergone a mystic transfiguration and had become a True Believer. And somehow, in his drugged state, he became separated from Anita, Keith, Jagger, Marianne, and several others in the party. He was stranded in a hotel in Tangiers with no money, no way of getting home, with Anita once more off somewhere with Keith. Anita never returned to Brian. It demolished him.

Alex never asked about Anita, of course, and Brian said very little. "He talked about her just a bit. Oh, the Anita Pallenberg thing was very heavy for him, and he couldn't talk about it. He talked about Morocco most of all, and I was always distrustful of that, his saying his whole philosophical bent had been changed so much since he'd been to the Middle East. Brian, Keith, and Anita. It was all involved with Morocco, he said. Morocco was an important thing to Brian. He talked to me more about the music there than the personal problems. He talked so little about Anita that one was well aware of her effect on him. He did say something once, but it was just a sort of throw-away thing. 'I'm not interested in Anita anymore.' That's all he said. Deliberately not making a play on the situation between himself and Keith over Anita. He could never bring himself to believe that Keith had actually taken her away. That would never come into any statement of his."

By the third or fourth week in the spring of 1969, as he and Alex began to seriously plan for Brian's return to music, he calmed down considerably. He began to seem closer to the old Brian, up high with excitement and enthusiasm about the music, desperately needing to make it, flashing once more that very strong drive to make it big as a musician that he once had in the earliest days of the Rolling Stones. Alex was planning a tour of Germany and Scandinavia with a group he had just formed, New Church, and Brian wanted to join them. But Alex gently talked him out of it. Brian wasn't quite together enough to play with a group, Alex felt. But most of all Alex was a little frightened because Brian had always been considered the leader of the Stones in Germany, had always been more popular there than Jagger, and New Church would have insurmountable security problems with Brian along. Brian then suggested that if he couldn't fit into New Church, why didn't they form another band together? A blues band.

"He talked a lot about the old days, as if I wanted to hear about getting back to the old days. I'm not in favor of revivalist movements, I didn't want to go back over the old ground. I dug some of his ideas, the things he wanted to do with Creedence Clearwater bits and the James Cleveland gospel bits, but I didn't dig going back to doing the Muddy Waters and Elmore James thing, didn't dig his ideas about using the Mezzrow-Bechet with soprano, either. Those are some of the things Brian was talking about, musically, the kind of band he had in mind. It seemed for me, personally, like a retrogression. That's why I withdrew immediately from any possibility of forming a band with him. That's why I cut out. But Brian never knew that. I kept that secret from him because, even though I couldn't go back over the old ground, I had no intention of undermining Brian's need to go back. So I told him that I couldn't personally handle the old stuff, that I wouldn't feel comfortable at it and wouldn't sound fresh, and I would just mess up his music. And what we then decided to do was that I would help Brian get the proper musicians for him, he would play his part in the band, and I would act as a sort of musical director to see that all parts fitted together. I would be more help to him that way because I couldn't sit in the band and play and also stand outside it at the same time and hear what it sounded like. And he began talking very excitedly about the things he wanted to do, the music he wanted to play. And he was getting happy again, really enthusiastic about the band."

Alex went down to Cotchford Farm several times during the next couple of weeks. Brian had almost completely stopped complaining about Jagger and Keith, and his anecdotes about mistreatment by people in "the office" seemed a thing of the past. Neither Jagger nor any of the Stones tried to contact Alex or Brian, and Alex had a feeling there was an attitude of disentanglement on both sides. And Milne's house, Alex believed, had a subtle way of calming Brian. Alex didn't know it but during Brian's most dejected period, after Anita had left him for Keith and he had plunged so heavily into drugs that he could barely function, Brian visited his parents one Sunday afternoon. Brian's chauffeur was out on the front lawn talking to Brian's father, and he saw Brian looking out at them from an upstairs window, staring at them in a strange way, appearing young and child-like. When the chauffeur went into the house later he asked Brian: "Why were you looking out at us like that?" And Brian replied: "I just wish I could be back here, in this house."

And Alex felt strongly that Brian had found a home in Milne's former house. "Brian was very much into the idea that it was Milne's house, in which he'd written *Winnie the Pooh* and *Christopher Robin* and various things, and he was very much taken with the sundial in the garden that has an inscription from one of the Milne books on it. He was fascinated by all of it. That had an effect on him, too, of calming him. That house was good for him in many ways, and I'm sure that if he'd been living anywhere else I wouldn't have been half as useful as I was. I was there because the overall vibes of the house and the gardens were such that you could get through to gentler feelings. The house did that for Brian."

The official announcement that Brian had left the band he created came on June 9, 1969. "BRIAN JONES QUITS THE STONES AS GROUP CLASH OVER SONGS" was the headline in the *Daily Sketch*. The Stones publicity organization churned out the official line: Brian had *left* the Stones because the band no longer played the sort of music that interested

26

him. A journalist reached Brian at his home in Sussex, and he went along with the charade: "I no longer see eye-to-eye with the others over the discs we are cutting." Brian had agreed to the public relations falsification months before; Jagger and Keith had gone to see him, had told him what he already knew—that he wasn't wanted in the group any more—and had gotten him to agree to the story that he had resigned because he wanted to go his own way. That story, they told him, would be better than letting the truth be known because the truth would hurt them all. Brian went along, licking his wounds for the next few months of life left to him.

Jagger, in his brief statement about the change in the Stones, announced that Brian had already been replaced. The new man was Mick Taylor, bass guitarist, a relatively unknown twenty-year-old who had just left John Mayall's Blues Breakers when he got a call from Jagger to sit in on a recording session with the Stones as a form of audition. "I've been looking at Mick Taylor for a long time," Jagger told the press. What he also neglected to say was that he had asked Eric Clapton to join the Stones as Brian's replacement, but Clapton had turned him down because he was involved with the hyped-up superband called Blind Faith.

A couple of days after Brian's dismissal had been turned into the official pronouncement that he had quit, Jagger and Marianne drove down to Clapton's home for dinner. As they sat at an enormous table in Clapton's ballroom-sized dining room, Eric invited Jagger to a Blind Faith concert the following Sunday in Hyde Park. It was a free concert, and Blind Faith—Eric, Ginger Baker, Stevie Winwood, and Ric Grech—was the first supergroup scheduled to play in the park since the free concerts had begun the summer before.

When Jagger arrived at Hyde Park that Sunday with Marianne and a few friends, he was impressed by the size of the crowd. About 150,000 of them, more people than he'd ever seen assembled in one place in his life, the monster sort of crowd that Jagger would just love to work his magic on. Backstage, behind the amps and trucks and police lines, Jagger asked where he could find the man responsible for the concerts. He was introduced to Peter Jenner, director of the organization that had convinced government officials to permit the concerts. Jagger asked Jenner: "Would you be interested in a concert by the Stones?" Jenner didn't have to be asked twice. The Stones free Hyde Park concert was set for Saturday, July 5, and the announcement went out.

Alex drove down to Brian's estate a few days before the official announcement of the split in the Stones, and he brought with him his daughter Sappho, who is a singer, and Peter Thorup, lead singer with New Church. Brian again talked excitedly about the band he would get together and said he was looking forward to going on the road again with a band that played real music. He also said he wanted to help Sappho make a record of her own, to produce her, because he very much dug what she was doing. And Brian called Cleo Sylvester, a young black Londoner who had met the Stones in 1962, when she was in school and the band was just being formed. Cleo had almost become a Rolling Stone back then; Jagger had asked her to find two other black girls who could also sing, because he wanted the black chorus behind the band to create some further excitement. But it never came together. Now Brian called her and asked if she would sing on his first recording, once he got his new band together. Cleo laughed, thinking, *Oh, Brian no. Why do you want me recording with you? You don't need me.* Brian told her not to laugh. "I'm very serious, Cleo," he said. "You can help me with the kind of music I want to play." And Cleo promised to do whatever she could to help: "Just let me know when you want me to come in for rehearsals." Brian said, "Great, I'll ring you."

Alex Korner: "Those were all the things that Brian was going to do, things he could give himself to think about doing and maybe eventually doing. Which clearly helped him very much to calm down. He wasn't faking his enthusiasm for the band. We were constantly on the phone when I wasn't down at his place, and I was saying: 'If the first guy didn't work out, try so-and-so, here's his phone number, or would you rather I ring him and ask him to come in and try out?' And Brian would be very well into ringing musicians, and he would ring me back and say he's tried this or that musician: 'I don't really dig him but this other guy has come up, do you know anything about him?' He was really into it.

"But he was the same old Brian Jones. He'd ask me to handle it for him and then he'd go off and do things on the side himself and we'd get duplications. I didn't say anything about it, because the enthusiasm about the band and the work he was putting into it was calming him down, getting him off the hatred and bitterness. But the way he was doing things, I understood he was the same old Brian. He didn't change. He just died."

Jagger's Hyde Park concert was set, just a week away. He seemed excited about it, for this was the first Stones concert in two years. It was also the first concert without Brian. Jagger decided Brian should be at the concert, and he had Keith and Charlie Watts and several employees of the organization ring up Brian and ask him to come. To say "Hello" to the crowd and to wish his replacement, Mick Taylor, good luck. Jagger told his associates he wanted Brian there to show the world that he was in fine condition, despite the rumors that he'd been wiped out of his skull, and to demonstrate that there were no hard feelings between Brian and the Stones.

But there were other motives beneath the surface, some who were close to Jagger insist. The concert was an ego trip for Jagger. He was scheduled to fly to Australia to begin work on Tony Richardson's film *Ned Kelly*, but he postponed his flight because he simply had to draw to Hyde Park the largest crowd of freaks and heads that Britain has ever seen. And some of them believed Jagger had an even darker reason for wanting Brian to attend—to make it clear that the Stones, with Jagger firmly entrenched at their head, was still supreme in pop even without Brian; to demonstrate to the world that the group had not been diminished by Brian's departure.

Brian received several calls asking him to attend the concert in the week before the performance. But Jagger didn't ring Brian himself. On the Monday before the concert he sat in his office with Shirley Arnold, who had been director of the Stones fan club since 1962, when they were a little known group playing small clubs on the edges of London and stirring a wild excitement among pubescent girls and young rock musicians.

"Did you speak to Brian yet?" Jagger asked her. "Is he coming to the concert?"

"I think he may come."

"Be nice if he comes, maybe even play with us."

"Why don't you ring him?" Shirley suggested. "Invite him yourself. He'd like that."

Jagger seemed to be thinking it over for a moment. Then: "I don't know. Got lots of things to do, getting the concert together, get ready for Australia. Look, I'll try to call Brian. But you keep after him. He should come on Saturday. Alex and his new band're gonna be there. Brian'll dig that."

Brian Jones died three nights later.

He was at Cotchford Farm with his latest girl friend, Anna Wohlin, a twenty-two-year-old Swedish student; Frank Thorogood, a building contractor; and Janet Lawson, his nurse. Brian had been drinking heavily and dropping downers. He slipped into a pair of swim trunks around midnight, and his nurse objected: "Brian, don't go into the pool. You're in no condition to be bathing." Brian ignored her, stepped outside and dove into the water. With powerful strokes, for he was a good swimmer, he quickly made several laps of the pool.

Frank Thorogood had eased himself into a lounge chair to watch Brian. But after a while it was obvious that Brian was swimming well and diving from the board well, and Frank went into the house for a cigarette. He was gone only a few minutes and when he returned there was no sign of Brian. Frank stepped quickly to the edge of the pool. Brian was at the bottom, not moving. Frank began to take off his clothing, shouting for help at the same time, and Anna came running out of the house. She dove in, fully clad, and raised Brian to the surface. They pulled his body out of the pool, and Anna attempted to revive him by forcing his mouth open, placing her lips on his, and breathing hard into his lungs. In newspaper articles bathed in bathos, some writers called Anna "The Kiss of Life Girl." But her kiss was futile. Brian was pronounced dead on arrival at the hospital.

An inquest was held a week later. Coroner Angus Sommerville of East Grinstead ruled that Brian had died "due to immersion in fresh water . . . under the influence of drugs and alcohol." The coroner reported "severe liver dysfunction due to fatty degeneration and ingestion of alcohol and drugs." His official verdict: "Death by misadventure."

Even before Brian was interred, a rather obscene debate broke out. Question: Did Brian Jones commit suicide?

On the yes side of the debate were most of the stoned of London, who didn't know Brian at all, but who knew all the answers because to be omniscient about superstars makes their own lives seem less petty, more glamorous. And some of them had the most delicious bit of gossip to substantiate the suicide theory: Brian had been planning to come down to London to a party, the story went, with a new girl he had just met and quite fancied, but Jagger had persuaded her to go with him instead. And Brian remained at home with his friends, growing ever more despondent, until he decided to drown himself. But all those who talked so knowingly about Jagger's perfidy were unable to supply names, dates, anything concrete. Actually, Jagger was in the recording studio when Brian drowned. But those unfounded rumors are still whispered along London's pop underground.

The anti-suicide debaters were in the minority, but they included almost all those who knew Brian well. Alex Korner summed up the argument in a statement that is touched with a bit of honest doubt:

"To commit suicide you have to plan to kill yourself, and I honestly don't believe that Brian planned to die. It's possible that in a moment of paranoia, down at the bottom of the pool, he suddenly decided it would be easy to die. But I don't think so. I really think it was a goof. I don't think he deliberately planned to commit suicide. I would have felt more sorrow for him and less for me if it had been intended, but now I feel more for me and for all of us, and less for him, because he isn't here. Most of the sadness is for me, because I miss him, but I can't help thinking that if Brian had to die that was a good time for him to die. Because he was happy when he died. If it had happened six months earlier it would have been much sadder for him, because he was in a state of severe depression. At least he died when he was beginning to feel happy."

Within hours after Brian's death, the Stones and their employees came together in the Stones offices, seeking comfort in one another. Shirley Arnold got to her desk before 7 a.m., and the band members arrived soon after. Shirley sat there, sobbing quietly, and Charlie Watts tried to comfort her through his own tears. Eventually, someone raised the question of the concert: "We've got to cancel it." They all agreed: It wouldn't be right to go on with it now that Brian was dead. *They're all shattered, really shattered*, Shirley thought. She got up to look out a window, daydreaming about Brian: *He was a pain and a joy to know; so many people have screwed up Brian, all that wrong crowd he got into from the very beginning except for Alexis . . .* and then Charlie suddenly shouted:

"Let's do it for Brian! Play the concert for Brian."

"Yeah, right," Jagger said. "A memorial for Brian."

Later, when they announced the concert would go on as planned, and a journalist questioned the propriety of putting the *new* Stones on stage only two days after Brian's death, Keith Richard threw the man down a flight of stairs.

There were about 500,000 people at Hyde Park on Saturday, packed tightly together under the hot July sun, the odor of new-mown grass lost in the stench of collective perspiration, an odor not unlike the locker room at Wembley, but no one seemed offended as band after band warmed up the crowd for . . . the Rolling Stones! A mob of Hell's Angels, hired as bouncers and protectors of the body of Mick Jagger, had been lined up in front of the stage like a line of ancient harlots waiting for trade. But when the last warmup group completed its set, and a hush fell over the audience in anticipation of the Stones' grand entrance, the Angels reached for their implements of authority—tire irons and chains—to discourage any attempt by groupies of either sex to reach the stage. On a ladder to an elevated platform which held a few loudspeakers at the right of the stage, Suzy Creamcheese and Marsha Hunt (in white buckskin) sat perched, unmolested by the *machos* in Nazi helmets; Suzy was, after all, practically a founding member of Frank Zappa's Mothers of Invention, and Marsha would bear Jagger's first child a little over a year later.

As the stage crew began nailing up large color photos of Brian the Angels joined hands and crushed back the crowd, for this was it . . . the Stones are coming! Murmurs from the celebreties on and behind the stage elevated to a roar and suddenly, there he was! Mick Jagger, in a dress—a white, billowing frock with bow buttons down the front, over tight-fitting white pants cut to the tearing point in the crotch to emphasize his genitals and promote at least psychic mastur-bation, and a gold-studded leather collar around his neck to stimulate the s—m set.

The assembled congregation had been told a number of times during the day that it was the Stones' wishes that a moment of silence be observed for Brian, after the band came on stage, but at the first sight of Jagger in a white dress the crowd began to shout and applaud, and Brian was forgotten. Jagger tried to hush them. "NOOOOooo . . ." he shouted and was ignored and finally surrendered to the audience.

"Yeah!" he screamed. "We're gonna have a good time, all right?"

The crowd roared back at him—"All right!"—and Jagger held up both arms, his dress billowing, his makeup garish in the daylight. "Cool it for a minute," he ordered. "I would really like to say something about Brian." The audience cooled it. Jagger began to recite from Shelley's *Adonais*, sounding at first like a schoolboy forced to read in front of his classmates and dreading every moment of it:

> *Peace, peace! he is not dead, he doth not sleep—*
> *He hath awakened from the dream of life—*
> *'Tis we, who lost in stormy visions, keep*
> *With phantoms an unprofitable strife,*
> *And in mad trance, strike with our spirit's knife*
> *Invulnerable nothings.—We decay*
> *Like corpses in a charnel; fear and grief*
> *Convulse us and consume us day by day,*
> *And cold hopes swarm like worms within our living clay.*

Marianne, who had suggested he read part of *Adonais*, cringed at Jagger's reading. But several girls in the front row had begun to weep at the first line, and Jagger appeared to catch the flow from them, apparently knowing that he had reached his audience and was manipulating it, and he threw himself completely into the poem. Jumping Jack Flash, stomping on Shelley's grave, and Brian's, now dancing in a frenzy, primping for the television crews and the still photographers, pumping and thrusting his pelvis. And sounding as if he were reciting Chuck Berry or Screaming Jay Hawkins, not Shelley; turning *Adonais* into "Roll Over Beethoven":

> *The One remains, the many change and pass;*
> *Heaven's light forever shines; Earth's shadows fly;*
> *Life, like a dome of many-coloured glass*
> *Stains the white radiance of Eternity,*
> *Until Death tramples it to fragments.—Die,*
> *If thou wouldst be with that which thou doest seek!*
> *Follow where all is fled,—Rome's azure sky,*
> *Flowers, ruins, statues, music, words, are weak*
> *The glory they transfuse with fitting truth to speak.*

By the time Jagger had begun to recite that final stanza, his rendition sounded something like: Oooh babba, daladaladala, boompa screech woo baby yip yip yip . . . And if any in the crowd understood this performance was rather gross, any protest that might have been made was drowned out by the sobs of those who actually believed they were hearing a eulogy rather than another kind of rock performance. At Jagger's last yip-yip the stage crew lifted the lids of small brown boxes that had been placed on stage earlier, and out fluttered several hundred little white butterflies (white to match Jagger's costume), in the final breach of good taste that the Head Stone called a memorial for Brian. Many of the butterflies flew off a few feet, and then dropped to earth, dead.

Then Jagger led his group into their rehearsal for the American tour. Musically, they were quite a mess, but the little girls didn't care; they tried to storm the stage and were hurled back into the crowd by the Angels. In a little while, after eight or ten numbers, Jagger was kissing everyone goodbye and prancing off stage, a wedge of Angels clearing a path to his military green armoured car while someone on stage was shouting into the microphones: "That's the Rolling Stones. Wow! The greatest rock-n-roll group in the world!" . . . Well, not quite, not on this performance. Of all the groups who played for the congregation, only Alex Korner's New Church came through with a set that could be considered worthy of Brian's memory, which is what the occasion was supposed to be all about.

Jagger and Marianne flew to Sidney that night to begin work on *Ned Kelly;* Marianne was cast as his sister. She had cut herself off from heroin just a few days before, to be fit for the film and to bring some sanity back to her disarranged life, and her body and her mind were being torn apart by withdrawal symptoms when the plane touched down in Australia.

She revived from her heroin haze in the hotel room. Feeling dreadfully ill, she stumbled into the bathroom and looked at her face in the mirror. She had cut her hair shortly before Brian died, cut it as short as Brian's, and now the face staring back at her from the mirror was Brian's face, not Marianne's. The trauma of heroin withdrawal, and her inability to be certain whether she was really Marianne Faithfull or simply an extension of Mick Jagger . . . she had been asking for a long time, "Who am I?" . . . and now she was seeing Brian's face in her face. Brian's death was on her conscience because she had known he would die, and she couldn't save him from death. And she thought: *It's logical that I should be dead, too. I've always been very connected to Brian, always felt I was a part of him and he a part of me.* She stared at that face, Brian's dead face in the mirror. Slowly, he began to wake: He was dead, he knew he was waking up somewhere beyond life, and

Marianne heard him say: "Where is my Valium? God, I feel awful."

And she felt even more strongly, then, that Brian had not committed suicide, that it was an accident—he had an asthmatic attack in the pool and drowned. Brian continued to speak, but Marianne heard only an occasional word. Yet she understood what he was saying, and she thought: *Brian could swim like a fish, but he was on downers, and they do make you feel like you can do things you really can't do. I think he's saying he was on downers and was overtaken by cramp and asthma and no one was around to help him. That's what he's telling me, that he feels awful because he did have suicidal moments, but not this time. And because he didn't do it on purpose he doesn't know what's happening to him. It's tragic. Realizing he's there, very cold, no friends, no Alexis, no doctor, no nothing.*

She stared at Brian, unable to speak. Finding it unnecessary to speak because she understood something very clearly: *I am Brian. I must kill myself because Brian is dead and I am Brian.*

Marianne swallowed several score Tuinol capsules, slipped quietly back into bed next to Jagger, and waited to die. And she thought about why she wanted to die: *There's something more than seeing Brian's face in my face. It's like Oscar Wilde being in prison and looking for someone to blame so he blamed it on Douglas. I'm looking for someone to blame. No addict wants to blame himself. So I'm blaming it on Mick. In many ways he let me down, as a woman, in our relationship. He failed me in so many ways, and becoming an addict and then killing myself is my revenge.*

The Rev. Hugh Hopkins, who had confirmed Brian fourteen years before, officiated at his funeral services in Cheltenham. He offered a prayer for Marianne's recovery and then read from Scriptures the story of the Prodigal Son. All the Stones were there, except Jagger, and hundreds of mini-skirted young women decorated the church. Rev. Hopkins, not to be overawed by this display of modern pop idolatry, delivered a eulogy that sounded at times as if he were blaming pop musicians for all the ills that had occurred in Western society since the Industrial Revolution: "Brian was the rebel, he had little patience with authority, convention, tradition . . . Typical of so many of his generation who have come to see in the Rolling Stones an expression of a whole attitude toward life. Much of what this ancient church stood for, for 900 years, seems actually irrelevant to them."

From among a group of musicians sitting in a forward pew came, at the end of the eulogy, a loudly whispered comment:

"At least there are no butterflies at this bloody memorial."

A short while later, as the funeral cortege drove through the gates of Cheltenham cemetery, a policeman on duty snapped a salute at the hearse, at Brian in his coffin. And Charlie Watts laughed at the absurdity of it all. And then grew angry:

"Now the bastards salute. I just hope Brian is around to see this. *Saluting* him . . ."

BOOK TWO

ONE WINTER-CHILLED afternoon in 1959 Michael Philip Jagger sat in front of a tape recorder in a rear bedroom of Dick Taylor's home, waiting for the three other boys seated around him to tune their guitars and set up the drum kit so that he could sing for them. They had been playing together as a blues group for almost a year but this rehearsal was something special: A week earlier Jagger had been in a gym class at the Dartford Grammar School, performing a set of strenuous calisthenics that were the educational system's hangover from the physical fitness programs of the war years, when he slipped and fell while trying to complete a frontal somersault and bit off the tip of his tongue. It bled a lot and hurt like hell, and Jagger couldn't talk or sing for a few days, which pleased the school masters enormously. When he did start singing again a few days later it sounded as if the quality of his voice had been changed, but he couldn't be certain because a singer's voice sounds different bouncing around inside his head than it does to everyone else hearing from the outside. He asked the other members of his band to listen to him carefully, to tell him whether something had happened to his voice.

He didn't play an instrument and really wasn't much interested in anything but singing the blues because he seemed to understand intuitively that the blues which he loved so much was a vocal music. All Afro-American music is, in its fullest form, vocal music more than instrumental; the best blues is sung blues, just as the best gospel music is music that's sung. Jagger said he felt enormous emotion about the blues and the sound of a blues voice crying out its personal pain. "I just dig the sound because the sound is so exciting," he would tell his friends, "but I can't tell you why I dig to sing it so much." Years later he would try to analyze what he felt as a young man but right now all he knew was that he simply must sing to express himself and that singing was the most viable form of expression for him. It's possible to reach more people with your voice than with an instrument, since the voice can be a very emotional instrument. Especially in the blues, which is the most emotional form of music ever created.

Jagger stood up and paced the room, his energy overload making it impossible to sit still for more than a few minutes. Dick Taylor set up the small drum kit he had inherited from his grandfather, Bob Beckwith tuned up the inexpensive guitar which was plugged into a primitive six-watt amplifier no larger than a portable radio, and Allen Etherington fondled his maracas. Finally, when they were ready, Jagger pressed the *Record* button on the tape machine, called "One, two, three," and the band banged its way into a Chuck Berry number. Jagger began to sing: "When the joint was rockin'/ Goin' round and round."

Jagger cut it off after one complete run-through, and the band ground to a halt. He asked what they thought.

Bob said he wasn't certain, there did seem to be a slight change in the quality of his voice but he didn't know precisely what it was. Dick Taylor tried to pinpoint it. He said Jagger's voice now had a fuzziness that wasn't there before, his diction and pronunciation seemed lazier, more drawling. "That's what it is," Allen said. "You've got a lazy tongue action because you bit off the tip. You can't sharpen the consonants and you sound more Negro, your voice is blacker."

Jagger played the tape back several times and then said he didn't agree; he would always deny the accident in school had changed the structure of his voice. But if the guys in the band liked it and thought he sounded more like Chuck and Muddy and Leadbelly, well . . . Over the last couple of years he had listened to the records of black American artists, even sent away to Chess Records in Chicago for recordings not available in England, and he had carefully mimicked the singers he listened to. He was pleased that the boys said his voice now sounded more like a black man's because the only thing that was important to him was to sing the way black bluesmen sang. Just a few months earlier he had read an interview with Fats Domino in one of the music papers, and Fats had said, "You should never sing the lyrics out very clearly." And Jagger had understood immediately how important a clue that was to the emotion behind the blues, because he would spend hours trying to decipher the slurred lyrics of Afro-American singers, only vaguely understanding until he read Fats Domino's remark that obscured lyrics contributed immensely to the emotion that envelopes and defines the blues. And now, if the boys believed the damage to his tongue had created a black slurring in his vocal delivery, that was a large step forward in grasping the sound of the blues.

He had a remarkable talent for mimicking any singer he heard on the radio or phonograph, Mrs. Eva Jagger always told anyone who asked—and sometimes complained—about her son's very noisy and discordant band. "Michael could be a very good impersonator if he wanted to; he could probably make a living from it. You know, he just sits there all day, lapping up the hit songs. Ever since he was a little kiddie of eleven or so he had this knack of listening to a hit song over the wireless just a few times and then he'd stand up and sing them over just like the originals. He's so serious about it, there's no half-measures with Mike. When he's imitating something, it has to be got off just right. But now he sits there all day imitating this Chuck Berry person . . . ."

It wasn't exactly driving Eva and Joe Jagger crazy, but like so many other parents in the late Fifties they didn't quite understand or approve of their son's love affair with rhythm and blues, with that dreadful new sound everyone was carelessly lumping together as rock and roll. Jagger's infatuation had started some time in 1956, when the film *Blackboard Jungle* was released. All over the English-speaking world young kids—Robert Zimmerman in Minnesota, who would become Bob Dylan; Jagger and Keith Richard in the suburbs south of London; Eric Clapton and Eric Burdon farther north; Lennon and McCartney in Liverpool—were shaken by the music from the film, Bill Haley and the Comets doing "Rock Around the Clock." Keith Richard's reaction was typical of them all:

"People were saying, 'Did ya hear that music, man?' Because in England we had never heard anything: the BBC controls it and won't play that sort of music. But everybody our age stood up for that music and the hell with the BBC. I didn't think of playing it when I first heard it. I just wanted to go and listen to it. It took a year or so before anyone in England could make that music."

Three years later Little Boy Blue and the Blue Boys were making that music in one part of Dartford while Keith was learning to play in another part of the town. When her son first began to sing the blues Mrs. Jagger's reaction was a mixture of pride and condescension: "We used to sit in the next room listening to their band play and just crease up with laughter. It was lovely but so loud. I always heard more of

42

Mike than I saw of him." But after a time it seemed more loud than lovely to the Jaggers and their neighbors, so the boys had to find another place to rehearse. On weekends Etherington's parents usually went off to the country, and Allen remained home so that the Blue Boys could work up their routines without adult complaints. During the week, after school hours, the Blue Boys' sessions were held at Dick's house in Bexley Heath.

Eva Jagger explained to her son that she didn't object to his singing, but that the neighbors were complaining about the noise of the band and she had to keep peace with the neighbors.

Eva Jagger had been born in Australia, had immigrated to England with her family when she was a child, and had married Joe Jagger, a physical training instructor. The small and comfortable home in Dartford where Michael Jagger was born on July 20, 1943, in the final years of the war, had an air of middle-class suburban gentility; Mrs. Jagger had always been annoyed by the English habit of treating Australians as less than worthy foreigners, and it seemed to so many who knew her that she was trying to prove she was more English than her neighbors who were born there. Her very mild and harmless pretensions to class would annoy Jagger years later as he began to climb out of his class through pop music. (For most pop stars the need to reach fame and financial success was at least in part a need to climb above their class, the only way out of the structured class system, similar to the discovery by prize fighters and other athletes in earlier decades that their talents could give them heroic stature and popular success and make them almost immune to class stratification.) But Jagger never expressed annoyance about his mother's attitude toward his band when they were forced to hunt up a place to rehearse to avoid the wrath of parents and neighbors.

No matter how much of a rebel Jagger seemed to have

become, in his later public image, he was almost rigidly conventional as a boy. There were a few things that set him apart: his talent at mimicry; his excessive energy that made it impossible for him to remain in one place for long; and, when they were twelve or thirteen, what other boys his age considered his remarkable ability to persuade neighborhood girls to sneak off to the woods with him for a spot of adolescent love-making. But on the whole, Jagger was in no way out of the ordinary. He wasn't any kind of outcast or loner. Although, like most kids, he didn't much enjoy the outer trappings of school, the uniforms, and the compulsory sports programs, he was a good student. To a few of his teachers, he appeared to be one of the few students who never dozed off, who was alive and was able to question accepted dogma. But intellectually, not as a form of rebellion. His friends thought he was very career-oriented. He told schoolmates he was aiming for a career in either business or journalism.

And he never appeared to object to the physical regime his father put him through, except on hindsight, after he had become a rock star and was building the Rolling Stones as the rebellious and raunchy antidote to the Beatles. But when he was Little Boy Blue he was proud of his gymnastic ability; basically shy, he nonetheless enjoyed showing off his talent at gymnastics. His father insisted that Jagger perform certain physical exercises daily: push-ups, weight lifting, several dozen laps around the garden every evening. Dick Taylor once came by to call for Jagger for a band session at Allen Etherington's home and, as they were going out the front door, Joe Jagger called: "Michael, before you go out do your weight lifting." Jagger obediently went into the garden, dragged a set of barbells from the shed, and pressed and lifted the weights for the required fifteen minutes. Dick stood there watching, thinking it monstrous that Jagger accepted his father's demands without protest, without even being aware that an adult's will was being imposed upon him simply because he was considered a child. Jagger would sometimes display annoyance at his father's orders, mostly in the expression of his very plastic-liquid face. But he didn't seem to be aware that it was possible for a seventeen-year-old son to object to those orders.

Jagger and Dick had become classmates at Dartford Grammar School beginning around the age of twelve, but they didn't really notice one another until they discovered a mutual interest in rhythm and blues about two years later. Independently, they had begun listening to the "pure" blues first—Leadbelly and Big Bill Broonzy and Robert Johnson. Around the time the white rock-and-roll imitators of R & B were making a splash, Jagger and Dick had moved into Chuck Berry and Little Richard and all the electric black-urban blues that was coming over from America. They were more interested in the pounding, driving, and raunchy side of the blues than in the folk side. The R & B style was a natural urban extension of the original Southern country blues. Younger musicians working in small bands in Kansas City, Detroit, Oklahoma City, in all the black ghettos of America, had come to feel that the original blues was a sharecropper experience that had little to do with life on the streets of the big cities. They considered the "pure" blues an effete art form. Beginning in the late Thirties a number of younger blues singers became "shouters"—screaming out their blues-oriented songs over crashing rhythm sections and blaring brass sections. These shouters sparked the development of rhythm and blues, which became the pop music for American blacks. The singers and the huge rhythm units behind them still had very legitimate connections with the older blues forms, but they were more involved in the performance of the music, in stage acts that would create a certain electricity between performer and audience, than in the simple purity of the blues.

And Jagger was a natural performer. In spite of a shyness, a tendency to hold back until he was certain he'd be accepted, his every cell ached to get out there and perform. When he learned that Dick Taylor had been playing that kind of music with a group of neighborhood boys for some time, he joined them, singing R & B songs with Dick and his two friends backing him up. They were fourteen or fifteen when they started playing together, copying instrumentation and vocalization note for note from the records, and eventually they called themselves Little Boy Blue and the Blue Boys because Jagger wanted everyone to know they were playing blues and not rock. It was a distinction that did nothing to overcome their parents' vexation about the decidedly unprofessional noise they were making.

Neither Jagger nor any of the members of his band had any intention of going professional or in any way trying to earn even a second income by playing the blues. They were more level-headed than that. Jagger's parents disapproved of the music and were guiding him toward a career. Joe Jagger occasionally wished his son would be more interested in formal sports because he felt strongly that the boy would make a good soccer player or cricketer, and might even be talented enough to become an athletic star; but he was realistic enough to settle for a professional business career for the child. Most of all, however, Little Boy Blue and his group believed they were probably the only persons in all of England who were tuned in to black American music, so they played and sang that music for enjoyment only. For the kicks of imitating their favorite songs on the few records they were able to import from America.

It wasn't until Keith Richard came along, infected them with his enthusiasm, after playing with them for a year or more, that they felt it was possible to earn some money from the music they loved, perhaps by playing as a semi-pro band on weekends.

Keith was born in Dartford six months after Jagger. When they were about six or seven they attended Wentworth County Primary School together and became friends, playing after school. But the Richards (the family still spells it with the *s* which Keith later dropped) moved to a house just outside Dartford, and the boys lost contact. Keith's father was an electrical engineer and wanted his son to take up the same trade, but Keith would have nothing to do with studying. He was known as a bad-ass cat even as a young boy. While Jagger would participate in school athletic programs because he felt he must, Keith approached it from a different slant:

"They'd get us all out for the cross-country running, and I didn't want any part of that. So I'd start out with the whole bunch of runners and begin to fall behind and when I got way behind I'd sneak into the woods and light up. A quick fag made me feel as right as rain. It was just a matter of hanging on until the others came back, all blown out and exhausted, then tack myself on to the last few and run back to school with them."

That was on the days that he bothered showing up at school at all. By the time he was fifteen and at the Dartford Technical School, a slag heap for students who weren't expected ever to amount to much, Keith was a confirmed truant. Ultimately, his principal informed him that even a slag-heap school was no place for his layabout kind, and Keith was expelled. He ended up at Sidcup Art School, another kind of refuse pile that took students who couldn't fit anywhere else; like most such art schools, including those which John Lennon, Eric Clapton, and Pete Townshend were attending about this same time, a student didn't need any artistic ability, or even leaning, to enroll in the school. The basic objective was to keep a boy off the streets until he's old enough to get a job.

Keith's lack of enthusiasm for schooling was equalled only by his obsession with the guitar and with Chuck Berry records, and caused by that obsession. Once he heard Bill Haley and the Comets and realized he could play that music if he tried hard enough, the music became his only discipline. His grandfather played violin and guitar and had run a dance band in the Thirties, and Keith begged him for guitar lessons. Once he had the rudiments, Keith simply flew off from there, determined to become the best rock guitar player in the world. He could play most of Chuck Berry's solos, note for note, at the time he entered the Sidcup Art School.

Dick Taylor went off to the same school after Dartford Grammar, "Because I didn't know what the hell I wanted to do with my life, and some guy had a prospectus from the art school and said, 'Look, I went to Sidcup to check it out, and you don't have to work much and you can stave off working for a few years,' and I said, 'Okay, I'll come along.' " Dick continued playing music with Jagger and the group around home and was listening to much jazz and also playing folk guitar at school—by now he had given up his antique drums for a new, inexpensive guitar. When Keith showed up at the art school a year after Dick had enrolled there, Dick was playing with several people in informal bands. A little jazz, a bit of country, some folk. But never getting it confused with the *real* music, R & B. Keith began coming round, getting friendly with Dick, sitting in with him at informal sessions, and turning them all on to his own special favorites in rhythm and blues.

Keith was a rebel, if any kids were rebels, Dick recognized immediately: "He was a real Ted, just a hooligan, and I used to really like him for that. I remember once the art school took us on a trip to Heal's, the furniture shop, because we were studying graphic design, and they wanted us to see well-designed furniture. And Keith was sitting in this really nice sofa worth hundreds of pounds and quite casually dropping his cigarette on it and burning a hole in it and not giving a monkey's ass about it. And going around ripping off ashtrays and trying to rip off lamps and things. He was a hooligan, a rocker. He always used to wear at all times a lilac-colored shirt, Levi's and a Levi jacket. No matter what the weather was he'd walk around in this perpetually. Never wore anything else from the moment I met him."

Keith, always angry that the need to attend classes was stealing time he would prefer devoting to music, expended a large amount of energy complaining about school:

"Dammit, you know what I discovered? I really wanted to learn when I was a kid. I really did. I mean, I wanted to watch how things are done and try to figure it out and leave it at that. I was going to school to do something I wanted to do, and then the assholes manage to turn the whole thing around and make you hate 'em because they have to run their little Hitler numbers, and then you just hate the learning thing. You don't wanna learn anymore. Because school is just like the nick. So you get thrown out of schools and you get into art school, and it's the same thing. And the best that's going on is in the bog [toilet] with the guitars. I mean, it's just great here, you go take a piss, and there's always some cat who's sneaked out to the bog, and he's going through his latest Jack Elliott or Woody Guthrie tune, and you discover Robert Johnson, and it all comes together for you. Art school is great—out in the bog."

Jagger had entered the London School of Economics on a government grant by now and was commuting from the suburbs each day. Keith was taking the same British Railways train to Sidcup. They met one day in the spring of 1960. Keith was carrying his guitar, and he recognized Jagger immediately and was surprised to see the record albums under his arm: Chuck Berry, Little Walter, and Muddy Waters albums.

"You really into Chuck Berry, man? What a fuckin' coincidence!"

Jagger showed him the albums, among them *Chuck Berry Is On Top*. "I got a few more albums like these," Jagger said.

"Been writin' away to this company, uh, Chess Records, in Chicago. You know? And I got a mailing list from them . . . just tryin' to get it together."

"Play a guitar?"

"No, no. I just dig to sing."

Keith asked Jagger to come by his house on the edge of Dartford that afternoon, for tea. "And bring your records." When Keith got to school he asked Dick: "You know a guy named Jagger? From Dartford?"

"Sure, I play with him in a little group from down there. He's our singer."

"Fuckin' coincidence. We grew up together, and now I meet him on the train after not seein' him for years, and he's into the same music as me." It was still rare to meet anyone in England who had even heard of Chuck Berry.

Dick invited Keith to join them in their band session, and that afternoon when Jagger came by Keith's house and played the records for him, Jagger extended the same invitation: "Come round and join our group."

Over the next year or two Little Boy Blue and the Blue Boys met several times a week at Dick's house. Bob Beckwith had also gone off to the LSE and had drifted away from the band, and Keith was now second guitarist. They soon began thinking about the possibility of earning a little money as a group, especially Keith. "Maybe not a full-time thing, as professionals, but we sure can play occasional gigs for the kids, to get spending money." Jagger, Dick, and Allen shrugged off Keith's idea: Who was going to pay money to listen to a rather dreadful band play music no one had heard of before?

But there was something that they very desperately wanted to do with the music. In their youth and excitement and naïveté, they were hoping to educate kids of their own age to love the blues the way they loved it. "It's the best music we know, and we have to turn people on to it," Jagger said one night as they talked about the future of the band. "No one else is playing this kind of music, and we gotta get them into it." The music was the true cause, the road to truth, and Little Boy Blue and the Blue Boys would show the way. They seldom talked about it in precisely that fashion, but the feeling was there, Dick Taylor remembers: Let's show them what the one, the only *real* music, is all about.

Then they discovered, in the 1962 announcement in *Melody Maker,* that Alex Korner was actually performing the music publicly, up in Ealing, and they drove into London to see and hear it for themselves. The first Saturday night that Jagger and his group watched Blues Incorporated perform, they were totally transfixed by the music. They returned the second week and were still amazed that it was all happening. But on their third trip to the Ealing Club Jagger was saying, "Well, *fuck* it, this is pretty awful . . ."

Blues Incorporated was a relatively polished group playing urban blues with a jazz influence, and the Blue Boys thought the style was a pandering to the public taste which demanded trad jazz and Dixieland. Jagger's group was playing much cruder music, partly because they were cruder musicians but mostly because they had taken the blues a step further into the more ballsy Chuck Berry, Bo Diddley, and that rocking rhythm and blues end of the blues spectrum. Jagger, Dick, and Keith sat at the bar that third night complaining that Korner's group wasn't playing the true blues.

"Fuckin' saxophone," Jagger said as Dick Heckstall-Smith blew a long solo on tenor sax.

"Yeah, I know what you mean," Keith whispered. "Kind of stuff my grandfather played thirty years ago, but a little more jazzy. Just thirty-year-old big band kind of shit."

They sounded more snobbish and purist in their own way than the blues purists who insisted a man must be black—preferably the son of a slave or a sharecropper—to play the music that came out of the black experience. As they sat there, criticizing and laughing at the performance of Blues

Incorporated, their attitude was: "We can do it better than that. We know more about black music than these cats do. We know the only direction is rhythm and blues."

But there was one event about blues night at the Ealing Club that really impressed them: the performance of a kid about their age, small and slim and delicate, with a mop of gold hair cut in wispy bangs over his forehead but still very short all around, and a skin that seemed touched with a brilliant sunlight even in the darkened club. Cyril Davies, the harp player for the group, had introduced him: "Now, here's Brian Jones from Chelt'n'am. And he's accompanied by the world famous P. P. Jones—Perpetually Pissed Jones—just come up from Oxford to play for us."

And Brian Jones and Paul Jones—no relation—played a couple of Elmore James numbers and Muddy's "Rolling Stone," and Jagger stood at the bar gaping at Brian. He was playing a bar slide guitar, and Jagger had never seen anyone play that instrument before and he simply couldn't believe the way Brian made it sound like a second voice in harmony with Paul Jones. An unreal voice from that guitar which sounded as if it came from somewhere down in the center of his soul.

"That cat's fuckin' incredible," Jagger said repeatedly through Brian's set. Keith was just as overwhelmed: "It's Elmore *James,* man. That cat's really Elmore James. What the fuck is this? Playing the bar slide guitar like that!"

They were finishing up their set with an Elmore James song that was a special favorite among English blues enthusiasts, "Dust My Broom." Paul Jones was singing it a little too commercially, just a bit too sweet, Jagger felt. Besides, none of the boys could really spend much time listening to the lyrics they knew so well:

> *I believe, I believe my time ain't long*
> *I believe, I believe my time ain't long*
> *I ain't gonna leave my baby*
> *And break up my happy home.*

Because at the end of that last verse, just as on Elmore James' recording, the slide guitar created a sound that seemed to soar away like a bird in flight, playfully darting to earth and back to the sky in a definite rhythm. But this was no gnarled black American up there on the bandstand. That guitar was being caressed by a golden English kid. Brian Jones.

When the set ended with that song, Keith was so excited by what he'd just heard that he ran over to the stage and dragged Brian back to the bar and made introductions all around. And they began talking about the music they'd been playing and how they first got turned on to the blues. Brian said he was demolished. He thought all along that *he* was the only cat in the world going ape over the music and then he discovers Alex and Blues Incorporated and now some kids his own age who've been hanging around down in the suburbs and getting into the same kind of scene. But not precisely the same, they discovered: Brian was more into the jazz-blues end of it and Keith began raving to him about Jimmy Reed and Chuck and the Chicago R & B music. "Look, it's all the same shit, man, and you can do it," Keith said. Brian promised he'd give it a try, he'd try any kind of blues that seemed to turn someone on.

Brian began to tell them a little bit about himself, and it flashed on Jagger and Keith that he was a little more together, musically, than they. He'd been seriously working at it for a long time. He was still living in Cheltenham, ninety miles away near the Wales border, but coming up to London weekends and sleeping in the spare room or on the kitchen floor at Alex's flat. He was getting a band together and was just about to move up to London permanently with one of his women, who had had a son by him. They were amazed that he was a father, yet was just their age, and they were certain he was sending them up when he said he wasn't married and this son wasn't his first; he'd split for the Continent the year before because he had made another girl pregnant, and she insisted on having Brian's baby, which scandalized everyone in Cheltenham.

"I'm trying to find a pad in London for my old lady and the kid," Brian told them. "Played a lot down around Chelt'n'am with some jazz bands but I really dig the blues and you must be in London to play the blues. London's the only place you can make it, and I'm having a go at makin' it. Don't know if I'm good enough, but I'm givin' it a go."

"You're the best fuckin' guitarist I've ever heard," Keith shouted.

Cyril Davies joined the group, ordering a pint of bitter for himself and looking half-drunk now that he was off the bandstand. As Cyril turned to the boys, Keith was telling Jagger that if Paul Jones could get up there and sing, he could too. Cyril didn't say anything at first. He took a long swallow of his brew, belched almost silently, then put his hand on Keith's shoulder.

"You think you can do it, go up and do it," he said. "Anybody who wants to blow can have a blow."

"Ya mean it?" Keith asked.

"Damn right. The way I see it, nobody's going to be stupid enough to get up there and play unless he's good enough. You boys think you're good enough, then do have a blow."

Jagger held back, but Keith was excited and urged Jagger to do a number. Eventually Jagger overcame his shyness and permitted Keith to lead him to the bandstand.

Jagger stood there awkwardly as Keith plugged in and Cyril began to introduce them after checking out their names once more, because he hadn't caught them during the introductions at the bar. Charlie Watts, a member of Blues Incorporated, sat down at his drums, and Cyril started searching through his bag for his harp. Jagger looked terribly nervous. He had never sung in public before and now he was about to sing in front of some really serious blues musicians and an audience of about 100 totally devoted blues freaks. He had never even considered the possibility that anyone else was as interested in the music as he and his Blue Boys were, and suddenly he was standing in front of a room full of people who apparently knew a great deal about the blues. He remained almost frozen at the edge of the stage. Keith was plugging into the band's amplifier, the biggest amp Jagger had ever seen, and he worried that possibly Keith wasn't experienced enough to handle all that electrical power. And the club's primitiveness added to his anxiety. The place seemed to be leaking with damp from an ancient roof that could barely hold back the rain and from the humidity of a hundred bodies throwing moisture into an airless room. Cyril had put a sheet over the bandstand to catch the moisture, and now in its third week it was so filthy and so rotted that the condensation dripped from the sheet onto the amps and microphones, and it occurred to Jagger that someone would be electrocuted.

Keith had finally tuned his guitar and looked to Jagger for the cue that he was ready. Jagger nodded that he was all set to sing. Keith jumped right into "Around and Around," and if anyone in the audience was into Berry he'd recognize that Keith was slavishly imitating every note. But the Ealing Club was filled with "pure" blues devotees, and Keith was playing something close to that dreadful rock and roll, and the air was thick with muttered complaints about the desecration of the blues. From the bar, one purist summed it up, quite loudly: "What the fuck kind of music is that?"

Then Jagger began to sing. He stood at the edge of the stage, flat-footed, the mike in his hand, and started screaming out the lyrics. He sang in a deep and husky voice that caught many of the intonations of Muddy and Broonzy and Memphis Slim and a dozen others who had clearly influenced him. Jagger barely moved as he sang. Except for his oversized head, which he was shaking in rhythm with the beat as if to emphasize some of the harder-hitting phrases in the lyric that were difficult to understand because of his slurring. Jagger's hair moved in time to the music. Alex Korner edged closer to the stage to watch this kid and he was struck with a thought: *He's a hair fetishist.* Alex simply stared, always fascinated by fetishists, and he barely paid attention to the singing; Jagger's performance of the music was more striking than the music itself, even though he barely moved his body beneath the shoulders. The bouncing hair was a performance in itself.

When their single number was completed they received a polite bit of applause from some, stony silence from many, but they didn't pay much attention as they rushed back to Dick and Brian at the bar. Cyril joined them. "Good voice you got," he said to Jagger. He pointedly ignored Keith. Dick Taylor, sitting it out as a member of the audience, felt strongly that everyone in the place had hated Keith's Chuck Berry routine and regarded Keith as a rocker.

"They didn't seem to know what the hell you were doin' because they don't know about Chuck," Dick said.

"Fuck 'em, they'll learn," Keith responded.

Jagger tossed back a drink, not saying much. He appeared, to Dick and Alex, to be so excited by his first public appearance that he was unable to say a word or even consider the dreadful audience response to Keith's playing. Jagger had done it. He'd played in front of 100 people, and his friends told him he had pulled it off.

The next day Jagger carefully sealed the box containing the tape on which they'd recorded the five numbers some months earlier, wrote "Little Boy Blue and the Blue Boys" on the outside, and posted it off to Alex with a letter that said he was "keen to sing the blues," had been singing all his life, and asking to come to London to talk about the blues.

As Jagger was dropping the tape into the mail, Cyril Davies rang up Alex and asked him, "Where can we find the boy who sang that Berry song and shook his hair all night?" Alex said he didn't know anything about him, and Cyril asked him to find the kid because he was damned good and should come back to Ealing and sing again. Jagger's tape arrived in the post the next day, and Alex found it waiting when he returned from a gig late that night. He immediately phoned Cyril and said: "Cyril, you know that young boy? The one you were searching for? Well, I found him for you." Alex's wife, Bobbie, was half asleep and overheard that part of the conversation and thought it was a strange way of putting it, almost as if Alex were procuring for Cyril. Alex laughed when she told him her thoughts: "Hell, no, I haven't gone into pimping. That was about a kid from Dartford who tried a blow at Ealing Saturday night. He was damned good, and Cyril wants me to get him as a band singer."

Jagger slid easily into Blues Incorporated and the scene at the Ealing Club just as pop music audiences in England were edging toward an interest in the blues, much to Alex Korner's surprise and delight. Alex had become obsessed with the blues after years of classical piano lessons. He was living in Paris with his family when he started piano lessons at age five and didn't really like playing much because it seemed to be mostly the usual thing of piano teachers flattering fathers: "He can be brilliant if he studies at it. Just brilliant." The Korners moved to London in the summer of 1940, when Alex was twelve, and he became involved with a crowd of kids whose major delinquency was to go to the street market at Shepherd's Bush and steal 78-rpm records. One of the first records Alex stole was a Jimmy Yancey hot blues, and it was the first music that completely turned him on. He wanted to play nothing but blues and boogie woogie piano from that point on.

Father, of course, objected. He had been an Austrian cavalry officer in the first war. In 1917 he led a charge through the lines, with his troops behind him, and surrendered himself and all his men to the Russians. He had simply decided that the Russian Revolution was correct, and the Empire was wrong—he could no longer accept what the Emperor Franz

Josef or the Kaiser stood for—and he went over to the more politically viable side. Somehow he managed to get his first wife and their children to Russia during the war, and he eventually became a geological engineer. Alex remembers his father telling him stories about geological expeditions into the Caucasus to do oil research, but is still unable to understand how his father had time to become a geological expert.

The elder Korner appeared in London in 1922, still an Austrian national but attached to a Soviet agricultural mission. He married Alex's mother in London in 1927—she was Greek and Turkish—and Alex was born in Paris in 1928 because his father thought it would be a good idea for a future diplomat to have a Continental birth and rearing. Mr. Korner desperately wanted Alex to be a diplomat—although Alex is still confused as to how he would have worked out the problem of multi-nationality—and the piano lessons were part of Alex's future assult on international diplomacy. His image was of Alex as a dashing diplomat who was such a brilliant dilettante concert pianist that everyone says, "Oh, my God, you should become a professional pianist." Alex suffered through piano lessons, largely hating them, until he stole the Yancey record and went wild over the blues.

His father went even wilder. He'd come home to supervise Alex's lessons, find Alex playing Albert Evans' licks, and slam down the piano lid and shout, "I'm not paying good money on lessons for tripe like this." Alex got sent away to boarding school. He went on playing the blues. When he was with the Army in Germany in 1947, Alex began playing the local dance bands and got paid for it. He'd return to London on leave periodically and blow with the Chris Barber band, a jazz band, and became a semi-pro musician, as he calls it. The Barber band played jazz, but Alex played in a blues quintet within the band, doing a half-hour set a night as a relief group.

"I was playing a couple of nights a week and working days in the City as a clerk. The Greek side of the family had a shipping concern and they wanted me to go into that, become a junior director, and all. Which I just couldn't see. I couldn't get into the idea of money for its own sake, or the idea of actually enjoying the *earning* of bread as pleasure. I didn't dig their life style at all because it was based on the fact of impressing others that they were wealthier than they actually were—although Lord knows they were wealthy enough—and also based on the act of acquisition being more important than what you did to acquire it or what you did to enjoy it once you acquired it. We were so far apart on everything that I finally left the City shortly before I was going to be made a junior executive."

Alex continued playing with the Barber band for a while, left to do a variety of odd jobs in small record companies, then joined Ken Colyer, a trad jazz band leader. Ken had just returned from a working trip to New Orleans and asked Alex to form a skiffle group to work within the regular band. It was more a blues-based folk band than anything else, but promoters insisted on calling it skiffle because that loose down-home style of playing was all the rage in England that year. He eventually left that band, dissatisfied with the music, and in 1953 teamed up with harp player Cyril Davies, playing as a duo in a number of clubs in London and attracting friends such as John Baldry and Davey Graham, who would sit in.

Years later, after the blues became quite popular in England and the Rolling Stones were superstars, the music press tagged Alex with the label, "Father of the white British blues," to which he strongly objects.

"I didn't do it. I just happened to be there when the thing took off and I lent encouragement to a lot of kids. But I didn't start it. It was really Chris Barber who got it all started, not me, but Chris never gets any credit for it. In that period between 1956 and 1960, when Cyril and I were playing duos and things, and I was still just semi-pro, trad jazz was the big pop music here. That's what the public wanted to hear, and if you didn't play trad jazz you didn't get booked into too many clubs. And Chris Barber was the big trad jazz band. Chris asked us to come back again, and he used us as an electric rhythm and blues unit within the band. He also started bringing over electric blues players from the States—Otis Spann, John Lee Hooker, Muddy, people like that. And he was cutting his own throat and killing the trad jazz scene by having this R & B unit within the band. He knew exactly what he was doing, fostering the thing which was going to come next in music. It had to come next because trad jazz by then had become so formalized—not that the blues isn't—but so formalized in the three-part front-line way that everyone knew exactly what the clarinet was going to play, and the rhythm section always played that very straight common time, four, with no feeling for landing on two and four, and no three feel anywhere in the slow things. It was real Mickey Mouse music by then. And Chris brought in the blues guys from the States, brought us in as a rhythm and blues unit, even though he has never been a fool about this business and must have realized he was bringing an end to his big money years. I think once Chris made enough bread out of the jazz thing to satisfy himself, he was prepared to go with the other thing he'd always been hooked on as much as jazz, which was the race blues."

Alex's rhythm and blues unit toured a great deal. One performance they gave was down in Cheltenham, and after the set by Alex and Cyril a young man came up to talk to them. He said his name was Brian Jones, he was blowing with the local jazz band, but he would rather be playing blues. Most of all, he had to break away from the architect's office where he was working as an assistant and loathing it. Alex gave him his address and phone number. "If you ever come up to London give me a ring. You'll find a meal and a place to sleep."

Cheltenham, where Brian lived, is a very genteel, refined

60

town almost 100 miles from London. It's filled with little old ladies who are still living the style of the late 19th century, when aristocrats would go down from London a couple of times a year to take the baths at Cheltenham Spa, which is fed by spring water that reputedly cures anything that may ail the upper classes. By the time Brian was born there on February 28, 1944, Cheltenham had gone slightly seedy, but it was still full of aspirations to be an aristocratic town, aspirations that rubbed off on its citizens.

Brian's father was an aeronautical engineer who played the piano and organ. His mother was a piano teacher. Brian grew up in an atmosphere dominated by music and became proficient at the piano before he was ten. His mother decided he had become so good she couldn't teach him anything more, so she sent him off to a more advanced teacher. He was very fond of church music, hymns at the beginning, and Louis Jones remembers that by the time his son had reached his early teens music had become almost a religion to him. He quickly learned to play the clarinet when he took a fancy to the instrument, and his mother would accompany him on the piano when Brian played classical pieces. The Weber Clarinet Concerto was one of his particular favorites, and one that he handled with extraordinary skill.

Then he discovered jazz and became almost a fanatic about the music coming from America on jazz recordings. When he heard Charlie Parker for the first time, on a series of six old recordings pressed in England on the Spotlite label shortly after Bird died in 1955, Brian convinced his parents to buy him an alto saxophone because no other instrument seemed worthwhile after hearing the near-miraculous sound that Parker coaxed out of his horn—a double-edged tone that combined into one, as if two sax masters were playing, the first blowing a thin transparent sound and the second a fat thick one. Brian quickly became a fine sax player—he had that blessed ability to master any instrument in a matter of weeks—but he was always disappointed that he couldn't come anywhere near the sound he heard from the records of the musical genius who had already become a legend.

Brian was restless, hurt, very introverted and paranoiac even as a teenager. His father remembers: "Brian was a normal, conventional boy who was well-behaved and well-liked. He was liked because he was well-behaved. Then a peculiar change came over him in his early teens, when he began to become a man. He began to have some resentment toward authority. He started a mild rebellion against authority which became stronger as he became older. He rebelled against parental and school authority. He would say, 'Why should I do something I'm told just because the person telling me to do it is older than I am?' "

His parents worried a great deal because his school work, which had always been quite good, began to deteriorate as Brian became more fanatical about jazz. "We were just average parents, full of the orthodox careers that were open to him at that time, and I was disappointed and full of anxiety when he became so wrapped up in his love of jazz that, in spite of all I could do or say, he went off to his music."

The Joneses were unable to recognize it at the time but Brian was withdrawing into himself until all his frustrations, all his paranoia, all his hurt and anger, began to bottle up inside him, and the only outlet was his music. For Brian, music was not simply a way to break out of the class system, or the path to fame and riches; music was the only avenue of escape from the psychic poisons eating at his soul. What his parents saw as rebellion on the surface was a manifestation of a deeper torment which would slowly destroy him.

When Brian was fifteen and still attending the high-toned Cheltenham Grammar School, he joined a jazz band that played weekends around small clubs in the West Country, earning a few shillings a night. But within a few months Brian tired of the monotony of trad jazz, and when he graduated soon after and took a job in an architect's office he felt almost that his life had come to a dead stop because of the routine of the music and the routine of office work. In addition, a fifteen-year-old girl whom he had made pregnant was about to give birth, and Brian faced a three-pronged crisis: The band was unsatisfying, work was unsatisfying, and the responsibilities of being a father were frightening. So he packed up his sax, the guitar he was just learning to pick, withdrew the few pounds he'd been able to save from his job, and fled to the Continent. He hitchhiked and wandered around Scandinavia for a few months, got turned on to the blues and became proficient with the guitar, then returned to Cheltenham when his funds ran out.

He joined another small band and held a succession of mindless jobs and hated it all because jazz was all that anyone ould pay to hear. Jazz that wasn't real jazz, that was the distressing part of it all, an English pop version of the incredible things that Parker and Dizzy Gillespie and so many others were doing over in America. So Brian turned more and more to the blues. He picked up a couple of very rare Elmore James records—even in America James was barely known to more than a few dozen whites—bought himself a slide guitar, and almost overnight had the James style mastered, but with his own improvisations that put his private brand on the music.

When he met Alex in the spring of 1960, Brian felt strongly that he must move up to London and make it as a blues musician. The first weekend after meeting Alex, Brian showed up on his doorstep in London, broke and hungry because he'd spent his last bit of spare cash on the train fare. Bobbie Korner fed him and gave him a place to sleep—on the kitchen floor because several other musicians were also spending the weekend. From that point on Brian would travel up to London every weekend to blow with Alex and Cyril. Eventually Brian became a member of Blues Incorporated and when Alex was finally convinced by Chris Barber's band manager, Phil Robertson, that Blues Incorporated should go professional, Brian was already an integral member of the group.

Blues Incorporated's audience at the Ealing Club had begun to build by the time Jagger returned by request for his second gig. Alex recalls: "The Ealing Club was a drinking man's pub, and the only music ever permitted to be heard inside its doors was trad jazz, and even that was only one night a week. We came along, and the trad jazz fans hated us. We thought a few times there were going to be punchouts over the music. We drew our support from the folk area because people who were into folk began to come into blues bit by bit. And all the cats coming into blues at that time became fanatics on the spot or hated it and never came back. The club held only 200 maximum, and our deal with the cat running the club was that he took the bar and we took the door, and of course he made more at the bar. There were no more than 100 people in London into the blues and they showed up, and the next week cats who had heard us on tour—especially cats from Croydon and Ipswich, where there had been punchouts because the trad jazz people hated us and the blues people dug us, and they settled it with their fists and tore the concert halls apart— those people who were on our side back then also showed up. And this club that held only 200 was packed to the gills within four weeks. People were traveling down from Scotland for a late night session and traveling back the next day, and our membership lists had gone up to 800 at the end of the fourth week. By that fourth Saturday night more people were showing up than we had room for, and the doors were being closed a half hour before the first set, and cats were offering a pound, which was a lot of money in those days, to be permitted to crowd in for the last number. And word got around town that there was something strange happening at this club in Ealing opposite the Irish pub, and a tremendous atmosphere developed because each of us was discovering that the other guy had been into blues for a long time and always believed he was the only man in England listening to that music."

The band was a strange one, Alex used to think at the time, because it held such a strange assortment of musicians trying to get things together: Brian was still sleeping on Alex's kitchen floor on weekends; Jagger and Keith were coming up from Dartford (although Keith was not permitted to play in the beginning); Charlie Watts, who Alex had played with occasionally in a jazz quartet for about a year before this, was on drums; someone called Keith Scott was on piano; Cyril on harmonica; Andy Hoogenboom on bass (replaced after a fortnight by Jack Bruce); and Dick Heckstall-Smith on tenor sax. The singers at the time were Cyril, Eric Lister, who was the first blues singer Alex ever heard in England, John Baldry, Paul Jones when he came up from Oxford, and Mick Jagger with his three songs, the full extent of his repertoire —"Bad Boy," "Ride 'Em On Down," and "Don't Stay Out All Night." Alex also sang occasionally, but only when all the equipment broke down and someone had to get up on a chair and belt out the songs without a mike; Alex was the only one who could belt.

After the early fear and nervousness the first time he got up on stage to sing at the Ealing, Jagger became enormously excited about performing because the audience was beginning to loosen up and enjoy what he was trying to do. He would drive back to Dartford with Keith early Sunday mornings and talk about what he'd been feeling. "The thing I'll always remember is waiting at the side for Alex to ask me to sing. I just stand there, waiting, and getting more impatient while the other cats are blowing because I want to get in front of that microphone more than anything else in the world. I just have to sing to that audience, that's all, I just have to sing."

One night, on the way to the club, someone lost an amplifier lead and, since none of them was really together professionally yet, no one had a spare. All of the musicians were generally out of their minds trying to find a spare or to work out a way of improvising from a light cord. And Cyril Davies was simply furious. He picked up his bag filled with harmonicas and all sorts of junk and rubbish and emptied it out on the floor, shouting: "Fuckin' blues players, fuckin' blues players. Out of my mind to be workin' with bloody bluesmen." Everything was sorted out by and by, but Alex came over to Jagger and whispered: "I don't think it's very wise if you sing tonight, Mick. I don't think Cyril wants you to sing at all." Jagger knew that Alex was right, but he couldn't understand why Cyril seemed to have taken a dislike to him. Especially since Cyril had gone out of his way only a few weeks before to bring Jagger into the band as a singer.

But it didn't really matter. The audiences were filling the club, listening to his three songs and listening to the blues. Like Alex, Jagger couldn't understand how anyone who heard a good blues record would not be turned on by it immediately and forsake trad jazz and pop and all the other dreadful sounds around that passed for music. Now that the Ealing was being packed every night they all felt even more strongly that they must spread the sound of the black bluesmen.

And it was indeed spreading. On the fourth Saturday night Harold Pendleton, who managed the Marquee Jazz Club in Soho, dropped in at the Ealing to see what all the excitement was about. Pendleton's club was empty on Thursday nights; he had tried everything to draw even a small crowd into the Marquee on Thursdays but nothing seemed to work, and he hoped the fuss being created at the Ealing could be transposed to the Marquee. When he finally fought his way inside the Ealing, past a crowd of several hundred standing in a drizzle outside waiting to pay their way in for the next set, Pendleton decided he didn't care much for the music. But he was a good businessman who refused to permit his personal taste to interfere with a chance for profit, and he asked Blues Incorporated to play the Marquee on Thursday nights. Alex and Cyril said they'd give it a go.

Within a few weeks Pendleton was making a tidy little profit and the band members were getting a couple of pounds each from the take at the door as young kids, who couldn't stand trad jazz and who had turned away from the sterile pap that rock and roll had become, wandered into the club to join the 100-odd members of the Ealing Club who had followed the band to the Marquee. The kids didn't care about musical classifications: Blues Incorporated was giving them something raw and raunchy and they stood up on the tables and rocked and danced and shouted to the hard-assed blues. Up in Liverpool, in a cellar club called the Cavern, the Beatles were playing the same kind of power-driven music and creating a similar sort of excitement, kids clamoring over them and pursuing them with junkie urgency.

On the night of the fourth gig at the Marquee Jagger strolled into the club with Keith at his side, as usual, grinned sheepishly at Alex, and held up a small newspaper cutting. His first press notice, a tiny item in the music paper *Disc*, on May 19, 1962, headed "Singer Joins Korner":

"A nineteen-year-old Dartford rhythm and blues singer, Mick Jagger, has joined Alex Korner's group, Blues Incorporated, and will sing with them regularly on their Saturday night dates at Ealing and Thursday sessions at the Marquee Jazz Club, London.

"Jagger, at present completing a course at the London School of Economics, also plays harmonica."

A two-sentence item, with one half-error: Jagger was playing around with the harmonica but he hadn't developed enough confidence to play it publicly. Jagger said he didn't mind the error because singing was the only part of music he cared for. He was reaching his audiences; you could feel the interplay between him and the audience. He and the audience were like one. He couldn't know precisely why it worked that

Michael Philip Jagger was so exciting a performer because his performances were completely natural, not contrived. Jagger, onstage, was an extension of Jagger offstage, his natural self, a public expression of what he was feeling about the music and the singing and the act of performing. Jagger transmitted his obvious excitement to his audiences. His performances were honest.

Working behind Jagger at each gig, Alex would sometimes reflect on why Jagger's performances went over so well: *Because he makes a total thing of singing a song.* No matter how badly he sang—and his singing was often dreadful—the total drive he put into shouting the blues in a hurtful, hateful voice created a strong flow of energy waves that swept over an audience; those waves, bouncing back in a cross-feed, stirred up an even greater excitement in the singer. The hair fetish image that struck Alex so sharply when he first saw Jagger sing was an important part of his empathizing with the audience. You felt he was shaking his hair to further stimulate himself, because the hair flouncing on his neck felt good, felt sensual, fit the mood of the innate sexiness of the blues; it was part of the sensuality of the performance, the performer, and the music. Jagger was highly sexy. But it was a natural sexiness, part of his drive and presence on stage. Back then, he wore baggy trousers and plimsolls and didn't need the campy makeup and dress, the coarse suggestiveness, that he'd later resort to to turn on his fans. In his first months and years his performances worked so well because his art was built on a reality within himself: sex and anger.

Jagger's performances created conflicts within the band. Several times, playing guitar behind Jagger, Alex thought: *Hey, man, they're going to pay more attention to him than the music.* Alex was a blues purist. The music was more important to him than the performer. And here was Jagger, turning it all upside down. But Alex didn't say anything about it to Jagger directly. He was too shy, too worried about offending with directness. And when he'd think about possibly suggesting that Jagger tone it down he'd hold back with the thought, *Perhaps Mick's right, and the purists are wrong.*

Sometimes, however, Alex and Jagger did explore each other's views of the music they were playing. And Alex soon understood that Jagger's strongest drive was the performance that would display the basic crudeness of rhythm and blues, understood that Jagger was young enough to have grown up with the electric shouting end of the blues and so didn't have to be concerned about the purity of country blues.

One evening in Alex's kitchen Jagger said he didn't give a damn about the finer points of the blues. The crude and raw parts of it turned him on, the full frontal music. That delicate guitar picking was too fine for him, he said; the heavy solos behind him got it all moving.

"Yeah, but does the crude side of it have musical value? Are those harsh solos effective musically?" Alex asked. "I mean, do you get better results using a cudgel or a rapier?"

Jagger preferred the cudgel, to bash their bloody heads in, he said.

"No, no, you do more by knifing your way gently, not bashing 'em over the head with sound. Slice your way into your audience."

During these conversations, Jagger would occasionally jump off his stool in front of the bar that broke the large kitchen in two and prance over to the old-fashioned stove to boil more water for their tea. Bobbie Korner smiled; when Jagger first started coming around to talk to Alex she'd insist on being the hostess and fetching whatever was needed, but she soon gave that up when she realized that Jagger was so speedy he simply had to do something . . . anything . . . to use up his excess energy.

The Chicago sound moved him the most, Jagger said. The electric city blues, not the country blues from Mississippi.

"But that's a vulgarization, that electric sound out of Chicago. It's electric country and it's a vulgarization of everything that's come before, all the country blues like Blind Willie McTell and Robert Johnson and all those extremely fine guitar pickers."

If it was vulgar, it was fine with him because that sort of vulgarization was the only way to make the blues popular, Jagger insisted.

Those arguments went on until it was time to run down to the club to do their sets. And as Alex watched Jagger perform after one of these discussions he'd wonder if perhaps the kid was right: Alex and the other members of the band were constantly arguing about the chances of the blues ever becoming a popular art form, and Jagger was up there singing as if he were certain that it would be popular. Every sound from his throat, every movement of his over-large head, demanded that the audiences wake up and recognize that this was the music to listen to, and Jagger was going to be its popularizer. He had a lot of gall, but he certainly seemed to have the determination, Alex thought, and he might just pull it off eventually.

The electric, supercharged nature of the performer's art excited Jagger, fascinated him, Alex felt. Jagger seemed to be learning to bend an audience to his wishes, to manipulate it. Sometimes, when a performance worked especially well, Jagger seemed almost like a puppet master. It didn't happen too often, yet often enough to make Alex realize that Jagger was learning his craft, was discovering the art of rousing an audience's emotions, pulling from it the precise response he demanded. Not that Jagger knew or studied every stimulus and response, not that his act became deliberate and calculating. No. He didn't understand it, intellectually, Alex was certain, but he did give the feeling that he knew he had within him the power to excite and stimulate. And it looked as if the audience excited him in turn, drove him further. The foot-thumping of his audience, the kids jumping up to dance, the loud, raucous sound of the band behind him, forced to follow the singer. And the lights, the props, the microphones and amps, and even the perspiration hanging heavy in the air, that locker room odor of sweating dancers and musicians . . . the total atmosphere of a club as seen by a performer from the stage, seemed to give Jagger a sense of timelessness. The intimacy of performers and musicians, the bickerings and the aimless conversations and jokes, the petty jealousies, all the words used to make contact or turn it aside, made them feel that normal human language is trivial compared to the force of the music. When he sang it was as if his voice, his body, were drawing out of himself his deepest, most personal self. And drawing out of the band a power that was absolute control, bent to his needs. He seemed almost subordinated to this power—the power of the band, which he controlled, and the power of his own performance. The sum of these was bringing from somewhere inside him a force no performer could explain, not even to himself. If anyone were to give it a name, he'd have to call it magic.

So what did it matter that some strong negative feelings had begun to grow between himself and Cyril? Jagger knew that Cyril didn't like the songs he sang, didn't think he sang the blues, thought he was singing well but it sure as hell wasn't the blues. Cyril was hoping Jagger would take his singing elsewhere, but he was creating a chemistry between himself and the people out beyond the lights, and he was usually able to dismiss Cyril's attitude. He knew Cyril was more of a purist than anyone else playing the blues. Cyril was so essentially a country blues man that the furthest step he could make, grudgingly, was to Muddy's electric blues playing. But no further. Certainly not so far as the shouters, the R & B men who had brought their ghetto pollution to the blues. Jagger could dismiss Cyril's criticisms and antagonism because it was clear that Cyril was questioning his taste, not his talent.

Among some members of Blues Incorporated and their wives, crew and associates, there was a strong feeling that Jagger had abandoned Little Boy Blue and the Blue Boys, that he had broken up the group by becoming a singer in Alex's band. Keith most of all appeared stranded by Jagger. Keith was always tagging along at Jagger's side, the friend with the guitar who watched from a table out front but was never permitted to play because he was a rocker. Alex's wife, Bobbie, started worrying that Keith's feelings had been hurt by Jagger and by her husband, who had brought Jagger into the band. As she sat with Keith one night in the Marquee she asked him:

"What about you and *your* band, now that Mick is working with Alex?"

"It doesn't matter. Mick is so good," Keith said. "As long as *he's* heard *we* don't mind, man. We really believe in him. He's going to make it."

Bobbie stared at Keith for a long while. She concluded that he honestly felt that strongly about Jagger's talent. But she didn't know—no one outside knew—that Keith was holding something back—the boys had formed a new band, the Rolling Stones, and were rehearsing as often as they could. They were very secretive about the band and never let Alex or anyone else know that they had put together a new group.

Jagger, most of all, kept his plans and ambitions to himself. He was very shy and difficult to talk to, wouldn't open up with anyone, not even Alex. Jagger also appeared very conscious of the age difference between himself and Alex. He would often call Bobbie Korner "Auntie Bobbie," though she wasn't yet thirty, little more than ten years older than he was. John Mayall's wife, Pamela, was about the same age as Bobbie, yet Jagger would call her "Old Mother Mayall." He was very guarded and distant with anyone not his age, left some of them with the impression that he fancied the older generation faintly amusing, that he felt an entire generation separated him from Alex and all the older people in music and that only musicians his own age would understand him. From the very beginning, the Rolling Stones seemed to possess a sense of their own security as a complete unit of friends and musicians not dependent upon anyone else, and not fully trusting anyone else.

The Rolling Stones had come together within weeks after Jagger and Keith had been so impressed by Brian's performance. Immediately after that first meeting Keith and Brian began playing together, bouncing riffs off one another, turning each other on to his favorite artists. Brian at the time was playing several nights a week with a jazz band, to earn money and for the chance to get out and perform, even though he hated the leaden music of trad jazz. He brought Keith along several times to sit in and blow with his group and, once again, Keith's rock sound was simply too much for the rest of the band, and he wasn't permitted to play. They talked a lot about Keith, Dick Taylor, and perhaps Jagger joining the group Brian was blowing with, and perhaps transforming it into a blues band, but Brian decided they'd be much wiser to form their own group.

The Rolling Stones was created out of their need to play their own kind of music. The band consisted of Brian as leader, Keith, and Ian Stewart, whom Brian had just met in a jazz club and who played the sort of straight boogie blues piano that none of them had heard before except on Albert Ammons recordings. Dick Taylor played bass. Bob Beckwith rehearsed with them for the first couple of weeks, then drifted away to concentrate on his schooling. Charlie Watts came by to play several times but he was Korner's drummer and couldn't afford to give that up for the Stones, so the group picked up a drummer named Tony Chapman. Tony was a salesman from Liverpool who would miss about half their rehearsals because he had to get on the road and do his selling. And finally there was Jagger. He seemed to be along at first just to be singing with his friends, but as the weeks passed and

Cyril was making it more obvious that he didn't like Jagger personally and thoroughly loathed his desecration of the pure blues, Jagger was almost forced to become more serious about the band that his friends had formed.

The group was no longer Boy Blue but the Rolling Stones. It signified the philosophical split in musical taste between Brian and Jagger. Pre-electric Muddy was the old blues style; Jagger and Keith conceived of this new band as rhythm and blues, the shouters backed by the heavy beat and raw amplified power. But the split would not be obvious for a couple of years.

When Brian suggested the name for the band Jagger said, "Let's call it the *Silver* Rolling Stones," unaware that up in Liverpool a group playing the same kind of raunch music originally called themselves the Silver Beatles, but quickly discarded "silver." It was the Silver Rolling Stones for a short period, then simply the Rolling Stones.

For kids from the suburbs, the seamier side of London life was an enormous jolt of electricity. And nothing seemed more seedy or more charged than the Bricklayer's Arms, a pub in Broadwick Street, Soho, that was the meeting place for whores, street traders, and businessmen. Ian Stewart was a regular at the "Brick," and he introduced the boys to a part of English life they'd never seen before. Most days, after classes at the LSE, Jagger would take the Tube down to the Leicester Square station, wander past the drunks and pensioners in Soho Square and over to the Brick. Usually, Ian's huge old racing bicycle was stashed just inside the front door, and Ian would be sitting at a table with his back to the wall, in cycling shorts, his feet up on the table, nibbling away at a pork pie to make it last through several pints of bitter.

The Brick's atmosphere was as earthy and raunchy as the music the Stones were trying to create. One of their favorite barroom ladies was a large woman of indeterminate age, ex-

74

cept that there was much age showing in her face and sagging body, and she provided the boys with an enormous number of insider jokes. Especially the one about her "minge," a word they had never heard before but which they correctly assumed to mean her vagina. She arrived one evening, quite angry, ordered her usual gin, neat, and complained to everyone in the pub:

"Riding on the Tube, and this young bloke sitting across me, trying to stare up me dress. Closed me legs tight and 'e stared even 'arder. Gave 'im a nasty look. 'E came and sat 'is fat arse next to mine and said, 'I want to look at your minge, it must be lovely.' 'It 'im with me bag, I did, and 'e ran off the train. 'Ere now, 'e wanted to look at me minge. The bloody nerve askin' to see me minge."

The Rolling Stones began rehearsing in a room above the pub which the landlord let them use for ten bob a night. Jagger had spending money from his government educational grant, Keith had a small allowance, Brian worked as a clerk in the electrical department at Whiteley's, and the others managed to scrape together a few pence each to contribute to the cost of the rehearsal hall. As soon as they had a steady place of their own to rehearse in, the boys set about upgrading their equipment. Dick Taylor bought the largest bass guitar he could find, at least four and a half feet long, but he couldn't afford an amplifier so he plugged into one that Brian got from someplace, in some mysterious way. Jagger put the bite on his parents for a loan to enable him to buy more professional equipment. Joe Jagger, afraid that music might further distract his son from a proper education, refused at first. Jagger then went to work on his mother, promising not to drop out of school until he finished his courses, at the same time ranting on about the potential rewards of show business. He told them that if he worked at it he could become wealthier than they could possibly imagine, perhaps a millionaire. But he added that he couldn't do it without the proper equipment for his group.

Eventually Mrs. Jagger gave in and loaned her son £30. Keith picked out two Harmony amps. They were no larger or more powerful than inexpensive phonograph speakers but when Jagger and Keith brought them round to the Brick the other members of the group almost went out of their heads with joy because they felt the equipment was at least approaching the power and sophistication of Alex's equipment . . . and Alex was a professional.

They rehearsed several nights a week and went looking for jobs. There wasn't too much work around because trad jazz was still dominant, and the promoters weren't about to try something new and potentially dangerous to the safe and steady income the trad bands were bringing them. One gig the Stones did get was at a pub in the north end of London on a Friday night. It was their first real job, and they struggled all their equipment into the Tube and rode for what seemed like hours. When they got to the front door of the dance hall they found a small hand-lettered sign announcing "The Roling [sic] Stones" and a totally empty hall. They began to set up their gear, Jagger occasionally turning to shout at an invisible horde rushing the stage: "Stand back! Stand back, mates! Give the boys some breathing space!" And Brian tore off his leather belt, pretending to whip a girl trying to climb onstage. When the band blasted into its first number, there were exactly two paying customers in the audience. That couple soon left. But a crowd did begin to build outside. Neighborhood kids who threw stones at the building and demanded an end to the horrible noise inside. After a few songs the manager of the hall, afraid his windows would be smashed, ordered the Stones to pack up. The boys returned to the Brick, where they got as drunk as their near-empty pockets would allow.

The Stones began to play as a fill-in group for Blues Incorporated at the Ealing and the Marquee and got a somewhat better reception. But they never told anyone they were the Rolling Stones; they just left the impression with the other musicians that they were messing around together in their spare time, not in any serious way. And they continued to rehearse at the Brick, whose patrons were more accustomed to talk about soccer and horse racing than about Muddy and Elmore. The boys would have a couple of drinks when they met each night, then go upstairs to play through their repertoire. Everyone down in the pub believed they were crazy. But the patrons were pleasant toward these longhairs, treating them as a bunch of loonies you don't want to offend by letting them know that you know they're insane. On occasion other musicians, and sometimes even a straight customer with a musical ear and a drunken curiosity, would come storming up the stairs to see what was going on. One night, just as the band was about to pack it up so Jagger, Keith, and Dick could catch the last train to Dartford, a well-dressed little man walked in and said:

"Hello, there. I'm an artists' representative. Here's my card."

Brian reached out and took the card, glanced at it, and turned to hand it to Jagger. Brian's face was contorted by an effort not to laugh. Jagger handled the card delicately, Taylor remembers, appearing to study the inscription with exaggerated concentration. The card read:

Artistes Representative
Cockfoster

"I think you lads are on to something here," the artistes' representative said. "This country-and-western music can definitely do things for you, can definitely make you money. I can buy you some suits, take you to American bases in Germany, make you a large sum of money. Country-and-western is big among Americans . . ."

His long recital seemed to wind on for twenty minutes. The boys listened politely, stifling their laughter as best they could. Finally, Jagger said his mother would never give her permission for Germany, because she had lost four brothers in the "Big War."

"Oh, I'm sorry. But if you can convince Mother, I can make you boys rich," he said as Jagger led him to the door. When Jagger rejoined the group, thrashing around with laughter, one of them swung a guitar at him and said, "I never heard you talk about those dear dead uncles."

Jagger said he never had any.

Jagger saw his first big break come and go in an instant at the beginning of June. All the members of Blues Incorporated were gathered at the Marquee about an hour before the opening Thursday night set when Alex Korner came tearing in, late and somewhat out of breath, and called a band meeting.

"Just talking to a producer of the BBC's jazz program. They want us to do a gig on the telly next Thursday night."

"Incredible!" Jagger shouted. "A million people will watch us and we'll double the people who come into the club."

"Right. But there's a problem," Alex said. "Here's the situation, man. The BBC is willing to pay for only six of us. They know there're seven in the band but they said they don't need three singers to do a few numbers, they don't need more than two so they'll only pay for six of us. Truthfully, Mick . . . it's a drag, but they feel they don't need you because you don't play an instrument. A drag, but there it is."

"Fuck 'em, we won't do it," someone called out.

Jagger remained silent as the other band members shouted their ideas on how to handle the BBC. It must have occurred to him that if Blues Incorporated did the BBC show then the Stones could debut at the Marquee that night. Someone would have to keep the Marquee open, why not the Stones? They'd been rehearsing enough, they'd played gigs at the Marquee before . . . although not disclosing to anyone that they were a formal band with a real name. They were ready.

Jagger said that they must play the BBC, that they couldn't turn them down because the exposure would attract an enormous number of new customers.

Most of the band members were very excited at that idea, that an appearance on the BBC would make them famous, bring promoters crawling into the Marquee with more job offers than they'd have the time or energy to accept.

But it was absolutely necessary to keep the club open, Jagger said. The band wouldn't be able to play the BBC and the club at the same time, and so another band or two must be put together.

"Right. If we leave the club for just one night somebody else will get the gig and we might have trouble getting it back," Alex said. "Pendleton won't like us giving up even a single night at the Marquee just for the lousy BBC."

"We'll keep the club open," Jagger said. "The Stones will play the gig."

It was the first time Alex was aware that the boys had formed a group and were calling it the Rolling Stones. Cyril suggested, and everyone agreed, that Jagger and John Baldry would be in charge of holding down the Thursday night date at the Marquee: Baldry to put together the lead band and Jagger the relief band. It was the first appearance in London of the Rolling Stones—Jagger, Keith, Brian, Ian, and Tony Chapman on drums; Dick Taylor didn't play because he'd dropped out of the Stones a couple of weeks before to complete his studies at art school and go on to university.

Jagger wasn't the same boy he had been several months before. He was rather quickly being transformed into a personality his parents would have difficulty recognizing. The surface changes were the most obvious, as they would always be with Jagger in the future. Before coming up to London he spoke with a quite typical English suburban accent. Within a few months he was beginning to mimic the Cockney accents he heard in the Bricklayer's Arms and through much of working-class London, and very slowly but quite definitely the Cockney became a natural way of speaking. It was almost as if he'd decided to become a Cockney because he knew he could never get away with imitating a black American sharecropper, and Cockney seemed to be the closest equivalent that England had. And while his speech was changing the carefully groomed university look had given way to a scruffiness which was just as carefully worked out: jeans, boots, tattered shirts and sweaters . . . clothing picked up for a few pence at second-hand shops in Camden Town.

Inside, Jagger was going through another change Alex and others in the group felt. He made it clear to them that he was beginning to have second thoughts about completing LSE and going on to any sort of ordinary career. Alex understood that Jagger was coming to realize his involvement in music and performing was something over which he ultimately didn't have control, certainly not enough control to decide whether to drop it and continue his schooling, or to really push the music to its furthest possible limits. He was completing his first year at LSE and talking about giving it one more year, and yet indicating that even with another year at school he'd have to leave anyway and get out there and sing, and perhaps he should quit right now. But he couldn't bring himself to do it immediately, Alex felt, because he knew it would hurt his parents and he said he owed them something. He also had a debt to the government, which financed his education and had an investment in him, he said. Could he be so ungrateful as to quit now and waste the government's money?

Jagger sometimes complained to Alex about how deeply he hated the need to go to LSE, how much he'd like to quit but couldn't at this point, and during these talks Alex came to understand a little bit more about Jagger—that his need to perform, his overwhelming drive to perform, had produced in Jagger the total amorality that Alex believed an artist needed to get his art together. People count, certainly, but they don't count if they interfere with the music or the performance. Alex knew what Jagger was going through. Months before, when he had told his wife that he was going to take Blues Incorporated fully professional, concentrate wholly on his music, she said she'd take the three children and leave him if he did anything so foolhardy; Alex considered that for a while and decided that nothing could stand in the way of his need to play and perform. *She didn't leave me,* Alex thought after one of these conversations with Jagger, *but I sure know your need for the music gets you. It's got Mick, and he's got to admit it's got him if he's going to be able to survive. You have to believe in it that hard, if you're going to do it, you have to set up your own code for what you're doing and stick by that code, even if no one else understands your code. That's Mick's greatest strength, he's totally amoral, he just doesn't want to know anything about any moralities that may interfere with the performance of his music. This kid has it so strong he's going to end up doing something and doing it so big that everyone knows he's done it.*

Alex was a vital influence on that growing "amorality" in Jagger, contributed much to it. Alex had three children to support, no independent income, and when he turned professional in a very risky business he clearly wasn't worried about the security of a steady job. Jagger was very much aware of Alex's attitude and was affected by it, Alex knew, because they discussed the lack of security in the music industry several times. And Alex always laid the same line on Jagger that he did with any other musicians who asked him about it: "When you're so damned young you just do what you have to do because you're physically fit to get yourself out of it if you need to. I mean, it doesn't matter if you run short of food for a bit, it doesn't matter if you have no place to sleep when you're nineteen or twenty. It's going to hurt a lot more when you're forty so you may as well do it now. What the hell, you've got plenty of time to survive."

Alex's role in the English music scene was that of the older more experienced man who looks after the younger musicians, points them in the right direction, and lets them run because they're going to run faster than you anyway. Music is a very tribal thing, each musician lending the other support, each knowing he could turn to one of the others for help when needed because they were all in it together, welded into a close community. There were no superstars, no riches, no screaming teenyboppers; just several score musicians who had come together in a very tight group revolving around Alex and Blues Incorporated. Their only concern was in music. How well you could play. What music you played. Very often they didn't like one another on personal levels but it didn't matter because the moment they began tuning their instuments they'd forget everthing but the music, which is all that mattered. Not one of them could explain why they played with people they didn't always like, except that they played so well you had to go and blow with them. They were a part of your tribe. And that sense of community was reinforced by the antagonism of the jazz musicians and the promoters.

By now, as the Stones had become a working band and were being paid a few pounds a night for playing, the jazzmen's hold on English popular music was slipping. The Beatles were breaking it down in Liverpool and were about to assault London, the Animals in Manchester were attracting notice, Eric Clapton was blowing tributes to Elmore in small London clubs, and so many other of the younger musicians were playing the blues. And great numbers of jazz musicians, managers, and promoters were beginning to understand that rhythm and blues was destroying the cozy jazz scene, and were signing up blues bands, leaping in before their rivals could get the edge. It started there, that summer Blues Incorporated played the BBC show and the Rolling Stones came out of the Bricklayer's Arms as a working band. By the following winter, some nine months after Alex and his group opened it all up at the Marquee, there would be a complete upset on the music scene. Clubs, managers, and promoters would turn their backs on the jazz bands and sign up any musician who appeared even slightly capable of forming a blues band.

And in that summer of 1962, as jazz musicians were beginning to sense their loss of dominance, much bad blood began to flow between the two camps of musicians. The antagonism was heightened when Alex, sitting around talking about the impending changes with a number of musicians from each camp, said, "I'm going to break down this goddamn Mickey Mouse jazz scene and produce some real music." That line was quoted and requoted in every club in London, and the antagonisms grew so large that Keith, angered at Harold Pendleton's obvious partiality for jazz, swung his guitar at the club owner's head; and some jazz players stopped talking to blues musicians. The bluesmen didn't really give a damn because record company A & R men were now slipping into the clubs to listen to the blues groups, and English recording firms were releasing Chuck Berry and Muddy Waters albums for the first time. The blues era was obviously arriving and the jazz stranglehold ending, and Jagger was ready to capitalize on it.

When the school year was out Jagger decided he must move into a flat in London to be in the center of the musical universe while everything was so fast-changing. He persuaded Brian and Keith to share a place with him. Jagger had some money from his government grant, Brian was working at odd low-paying jobs, and Keith received a small allowance from his family. Their combined income didn't add up to very much but they felt certain the band would be getting a greater number of paying gigs and they'd be able to at least scrape together enough for the rent, for food, and for the rehearsal hall at the Brick.

The bedsit they found was in Edith Grove, off the Fulham Road in Chelsea, a tiny hovel that had electricity—one bulb dangling from a cord in each of the two rooms—and little else to make it livable except that it was cheap. The water taps leaked, wallpaper was flaking off the walls, and sometimes the walls themselves seemed about to flake apart, the furniture provided by the landlord and the odds and ends they dragged up from the street just a step ahead of the dustmen collapsed with predictable regularity. There was a communal toilet two flights up, rather unclean and completely unlighted—to use it after dark the boys had to carry a candle. About the only equipment that worked properly was the record player they brought along and the very large fridge, which became a standing joke among friends because it was always empty except for pint bottles of milk crawling with mold.

Their greatest problem was food. They had misjudged their wealth and the band's ability to earn a few pounds a night and soon discovered there wasn't enough money to feed them properly. Mrs. Richards sent parcels of food every couple of days. Cleo Sylvester, a young black student and singer who had met the boys at the Marquee, where she occasionally sang in a backup group with Blues Incorporated, bought them food whenever she could spare money from her allowance. Their staple diet was potatoes. Mashed, usually, because none of them knew anything about cooking. And Brian insisted on adding fried eggs to the potatoes whenever they could get enough money together to buy a few eggs. "It gives the spuds a colorful look and it also boosts the old calories," Brian said. "No sense dying of starvation just when this band's about to tear the country apart with its great music."

They never did come close to starvation, in part because they were pretty crafty at nicking their neighbors. On the floor above them lived two young men in training to be school-teachers. They'd hold several parties a week—beer and sandwiches with friends, and dancing to Duke Ellington records. When the parties ended and everyone was passed out, Brian, Keith, and Jagger slipped into the flat with paper bags and filled them with the leftover sandwiches and empty bottles to return to the pub for the deposit. The flat below them was shared by four middle-aged women from Liverpool, come to the big city together because times were bad up north. The boys didn't know what the women did for a living and cavalierly decided they must be whores. But the women took a liking to these scruffy nineteen-year-olds and often fed them and helped hold them together when things really seemed to be bad and the boys appeared about to collapse—a look they learned to cultivate for its most rewarding effect.

Their financial crisis came about mostly because they continued to buy equipment for the band on hire purchase and the weekly payments had to be made to the shops. They'd hide money away in an old tin in the flat to make the repayments, but some of the cash seemed to be vanishing each week. Eventually Jagger and Keith discovered that Brian—who had the only steady income and was contributing more than his share—was periodically dipping into the money tin. They became angry at Brian, and several arguments shook the flat. But Brian was then the leader of the Stones, he was such an incredibly fine musician that he learned to play the mouth harp like a professional in a single day while sitting around the flat, in no way could the Stones at that time survive without Brian for he had fused them into a functioning unit and held them together, so Brian was usually forgiven his petty thefts.

The band's paying jobs were few. Much of the time they played for nothing, because no one would pay them. But they weren't too often discouraged. Brian would sometimes say he was going to quit because he didn't think he was good enough to make it—and he needed very badly to make it—but Cleo or one of the other young women who visited Edith Grove would bring him out of his dark moods. Those periods of depression didn't come too often except for Brian, who was careful not to appear discouraged when Jagger was around. Most of the time the boys were optimistic and they spent many hours discussing their future.

One of those conversations was kicked off after the band completed a date which was rather disappointing because only a couple dozen fans turned out to hear them. As the Stones were packing up their gear after their last set a blonde and attractive young woman, one of those pre-groupies who were beginning to follow the band from date to date, came up to chat with Brian.

"We're all on your side, we love the music you play, but a lot of people just hate you," she said.

"What does that mean?" Brian asked.

She told him that while she was waiting outside, before the doors were opened, a man prominent in the jazz world came up to her, glared at the Stones poster, and asked if she was a fan. She said she certainly was and he smiled and said:

"Forget them. By the time we're finished with that little lot they won't get a job in any club in England."

The boys talked about that incident on the way back to Edith Grove. Jagger summed up their attitude: "To hell with the lot of them. We'll just keep hammering away and we'll make it in spite of them all. Anybody who laughs at us can get on with it."

Keith and Brian shouted their agreement. But when they returned to their flat they talked about their future almost until dawn and continued to discuss it in the following weeks. Jagger said he was concerned about their parents. They'd put a lot into giving them a good home and a good education, and he said he knew his parents were upset about his interest in the blues, playing in the band. He wondered whether he was doing the right thing by not working harder at school and looking for a worthwhile job, and perhaps forgetting about this mad music bit.

"Maybe yer right," Brian said. "Suppose we fail?"

"Why should we fail?" Jagger said. "I don't think about failure because we're going to make it. What it comes down to is, we really have to go for what we believe in. The blues."

Keith said he was right. That's what they had been feeling down in Dartford, that they had to push rhythm and blues over to a wide public. "We got to get *our* idols idolized by everybody else, turn 'em on to Chuck and Jimmy Reed and all those cats."

"All right, so we carry on with it and we know we're going to make it," Jagger said. "Look, there's something Alex keeps telling the cats. I don't remember just how he put it but I think of it this way. Even if we do flop, even if we just scrape along making a few bob a night. Does it matter? At least we tried. We'll try to the best of our ability and we'll have nothing to regret in later life no matter how it turns out. Maybe we'll all be working in offices and married and settled down with kids in some suburban house. But if we don't give it a proper fling we'll probably end up kicking ourselves."

"Yeah, because we'll never know how good we could have been," Brian said. "And a lifetime of regret, of looking back and kicking ourselves for not giving it a proper fling, would muck us up forever."

Jagger said it was settled, they must carry on with it. And if they had to give up everything for the music, then they'd give it up. But the first thing they must do is join the National Jazz Federation.

Brian and Keith chorused that Jagger must be stark raving out of his bloody mind, that the jazz bunch were their enemies, but Jagger explained that the problem was that the trad boom was dying. A lot of clubs using trad bands were feeling the pinch and closing down. Or changing over to the kind of music that Alex and the Stones were playing. They had talked to the kids, Jagger said, and they knew the kids were looking for something different. Not trad jazz or the Shadows and Bobby Vee kind of pap. What they were looking for would be the Stones, even if they didn't know it yet. "Thing is, though, that the trad scene has been dominated by older musicians, like Chris Barber and Humphrey Lyttleton—Acker Bilk and Kenny Ball, too, if you like, on a more commercial level."

"So why join the Jazz Federation?" Brian asked.

It would mean they'd have direct contact with all the top people in the business, Jagger said, get them to think the Stones were jazz musicians trying the new music fad that Alex had started. That way, when the blues pushes the last of the jazz musicians out, and some of them start to switch over to the blues to keep working, the Stones would be there first.

They promptly signed up with the National Jazz Federation. It was a delicious feeling, infiltrating the enemy and nibbling at them from within.

With Dick Taylor gone because he had been accepted at the Royal College of Art, the Stones were forced to search around for a new bass guitarist. Keith asked Tony Chapman, their regular drummer, whether he knew any good bass players who were looking for a group to join. Tony said he did know one cat who was damned good and would bring him around to the Wetherby Arms, in the King's Road, where the Stones had begun to hang out and occasionally to rehearse because it was nearer their flat than the Bricklayer's Arms.

The bass player, Bill Wyman, turned up with Tony the next evening, hauling a huge speaker and a spare Vox eight-thirty amp, the biggest amp any of them had ever seen. *And it's his bloody spare,* Keith thought. Tony introduced Bill all around, but only Jagger and Ian paid him much attention because Keith and Brian were deep into a conversation and their brew, which annoyed Bill somewhat. Bill thought Jagger was just a shade neater than the other two, as befits a student, but was pretty scruffy nevertheless, hair growing long, clothes looking as if they hadn't been cleaned or pressed in ages.

After chatting a while with Jagger and Ian, whom Bill had met before at rock clubs in Surrey, they got down to playing a few numbers together in a room back of the pub. Bill was edgy because he didn't know whether he could bring off the blues sound this band wanted. He had heard a lot of talk about the Stones among other musicians, heard they were damned good. He wasn't certain of his own ability although he'd been playing in rock bands for about four years and was more experienced than any of them. *And I sure as hell don't like the name Rolling Stones, damned silly name,* Bill thought as they worked through a few numbers. When the informal audition was over Brian and Jagger asked Bill to join the band. He accepted immediately, even though he guessed he'd lose money at least for a while because the Stones had no real drawing power yet and Bill had been playing with bands which earned him at least a couple of pounds a night. He auditioned for the Stones primarily because he could no longer stand playing with the dreadful rock bands that were around at the time—bands imitating the Shadows, little dance steps, and an unvarying sound in every number—bands that had run out of musical ideas and were playing the same old draggy pop rock every night. And he joined the Stones because he felt the band was the only live and vibrant group he'd heard in a long while.

Cleo Sylvester got to the Marquee a little early, one Thursday night in December, and once more she felt a bit of surprise when Jagger came over to chat. She had known Alex and John Baldry and the other musicians since Blues Incorporated's opening night at the Marquee; as a black woman and a singer she wanted to learn all she could about the black American rhythm and blues, and the Marquee was an informal conservatory for her. Cleo had been present at almost every Blues Incorporated club date since the band was formed. And yet, though all the musicians—especially Baldry and Brian—were taken by her quick smile, her impish laugh, and warm good looks, and spent much time with her, Jagger was too shy and reticent to even say "Hello" for the first three months. When he did finally get up the courage to talk to her he asked her about herself and learned she was still in school and lived near Euston. "I know the neighborhood, I go to school there," Jagger said. He was so diffident about it that Cleo didn't even consider the possibility he went to LSE. She assumed he attended the Pitman Shorthand College, which was also near her home. When she learned he was a university student she was rather startled.

Over the summer Cleo and a girlfriend dropped into the Edith Grove flat regularly, occasionally cleaning up the place, laughing at them for being the sloppiest housekeepers in the British Isles, and Jagger had become warm and open with her. He impressed Cleo with his ability to withstand setbacks—or his need to pretend the unpleasant doesn't exist—and the way he'd deflect attention from his feelings by reeling off jokes. He seemed to be so aware of his talent and his potential that nothing else mattered, nothing could throw him off the course he had set for himself. Cleo went down to the Flamingo to see the Stones on their first night at this club in Wardour Street. There were no more than six people in the audience, and Jagger appeared very depressed for a time at the lack of turnout. The Flamingo was patronized mostly by blacks, and the Stones were resented for playing black music, and Cleo felt Jagger was hurt because he had often talked about popularizing black artists. Cleo could sense that immediately, the hurt Jagger felt and his depression. But by the time the group got out into the street Jagger was convulsing Cleo with old Bo

Diddley jokes, with a comic routine he had developed of spouting a string of long and unusual words and then suddenly breaking into a West Indian accent, of sending everything up. All the members of the Stones seemed to Cleo to be in deep misery because of the unenthusiastic response the band was getting in some clubs, but Jagger was expert at covering his feelings.

Despite their growing friendship, whenever Jagger approached Cleo, as he did now in the Marquee, she still felt a bit surprised that he had overcome his extreme shyness. That evening, Cleo recalls, Jagger got right to the point.

"Cleo, I'd like you to join the Stones," he said.

"Are you serious?"

"Sure I am. We've talked it over and decided we want some colored girls to join the group as singers. To back us up. We're looking for a little more of the American sound."

"Like the Ikettes?"

"Exactly," Jagger said. " 'Ooh-Poo-Pah-Doo' and songs of that sort. And we've decided on a name for the girls. The Honeybees."

"I'd love to give it a go," Cleo said.

"Do you know any other colored girls who'd be interested in singing with us? We figure we want you and two more."

Cleo said she'd hunt around for two other black singers, and Jagger told her to be certain they were English, not West Indian, because he wanted girls who could copy the distinctive sound of the Ikettes without that West Indian lilt. Cleo found one girl who said her ambition was to be a singer. They went round to Edith Grove the following Sunday, and the Stones, very excited about getting their black chorus together, rushed them down to the Wetherby for their first run-through.

It turned out the new girl couldn't sing a note or even follow the lyric: While the band banged away and Cleo sang "Ooh-poo-pah-doo" over and over again in response to the lyric Jagger sang, she was shouting "Ooh--poo-poo-poo," completely off key, and then suddenly breaking up with nervousness and shouting, "Oh, oh, oh. Oh God, what can I do? I can't sing." The rehearsal soon broke up, the boys telling Cleo she'd brought them a complete loon instead of a singer. The girl fell into the Stones circle, though, and became one of several young women who'd help clean up their flat and bring them something to eat on occasion. But the gimmick of the black chorus—the Honeybees imitating Ike and Tina Turner's chorus—was soon given up as an idea not worth the trouble. Cleo was too busy with school exams to get seriously involved with performing, and the Stones were getting so few paying gigs that to split up the take among three extra performers would reduce their income to a few bob each per week.

Brian and Jagger had been asking Charlie Watts to become their regular drummer for several months and by the end of the year, 1962, were almost begging him to become a Rolling Stone. Tony Chapman was still committed to his job up north and missed so many rehearsals and club dates that they brought in another drummer, Steve Harris, to sit in during Tony's absences. But Steve was primarily a jazz band drummer and he couldn't completely adjust to the blues idiom, or the Stones versions of the blues, and the boys desperately wanted Charlie to round out the group. The Stones were getting more work by now, mostly in clubs on the edges of London. They were being paid on a percentage basis with the promoters—the more customers they brought in, the higher their wages. And the customers were beginning to come in, the Stones were building a following. They could feel an enormous energy growing, out there beneath the stage, young girls winding tighter and tighter and then finally springing loose, leaping on stage to touch Brian or Jagger, the favored two; dozens of these adolescents who already looked like, and dreamed of being, full-blown, sexual, sensual women, dozens

of them followed the Stones to every gig they played, screaming over the performances as if they were being sexually
fulfilled by the music, by Jagger's gestures and Brian's sadistic
teasing, his flick of evil. Brian said he'd love to put the boot to
these little girls, to arouse them with his screaming thumping
soaring guitar and then kick them and whip them and bugger
them until they were so broken to his will that they could only
plead for more. And though he was at least only partially
fantasizing aloud, the feeling of evil sensuality flowing from
Brian created a love-fear chemistry that forced the women to
come back for more, to follow the Stones around the London
club circuit. And to spread the word among their friends that
the new kind of music, and performance, coming out of this
band was guaranteed to wipe them out of their minds and
inspire delicious little orgasms at the same time. The Stones
weren't exactly being mobbed, but their ability to borrow the
most sexually arousing forms of black American music and
project it as something fresh and wholly their own, created a
small but devoted following that was slowly building up. By
the final months of the year the band was splitting £25 to £30
a week.

But Charlie was still unable to decide whether he wanted to
join the Stones. He was getting enough work with the jazz-
oriented band in which he'd been playing for about a year to
satisfy his need to play and to supplement the paltry wages he
earned as an apprentice artist and designer in a Regent Street
advertising agency. The trouble was, he said, he didn't know
whether he wanted to become a full-time musician, and Brian
and Keith were making it plain they believed the Stones would
soon be a full-time professional band. Dreaming, perhaps . . .
Jagger, after all, was still at LSE pursuing his business career
and though he wasn't working too hard at being a student, he
still seemed to feel that he'd never get rich with his singing
and so must devote some of his energies toward a more orthodox way of making a living. Charlie could understand that.

He was level-headed enough to realize that music was a hazardous business, and he believed it would be the sheerest folly to give up even the £14 a week he earned in the design studio and perhaps starve as a musician. Charlie liked clothes—smart suits, shirts, and ties; Christian Dior's London headquarters was next door to the ad agency, and the models Charlie had begun to date weren't the types to be seen with the likes of a scruffy Rolling Stone.

Charlie was worried because none of the musicians he knew in the jazz end of the business had a good word to say about the Stones. They were complete outsiders, and no one wanted to know anything about the great sound they were making because everyone was too busy looking at the Stones as a gang of ruffians, layabouts, and long-haired freaks. Charlie knew the group was damned good, knew that attitude was completely wrong, but he wondered whether the Stones would ever beat the unofficial boycott and really make it big; he worried about his future as a Rolling Stone. He had been born in Islington in June 1941, the son of a lorry driver for British Railways who always impressed on him the need for a steady job and permanent security. He went to Harrow Art School, landed the ad agency job, and felt that his future was as secure as it could be. Then the Stones came along.

Other musicians, especially Alex Korner, felt that Charlie was being middle-aged cautious, much too security-minded for a nineteen-year-old. Alex had offered Charlie the slot as regular drummer with Blues Incorporated in November 1961, but he had turned it down because his firm was sending him to Denmark for a couple of months to do some work there and he didn't want to risk losing his job. He didn't join Alex's band until his return from Denmark, and then only as an occasional drummer. And a few months before Brian began pressuring him to join the Stones, Charlie had dropped out of Alex's group, replaced by Ginger Baker, because the band was getting so much work that it had become a strain on him, interfering with his work at the ad agency.

Still, Charlie sensed that the Stones and all they represented were the coming thing in pop music. Perhaps the public wasn't aware of it—the Stones had received no publicity, they weren't even a complete band at this point—but other musicians could feel it, other musicians talked about the marvelous sounds that were coming out of Blues Incorporated and the Rolling Stones. Those two groups and few others were talked about among younger musicians.

"Brian and Keith are really after me to join the Stones," Charlie told Bobbie Korner as they sat in the Flamingo one night before the Stones were to take the stage. "I just don't know what to do."

"Are you working with anyone now?"

"Just a few gigs with Blues by Six. Nothing much. And I'm getting bored with their music. It's dead, compared to what Alex is playing, and the Stones."

"Then join them. Why not take a chance?" Bobbie said. "You don't have to be so cautious at your age. If it doesn't work out, there are a lot of other jobs around, and a lot of other bands. There certainly is nothing to lose by joining them. You're still very young and you have plenty of time to see about a regular job later if the music doesn't work out. But I think it will work out. Alex feels the Stones have a very bright future."

Charlie became the Stones' regular drummer in the first weeks of 1963.

The Stones had overcome the early resistance of the Flamingo's patrons, were pulling fair-sized audiences of screaming wriggling girls (and boys) into the club, and were given a steady Monday night date there. Other jobs were coming in with greater frequency, mostly in small clubs on the edges of the city whose owners worried less about the jazz-blues arguments than they did about filling their places with paying customers. By February 1963, the Stones were working at least four nights a week and earning about £7 apiece. With no newspaper write-ups, no manager, no real professional experience, Jagger was earning as a part-time singer half what Charlie was making at the ad agency each week. When he went home to visit his parents and his brother, Chris, who is five years younger, Jagger told them about the band's progress, their growing earning power, his feeling that he was on the edge of breaking things open in the music world and might perhaps someday really become wealthy as a singer. His parents, of course, worried a great deal and talked long and often about how to bring their son to his senses, how to make him realize that his infatuation with music and performing could only lead to disaster in the future. They sensed that he was seriously considering leaving LSE and felt they must steer him away from this insanity. But nothing they directly said to him seemed to have any affect; he simply assured them he was continuing his studies and working hard at them.

Alex recalls that one afternoon shortly after the Stones became the regular Monday night band at the Flamingo, he received a call from Mrs. Jagger. From her opening remarks, it was immediately clear to Alex that she was sounding him out about Jagger's growing determination to leave school and risk everything on the Stones, and also trying to learn whether Alex had been responsible for the change in her son. After telling Alex how glad she was that her son was enjoying himself with his hobby Mrs. Jagger asked:

"Tell me honestly, do you think he has any future in the business?"

"He certainly does. I think he has an enormous future. He's one of the best singers I've heard and he'll go very far with it."

"*Really?*" Mrs. Jagger said, sounding to Alex incredulous. "I must say that *my* side of the family has always played music and sung a lot, and I've always felt that Mick is probably the least talented of us all. The whole family feels that way. I'm very surprised to hear you say that about his singing."

Alex could feel her need to be reassured. She was obviously quite anxious that Jagger was doing the wrong thing, with the Stones, and she simply must talk to someone who could really judge pop music, needed to know what a man of Alex's experience actually thought about her son's talents and his chances of succeeding.

"I don't know the members of your family. But I totally disagree with what you say about Mick's talent," Alex said. "You're completely wrong in your assessment of him. I think he's going to be enormous someday. I'm convinced he's going to be very successful."

Mrs. Jagger continued to ask questions, and Alex was embarrassed: He felt she was invading their privacy, violating the integrity of the musician's tribal privacy. He tried to end the conversation as quickly as possible, thinking: *I don't mind being some sort of father figure to Mick if it's any use to him but I'll be damned if I'm going to be a same-generation figure to his parents. That's quite another matter. This world we're involved in, my relationship with Mick, is a musical-personal one. It has nothing to do with his family, his background. I don't know his parents, I don't want to know anything about the people I'm working with except in our capacity of working together. That's a special world and parents have no place in it.* Mrs. Jagger continued to ask questions, feeling Alex out as to what Mick was doing, whether he'd become a layabout, possibly getting in with the wrong crowd. Alex simply reassured her that everything was fine, and eventually she thanked him and rang off.

Alex turned to his wife. "I'm not about to put up with people ringing me and asking me to tell them about their children," he said.

97

"You're absolutely right. Mick keeps his background separate from his music. You've been his escape from his background and . . ."

"And I'm not going to get involved in his past and destroy the relationship of the present. I'm not interested in knowing musicians in other worlds outside of music, and for someone's mother to ring up . . ."

Giorgio Gomelsky, a flamboyant eccentric bearded White Russian *émigré* film-maker who had first introduced Chicago blues artists to English audiences by promoting the National Blues and Jazz Festival, was running the Crawdaddy Club at the Station Hotel, Richmond, Surrey, a quiet Thames-side country town forty minutes from Soho by rail. Gomelsky's club acts had always been jazz bands up to the previous summer, when Alex's gigs at the Ealing and the Marquee prompted a demand by teenagers for blues-based music they could dance to. Gomelsky hired a blues group, the Dave Wood Rhythm and Blues Band, which became the Crawdaddy's resident dance band. Several of the Stones had visited the Crawdaddy over the months and got to know Giorgio. In turn Giorgio had dropped into clubs where the Stones were playing—in London and at little clubs in Windsor and other towns near the city—and their raw-edged approach to music appealed to him personally and as a businessman. Wherever they played the Stones were pulling in crowds and generating a remarkable visceral excitement that seemed refreshing to Giorgio after so many years of watching jazz audiences that were barely alive enough to wriggle their toes to the beat.

Giorgio took an almost paternal interest in the Stones, encouraging the boys whenever they seemed to become depressed about their future. Jagger and Brian particularly had such an enormous drive, an almost manic need to make it, to become famous and successful and sought after. Giorgio bolstered their confidence whenever it fell and offered an occasional suggestion or bit of advice: "I think you'd be more effective if you varied the volume of your songs a bit. The amps can be used to bring another dimension to your music, louder on some numbers, softer on others, to change the mood and let your musicianship come through." The boys always listened, experimented with his ideas, worked hard to develop a special Rolling Stone sound, bringing a little bit more professional backing to the sexual feel of Jagger's performances and the compulsive evilness of Brian's.

Brian traveled down to Richmond as often as he could, to sit and talk to Giorgio, promoting himself and the Stones. He and Jagger desperately wanted the kind of steady gig at the Crawdaddy that Dave Wood's band had because the Crawdaddy's audiences were younger and more excitable than the Flamingo patrons; there weren't any jazz-oriented people coming to the Crawdaddy and harping about the blues' crudeness as there were in almost all the clubs in London. The boys talked sometimes about how to ease the Wood band out of the Crawdaddy and get the Stones in. Then they heard the Dave Wood group was about to leave the club to take a better job in London, and Giorgio was looking for a new group to replace them. Brian said they must call Giorgio right now, this very moment, chat him up, tell him we're available, *beg for the job if we have to* . . . and Jagger was voted the man to make the call. They raced down to the King's Road, to a call box, and rang Giorgio. Before Jagger could do more than tell Giorgio his name, Giorgio cried: "You must be psychic, Mick. I was going to call *you*, this very day, to ask if the Rolling Stones would come to Richmond and take over the Sunday afternoon dance sessions."

Jagger said they'd be right down to talk about it. They flew back to the flat, dug into the tin can for a few pounds, and boarded the next train to Richmond. When they arrived they almost fell over one another to get across Kew Road from the station to the Crawdaddy, more excited about this job than any other because the Crawdaddy would be a place of their own, a showcase for the Stones and a proving ground where they could experiment with musical ideas and get a feedback from kids their own age, the sort of audiences they had to reach and command and suck into their music if they were going to ever catch that gold ring.

Giorgio told them that he couldn't afford to pay them much, they'd have to pull audiences in if they were going to earn any money. He offered them a basic minimum of £6 a night for the band (£1 a man) or 50 percent of the take at the door, whichever was larger. They accepted immediately. The first Sunday afternoon they attracted almost seventy teenagers into the Crawdaddy, and the band made £7.10, more than they had hoped. On the second Sunday the audience, and their wages, doubled. By mid-March the Stones had created, down in Richmond, a vital force on the pop music scene. The Crawdaddy was the place to be on Sunday afternoons. Long before the Stones were scheduled to take the stage the kids formed long queues in Kew Road, so strangely dressed in riotous colors or the American cowboy look, so absolutely beyond the most vivid imaginings of Richmond's gentlemen and matrons that the local paper, the *Richmond and Twickenham Times,* sent a man down to see what was going on. He wrote a story about the weird kids spilling out into the roadway, the near-riots that sometimes occurred when the Stones completed their performance and the kids were turned out into the streets, the perverse look of these musicians who didn't even wear suits and whose hair was creeping down to their shoulders. But the writer did say that the Rolling Stones were a different sort of group from the deadly bores that were playing across England, that their music was new and exciting and was perhaps the wave of the future in English pop music.

The boys were carried almost out of their minds when that

story appeared. Their first publicity. The very first recognition, in print, of their ability to excite and stimulate, with their music and their outrageous performances. Brian was more exhilarated than the others by that half-page feature article. He cut it out of the paper and stuck it into his wallet and pulled it out so often to demonstrate to any who'd listen that the band he formed was truly something special, that in a week or so it was tearing and disintegrating.

It wasn't only the teenage fans who considered the Crawdaddy the place to be on Sunday afternoons. Giving up Sunday lunch to make the trip to Richmond became, for London's growing hip set, the chic thing to do. The Crawdaddy was a must appearance for the Jean Shrimptons, the David Baileys, the Eric Claptons, for the hip, the camp—especially for the queens who found Jagger so very desirable—and the groupies: models, actresses, even young ladies of the aristocracy who found it impossible to ignore Jagger's exotic sensuality, so appealing to both sexes, and who were charmed by his rough Cockney edge.

BOOK THREE

CHRISSIE SHRIMPTON, tall, lithe, and delicate, with silky brown hair framing a face that's just short enough of perfection, and artificiality, to lend her a special allure. One of those Englishwomen who, when they are beautiful, are exquisitely provocative. At seventeen Chrissie was beautiful, perhaps not in that kooky Bailey-created manner of her older sister, Jean, whose face was beginning to be seen in all the fashion magazines, but the beauty of those wholesome North Country women.

Chrissie had been going to the clubs to see and dance to jazz bands since she was fourteen and had begun to date, and when Alex stirred an interest in the blues she went to see his band. She had watched Jagger perform in his first weeks with Blues Incorporated, when he had only one song memorized, and she thought he looked so cute, so small next to towering Long John Baldry—not realizing that Jagger felt so diminutive next to Baldry, so unimportant because all the other band members seemed like giants next to him. Now that the Stones were playing at Richmond and Windsor and other towns near her father's farm in Burnham, west of London, she went out to see them. Chrissie was usually the most striking young woman in the audience, and it seemed to her Jagger was directing his songs at her, singing to her as if she were the only woman in the room. It didn't seem to be very sincere, it was obvious Jagger was trying to pull her. Chrissie enjoyed it and wondered why Jagger was too shy to approach her and chat her up. She'd stare back at him, teasing, and pleased that he was paying her attention.

One evening the Stones played at the Maidenhead International Club, a rather dreary place frequented by the au pair girls of the area. Chrissie went to see the band with a boy friend who claimed that he knew Jagger, and she realized that knowing Jagger was a kind of status symbol, a sign of being "in" for the Richmond Art School set, the kids who wore "groovy" clothes and tried to be very hip. She was certain few of them, including her date, had more than a passing acquaintance with Jagger.

She was in a playful mood, talking to her date about Jagger's obvious interest in her, his shyness, his inability to make the first approach. Her date said Jagger was so shy that he'd be willing to bet Chrissie couldn't even entice him into kissing her. Chrissie responded, "Make it a ten-bob bet. He'll kiss me." When the Stones finished their set the foreign girls were hanging back, bashful, wanting so desperately to simply touch one of these boys but almost afraid. Chrissie brazenly walked up to Jagger.

"Will you kiss me?" she asked.

Jagger giggled a bit—he was often very giggly around women—but he stepped closer and leaned over and kissed her on the lips. Chrissie put one arm on his shoulder as she was being kissed; her right hand was extended behind her, palm up, asking to be paid the ten bob. Jagger giggled again after the kiss, and Chrissie studied him. "He was very giggly, very pretty," she said. "I guess he was very camp then, without me realizing what camp was. He was like camp without knowing it himself. I thought he was very groovy. He looked very young and he was very spotty, very pimply. I was very impressed with him."

He asked her for a date ("I'll take you to the pictures"), and they arranged to meet in Windsor a few days later. Jagger sat primly at her side on that first date, seeming to be absorbed in the film, incredibly shy; the conversations he began were like green logs, smoking but unable to catch fire. When the film ended and they went out into the street the other members of the Stones showed up—they had another gig in town—and Jagger made Chrissie promise she'd come see him at the club. The promise extracted, Jagger ran off down the street, shouting at his group. Chrissie was trying hard to make sense of what he was saying but she couldn't understand a word because of his strong London working-class accent.

Giorgio was beginning to feel certain he had the next hit group on his hands—the next Beatles perhaps. Not so huge as the Beatles, possibly, for after all they were stirring the sort of excitement that hadn't been seen since Sinatra did it back in the States twenty years before, but certainly big enough to make hit records, command large audiences. Why, even the smart hip London people were coming down to see the Stones, even a Beatle was coming to see them—George Harrison himself, chatting them up and returning to London to rave to others about them. So Giorgio became the Stones manager, under a verbal agreement. He immediately set about promoting them, using his contacts in the music press to get these kids written about. One call was to Peter Jones, a free-lance writer specializing in pop music. Peter tried to make his excuses. He didn't want to give up a Sunday afternoon with friends just to see another new group, and certainly not all the way down to Richmond. But Giorgio has a cunning habit of pretending he doesn't understand when someone fails to agree with him, his accent getting thicker, his ears unable to hear much, and Peter finally agreed to go down and see the Stones.

He walked into the saloon bar of the Station Hotel the following Sunday afternoon. It was half-filled with the usual Sunday drinkers leaning over their pints of bitter, but this lot was trying very hard to ignore the heavy drum beat and the loud guitar wails coming out of the back room, the Crawdaddy Club. As Peter headed toward the club door he could hear a man at the bar grumbling about the music. "Turn the radio on, drown out that ridiculous rubbish," the customer asked the bartender. Peter chuckled and pushed through the door. The Stones were up on a small stage, standing around looking bored, a handful of teenagers watching and adoring them, while Giorgio gave directions to a cameraman. He was getting the Stones down on film, his favorite medium, hoping eventually to use the result as promotion and perhaps a *cinéma vérité* feature. Peter's first thought on seeing the Stones was, *they're so hairily disarranged.* Most young Englishmen were permitting their hair to grow long, but this was the longest Peter had seen. The group broke for lunch after a little while, and Peter went out to the bar with Brian and Jagger.

"How are the Stones doing?" Peter asked.

Jagger started to say something about how great life was for them, but Brian cut him off. "It's pretty down. We've got the best group in England but we're not getting anywhere because of the blocks being put on us," he said. "The jazz people, they're making it impossible for us to break through, they're against rhythm and blues."

"Yeah, it's all sort of like, trad is trad, and modern is modern, and your mainstream's your mainstream, and your blues is your blues, and all that down the line," Jagger said. "And you can't play rhythm and blues in here because this is a jazz club. We can't get much work because people want you to play jazz, in some form. We're playing just very basic blues, twelve bars to twelve bars, and the jazz people hate us."

They went on about the hurdles being put in the band's way, and Brian sounded very despondent. But he brightened suddenly and fumbled in his wallet for the cutting from the local newspaper, talking more rapidly now about the following they had built up in Richmond, displaying the newspaper article to prove his point.

The Stones went back inside after lunch to play a couple of numbers for the cameraman, while the teenage extras danced about. One song was "Pretty Thing," and Peter Jones was deeply impressed: *This is dynamite . . . everything's happening up there that should be happening in music . . . these kids are one of the most potent little outfits on the scene . . .*

When the set was over Brian came up to Peter. "Sorry the music wasn't up," he said. "We need an audience to get us really swinging, and these kids are just a few extras Giorgio brought in. If you'll stay around till our real set . . ."

Peter thought, *He's actually sorry . . .* "Brian," he said, "I think the Stones are excellent, I really do. You're authentic and you deserve a break. I mean that sincerely. I'm going to get a couple of real hardened rhythm and blues fans to come down and see you, and see if we can get a bit of publicity going for the Stones."

Jagger and Keith had come over to join Brian, and they all seemed pleased enough at Peter's promise. But Peter could sense they were trying to hold down their enthusiasm—*probably because they've been promised all sorts of things before and have been disappointed*, he thought.

The next morning Peter went into the office of *Record Mirror*, the paper to which he contributed, and talked to journalist Norman Jopling about the Stones, asking him to have a look, to judge for himself whether the Stones were the most exciting group on the music scene. Jopling agreed to go down to Richmond the following Sunday, with a photographer, and to write a feature if he felt the group warranted one. A couple of weeks later a headline screamed across five columns in an April issue of *Record Mirror:*

THE ROLLING STONES—GENUINE R AND B

And the Jopling article, the first in a trade paper about the Stones, was filled with praise for the group and the music they were playing. He wrote:

"As the trad scene gradually subsides, promoters of all kinds of teen-beat entertainments heave a sigh of relief that they have found something to take its place. It's rhythm and blues, of course—the number of R and B clubs that have suddenly sprung up is nothing short of fantastic.

". . . at the Station Hotel, Kew Road, the hip kids throw themselves about to the new 'jungle music' like they never did in the more restrained days of trad.

"And the combo they writhe and twist to is called the Rolling Stones. Maybe you've never heard of them—if you live far from London the odds are you haven't.

"But by gad you will! The Stones are destined to be the biggest group in the R and B scene—if that scene continues to flourish. Three months ago only fifty people turned up to see the group. Now Gomelsky has to close the doors at an early hour—with over 400 fans crowding the hall.

"Those fans quickly lose their inhibitions and contort themselves to truly exciting music. Fact is that, unlike all the other R and B groups worthy of the name, the Rolling Stones have a definite visual appeal. They aren't like the jazzmen who were doing trad a few months ago and who had converted their act to keep up with the times. They are genuine R and B fanatics themselves and they sing and play in a way that one would have expected more from a colour US group than a

107

bunch of wild, exciting white boys who have the fans screaming and listening to them.

"... They can also get the sound that Bo Diddley gets—no mean achievement. The group themselves are all red-hot when it comes to US beat discs. They know their R and B numbers inside out and have a repertoire of about eighty songs, most of them ones which the real R and B fans know and love.

"But despite the fact that their R and B has a superficial resemblance to rock 'n' roll, fans of the hit parade music would not find any familiar material performed by the Rolling Stones. And the boys do not use original material—only the American Stuff. 'After all,' they say, 'can you imagine, a British-composed R and B number? It just wouldn't make it.' "

Chrissie was commuting into London every day to attend secretarial college. She and Jagger would meet after their classes, walk through the park, sit on a bench for hours, talking ... both amazed and joyous, almost overwhelmed, because they had fallen in love. They swore it was the first real love for either of them. *He's the first man who's ever really turned me on, he's someone incredibly special,* Chrissie found herself thinking. And Jagger seemed to feel the same way. He continually expressed annoyance that she had to go home each night. He said he wanted her to spend the night with him at the Edith Grove flat, but was upset because he couldn't take her to so dreadfully filthy a place. But he impressed her with his need to spend the night with her, every night, to make love to her.

A couple of weeks after they'd met, Chrissie's parents went away for the weekend to celebrate their 25th wedding anniversary, and she asked Jagger to come down and stay with her. From then on they hitchhiked to her home after school, or after a Stones gig, and Jagger sneaked into her bedroom after the Shrimptons had gone to sleep. In the morning he rode back to London on the train with her. The Shrimpton neighbors, and Chrissie's contemporaries, tried to bring her to her senses, to deaden her infatuation for Jagger. They told her he looked peculiar and ugly, with his pimply face and huge red lips and hair almost as long as a woman's; they said they couldn't understand what she saw in him, that he was a strange man for a well-bred middle-class young lady to be dating, to have fallen in love with. But just another few months later all the young debs of the area would be begging Chrissie to bring Jagger to their parties, for the Stones had become fashionable. Especially Jagger. He was so camp, so strangely pretty, so outrageously androgynous. Jagger seemed to have that special quality of women, so much more attuned to their bodies, to the physicality of themselves at almost every moment of their lives, listening to and feeling every pain, every pleasure, every sound in their bodies, and not simply on a sexual level. Jagger's androgynous nature was more than an outer cloak he wore for shock effect, it was an integral part of his personality. He projected that from the stage and in his private life. And Chrissie wasn't even certain he was conscious of it. Yet when she did think about it, sometimes, she realized that several bisexual musicians, and the queens who hang around musicians, were as grasping toward him as any pubescent groupie. So perhaps he was aware of it, Chrissie felt.

The Stones had begun to play at the Ealing on Tuesday nights, making only £1 or £2 for the six of them but glad to be working for the experience. The band was never very successful those nights. Only about ten or twelve customers would wander around, and it was so cold that winter that even the musicians left their coats on; the water leaking from the roof always seemed about to form icicles. Eric Clapton came in most Tuesdays to sing the only song he really knew, "Roll Over Beethoven," with his eyes glued to the floor so he wouldn't have to look at the empty club, and Jagger said that

Clapton couldn't really play guitar, that he was trying damned hard to get it together but hadn't mastered it yet. But a deep affinity grew between Jagger and Clapton, the blues—Robert Johnson and Elmore and all the others—and something on a very personal level. They were both young and so very sexually attractive and shy and tentative, and they became very close.

In spending almost every day, and many nights, with Jagger, Chrissie began to understand that his shyness and gentleness were only one facet of his personality. He was very soft and feminine but he also had a very strong ambition, she felt, and wouldn't ever let anything stand in his way—not a woman, or another musician, not Brian or Keith or anyone. She felt he could be unscrupulous, if he had to be, that Brian was ostensibly the leader of the Stones but that Jagger was actually the strongest, the toughest. He hadn't bothered to dominate the group in actuality because there was no need for him to step forward. But he would, Chrissie knew, when he believed it was necessary. The contrast between his softness, the ease with which he was brought to tears on occasion, and the vein of toughness inside fascinated Chrissie.

She saw other contrasts in him. He seemed to be quite rebellious, anti-authoritarian, almost anarchist, hoping that someone would tear down society and start it all over again. Correctly this time. But he constantly wavered between loyalty toward the Stones and a feeling of debt to the government and the LSE. The way he worked so hard at his studies, although in spurts, made Chrissie feel at one point, in the first months of their relationship, that he would complete his studies at university even if it meant breaking up the Stones. Jagger also insisted that he didn't give a damn what society thought of him, that he wouldn't conform just to win society's approval and he'd certainly never get married because that would be the ultimate conformist behavior. Then he promptly asked her to marry him. They began to seriously discuss getting married, soon, perhaps when he was making enough money they'd be married . . . But he also said money wasn't important, just a societal hangup, that he was interested only in spreading the blues, making people understand about the incredible black musicians out there who were playing the best music in the world and who deserved fame, recognition and riches . . . Then he'd sit with Edward Shrimpton, Chrissie's father, and discuss economics, ways of making money, keeping it, making it grow for you, talking about money for hours on end.

Chrissie was very surprised that Jagger got on so well with her father. Mr. Shrimpton had always been money-minded— Chrissie often teased him about that. He never really liked any of the young men Chrissie and Jean would bring home because none of them had much knowledge of, or interest in, financial affairs. The young men were usually well-dressed and proper gentlemen but they didn't seem to be the sort who would support his daughters in the traditional way. Chrissie said her father was very much influenced by appearance and should have been appalled by Jagger's scruffiness, but got on well with him. Chrissie eventually understood that it was because her father could see through Jagger's deliberate image of unwashed poverty and into his head, and his ability to make money. He respected Jagger for it, telling Chrissie he had a deep respect for Jagger's mind because the boy was bright and intelligent and understood that individual freedom and dignity are more readily attainable if one has money, and the power that money brings.

It was difficult for Chrissie to believe that about Jagger, at first, because his life style was so peculiar. She had seen the flat in Edith Grove that he lived in with Brian and Keith and had been somewhat appalled by it. And the normal bachelor sloppiness had increased geometrically with the addition of a fourth roommate, a young printer named Jimmy Phelge whom they'd met in a pub. They loved Jimmy because they felt he was more insane than they, foul and grotty. They called him Nanka Phelge to indicate their distaste and attraction toward him. Jimmy turned the place into more of a hovel than it had been by introducing spitting contests. Phelge added to the general derangement in novel ways—his favorite was tacking obscene notes on the door, his form of love letters to young girls who had begun coming around seeking out the Stones, and their beds, describing an enormous variety of rapes and destructions and enslavements the Stones would wreak on them if they stepped past the door. Many of the girls just couldn't wait.

Jagger would never permit Chrissie to visit the flat. She'd stop by on occasion, and if Jagger hadn't returned from school she'd be forced to wait downstairs because Keith refused to permit her inside: "Much too filthy, love." There was also another embarrassment: a young American girl who had moved into the flat upstairs, a very fat, slovenly woman who wanted desperately to go to bed with Jagger; he had borrowed a few pounds from her, and she told him he didn't have to repay it if he'd only make love to her. Jagger giggled when he told Chrissie about it, said he hoped he'd never get that poor. But he seemed to like the girl. She fancied herself a fortune teller and astrologer, and she drew Jagger's chart: He would soon be famous, the stars told her, Jagger and the Stones would struggle for just a little while longer and then achieve a popularity awarded to few other groups; they would be held down for a while, by the fame of another band, but in a few years that group would disband and the Stones would be at the top of the mountain by themselves and Jagger would be the most famous performer in the world; but despite all the fame and even notoriety, Jagger wouldn't find personal happiness until he was thirty. Jagger said he believed her, quite strongly.

Only after Jagger took Chrissie down to Dartford to meet his parents did she begin to understand some of the conflicts and contrasts within him. Chrissie found Mrs. Jagger a pleasant, good-hearted woman who immediately treated her son's girl friend as her own daughter. But she was also annoying because she giggled a great deal *(Was that where Mick gets it from?* Chrissie wondered) and she seemed to thrive on gossip, any sort of gossip. Mrs. Jagger seemed annoying, most of all, because she kept after Jagger about the band, how the music was interfering with his scholastic career, and Chrissie felt she wasn't sophisticated enough to understand Jagger's needs. She also felt dreadful that Jagger had no patience with his mother, not enough patience to try and explain what the Stones meant to him, how they fulfilled a very important need. *She loves him very much,* Chrissie thought, *but Mick isn't very much into her . . . he's not being too nice . . . she's no more demanding than any mother, and he should be a little kinder to her . . .*

On meeting Jagger's parents and his younger brother, Chrissie also learned that Jagger's Cockney accent was faked, that his background wasn't much different from her own, that he was trying to break out of a suburban mold by pretending to be something he was not. And she began to understand that her father actually was able to see past Jagger's rebellious veneer and into the middle-class kid beneath it.

A few days before *Record Mirror* ran its feature on the Rolling Stones, Peter Jones was making the rounds of record companies and press agents, looking for feature material. He ran into Andrew Oldham. Andrew was nineteen, a small, slim, gingery and fast-talking manic, the first English hustler of the new pop era; he had an enormous drive and a strong need to leave his mark on the public consciousness. Andrew had first shown up on the music scene about two years earlier, billing himself as Sandy Beach, a singer-compère, running around to newspapers trying to get his name publicized. Nothing seemed to work; show business ignored him. So he

changed his name again, selecting another absurdity—
Chancery Laine—and continued his assault on the big time.
He failed again. He supported himself by working for Mary
Quant as a promotion man and general factotum, more successful at getting publicity for others than for himself, and
after a few months as a doorman at Ronnie Scott's jazz club in
Gerrard Street he became press agent for a young singer
named Mark Wynter. Andrew was hip, the quintessential
mod. While the young in America were imitating the
Kerouacs and Keseys and other members of the Beat Generation and taking to the road, in England the coming of age of
the war babies and the abolition of the draft created another
kind of existential army of teenagers—their energies poured
into sharp clothes, flashy and plastic, and American music.
They formed a subculture that was powering the Beatles into
the headlines as their "spokesmen" and that was searching for
other groups to adore, bands which were transforming American rhythm and blues into British hard rock.

Andrew Oldham was in the center of it, a part of the youth
culture and a hustler trying to capitalize on it, to bend this
strange new force to his own ambition. He was enormously
successful as a publicist, getting a large amount of newspaper
space for his client. He seemed to be everywhere at once, on
the make, turning up at newspaper and magazine offices,
parties, concerts, television studios. It was paying off, Andrew
was certain, when he attended a taping of the TV program
"Thank Your Lucky Stars" in January 1963 and met Brian
Epstein, the Beatles' manager. Epstein was impressed and
hired Andrew on the spot to help promote the Beatles second
record, "Please Please Me," which had to break into the charts
to sustain the drive that had been created by the Beatles and
demonstrate that they were not a one-shot recording group.
That second Beatles recording crashed into the charts at
number nine at the beginning of February, and Andrew got
music papers to run long features on the Beatles.

But now, as he met Peter Jones, Andrew was down to his single client again. The Beatles were becoming so large a property that it was obvious they needed a full-time publicist, so Andrew was eased out in favor of Tony Barrow. He didn't seem to let another defeat bother him. He had high energy, kept plugging away, and now he had been given a desk in the office of show business agent Eric Easton, with the possibility of a management partnership if they could find the right acts. Andrew asked Peter Jones to do a feature on Mark Wynter, but Peter wasn't much interested. Andrew dropped that subject quickly, and asked Peter: "If you hear of anything going in music that's at all interesting, let me know. I could use something in a part-time way." Peter said he'd keep that in mind, and Andrew continued:

"I've got a hunch the Beatles are going to be the biggest thing in the business in a few months. There's no stopping them. I'm just hoping I can find another group like them, then I'd have a go at management. If I find something I can work out a partnership with Eric Easton."

"There's this group called the Rolling Stones I saw down in Richmond. They're wild, really wild," Peter told him. "It looks as if rhythm and blues is going to be the next big thing. *Record Mirror* is saying that in the next issue, a long story about the Stones. Why not have a look at them?"

"Do they have a manager?" Andrew asked.

"I'm not certain. They're working for Gomelsky, but I don't know if he's signed them to a contract. The band is pretty brought down right now because they feel things aren't happening fast enough for them. But it's going to happen soon, people are talking about them. George Harrison has been down to see them a few times and he's raving about them. You really should go have a look."

Andrew said he might do just that. He didn't have to give it much thought: If *Record Mirror* was doing a feature on the Stones perhaps they really did have something, and if they did a lot of people would be trying to sign them up as soon as the newspaper came out. Andrew had to get there a step ahead of everyone else. He hurried back to Easton's office in Regent Street and told him about the big tip from Peter Jones, speaking fast and exuberantly, trying to convince Eric to go down to the Crawdaddy with him. It wasn't the first time that Eric had been touted on the coming sure-fire hit, and been disappointed. But he had given Andrew a spare room in the office primarily because he felt Andrew was a part of the pop scene, very much in touch with teen fashions and fads, as up to date on current pop trends as anyone else around and a man who seemed able to predict future trends. After all, Andrew had been saying for months that the Beatles were going to become the biggest act in the world, and it was beginning to happen just as he predicted. Eric couldn't very well ignore Andrew.

They drove down to the Crawdaddy the following Sunday afternoon, April 28, 1963. Eric kept thinking, during the drive, that he hoped he wasn't wasting an entire evening when he really preferred being home with his wife and children. The thought fled as they approached the Station Hotel. Outside, in a long queue, were several hundred outrageously dressed teenagers. Inside, after a long wait on the end of the queue, Eric kept thinking it was the first free Turkish bath he'd ever had. Every inch of space was jammed with kids, until the air filled with steam. And when the band came on Eric felt he was being lifted from his seat by the music. He told Andrew it was the most exciting thing he'd ever heard. The Stones seemed to be hurling their music from the edge of the bandstand and driving the kids wild with pleasure, 400 pairs of arms waving in beat to the music, barely able to dance because they were packed so tightly. Jagger's mouth was glued to the micro-phone as he belted out the lyrics, Brian chugging and thundering on the harmonica, both of them dancing as they worked, stirring up the crowd even further. Behind, the rest of the group pounded out a simple blues line around which Keith's guitar wove complex figures.

"That sound is fantastic, and the kids are finding it exactly right for them," Eric said, shouting into Andrew's ear to make himself heard over the pounding of the band and the roaring of the dancers. "You may be right, Andrew. The Beatles are making a big impression, everybody is going to look for a Beatles sound, to get on the bandwagon. That's one way to go. But the best way is to go for something definitely different, that's the secret of making it. These boys up there are certainly different. The beat's much the same, the guitars are featured in the same way, but the Stones are more basic, more down to earth. And a lot more exciting."

"Yeah, it's that Mersey sound, but way far ahead of the Mersey sound," Andrew said. "The Stones have got the music—a really special sound—and they've got sex. The chap singing, and the one on mouth harp, they're driving the girls crazy with the sex they ooze. They can't miss. We should get to them right away."

At the end of the set Andrew and Eric pushed their way to the bandstand, to Brian. "Are you the leader?" Eric asked. Brian said he was, pointedly ignoring the scowls from Jagger and Keith. They had, after all, talked at length about no one being the leader, all being equal in the Stones, and though they agreed that Brian had brought it all together they didn't much like to hear him say he was the leader of the band. "We'd like to chat with you boys, about what we can do for the group," Eric said. He told them he was an agent, representing such clients as Julie Grant, guitarist Bert Weedon, disc-jockey Brian Matthew, and that Andrew had worked for the Beatles, promoting the record that was now high on the charts. "Perhaps we can help you. Will you come in and see us?"

Brian and Jagger went to Eric's office the next day, arguing on the bus about the best way to handle agents: Jagger insisted that they must be somewhat distant and offhanded, perhaps even pretend they had had several offers of management contracts. When they found Eric's office and were seated across a huge desk from Eric and Andrew, Jagger asked:

"What do you have in mind for us, Mr. Easton?"

"Look, fellows, we're very interested in your group. If you'll agree to let us manage you we'll make a real go for you, but I must make it clear from the start that no promises are being made."

"What do you mean?" Jagger asked.

"Just that I'm not promising that I can get you on 'Sunday Night at the Palladium' or a hit record or a role in a huge film. No agent or manager in his right mind would ever say anything like that because you just don't know in this business. Making those sorts of promises is a waste of time.

"All I can promise is that we'll be honest with you, rather than make a lot of rash statements we can't live up to. We think you're good . . ."

"Why do you think that?" Brian asked. "What do you like about us is what I mean?"

Andrew leaned forward, intense, sincere: "I remember seeing the Beatles in Doncaster when they were eighth on the bill to people like Helen Reddy and Tommy Roe. I sat there with a lump in my throat. Just that one night, and you knew they were going to be very big. An instinctive thing. From that night on it's registered subconsciously that when they made it another section of the public was gonna want an opposite. I feel that even more strongly now, after working for Epstein and the Beatles. They're being dressed in suits, going cutesy, trying for the image of harmless adolescents . . . Even more now, the public are going to demand an opposite. And when I saw you perform last night I knew that other section of the public was going to want the Rolling Stones as the opposite. Again, it's just an instinctive thing. But I know you've got it, and I know I can make the public aware you've got it."

A few weeks before, Alex Korner had told a group of musicians after a Stones gig at the Marquee: "Only two good things are going to come out of this club—Blues Incorporated and the Rolling Stones." The most important blues musician in England, and now a hot young London publicist, both ranting about the Stones.

"We think you're really very good, very exciting," Eric said. "But the real success of anything depends on whether the general public agree. If the kids, the young fans you need, don't agree with us, if they don't want to accept the stuff you're doing . . . well, that's it. Nothing we can do is going to make any difference. All we can do is present you as a group exactly the way you are. We'll try to get you exposure but the rest is up to you.

"Well, that's about the lot. Do you fancy the idea?"

Brian and Jagger glanced at one another. They liked Eric's out-front talk and although he was fortyish, he did say he had a long background as a musician, and a manager and agent. And there was this Andrew chap. He was the same age as they, which was very important, and he was so clearly on top of things—he worked for the Beatles. "Okay, we'll go along with you," Brian said. "Anything you can do will be much appreciated. And we'll do our best to show the fans how great the Stones are."

They shook hands all around, and the boys got up to leave, to report to the rest of the group. Eric told them to sit down again, they'd just begun. He explained it was vitally important to be certain that the Stones had no connection with any other firm, had signed no contracts with any one. Brian assured him they had no manager, had never signed anything with Gomelsky, and if Gomelsky might later feel he'd been cut out, well, that would be too bad . . . But there was one thing, Brian admitted—they'd been recording in the IBC studios on Portland Place and had signed something, he wasn't certain precisely what it was, but he had a feeling that if the Stones demos worked out IBC would have a crack at handling the

119

group. "But the material is pretty bad, it's nothing any record company can use," Brian said. Eric disagreed; he promptly contacted an executive at IBC and offered to buy back the demos. The price was set at £100, the Stones to pay half of it.

"Now that that's out of the way," Eric said, "we must get a Rolling Stones disc out—fast. And we must form our own record company to do it." Eric explained that he and Andrew felt strongly the Stones were so far ahead of their time that it'd be too much to expect the ordinary artists and repertoire men at the major recording companies to understand the sound the band was trying to project. They—the band, Eric, and Andrew—would do the entire thing themselves—record, produce, package, and so keep control over every aspect of a disc, then sell the finished product to a record company. It was a daring concept, for England, but Phil Spector and other American artists and producers had taken that route, and it was well worth the attempt. Especially since it meant they would keep a higher percentage of a record's income; they could earn more money by selling a finished product rather than simply becoming another group in a large company's stable. So Impact Sound was created, a label whose only assets and employees were the band and their managers. It was the first independent record label in England.

Less than two weeks after Eric and Andrew drove down to Richmond to see the Stones, the band carted their equipment into the Olympic Sound recording studios, hoping they could get two good sides onto tape in one session. The studio seemed cavernous and bare: just the six Stones, Andrew as producer, and recording engineer Roger Savage. Only Roger really understood the mysteries of studio consoles and tape decks and remotes. On the way to the studio Andrew had come right out with it:

"Look, this is the first recording session I've ever handled, I

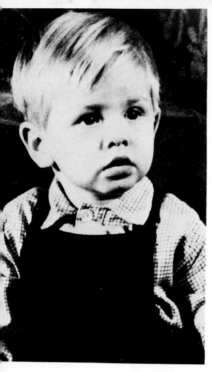

Brian Jones, age 2, and Jagger, age 10, on holiday with parents (Syndication International).

The Rolling Stones, 1968 (Michael Cooper).

Brian with Anita on her arrival from Munich, 1966 (Syndication International).

Chrissie Shrimpton and Jagger leaving for New York, 1966, to do the Ed Sullivan Show (Syndication International).

Brian rehearsing with Jagger and Keith in Keith's mansion, 1969 (Michael Cooper); Jagger in Brian's flat, 1966, when Brian was still "leader" of the Stones (Michael Cooper).

Brian and his hookah, with Jagger and Keith at Achmed's, Tangier, 1966 (Michael Cooper); Marianne and Jagger in Tangier (Syndication International).

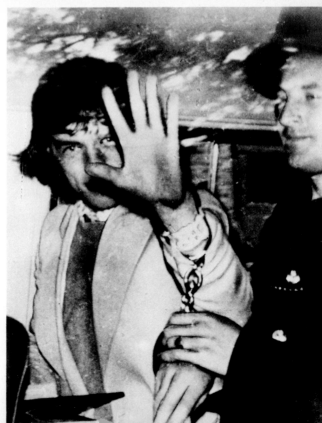

Keith and Marianne—"the girl in the fur rug"—amused by the drug trial headlines (Michael Cooper); Jagger, in handcuffs, on way to prison after drug conviction (Syndication International).

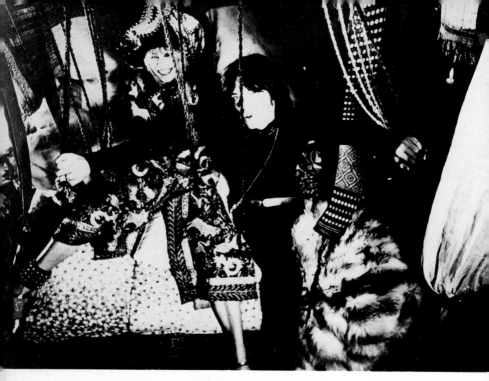

Jagger and Anita in costume on set of Performance *(Michael Cooper).*

Marianne's first night out after losing her baby, with Jagger and Lord Montagu (Syndication International).

Brian and Suki Potier in Marbella, Spain, 1967 (Syndication International).

Brian and Keith sharing a puff, 1968, before the final break (Michael Cooper).

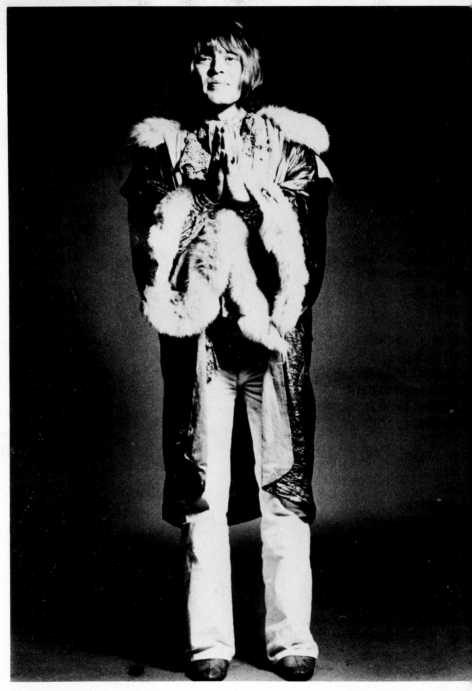

The last photo of Brian, taken by Michael Cooper a week before Brian drowned (Michael Cooper).

don't know a damn thing about recording, or music for that matter.''

"So we'll all be in the same boat, ignorant as 'ell," Jagger said. "A bunch of bloody amateurs gonna make a 'it single.''

"Right," Andrew said. "Anyway, I'm sure I know the sort of sound that's gonna prove commercial, that will sell. We'll just get in there and play it by ear and not get panicky—except we must remember we've booked the studio for three hours, and it's costing a great deal of money.''

"Sure, don't get panicky but get it all done in three hours," Jagger said.

They got down to business and cut the first track, what they considered their best and most commercial song, "Come On," a Chuck Berry number. The song was a disaster. The Stones were tense and sounded almost amateurish; Jagger complained that they couldn't get started in the sterility of the recording studio, that they needed a live audience to respond to them and provide a challenge and a crossfeed, to force them into their best and wildest form, that he couldn't deliver the kind of *performance* in a studio that he belted out from a live stage. But time was running out, and they had to settle for the version of the song that they got down on the tapes. When the three hours were up and the Stones first recording session came to an end, the studio engineer asked Andrew:

"What about mixing it?''

"What's that?" Andrew replied.

The engineer explained patiently: They'd been recording on four tracks, Jagger's singing out front on one, Brian's wailing harmonica on another, and so on, and the tracks would have to be mixed down onto one tape, a tedious job but the most vital part of record-making, for the proper mix could mean the difference between a hit and a reject; it could make the band sound like a live driving hard rock blues band, or a flaccid imitation of Bill Haley and the Comets . . . all the while, during his explanation, looking at this kid Oldham as if he were the most ignorant producer to ever step into a studio. And Andrew said:

"Hell, you take care of all that. I'll be back in the morning."

The result was predictable: Decca Records informed the Stones that the tape was dreadful, they'd have to return to the studio and re-record "Come On." Professionally, this time. "Bunch of Erdies," Jagger moaned—his favorite expression, this season, Erdies denoting all those faceless and mindless men who weren't hip, who were trapped in jobs and careers and prisons of the mind. "Bloody Erdies not only want us to record again but they probably want to take us over completely and 'ave us coming out with a load of shit instead of real music. Decca. Erdies."

In spite of their complaints as they drove to Decca's studios in West Hampstead, Jagger and the others were terribly excited at how fast everything seemed to be moving for them. Eric had persuaded Decca to sign the Stones, at a royalty equal to that given the biggest recording stars in the business. Eric had been quite cunning about it. He had created an interest in the Stones among executives of several other recording companies and had then worked on Dick Rowe's wounded pride; Rowe, a Decca official, had turned down the Beatles only two months before, telling their manager, "We don't like your boys' sound, guitar groups are on the way out," and since then he'd taken a lot of vicious ribbing. Rowe had heard about the Stones, he was anxious to find a group to replace the lost Beatles and restore his own good name, and he jumped at the chance to sign the Stones even though the arrangement demanded by their manager was rather unusual: The Stones would lease their tapes to Decca, maintaining complete control over the music and, most important, the band and their managers would own the masters of their recordings, which meant that if the Stones became extremely popular at a later date they could use those masters to bargain for enormous future advances. Decca executives, anxious lest EMI dominate the market with the Beatles, agreed to Easton's demands. But they insisted the Stones would have to re-record "Come On" before it could go out under the Decca label.

The second session was no better than the first. Nor was the third. But finally the Stones laid down a tape that satisfied Decca: "Come On" backed with "I Want to be Loved." The single was released on June 7. That evening the group made their first television appearance, well down on the bill of "Thank Your Lucky Stars," a pop music program. Andrew and Eric dressed the boys in checkered suits, and there were violent arguments about that, Jagger insisting he'd be damned if he'd get dressed for a TV show, it was too close to selling out.

"You have to make some compromises," Andrew told them. "Just to get started in this business you have to compromise a bit." Andrew didn't mention it just then because he knew Jagger would be hurt, but a TV producer had told him the Stones would have to get rid of that vile-looking lead singer if the band was ever to get past a BBC audition. "The TV people are used to dealing with groups like the Searchers and the Swinging Blue Jeans," Andrew continued. "If you guys dress the way you do in a club you won't even be allowed inside the building. You must make this compromise, you must wear some sort of uniform to get on the show. And doing the TV is the only way to get exposure for your record."

Jagger finally agreed. But despite Andrew's attempt to clean up the band's appearance a bit, a number of viewers were furious about the disgraceful trash that was being presented on English television. One newspaper published a letter from a viewer who said: "I have today seen the most disgusting sight I can remember in all my years as a television fan. The Rolling Stones . . ."

Jagger was angered at the reaction, since most of the letters to the papers and the television station singled out his long hair and his blatant sexuality. But Andrew seemed jubilant that a minor controversy had been created.

"Just wait and see. If we upset enough adults we're going to hook the kids," Andrew predicted.

The Stones' first record fell with a dull thud on the industry and the public. The tone of the song, as done by Chuck Berry, was of frustration and barely-concealed fury: "Couldn't get my car started . . . I wish somebody'd come along and run into and wreck it." But Jagger's version was much toned down (for the words "Some stupid jerk," Jagger substituted "some guy"), and he wasn't nearly as much in control of the vocal as Berry had been. It was a rather vapid imitation of Chuck Berry. While some reviewers predicted big things for the Stones, most dismissed the record as a pleasant introduction for a new group but nothing very important, musically. And Norman Jopling, who had written the first important article on the Stones several weeks before, said of their record:

"The disc doesn't sound like the Rolling Stones. It's good, punchy, and commercial, but it's not the fanatical R and B that audiences wait hours to hear. Instead, it's a bluesy commercial group that should make the charts in a smallish way."

Jagger and the others were discouraged by the reviews but Andrew ran around to newspaper offices trying to stir up excitement and a feature on the Stones. But no one was interested unless the record got fairly high up on the charts. At the end of June it did come in at the bottom, number fifty, mostly because Stones fans in the London area had concentrated their buying of the single in a vital one-week period.

"Fifty's better than nothing," Andrew said. Jagger agreed; his first recording, a singer and a group barely known outside a small circle of fans, *and they were on the charts*. Jagger kept looking at the music industry charts. The Beatles way up near the top with "From Me to You," those incredibly lucky Beatles who seemed to get all the breaks, four provincials from Liverpool, of all places, who were bouncing around London as if they owned the town.

"We'll pass them yet. Maybe not this single but the next

one, we'll get up higher on the charts than the Beatles," Jagger said.

"Oh, come on, we're not competing with anyone," Charlie said. "We just have to go out there and do our own music and if we're any good the public are going to buy it."

Andrew sat in his chair, watching closely Jagger's petulance and Charlie's more realistic attitude and something that had been tugging at Andrew's mind since his first meeting with the group began to take concrete form: *Charlie is his own person, he isn't looking for an identity. He already knows who Charlie Watts is. But Mick is still looking for an identity, he's going through a lot of changes trying to find out who he wants to be.*

With the record on the charts, Andrew made another round of newspaper offices, promoting the band. He met with greater success this time, helped considerably by advance reports from the trades which indicated the Stones would hit somewhere around the thirty-five spot the following week. Andrew showed more recent photos of the Stones, hair even longer than the Beatles, and journalists, ever looking for a gimmick to inflame middle-class readers, reached out for the hair. Several of them showed up at Eric's office, with photographers, to interview the band. Few questions were asked about the music the Stones played; the newspapermen seemed to be interested only in the length of the boys' hair. Jagger and Brian, the two main spokesmen, had been primed by Andrew: "They're going to make you a controversial band, asking all kinds of dumb questions," he said. "Just be as tough with your answers as you like, don't try to be nice. Controversy sells newspapers, and it'll sell the Stones to the newspapers." And when the reporters asked whether the Stones had copied their hair styles from the Beatles, Jagger, hands on his hips, his sweater askew as he shook his shoulders angrily—emphasizing the gesture as photographers shot his picture—Jagger snapped:

125

"Art students have had this sort of haircut for years—even when the Beatles were using hair cream."

And Andrew smiled broadly when Jagger, in response to a question as to whether the Stones were toning down their act in imitation of the highly successful Beatles, said:

"Never, no way at all. If people don't like us as we are, well, that's too bad. We're not thinking of changing, thanks very much. We've been the way we are for much too long to think of kowtowing to fanciful folk who think we should start tarting ourselves up with mohair suits and short haircuts."

At the end of the interview session Andrew said: "It was perfect, just perfect. They're going to plaster your pictures and your terrible, terrible statements all over the papers. Those dirty Rolling Stones, that's what you are. The opposite of those nice little chaps, the Beatles. It's working, it's sure as hell working. We're gonna make you famous."

Jagger asked him to define fame.

Andrew thought about the question for a moment. "This is how I see fame—every time you go through an airport you get your pictures in the papers. I'm going to make you that famous."

The Rolling Stones photos and interviews began appearing in the press with regularity, the long hair the main focus of all the articles; the Stones were singled out as the prime example of what was wrong with English youth. The boys were annoyed that no one seemed to pay attention to the music, but Jagger told Chrissie that he understood Andrew's tactics and appreciated them—shock the hell out of everyone, especially the parents, enrage the parents so much that their children will be forced into an anti-authoritarian stance, will stick their tongues out at Mum and Dad by buying Stones records, attending their concerts, championing them.

Jagger pushed Andrew a step further. "No more suits," he said. "The Stones are never going to dress up in suits again." After a bit of an argument, defending his decision to compromise for the sake of a TV appearance, Andrew agreed. From that point on Jagger would slowly come to involve himself in the business. Shirley Arnold, head of the fan club, watched with some amusement at first as Jagger started to make decisions as to what was best for the group, the songs to be put on records, the sort of publicity to be aiming for, the writers he wanted to favor with exclusive interviews because they seemed most able to understand the Stones and their music. Jagger even ordered Charlie Watts to let his hair grow longer—"You still look like a jazz drummer, Charlie," he said—so that all six of them would present the same threatening image when their photos jumped off the newspaper pages and slapped those Erdies in their vapid faces.

Chrissie was shouting at Jagger, shrill and angry. Her arms were swinging, the open hands trying to slap him. Jagger's eyes, his face, were rather bruised-looking in the morning light that streamed into their flat in Kilburn. He held her wrists, and she kicked at him, kicked for his shins and his groin, and he performed a series of one-two dance steps to take the kicks on the fleshy part of his legs, and on his buttocks.

"Aw, come on, now . . . you know why I had to do that . . ."

"Your bloody image, your bloody career . . ." Chrissie certainly did know why he'd embarrassed her, last night, hurt her, made her feel so cheap and unwanted and . . . well, just a piece of baggage carried by a rock-and-roll star . . . a minor star, but a star. They had been walking along the street last night, a cold night in December 1963, after a Stones gig in Soho. Jagger, Chrissie, Keith, Brian, and two girl friends. As they approached the flat that Jagger and Keith had leased for the outlandish sum of £50 a week the previous summer, a half dozen wailing fans rushed out of the shadows. Young girls intent on rape, or at least the boys' autographs. Jagger had quickly taken his arm from around Chrissie's shoulder. Had whispered, "Get away for a moment." Then almost shoved her from him. He'd been doing that for weeks, now that the Stones had a fan club and were attracting thousands of letters requesting photos, locks of hair, trysts, and gang bangs. Andrew had told them not to be seen with their girl friends, and Jagger had agreed that that was best for the group's image. John Lennon's wife, Cynthia, had given birth to a son the previous April, and the rumors of the boy's existence had stirred angry grumblings from Beatles fans; their manager was still trying to keep the birth a secret because he was afraid the domesticity surrounding parenthood would lose the Beatles thousands of record sales. Chrissie knew that Jagger's attitude toward any member of the Stones publicly acknowledging they had girl friends was: Don't admit it at all, keep the women far in the background. It was very important to their image, he told her, it was quite vital that none of their fans' daydreams about meeting and going to bed with a Stone should be shattered, and Chrissie believed Jagger's primary concern was their image, before their personal lives. Chrissie shouted this accusation at him now: that he cared about only his image, and his career, he was so callous about it that he had *ordered* Charlie Watts not to marry his girl friend, Shirley, had forced Charlie to cancel his wedding plans.

"Aw, stop it. You know I love you, that I need you . . ."

"Don't try to charm me," Chrissie said, struggling to free her hand from his grasp and get a slap at him. "Everybody lets you get away with everything 'cause you're so charming . . . but you're not going to charm me."

Chrissie only wanted his respect, to be treated like a woman with an existence of her own, not simply another musician's groupie. She caused scenes, fought with him . . . they'd often punch and slap each other, Chrissie usually punching first . . . so open about their battles that friends always talked of their relationship as "tempestuous." She would never let up on him until she felt she had his respect once more. Living with him for six months, Chrissie had come to believe that Jagger was strong and ambitious and unscrupulous on the outside but another part of him was so soft and gentle and . . . *lost* was the only word she could think of, *a little boy lost . . . so strange because he has a lot of strength and yet needs a very strong woman to make him feel weak.* Jagger's friends had told her of the duality in his personality, had described the weak half of it as a masochistic streak, and Chrissie realized he needed a violent relationship with a woman at least as strong as he was. *A woman who would give him a hard time,* Chrissie often reflected after they had settled one of their brawls, usually by making love, but only after she felt certain she had regained the respect she demanded, *I think that's a peculiar Leo thing, they are such strong, domineering characters that they need a woman who is their match.*

Now Jagger blunted Chrissie's attack, brought her into his arms to make love to him, the way he often did. He told her he wished to marry her, to have children by her; he seemed to Chrissie to be able to fix upon what was young and helpless in her, able to seek it out and use it to weaken her; at the same time he grew very apologetic and penitent, and very tender—Chrissie found that charming because the only time most men look tender is in defeat, but Jagger appeared tender even when he knew he was winning.

Chrissie's anger at Jagger's action the night before, at his constant need to put the public Mick Jagger before the private Jagger she lived with and loved, was intensified because she knew he didn't believe in the image—when Jagger saw another one of those idiotic stories pointing an accusatory finger at the unwashed hairy apes called the Rolling Stones he would sometimes laugh and sometimes get furious. But at all times, she felt, he knew it was simply publicity, that it had nothing to do with the real Mick Jagger. And Chrissie couldn't understand why he would put that public image before his personal life. She also recognized that there was something else bothering her: Andrew Oldham. He had come up with the image, the Stones as antidotes to those cheeky but adorable Beatles, he had insisted that the women be hidden, and his publicity program had proven so effective that Jagger considered him a Svengali guiding the Stones to number one on the charts. And Chrissie was annoyed at Andrew. It was something more than Andrew's manipulation of the press and the Stones. Chrissie had been hearing some disturbing things about the relationship between Andrew and Jagger.

She had finished up at secretarial college the previous spring and moved to London, to be with Jagger. She was searching for her own flat, insisting that she must maintain a degree of independence, but until she could find a place she had moved in with Jagger, and Keith, immediately after her eighteenth birthday, in May. And she had gone to work for Decca Records. For a few weeks she was simply another secretary in the office. Then it was discovered she was living with Jagger, and she was treated as someone special, never given much work to do except in connection with the Stones, free to leave when she liked, to attend concerts and gigs at clubs and go out on tours with the Stones. She thought it was hilarious because the Stones had only one record out at the time and although it lingered in the charts for months it wasn't exactly creating much of a fuss.

When Andrew set up his own office in Regent Street during the summer to handle the Stones in their quick-growing popularity, Chrissie went to work for him. Andrew was beginning to get very camp, it seemed to Chrissie, and everything about him and the office appeared to her to be continuous madness. She found Andrew very strange, a man of great charm who could also be nasty and almost schizoid: very clever, quick-witted, humorous, and incredibly bitchy and evil. He always had great dramas swirling around him, incredible scenes, and morally Chrissie was appalled by everything he represented; she'd had a convent upbringing, and

Andrew's style offended her sensibilities. Andrew wanted the women in his office to be very butch, to wear trousers, and sit with their feet up on the desk. He'd rush into the office at nine in the morning and ask someone to pour him a few ounces of vodka to start his day. And he loved it when the women teased him about the makeup he wore behind the dark glasses. He'd ask: "Is there something wrong with the color? Please go out and get me eye-stuff that's a better shade."

Chrissie's relationship with Andrew became quite tense after a number of bitchy queens started teasing her about how close Jagger and Andrew had become. "You know what it's like, you know what Mick and Andrew are like"—a phrase repeated so often, by several very campy men, that Chrissie was becoming very upset. She didn't quite understand, she couldn't see anything *wrong* in their relationship. But every time she heard the phrase or some variation of it she couldn't help remembering the night the Stones were rehearsing at Ken Colyer's club before going up to the Decca studio to re-record their first single: Andrew was teasing Jagger, about double trackings and their inexperience with studio techniques, and she realized they had become extraordinarily close in a few weeks, that they had a strong and unique friendship. Not something she could be jealous of, not back then. But now . . .

She had once told Andrew what was being said about him and Jagger, after she could no longer stand the queens' teasings. Andrew assured her there wasn't any truth to it, that he and Jagger were strictly friends and business associates. She could believe that, she had always felt the relationship was just a strong male friendship, nothing more.

Still, Chrissie was worried. She wasn't exactly going around arguing with herself about it, but she knew that from the moment she met Jagger other musicians—homosexuals and bisexuals—had been after him, as had many male fans. She was certain Jagger was aware of it, but she could never ask him his feelings. Her concern was heightened when Andrew moved into the flat with them, and Andrew's wife, Sheila, asked:

"Do Mick and Andrew sleep in the same bed?"

"Not when I'm there. Because I sleep with Mick," Chrissie said.

But Chrissie didn't dwell on it—what's there to worry about when your man is a good lover, when he is gentle and manly, as much concerned with your sexual pleasure as with his own? Besides, everything was happening so fast for the band that personal anxieties had a way of vanishing in the rush of professional joys. Back in September they had gone on their first concert tour, way down on the bill with the Everly Brothers and Bo Diddley himself—"We'll just have to be on top form to even *live* in the same theater as that bloke," Brian said after learning the Stones were booked on a tour with one of their heroes; the band quickly dropped all Bo Diddley numbers from its act. In a couple of weeks, starting January 6, 1964, the Stones would be touring again. This time they'd be on a bill with the Ronettes, an American vocal trio created by Phil Spector—brazen, shapely, enormously popular with teenage boys who didn't have the courage to lust after the girl next door. And, this tour, the Stones would have top billing—only their second tour of England, and they were the top of the card. It was a coup that Easton had pulled off, demonstrating how a shrewd manager can create an overnight sensation.

Easton did have a little help from the Beatles. Two of the Beatles, in any case: Lennon and McCartney. With "Come On" making it into the Top Ten on the pop charts in July, Decca demanded another fast single. The Stones tried for weeks to find a suitably commercial follow-up, arguing over hundreds of titles, dismissing out of hand Keith's suggestion they write their own songs, growing tense and snapping at one another. There was such an enormous storehouse of material in the records they owned and in the songs played by Alex and Baldry and so many others, and they still couldn't find a couple of three-minute songs.

Andrew was upset because he was anxious to get into the studio again, to learn studio techniques, perhaps to become the English Phil Spector, to become successful and rich and famous as a producer of hit records and the creator of hit pop artists, as Spector had done in America . . . why not? And now the Rolling Stones were unable to come up with a song.

Andrew was walking along Jermyn Street one afternoon, dark glasses hiding his makeup and his glazed eyes, walking in the curiously birhythmic manner of one stoned out of his skull.

"Hey, Andy," someone shouted. "Andy, get in here."

He looked around and recognized that choir-boy face of Paul McCartney sticking out the window of a taxi. John Lennon was sitting next to him. Andrew stepped off the curb, gingerly, and crossed over.

"Where you two coming from? Living it up with the London birds?"

"We've just got back from a big lunch at the Dorchester, a Variety Club do that was fab!" (Paul said that "Fab!" with an exclamation point in the voice; it was the season's hip expletive.) "We've been meaning to call you to talk some ideas over with you."

"I don't have any ideas for anyone—I need a couple of songs. The Stones have got to make another record soon, and they can't find the proper material. Driving me loon."

"We've got a couple of spare songs we just finished that are more up their street than ours," John said in that Liverpool accent that Andrew still had difficulty understanding. "You know we like the Stones, man, and we'd be happy to let them have a go at one of ours. We'd like you to hear them. Especially one we call 'I Wanna Be Your Man.' "

Andrew pulled open the cab door. "Get out of that taxi. I'm meeting the Stones right now in Ken Colyer's, and we can all hear your songs immediately."

They went round the corner to the club. Inside, the Stones were sitting around, dejected, a half-empty bottle of vodka and a general air of gloom evidence they still hadn't played through a song that would be suitable for their next recording. Jagger held back for a moment while the other members of the band asked the usual questions about the Beatles' success, and plans, and then suddenly broke in.

"What are you two doing here?" he asked.

"Andrew says you need some songs. Well, we have at least one song that'll be perfect for you."

"Play it for us," Jagger said, ignoring the other Stones' excitement over the offer. When they'd calmed down a bit, Keith and Bill handed their guitars to the two Beatles, who began to play their song while Charlie lightly brushed the beat. At the end of the first chorus of "I Wanna Be Your Man," John and Paul came to a stop.

"That's all we've written so far, just the chorus," John said.

"Oh, great. Very good song, we sure can use it, but how long can we wait for it to be finished?" Brian said. "We haven't got a lot of time, Decca's down on our backs."

A glance between John and Paul. "Listen, if you guys really like the main part of the song, we'll try to finish it up right away," John said.

"Yes, please do," Jagger said. "We badly need a song, and that's a good one."

The two Beatles went off to another room. They returned about five minutes later. "Forget something?" Bill asked. "Need a guitar to work with?"

"No. We've just finished the middle eight," John said. "See how this sounds to you." They played the song through and, after getting over their surprise that anyone could write a song so quickly, Brian and Jagger agreed that "I Wanna Be Your Man" suited them perfectly. It would be the "A" side of their new record. Later, Jagger told Keith that he may have been right—if writing songs was so easy, perhaps they should do their own.

The Stones went into the studio a couple of weeks later to record the Lennon-McCartney song. By then Andrew seemed to have despaired of anything working out properly, he had fallen into one of his "black periods" as he called them, and had gone off to the South of France. He had already given up on becoming a singer and a performer and seemed to be feeling so frustrated that he even shelved his plan to become a recording studio genius, at least temporarily. Eric Easton went into the studio this time as producer. He didn't have much recording experience but he had a wide background as a musician, something that Andrew lacked, and he felt certain he could help the band put together two good sides, could supervise them, guide them, offer suggestions, and let the engineers worry about the technical aspects.

As he sat in the control booth of the Kingsway Studios while the Stones were trying to get a usable version of the Beatles song on tape, Eric marvelled at the change in the band since their first studio sessions just a few months before: *They're getting the hang of this recording business. They were edgy and nervy on the first sessions, but now they're beginning to relax . . . to get themselves in the mood where they're really reproducing the sort of stuff they do in the clubs.* By nightfall the Stones had a hard-driving Elmore James style treatment of "I Wanna Be Your Man" on tape, and they were ecstatic that it had all gone so smoothly. As they were being driven home, Brian fairly shouted:

"Know why all that went so well? It's because we can feel that things are starting to happen for us at last. You know? We're not just banging our heads against the walls of different promoters. Now we've got someone doing the worrying for us"—pointing at Eric—"we're feeling that much happier and that much more on the way."

Perhaps Brian didn't have any more worries, but Jagger did: he was beginning to learn the business side of pop music, to involve himself in all the petty details of management and contracts and promotion; he said he enjoyed it, and he felt qualified because of his LSE training, but it could sometimes be a headache.

"I Wanna Be Your Man" was released on November 1. It quickly got onto the charts and began moving up, with enormous help from several quarters: Eric, working almost from a master game plan, got the Stones booked on a few television shows; Andrew created another round of newspaper controversy over the Stones haircuts, or lack thereof; some reviewers raved about the recording, the man from *Disc* magazine especially enthusiastic because the Stones had finally been able to get on a record the drive and excitement of their live act; but helped most of all by the fact that "I Wanna Be Your Man" was written by the songwriting half of the Beatles.

For, by mid-November, the Beatles had become the most exciting news to happen in Britain since Hitler's armies had collapsed eighteen years before. The Beatles had been causing riots in tours up North since May, and completely dominated the record charts through most of the autumn, simultaneously hitting number one in each category: single, extended play, and LP album. They had been booked into the London Palladium the night of October 13, 1963, topping the bill in a show televised as "Sunday Night at the London Palladium." Throughout the day the streets around the Palladium were besieged by Beatles fans, thousands of them trying to catch a glimpse of their idols, piling up presents at the stage door, fainting in the streets, cheering and chanting and generally mystifying the poor bobbies assigned to keep some kind of order. Journalists showed up as news of the crowds started getting around, joined by TV and radio newsmen. Britain hadn't seen anything like it in modern times—the start of the "Beatlemania" that was to sweep much of the world for the next few years—and the chaos that the Beatles caused was front-page news the next day.

The following Wednesday the Beatles were invited to play at the Royal Variety Performance, the biggest and most prestigious show of the year. The bill included most of the top stars in Britain, plus Sophie Tucker, Marlene Dietrich, and Maurice Chevalier, and the audience included the Queen Mother, Princess Margaret, and Lord Snowdon. That show was televised November 10, to a viewing audience of 26 million, almost one-half of Britain's population. The Beatles became a national institution, ranking up there with pubs, soccer, and the pools. Especially after John got in a cheeky but adorable joke at the Royals' expense: Before one number he asked the audience to clap in time, then nodded toward the Royal box and said, "Those upstairs, just rattle your jewelry." The joke made every front page the next day, and every writer was careful to point out that the Queen Mother, in talking to the Beatles after the show, had indicated she'd enjoyed the joke and loved those four lads from Liverpool.

The Stones single, "I Wanna Be Your Man," was being delivered to the record shops during that week, and the spillover of the Beatles insanity helped create a greater demand for the record than would normally have been expected for such a relatively unknown group as the Stones; Beatles fans rushed out to buy the record simply to hear the Lennon-McCartney song.

With the release of that record Eric and Andrew made certain that even the journalists could grasp the fact that something big was about to happen to the Stones, and the group's press coverage rose dramatically. *Daily Mirror* record columnist Pat Doncaster visited the Richmond Athletic Club, to which the Stones had moved their Sunday performance from the Crawdaddy Club, and he wrote a glowing article about them; the *Sunday Times* sent a photographer to shoot some pictures for the color magazine; a video team from BBC's "Monitor" shot a lot of film for viewers. Chrissie had begun to keep a press cutting file on the Stones months before but she gave it up now because it seemed an impossible task for one person to handle. The chore was turned over to Shirley Arnold, a fan from the earliest Crawdaddy gigs who had been hired by Andrew to put in a couple of hours a week answering the fan letters and who became full-time fan club president, with several assistants, as Post Office bags of mail began piling up.

Eric continued to build the momentum, booking the Stones onto the ballroom circuit when the second record was released, sending the band on a tour of halls in which couples usually danced to trad jazz bands or light rock groups. And Brian was regularly beaten up by men who didn't like the way he was aggressing from the stage, making violent love to their girl friends while putting the boot to the men; Brian didn't know when to pull back and cool off a situation and he was attacked several times. Touring the ballrooms in the back country outside London seemed to Jagger to be an insane thing to do, and he tried to persuade Eric to cancel. "We're used to the atmosphere in the little clubs, and there's a lot of hard nuts out there among the dancers who're not gonna fancy our hair and maybe'll try to scalp us," Jagger said. He seemed to Eric almost frightened after the first couple of shows—ballroom rockers demanding strange rock-and-roll songs and when the band ignored the request or insisted they didn't know the song, riots seemed likely to follow. But Eric reassured him: "You're a hot group right now. You must get out to the bigger places, pull in more fans, it's the only way to keep driving up. Don't worry about the hard nuts, just try to avoid any incidents." Avoiding trouble wasn't such an easy thing to do, not with Brian so ready to fight anyone who seemed to be insulting him or his hair or his music.

When he returned from the ballroom tour that late autumn, Jagger told some friends and journalists that he knew it had worked, he could feel something powerful happening within him; somehow his entire body felt different, up there on the stage, he said, he'd been experiencing something so sensual that he was unable to describe it even to himself. But he did know he was learning something about showmanship now, working with larger crowds, learning how to control the hysteria, to whip it up and tone it down; jerky movements of the hips, grasshopper dance steps, thrusting his pelvis forward rapidly in a parody of copulation, almost daring the girls out there to reach for his genitals, waving his arms in invitation, swinging around to present his butt. He'd begun to wear special jeans, cut tight in back to conform to the shape of his buttocks and tight in the crotch to emphasize the genitals. If those kids—girls and boys—needed sexual fantasies then Mick Jagger was going to supply them. And he did, obviously: The Stones were beginning to run into mass hysteria.

"You walk into some of these places, and it's like the Battle of the Crimea going on, people gasping, tits hanging out, chicks choking, nurses running around with ambulances," Keith later said. "You know that weird sound that hundreds of chicks make when they're letting go, when they're coming? They sound like hundreds of orgasms at once, they can't even hear the music, and we can't hear the music we're playing . . . Chaos . . . Going out of the theaters is the dodgiest—the chicks try to strangle you they want you so bad. One time I found myself lying in the gutter with a shirt on and half a pair of pants and the car roaring away down the street with the guys in it. Oh, shit, man. They leap on you. 'What do you want? What!' "

Brian knew what they wanted. He'd been the first to understand that the audiences wanted sexual stimulation, sexual fulfillment, the fueling of their fantasies, and he'd been the first to experiment with movements of his body and his guitar which simulated sexual activity and drove the audiences to a frenzy. While Jagger was still moving only his head, flouncing his fair, and clapping to the beat, Brian was bouncing around teasing with his entire body. Then Jagger began incorporating similar movements into his performance, and Brian felt Jagger was imitating him. When Jagger began to get more notice than Brian, which was inevitable because he was out front as lead singer, Brian grew jealous and more paranoiac. He felt Jagger was deliberately stealing his act, competing with him, trying to become the star of the band and leave everyone else back there in the shadows. Brian soon had tangible evidence to support his suspicions: Jagger was beginning to get most of the fan mail, and journalists were asking for interviews with Jagger. A tension was beginning to develop between Brian and Jagger, way back in those first few months of the band's existence. Brian would call up Shirley Arnold to complain about it: "I must tell you this . . ." and he'd cite several instances to illustrate Jagger's perfidy, Jagger's attempt to push them all into the background and seize the glory for himself. And Jagger began to draw a line, with him on one side and Brian on the other: Cleo Sylvester was talking to Jagger one night about the growth of the band's popularity and said something innocuous about Brian's musicianship. Jagger said, "You're on Brian's side." And Cleo thought, *It's not a question of being on anybody's side, but Mick seems to feel there is a side.* Jagger's remark made her aware that something was happening between him and Brian, made her notice and feel sad about the small disagreements that grew into large arguments and petty jealousies.

And now, at the end of 1963, when the band was earning about £1,000 a month, Jagger told Chrissie he wanted to marry her as soon as possible. He was making a lot of money with the band, he felt confident the Stones were going to become as big as the Beatles, music was his future, and the future looked brilliant. He was so confident that he'd finally dropped out of LSE after agonizing over it for a long time, unable to make up his mind. He'd talked to Chrissie again and again about leaving LSE, making a decision to quit and then backing down, wavering and uncertain—that trait friends and associates found so distasteful in Jagger. Sometimes Chrissie felt strongly that he'd finish up at university, then finally realized that he couldn't because he had a drive for performing that he couldn't turn back no matter how hard he tried to conform to his parents' wishes and despite his feeling of obligation to the government. Once he did make the final decision to quit there was no stopping him: He would assert his independence by leaving school and marrying Chrissie. Marriage was the inevitable next step: It was the first real love for each, and they talked much about living together as man and wife forever, having several children. But there appeared to be much conflict in Jagger because of his need to protect his public image by hiding Chrissie from his fans so that they wouldn't turn against the band, and his need for a woman he could call his wife. He'd tell interviewers that he was very much against marriage and would never marry; he'd tell Chrissie that he wanted to marry her as quickly as possible. He seemed unable to decide how he really felt.

But down at Chrissie's sister's flat one night Jagger announced that they were definitely going to be married soon. After the round of congratulations from Jean and her guests, someone suggested that Jagger had better call Andrew to break the news. Chrissie listened at Jagger's shoulder when he rang Andrew, waiting to be congratulated. But Andrew wouldn't talk to her about it. He was very broken up, and

Chrissie had the impression he was crying at the other end of the phone. Jagger was trying to comfort him, to reassure him that marriage wouldn't change anything. Chrissie couldn't understand why Andrew was so upset.

She also couldn't understand why Jagger refused to set a firm wedding date: "Someday, someday soon," he'd say when they talked about it. But months went by, and they were no closer to marriage. She didn't care very much about marriage, necessarily. She wanted to have children, to bear Jagger's children, she wanted to be a mother. She'd do it outside of marriage, if that's how Jagger really felt about it, she would risk the criticism and outrage of respectable society and bear Jagger's children without marrying him, for she desperately wanted to be a mother. Jagger said he also wanted children, her children. But as the months went by, through the Christmas holidays and into 1964, Chrissie came to realize that Jagger felt it would be destructive for his career to marry and have children. She sensed he was correct. *It certainly would be daft,* she thought, but she was terribly hurt by his attitude.

Chrissie knew that Jagger had kept a distance between himself and his image, that he hadn't been overwhelmed by the image and been swallowed up in it. He often laughed at newspaper articles portraying them as louts, hairy brutes who were corrupting the nation's youth. Andrew seemed to delight in the image, wanted to be a part of it; he seemed to have a strong need to make himself and the Stones over into characters out of Burgess's novel, *A Clockwork Orange.* He had photos taken of them, the boys viciously overturning a baby pram (presumably with an infant still inside). But Chrissie felt certain that Jagger was too clever and too perceptive to be taken in by his own publicity machine. He hated interviews, dreaded them, because they intruded on his privacy. *He wants very much to be a private person,* Chrissie thought, *he wants very much for the group to work and be a personal and financial success, but he wants to keep himself private and apart from that image of the rock-and-roll star.*

Whenever the line between star and private man seemed to blur, Chrissie would help him define it again by tossing out a standard accusation: "You're nothing but a rock-and-roll singer, you're an idol to everyone else but I know what you really are." Jagger would grow angry, but it would help him keep an emotional balance about his fame. He'd often tell her: "Where you are is home. All the rest out there is bullshit." Jagger's own tough defensive shield, his very conscious and shrewd manipulation of his image, combined with Chrissie's realistic appraisal of the whirlpool that stardom could become, helped save him from being sucked into his own public image.

And yet the image that was being manufactured, that of a rebellious young man who damned all society's conventions, was being slowly etched into his brain, Chrissie felt. A part of Jagger was beginning to conform to the new role, rebel: anti-marriage. More violence introduced into his act. A greater awareness of his bisexual image (he had a habit now of leaning close to the mirror, staring at his face for long periods, as if the image that stared back at him was the only subject that interested his soul). And, whenever the subject of parents came up, putting down his family out there in the suburbs.

That rejection of his family was noticed by almost everyone with whom he came into contact. During one conversation with Paul McCartney, Jagger made it clear he couldn't get along with his parents, that he didn't seem to like his mother very much; she was one of those "old" people. Paul said: "I don't hate old people. I like my Dad. He's 'old' people, and I like him. I get along with older people." Jagger didn't appear to understand what Paul was talking about, and Paul had a strong feeling that Jagger was a loner, building walls of anger to defend his psyche . . . from what? And Paul went away from that talk feeling very sad for Jagger.

There were times that Chrissie wondered how strongly Jagger really felt about the need to keep his public image totally separate from the core of his self. Usually, she felt he had too much intelligence to be corrupted by the idolatry of the fans, and the wealth. But occasionally a thought would cross her mind: *Is it possible he's not being fooled by the public image only because he knows he's too young and unsophisticated to handle it now? I'm beginning to think he probably wants it from afar but isn't able to cope with it yet so he'll likely stay away from it until he feels he can handle it . . . he's certainly aware of what he is . . . I wonder what he'll be like when he gets into it all the way? . . . he certainly won't remain the same because that scene is so sick. It's such a joke. Will he become a joke?*

BOOK FOUR

SHE CAUGHT EVERY man's attention, and every woman's, and she tried hard not to make them aware she knew they were fascinated by her. When they asked who she was they were told "Marianne Faithfull," but the name meant nothing. Except that they couldn't believe it was her real name; it had to be a stage name. She hung back near the door to the drawing room of this flat in Paddington, like a gatecrasher, appearing so out of place in her shirt and jeans as celebrities drifted by her in full evening dress. She was very beautiful, but there was something more astonishing about her than ordinary beauty, something both virginal and sensual. Andrew Oldham spotted it immediately: *a lustful purity,* his press agent mind wrote the newspaper headline as he stared at her from across the room. *She's part childhood sweetheart and part vamp. I can make her a star.* Her face had a fine, delicate bone structure, a guileless face, unable to tell lies. Her blonde hair fell coquettishly just past her shoulders. Her long lashes frequently drooped closed over the most brilliant, deep-set blue eyes. Her Dresden complexion was slightly flush-tinted. Her lips seemed so wet, so filled with the redness of her blood that many men created an instant daydream on first seeing her: those incredible lips flicking across their mouths, their ears and necks, up and down their bodies. She appeared to be possessed of all the mysteries in which men cloak woman.

Marianne knew her effect on men. She could feel them staring at her, along the streets, in restaurants, at parties such as this, but she seldom bothered to glance at them because most of them seemed slightly out of focus to her, existing simply to give her the prickly excitement of their curiosity and desire. Most men seemed small, awkward, they took quick, small, self-conscious steps and seemed to be daring her to kick them, sometimes making her want to kick them because they were such dwarfs.

Marianne was only dimly aware of Mick Jagger and the other Stones who were here with their girl friends. She knew about the Stones—the tours that created riots among little girls; their EP released in January and the single at the end of February that went to the top of the charts and were large hits; the raunchy image that was creating a cult around them; the controversy around them that led newspapers to publish such articles as, "Would You Let Your Sister Go With A Rolling Stone?" Marianne knew a great deal about what had been happening to the Stones since the first of the year because she and her boy friend had become friendly with some pop recording artists. But she hadn't ever really listened to the music of the Stones or to any rock and roll. Marianne seldom even listened to Beatles records, although she had met Paul McCartney a few weeks before; Paul had invited her and her boy friend to this Good Friday, 1964, party to help launch singer Adrienne Posta. Rock and roll wasn't something that a seventeen-year-old woman like Marianne would listen to. She was a bit of a snob, she would later realize to her amusement and, occasionally, regret: The daughter of an Austrian baroness and an English don of philology and Italian Renaissance art, she was studying classical music and drama. Pop music was something for the masses.

She smiled at her boy friend, John Dunbar, feeling a little nervous because that strange young man who was wearing makeup and dressed in a puff-sleeved satin shirt and velvet pants was talking to John, urgently and intensely, frequently nodding toward Marianne and openly asking questions about her. She would later learn he was Andrew Oldham. But she wasn't alone long enough to let the nervousness take hold. Guests were continually approaching her, chatting her up, asking the same questions that unusual man seemed to be asking John. Most of them were men, going through the pre-seduction rituals, but even women seemed to be drawn to her. One young woman left the crowded drawing room to cool off near the stairs where Marianne was standing and introduced herself as a magazine writer.

"Are you enjoying the party?" she asked.

Marianne sat on the stairs next to her and said she didn't really know too many of these people. John Dunbar, her boy friend, who was studying art at Churchill College, Cambridge, had brought her here. She had met John only the month before, at a St. Valentine Day student ball at Cambridge and hoped meeting him on that day was a lucky omen. John's father was a painter and tutor at the Royal College of Art, she said, which gave John access to various hip portions of London society, including the pop scene. She and John had met Jane Asher, a young actress who was dating Paul McCartney. And had met Jane's brother, Peter, who was one-half of the duo Peter and Gordon. Through Jane and Peter they'd met Paul McCartney, and through Paul they had arrived at this party. She said it all breathlessly, a litany of hip names. But not name-dropping from her lips, more an ingenuous excitement at her luck in being in the center of things. But she felt a little out of place among these strange celebrities, Marianne raced on in her soliloquy, she was still in a convent school in

147

Reading and only came up to London on weekends with John. But she'd just taken her first real holiday job and was feeling very daring but a little nervous. Soon she'd go back to school to take her A levels in music, and on to university. She had just turned seventeen.

Mick Jagger rose from the couch where he'd been seated for a long while, and it appeared to other guests that he pointedly ignored Chrissie at the other end. They were in one of their tempestuous periods, both sulking and refusing to have anything to do with one another. Jagger yawned, apparently to let everyone know he was bored—with Chrissie and her scenes, his gestures seemed to imply—and he walked over to Marianne.

"I'm Mick Jagger," he said—then very deliberately and dramatically poured his glass of champagne down the front of her shirt. Mumbling some vague East-End-accented apology, he began to mop the liquid away with his hand, roughly stroking her breasts, his lips wide in a grotesque pantomime of a leer. Marianne rose from the stairs brusquely, almost knocking Jagger over, and walked away, barely squelching her fury. *Here's the great pop sex symbol,* she thought as she searched for a towel in the kitchen, *and what line does he use to meet a bird at a party? He spills champagne on her shirt. Who in hell does he think he is?*

As several guests came to cluck over the accident, to make apologies for that boorish Jagger, Marianne said she didn't expect much more than that from a low-class pop star. "He's simply a dreadful, spotty, South London-speaking slob," she said, her anger almost boiling out of control. "He is just dreadful, and apart from that I can't stand his spots. I hate pimply men, and Jagger has more spots on his face than anyone I've ever seen."

Marianne asked John about Andrew after the party. Just

before she and John had left Andrew had introduced himself. "I want to record you," he said.

"Don't you even want to know whether I can sing?" Marianne asked.

"It doesn't matter. You're pop star material, you have a very commercial face, a very beautiful face that the newspapers and the public will love. And besides, John told me you *can* sing."

She laughed now as she told John about that brief conversation and how she had laughed at Andrew and practically brushed him off. John said that Andrew seemed quite serious about it. He had been stunned by her looks, by the aptness of her name, he felt she had star quality. And after John had told him she played guitar and could sing a bit, Andrew said he must record her, he would make her a star.

Marianne laughed again and said it was all so silly. She couldn't really sing, she didn't know anything about pop music, she had no desire nor talent to be anyone's star.

But when she received a telegram from Andrew at school a few days later, asking her to come up to London to talk about making a record for his company, she was intrigued. A part of her felt the entire episode was a bit of foolishness, that getting involved in it would interfere with the goal she had set for herself. But there was another influence, tugging her to London and the recording studio: a feeling that a whole new world had slowly been opening for her in the last few years, that she had once been so unhappy and miserable, as a child, that whatever happiness and adventures now coming her way were owed her, as compensation for those earlier years.

She had been born in Hampstead Hospital. When she was an infant her family moved to Reading, into a tiny house which she hated and called Reading Gaol. Her mother, Baroness Erisso, was a survivor of one of Austria's noted aristocratic families, and had been a ballet dancer. Marianne told friends that the Baroness had been tortured by the Gestapo during the war because she was a spy for the Allies, that her father had also been a spy and had met the Baroness in Vienna—she was his spy contact—and married her after the war. Some friends dismissed it all as part of Marianne's romantic fantasies—she had the most incredibly romantic dreams of young minstrels dressed in velvets and courting her in ancient castles, of ghosts, of Gothic romances—and they felt certain she was living out a dream fantasy. But Marianne's parents *had* told her they had been spies against the Nazis.

When she was a child Marianne had twice been stricken with TB. The second time she was taken by her mother to live in a castle in Austria that belonged to the Baroness's family. Once Marianne recovered, after about a year in Austria, she returned to Reading with her mother. The Baroness left her husband, who gave them the little house in Reading. Marianne was sent to St. Joseph's Convent School when she was eight; her grandmother was dying of cancer and came to England to be with Marianne's mother, and Marianne was sent off to the convent to protect her from the sounds and smells and textures of death. Marianne was not a Catholic—St. Joseph's was the only school with class that would take her without much cost to her family. She was a boarder, felt a complete outsider and very poor, and hated every moment at the school. She was not accepted by the other girls until she became a Catholic, converting only for social reasons, because of the pressures she felt from classmates and nuns. The Church, with its promise to answer all the mysteries, bestow special knowledge and rewards, seemed to be luring her to give up her life to it, but Marianne battled with herself to stay clear of that trap.

She had felt life was dreadful, from the moment she entered the convent school, because she wasn't very pretty in those years. TB had left her skinny and pale, and she was very shy and awkward because of her position as a charity boarder. Then, at fifteen, she suddenly became almost overnight, the prettiest girl in the school, and she began to rise above the terrors of her childhood. Being pretty was so important to her, and it felt so good—boys from adjoining schools kept falling in love with her, and her classmates were fawning on her, hoping some of the boys Marianne had no use for would dribble down to them. There was an agreement between St. Joseph's and the all-male Quaker school adjoining it that some of the convent girls would help the boys with dramatic productions, playing the female roles. The boys put on an opera the year after Marianne had so suddenly become desired, and she was the only girl offered a role in the production. The headmaster's son fell in love with her, and Marianne began to understand how life changes when a plain woman becomes beautiful and lusted after, which is what the boys were doing. By the time she was seventeen and had met John Dunbar she felt strongly that Marianne Faithfull was to be looked up to, would never again permit anyone to look down upon her. She was very conscious of being looked up to.

That year, her last at the school, all her classmates were making a big thing about who would be the first to lose her virginity. It was a natural reaction to the strictness of the convent; the girls had been instructed on their first day at the institution that immediately after bathing they must get into their shifts because it was shameful for them to look at their bodies. They were not only virgins, but were absolutely virginal. Many of them decided to change that condition as quickly as possible, once they became upper-classmen and had a bit more freedom. But being the first to sleep with a man was not so important to Marianne as was the kind of man with whom she'd make love. The other girls would take any ordinary public school boy who came along, if they had to; Marianne waited until she met an undergraduate at Cambridge, a man with a very good background and much future potential. And shortly after meeting John she was coming to London with him and getting involved in all the things her friends at St. Joseph's could only dream of doing—being friendly with the Beatles, having Mick Jagger pour champagne on her and stroking her breasts, and being furious at that lout of a sex symbol . . .

And now the offer, the urgent telegram, asking her to make a recording. *It could be fun,* Marianne thought, *a form of slumming.* She thought the pop scene very sordid, its celebrities not as intelligent or intellectual as John, but perhaps it would be exciting to get a little closer to it. But she was also afraid. She had a painful need to be accepted at Cambridge and a terrible fear of failing her exams. She checked and rechecked everything, fearful of making an error in her work; it was only in her imagination that she was no longer afraid of making a mistake, for she was going to be a great actress, a star, a woman admired by the entire world. She knew that making a pop record might just interfere with her dreams. Yet she seemed unable to resist the lure. She told herself that she would make the recording but that she didn't want to become involved in the pop scene or achieve the kind of fame that Jagger had, but another part of her reached out for it, as further proof that she was a beautiful and talented woman.

She was repelled by it, but couldn't stay away.

She went up to see Andrew and signed a recording contract. Andrew told her he had asked Lionel Bart to write a song for her, to be used as the "A" side of her first record. He added that Jagger had written a song especially for her, "As Tears Go By," which would be used on the "B" side. Jagger showed up that first day and tried to impress her that he'd written the song after meeting her, a tribute to her, a love song written by a pop idol to a very special woman. Marianne smiled at that, and thought: *He's saying that because he wants to get me into bed, it's probably just a song he has left over that the Stones can't use.* Which was precisely why the song came to be offered to her. Jagger and Keith had begun to collaborate some months before, Jagger writing the lyrics after Keith brought him a melody, and they felt their songwriting was going well: Gene Pitney, an American songwriter and singer who'd had a dozen big hits in succession in the States, met the Stones on the "Thank Your Lucky Stars" television show the previous June, listened to some of the songs that Jagger and Keith had just written and immediately recorded one of them, "That Girl Belongs to Yesterday." Pitney's record became a big hit in Britain. That song, like "As Tears Go By," the song Jagger offered Marianne, couldn't be used by the Stones because it was too sweet and gentle, too mushily sentimental, for their raunch image.

Everytime Marianne came up to London to rehearse the two songs Jagger would be there, making little plays for her, and Marianne began bringing a girl friend along in self-defense. When the sessions were over everyone would pile into the car to drive the girls back to the station, and there wasn't ever enough room for them all. Jagger was always the last one in, he would always have to sit in someone's lap, and each time he'd try to select Marianne. But she'd maneuver it so that he'd have to sit in her girl friend's lap. Jagger would get very cross about it. Marianne didn't care how he felt. She thought it all so funny that she was frustrating one of the country's latest sex symbols. She didn't fancy Jagger at all because of his generally uncouth behavior—she didn't realize then that it was an act: "I'm filthy and dirty and I never wash but aren't I sexy?"—and she much preferred the high tone of the undergraduate set.

Lionel Bart's song didn't work out too well, and "As Tears Go By" was chosen for the "A" side of Marianne's first record. Jagger stepped up his plays for Marianne, and she continued to turn them back, almost laughing aloud at the audacity of such a lout trying to seduce a woman above his class. She felt so superior to him and to everyone involved in the recording. In the studio, as Andrew and Jagger and the engineer gave her directions, she'd think, *Who do these people think they are? They all speak with accents and they're all so horrible, especially that dreadful spotted sex symbol.* But by the last recording session, when both songs had been taped to Andrew's

153

satisfaction and everyone was saying goodbye, Jagger didn't offer to drive her to the railroad station as he usually did. *It might have worked*, Marianne thought as she waited for her train, *I might just have accepted if he asked me to go home with him.* But she pushed the thought aside, not wanting to explore what she felt for Jagger, if anything.

New York, June 1964. Baby Jane Holzer, invented by David Bailey the summer before, almost as an afterthought to his creation of Jean Shrimpton, Angela Howard, Susan Murray. And now Baby Jane, the girl of the year, the darling of American underground society, fairly dances around in her seat in the Academy of Music, so carefully casual in her zebra coat, her blonde hair bouncing as she shouts to friends about the pop music sensation of the year. This is the year of sensations: Baby Jane, Andy Warhol, the Rolling Stones on their first American tour . . . Baby Jane the most sensational of all, so cool, so sophisticated, pretending not to notice how the boys and girls who have come to see the Stones are staring at her, the Baby Jane of *Vogue,* of *Life,* of Warhol films.

She twists around to shout to one of her friends. They're all here, the New Celebrities, come to see the Stones; Bob Dylan had returned from a concert tour of Britain two weeks before, raving about the Stones and the black American music they played, and if Dylan was urging his friends among the New Celebrities to see the Stones then, by God, they must do better than that—they must suck the Stones into their world of High Camp, and Baby Jane cries out over the heads of her friends, to a late arrival, that she has just been *backstage* with the Stones and they're *so-o-o divine*. Then turns to the actor next to her, interrupting his conversation with Warhol, and shouts at him.

"Wait'll you see the Stones!" she says, her voice quivering with the anticipated orgasm of their performance. "They're so sexy—they're pure sex. They're *divine!* The Beatles, well, you know, Paul McCartney—*sweet* Paul McCartney. You know what I mean. He's such a *sweet person*. I mean, the Stones are bitter, they're all from the working class, you know? The East End. Mick Jagger—well, it's all Mick. You know what they say about his lips? They say his lips are *diabolical*. That was in one of the magazines.

"When Mick comes into the Ad Lib in London—I mean, there's nothing like the Ad Lib in New York. You can go into the Ad Lib, and everybody is there. They're all young, and they're taking over, it's like a whole revolution. I mean, it's *exciting*. They're all from the lower classes, East End sort-of-thing. There's nobody exciting from the upper classes any more, it's a whole new thing. It's not the Beatles. Bailey says the Beatles are *passé*, because now everybody's mum pats the Beatles on the head. The Beatles are getting fat. The Beatles—well, John Lennon's still thin, but Paul McCartney is getting a big bottom. That's all right, but I don't particularly care for that. The Stones are thin. I mean, that's why they're beautiful, they're so thin. Mick Jagger—wait'll you see Mick."

The Stones suddenly appear in large white puddles of spotlights, wearing street clothes instead of uniforms, just like Dylan and all those real, suffering folksingers in Greenwich Village stirring up a revolution. Jagger's body is long and lean as he skips and dances to the microphone, and the audience tension starts building toward its ultimate mass orgasms as the band smashes into its fantasy about America, the America of Chuck Berry jam sessions, Muddy Waters Southern barn-yard picking, Little Richard's revival meetings . . . all subverted and manipulated to simulate the funky atmosphere of the Crawdaddy and Ealing in this theater that seats thousands. Jagger manipulating the audience, that mass of undifferentiated bodies quivering beyond the spots, manipulating them into believing they are the hippest because they are among the few in this amorphous society with enough sagacity to assemble for the Stones.

155

"Didn't I tell you they're simply *divine?*" Baby Jane asks Warhol as they fight their way backstage after the concert-/orgy for a personal audience with the Stones. "Didn't I tell you Mick is something beautiful?"

The next night is hip New York's party of the year, the Mods and Rockers Ball—a dance in honor of the Stones and also to celebrate Baby Jane's twenty-third birthday. Fashion photographer Jerry Schatzberg, who *is* the New Society—proprietor of the posh discotheque Ondine, breeder of horses on his Pennsylvania farm, dear friend of the Duke and Duchess of Bedford and of Dylan and Warhol and all the other sensations—Jerry is the host, and everybody is here in his apartment and studio on Park Avenue South: Baby Jane, Shrimp, Barbara Steele, all those people who get invited to New Celebrity parties. And Goldie and the Gingerbreads, four young women in gold lamé tights who will play rock and roll for the dancers—Nicky Haslam, *Show Magazine* art director, discovered them at the Wagon Wheel and hired them to play for Jerry's party.

Goldie and the Gingerbreads play a one-hour set, Baby Jane in her black velvet jumpsuit with huge bell bottom pants, frugging, Sally Kirkland, a young actress in a leopard print dress doing the frug with Jerry, everybody out there jumping, bouncing the studio floor up and down like a trampoline, getting off to this funky woman's band that plays hard rock with a drive equal to—yes, you had to put it this way—as good as any male band. When they take their break Goldie and her band go upstairs to Jerry's apartment to relax before the next set, and the next—it's certain to go till dawn—but the word flashes up to them that the Rolling Stones have arrived. *They* have actually arrived. And they're coming upstairs to the apartment that serves as the band's dressing room and as a refuge for those more interested in delicious little conversations and gossip than in dancing.

Carol McDonald can't believe what she is seeing, can't believe that these *slobs*—there's no other word for them—that these filthy-looking undernourished slobs are being touted as the musicians who will dethrone the Beatles. "They're the messiest things I've ever seen in my life," Carol whispers to one of the other women in the band. Their hair is greasy, their clothes filthier than any Bowery bum would tolerate, and the girls with them—Carol can't decide if the Stones brought them over from England or picked them out of the New York gutters—the girls are just as cruddy. All of them, the Stones and their girls, look as if they haven't washed their hair in months. Grease actually hangs from their hair. "They must have worked on the grease," Carol said, "there's just too much grease to be casual. Is there a hairdresser in town who plasters you with grease?"

"Koom over here, love, give us a kiss," Jagger orders one of the women in the band. Her look of sleet doesn't seem to deter him. All night long he plays the nasty East End hoodlum—*loudmouth*, Carol thought as she watched Jagger in action on the dance floor, ordering women around, demanding they dance, get him a drink, *kiss his ass . . . He's an obnoxious loudmouth.* But she wondered whether it wasn't an act, Jagger pretending to be butch and evil and vicious, playing the hip malchick because he thought it was expected of him.

She had seen that article in one of the English music papers, an interview a few weeks before in which the conversation once more turned to whether or not the Stones' image had been manufactured. And Jagger had said: "All this talk about an image. I don't think I've got the hang of what it all means, not yet. We've never sat down and told ourselves, 'We've got to get an image.' We've just gone on as we've always gone on, hoping that one day people would want to listen. Soon they'll be sending round psychiatrists to find out about us. All that 'caveman' chat—what does it really mean?"

And here is Jagger, in New York, behaving like a Neanderthal or its futuristic equivalent, Alex in *Clockwork Or-*

ange—who the hell is he kidding? Carol asked Goldie during one break.

Jagger wanders upstairs, and refuses to return to the party. A band of celebrities follows him, most of them somewhat self-conscious about their need to be around him, but obeying his unspoken command that they come to him: Baby Jane, very chic but exuding an almost desperate need to be near Jagger; Shrimp, curious about what is bothering her future brother-in-law; a dozen women who would grow furious if anyone called them groupies. But Jagger seems uninterested, to Carol and others, seems almost rude in his disdain of the party thrown in his honor—for it is understood in New York that Jagger is the Stones. Oh, certainly, there is Brian, who started the group. But Brian is too intense, he has too much of his soul invested in the music, while Jagger is Pop Art, the Warhol of the stage. There's something special about Jagger, something in his presence, that makes you think only of Jagger when you think about the Stones. Jagger gave the impression that he loved himself, loved the sound of his voice, loved the way people were forced to admire him, seeming to feel a great joy because he was admired, and setting up currents and waves that hooked other human beings to him, forced them to be bound to him through eternal emotions—not only from the stage, where his emotions bounce and collide off theirs, and take energy from theirs, but even more so here in Jerry's bachelor apartment, which was almost dripping with a boudoir intimacy that could have been created by the editors of *Playboy:* modern art on the walls, the finest stereo equipment, a tree-lined terrace outside—every American male's dream of making it. Here, Jagger played the boorish East End lout, and the New Celebrities simply adored it. As did their parents thirty years before, taxiing up to Harlem to see Cab Calloway and Louis Armstrong.

Jagger sat in the Stones' suite in the Park Sheraton Hotel the next morning. Young women appeared to be spilling out of every closet and draped over every bed and chair. Below him was Seventh Avenue, with its traffic and the people hustling along, and up the street was Carnegie Hall, where they would play later in the month. New York is pure energy. How very different from English tours, from the Midlands and the North, where the towns and the citizens are feeble, limp, simply passing through on the way to their graves. One city in the North was so impotent—that's what the dullness felt like, impotence—that the band's bottled-up energy finally exploded hours after the concert. Their hotel window overlooked a parking lot, dozens of cars ten feet below them, polished metal gleaming in the soft rainfall. Brian, quite drunk, had started it, as usual. He opened the window and leaped down on the hood of a Jaguar, smashing an enormous dent in the metal. "Come on!" he shouted, and Jagger followed, and then Keith—leaping down, smashing a hood or a trunk of an expensive car, staggering back upstairs to leap out again. Hundreds of pounds worth of damage because they felt depressed with the grayness of the North and because Andrew had gotten them into a *Clockwork Orange* violence.

The Stones didn't feel that sort of need in New York. And, hopefully, the rest of America would be as potent and vigorous as New York. For in this city that Jagger was exploring for the first time, they were celebrities. Their concerts had turned into riots, teenage girls invaded their hotel rooms, some armed with scissors to cut off locks of hair for their scrapbooks, others hoping to spend a few moments in bed with one of the Stones—it seldom mattered which—for a more memorable souvenir.

But when the Stones went out on tour a few days later, to the heartland of America where they hoped to reach the *real* people in all those towns Chuck Berry sings about in "Route 66," their fantasies about America smashed against reality.

The plane touched down in Omaha, and they climbed out into a hot summer wind so filled with dust that Brian's asthma kicked up and threatened to strangle him. No fans. There wasn't a single screaming teenager at the airport, nothing but strange-looking men with large bellies who stared at the Stones' long hair with anger and contempt. "It's like a desert, where the hell is everybody?" Jagger said. Almost on cue a dozen motorcycle policemen, looking as if they were auditioning for a Hitler Panzer division, roared onto the tarmac, followed by a limousine. The Stones were hustled inside the mile-long Cadillac, their luggage gathered up, and the caravan raced into Omaha with police sirens wailing.

"I didn't think anybody in Omaha ever 'eard of us, we really got it made," Jagger said as the procession flowed toward their hotel. Brian groaned through the handkerchief protecting his mouth and nose from the dust: "Yeah, we must be heavy here."

They sat in their dressing room that night, drinking whisky and Coke out of paper cups as they waited to go on. Several cops, big beefy men in Texas Ranger-style uniforms, walked in. "What's that you're drinking?" one of them asked Keith. He was actually drinking straight Coke at the time but he said: "Whisky and Coke." The cop said: "You can't drink whisky in a public place, it's against the law. Pour it down the sink." It flashed on Keith: Lenny Bruce had been making jokes about the Nazi mentality of American cops when he appeared at The Establishment in Soho just a few months before, but the jokes were truth: This policeman could shoot down Lenny and anyone else who angers him. "Listen, officer," Keith said, "I'm just drinking Coke. There's no whisky in it." Keith looked up to negotiate with the cop. A .44-caliber revolver was pointed at a spot between Keith's eyes. He poured his Coke down the drain.

Jagger bounced out onto the stage, leading his band into the spotlights of an auditorium built to hold 15,000 screaming fans. His body sagged visibly when he realized the house was empty. (By official count, later, there were 637 people in the audience, and at least fifty of them were policemen.) The promoter hadn't been able to sell many tickets to the concert but he did know the Omaha chief of police and persuaded the man to give the Stones a motorcycle escort. To impress the band and, hopefully, drum up a little more business.

"It's like we have to start all over again, here in America," Jagger said when they got back to their hotel rooms. "Nobody wants to know anything about our music."

"They will," Keith said, "they'll have to listen to us soon 'cause we're good. Wait'll we get to Los Angeles. It'll be a lot better, it'll be like New York."

But the further away from New York they traveled the larger the disappointment. They taped the "Hollywood Palace" TV show. The vogue for English groups touring America for the first time was to play the "Ed Sullivan Show," but Sullivan refused to permit the Stones on the program. He didn't like their image, not for his Sunday night family viewers, and Eric had no bargaining power at all: London Records, the band's American distributor, had released three Stones singles but each had sold so poorly they were withdrawn from the market.

Dean Martin, host of "Hollywood Palace," agreed to use the Stones because they'd be perfect foils for his brand of tipsy put-down humor. "And now I'd like to introduce the latest rave from England, the Rolling Stones," Martin told his audience—holding his nose. When the curtains parted, displaying the Stones to about 10 million viewers, Martin said: "Their hair isn't that long. It's just smaller foreheads and higher eyebrows." The camera panned to Jagger, who glared out from his painstakingly unruly hair and seemed to be saying, "Just let us play, man." But Martin wouldn't let up. After the Stones played "I Just Wanna Make Love to You" Martin announced there would be a commercial break: "Now don't go away, anybody. You wouldn't leave me with these Rolling Stones, would you?'' The little old ladies in flowered hats sitting in the studio audience broke up at that one, and Martin continued: "Actually, the boys are going back to England soon to have a hair-pulling contest with the Beatles.'' During the two-minute commercial break the Stones seriously considered walking off without performing their next number; Keith and Brian were especially furious over Martin's routine. But Jagger persuaded them to continue. When the camera returned to the band, Jagger sang "Not Fade Away,'' and the boys' first major American television appearance ended. Martin introduced the next act, a man bouncing on a trampoline, by saying: "This is the father of the Rolling Stones. He's been trying to kill himself ever since.''

The Stones were in Chicago when the Martin show was broadcast, sitting in their hotel room, drunk on whisky. And when Jagger realized the enormity of Martin's putdown he became so angry that he called Eric Easton in London and tore into him: "What the 'ell kind of manager are you, getting us into that?'' he demanded. "You really screwed us up, this Martin bastard ripping us apart, nobody comin' to see us at our concerts . . .'' Eric tried to tell Jagger to have patience, the fame would happen, the kids who saw the Martin show would understand why adults reacted that way and would rush over to the Stones *because* adults hated them, that exposure on any national TV show—even one as obscene as Martin's—was better than being ignored completely. Jagger refused to listen. Encouraged by the others on extension phones, he continued to scream at Eric, who finally hung up. Jagger put the call through several more times, continuing his tirade, and Eric kept hanging up on him.

Jagger was so very confused, Eric later said. He had been the toast of New York, all of the most important people had reached out to him, even Bob Dylan had championed the Stones, but now it suddenly appeared their future had been washed away before it had a chance to develop. He seemed unable to understand what was going wrong. Especially since everything seemed to be going so well back in England. Just before coming to America their incomes had risen to $500 a week each, they were among the highest paid bands on the British concert circuit, and there were more than 50,000 members of the Rolling Stones Fan Club, subscribing to the new *Rolling Stones Magazine.* They had recorded another single the previous January, "Not Fade Away" backed with "Little By Little," a song Jagger wrote with Phil Spector. Jagger had been very excited when Andrew lured Spector into the studio and Spector played maracas on the recording and helped produce it, and he was even more excited when Andrew told them what Spector had said:

"Listen, boy, these oddballs are just great. Wait till they get a good look at them in the States—the kids there'll flip. They've got an incredible sound going, and if the kids don't like the sound they can just look at them. That hair, boy, is going to be one great asset for the boys in the States."

If anyone knew what the kids in America would pay to see and hear it should have been Spector: He had become a millionaire when he was nineteen because he had gauged perfectly the music that American kids would buy. It was happening in England. Why not in America? Back in England "Not Fade Away" had been released in late February to rave reviews and had gone straight into the charts . . . while their first extended play record was still selling so briskly that it remained high in the charts, and the Stones were second only to the Beatles. In England, that is. In America "Not Fade Away" got as high as number eighty-two in the *Billboard* charts—high enough to give promoters the courage to book the Stones on their first American tour—but the record never went much higher.

What brought Jagger down most of all was that the American experience was so depressing it destroyed the thrill he should have felt from the latest news from England: The Stones' first longplay record, released a few days before they flew off to the United States, hit the top of the charts within two weeks . . . was number one right now . . . 110,000 English kids paying over £200,000 for the record . . . their first LP, and it had actually held back the Beatles' latest release. And George Harrison was telling an interviewer: "It's become the in thing for adults to say the Beatles are good or the Beatles are funny, it's in for adults to like us. So the real hip kids—or the kids who think they are—have gone off us. The in thing for those kids now is to be a Stones fan, because their parents can't stand the Rolling Stones." Most encouraging of all, *Record Mirror* held its first annual pop music poll, and the Stones placed first, well ahead of the Beatles . . . and Jagger personally was voted the most popular individual in a group, coming in ahead of George, Paul, John, and Ringo.

It was all coming together so beautifully in Britain. Even the songwriting, opening new facets of their career. Jagger was no longer hesitant about writing songs with Keith, or recording them with the Stones, no longer felt awed by John and Paul's ability to turn out dozens of songs for the Beatles. Jagger and Keith had begun writing in the summer of 1963, Keith producing the melodies and Jagger the lyrics aimed at adolescent emotions:

> *It is the evening of the day*
> *I sit and watch the children play*
> *Smiling faces I can see*
> *But not for me*
> *I sit and watch as tears go by . . .*

With Andrew as a third partner, Jagger and Keith formed a music publishing company. Brian Epstein had demonstrated the wisdom of creating a publishing company for Lennon and McCartney—no sense permitting one of the established publishers to siphon off 50 percent of the gross. In the beginning, with Marianne's hit record of "As Tears Go By," the songs were bringing Jagger and Keith an extra $250 or so every royalty period. Now, with some two dozen songs recorded by the Stones and by other singers and bands, that additional income soared to several hundred dollars a month. They never considered their songs good enough to be the "A" sides of their recordings because they were still slavishly copying black blues artists and were afraid they'd sound like fools if they wrote and recorded an "authentic" black blues number. They were limited in their thinking about the potentials of the Stones; Jagger, especially, was worried that the critics and the fans would react badly if the Stones reached out musically. "It seems funny farming out our stuff to everybody else," Jagger said. "Maybe we'll use more of our own stuff when we're better established."

Everything that had been happening to the Stones' career should have thrilled Jagger. They were so obviously on their way. But the empty halls in Detroit, in Hollywood, in Omaha, kept nagging at him, damping the exhilaration he should have felt. Worst of all was the feeling that he—they—were being ignored in America. Just before they flew off for the American tour, Andrew had told the British press that the Rolling Stones were not simply a band *but a way of life*. And, his words implied, our boys have become so significant, sociologically, that by god they must be treated with respect. Now that the Stones were important newspaper copy every journalist in Britain wanted an interview but it was just too bad, the Stones weren't going to be available to every journalist hoping to make a name for himself by generating another Stones controversy. Jagger, along with Eric and Andrew, carefully selected the writers to whom interviews would be granted. Of course, that meant writers who fit Jagger's concept of trust: much flattery, some understanding of the Stones' music and, most of all, youth. Jagger knew that the publicity had been important to the band and was grateful that the British press had at least paid attention even if too much had been written about their hair and other rubbish that had nothing to do with music. In Britain, Andrew could go to a writer for a major paper and suggest a story—"Would You Want Your Daughter to Marry a Rolling Stone?"—and get two columns of space and another contrived controversy, but here in America it was almost as if Jagger and the Stones didn't exist, so few journalists paid any attention. Most adults, in America and in Britain, dismissed other pop singers with boredom, annoyance, or contempt. Jagger provoked anger. The Stones were stuck between flights at Midway Airport, Chicago, for several hours, and wherever they went in the terminal angry adults would shout at them: "Are you a goil?" . . . "Look, it's the Supremes!" . . . "Cut your hair, creeps!" When they finally boarded the plane Jagger was leading the way down the aisle, and all the middle-aged passengers in their seats looked back to stare. Jagger stopped, turned, and shouted: "If anyone of you opens your mouth, I'll smash 'im straight in the teeth." All the passengers in their seats seemed to exhale at once . . . whooosh . . . and the band walked down the aisle in perfect silence. Jagger was giving the finger to the acceptable norm, and he was hated for it. Most especially in America.

He was depressed by that first American tour, he told Chrissie when he returned to London. "The Americans gave us a very 'ard time, everybody over there seems to be against the Stones except for some groovy people in New York," Jagger said. "But all the American ladies were outraged by us, they seemed to think we were going to rape them and cut them to little pieces. The cops just wanted to shoot us and the men beat us up. 'Jagger, you old queen,' some people yelled at me." Chrissie laughed, she couldn't help it, and Jagger's liquid face melted into a grin. "Sounds funny, now, but it was scary most of the time. And that bastard Dean Martin, he was so sarcastic. He really put us down worse than any sarcastic story ever printed over 'ere.'' And the Americans, he continued, well, they're incredibly exciting because they're so fast-moving, everything seemed so powerful, so full of energy. But there was something unpleasant about them. "Strangest thing is the way people over there are so nervous, they're kind of very on edge, very unrelaxed, even if they're being open. I like America, but I also 'ate it somehow."

Jagger and Keith moved to a flat in Mapesbury Road, North London, and Chrissie went with them. She continued to maintain a flat of her own, still not officially living with Jagger, but she spent most of her time with him. They lived quietly, despite newspaper stories that would have you believe the Stones were raving all over town deflowering virgins. They had a few close friends come round occasionally: Camilla Wiggin, one of Chrissie's girl friends, and Charlie Watts and Shirley. Jagger continued to insist they couldn't marry just yet, still dictating Charlie's personal behavior as he had dictated Charlie's professional behavior when the Stones were formed, telling Charlie precisely how he wanted the drums played. Charlie, and so many others around the Stones, was getting quite upset about the way Jagger and Andrew continued to hide the women from the fans, for the sake of the band's image. Jagger's attitude was beginning to affect Charlie quite badly.

A couple of months before the American tour, the Stones were invited to appear at the Montreux TV Festival, the first trip abroad for the group. Jagger said none of the women could accompany the band. But Keith's girl friend, Linda Keats, slipped aboard the plane at the last moment so Jagger couldn't send her back and really anger Keith. Chrissie was at Heathrow, saying goodbye to Jagger, and when she saw Linda board the plane she exploded, shouting at him, arguing that she should go, embarrassing him in public—but she didn't give a damn, she thought. He was behaving badly toward her, and Charlie and Shirley, and she wasn't going to stand for it. Jagger relented: "You can come on the next plane." Chrissie rushed home for her passport, tried to reach Shirley, but couldn't locate her. In Switzerland, there was constant bickering and arguing between Jagger and Charlie about Charlie's wish to marry Shirley immediately. Jagger, joined by Andrew, said he couldn't do that if he wanted to remain a Rolling Stone. Charlie began to drink heavily because he was worried about facing Shirley when he returned; he'd promised that he'd put his foot down about their marriage and get Jagger to agree. The whisky made Charlie terribly sick and when the group returned to London Charlie was so ill he had to remain in Switzerland an extra day. Chrissie thought it was hateful, what Jagger was doing to Charlie, and she was pleased that Shirley and Charlie decided to get married secretly. Chrissie was the only person outside the immediate families who knew about the marriage and she was dreadfully afraid to let Jagger suspect because she knew he'd be furious.

Chrissie didn't mind the lack of social activity in their lives; she enjoyed having Jagger alone at home because on the outside was nothing but insanity—fans grabbing at Jagger, threatening to murder Chrissie because *she* was usurping their dream place as Jagger's woman. She knew that Jagger desperately needed to be away from people when he wasn't performing, that he needed time to recharge his batteries. He was so fed up with the fans around him at all times. He'd go out the front door with Chrissie and shudder: "Ooooh, all these chicks are still around, what a drag!" and race to the car. Even worse than the young girls on their doorstep were the mornings they'd awake, hear giggles, and find a couple of girls in the closet who had sneaked in through the windows during the night. The flat was being invaded daily; several mornings Keith had to climb out the kitchen window on the ground floor to evade mobs of girls who had gotten into the building. Jagger told Chrissie:

"It was so great in the old days, when I used to be able to amble across the road to the pub, and nobody'd bother me. Now I got hits, and the Stones are so big, it all gets very 'airy. I really been thinking about using disguises. Especially at concerts. Try to get into a hall, and you're attacked by these crazy birds. Maybe I'll wear a false mustache. Or dress as an attendant or a copper. That way I can walk in like part of the staff. Got a greater idea—ride up in an ambulance and have them cart me in on a stretcher."

The fans were such an annoyance that every few months Jagger and Keith would move into another flat, until the fans discovered the new location and mounted their siege again. Keith soon went off to a place of his own, with his girl friend, and Jagger leased a large place in Bryanston Mews East in fashionable and well-policed Marylebone, close to the Swiss Embassy and near to where Ringo was living with his wife, Maureen. Chrissie went with him, although continuing to keep her own flat.

While Jagger continued to seem depressed over the failure of the American tour and the demands of his fans, Brian was gaining strength and confidence. The Stones music was more professional, had more drive and guts, and Shirley Arnold, back in the fan club office, was getting sacks of mail daily, addressed to Brian. He was exhilarated by the band's progress: "We're at the top in England after just a year, and right soon we'll be at the top all over the world." It was his group, Brian felt strongly, although he'd never say that in public; but he had created the Stones, they were his band. And now, with Jagger keeping somewhat out of sight because he was too down to give many interviews, Brian was out there exulting over the delicious feeling of it all:

"For me," he told Pete Goodman, a writer for a teen fan magazine who had been selected to write the Stones' "official" story, "for me, the most important part is the live performance. I feel the exitement of the audience come through to me, communicating like mad. I feel that I'm thoroughly alive—like I've lived a long time in the space of just a few minutes.

"It's essentially a two-way thing. You give . . . and you receive. The wilder the audience, the more there is in it for us. I mean it. Those moments when Stu, our road manager, is fixing the equipment on stage are full of excitement for me. I can hear the atmosphere, even if I can't see anything. And when the curtains part and you see a flailing mass of waving arms, it just does something to you. Right inside. There's a swaying and a roaring. Screams? I've heard some groups say they don't like them. Well, okay for them. But we like the screams. It's all part of it, the whole proceedings, do you see? That two-way thing all over again. Sometimes that atmosphere gets real tight. It feels as if it could snap."

Brian was getting so carried away by the thrill of it all that it seemed to some he was losing his senses. He was sitting in the Ad Lib one night, about a month after the American tour, drinking whisky with Keith, John Lennon, and an American journalist, Al Aronowitz.

"Just one more tour will do it for us," Brian said. "One more tour will make us the biggest band in the world." John snickered, but Brian rushed on: "No, seriously, one more tour, and we'll be bigger than the Beatles even, there's no holding us back, we're going to be the biggest group in the world."

"It's all right with me," John said. "But I wish you good luck. Once you have it, you'll hate it. You can have it, I'm thinking of quitting anyway."

"You're not," Keith said. "Seriously?"

"Been thinking about it seriously, it's too much of a drag. You can have the whole show. But it's not as easy as you think. You're not playing ballrooms in Blackpool anymore.''

"No, it's the big time now," Brian said.

"Right. And you've got to be perfect for the big time. You've got to be great. You've got to be strong. And hard, that's important, you've got to be hard."

"We're all those things, we're great, certainly, and we're strong and hard," Brian said.

"Are you?" John asked, leaning over the table, his myopic eyes squinting at Brian. "Are you all strong and hard? Is there one weak man in the group who might hold you back?"

Keith and Brian tried to evade the question, and John pressed them as they shrugged. Finally, both nodded, yes, there is a weak one in the group.

"Then get rid of 'im!" John snapped. "Get rid of 'im."

Brian nodded again, his face quite serious, then smiled. "We'll make it," he said. "One more tour and we'll make it."

It was all well and good that Brian was enthused, and Jagger depressed—that their career was totally dominating their lives—but for Chrissie, career was intruding on her personal relationship with her man and was filling her with pain. She tried not to complain to Jagger about the pressures of fame but she couldn't always smother her feelings, she was too open and honest to hold it back. "People are trying to make me into something because of my sister and because of you," she told him. "I've never been anything except me, Chrissie Shrimpton, and I never want to be anything but that but there's all this pressure that I should *be* something, an actress or something. Because of those two labels, 'Shrimp's sister' and 'Mick's girl friend.' It's painful." She actually enrolled in an acting class, because of the pressures, but soon gave it up because she realized she didn't want to be an actress—couldn't be an actress—realized she was surrendering herself to the unspoken demands of people who continually asked her,

"And what do *you* do?" She didn't *do* anything, and felt ashamed . . . ashamed that she wanted nothing more than to be a mother, to raise Jagger's children, while the world outside insisted she become a superstar in her own right.

She and Jagger were seldom really alone, that was the worst part of their relationship, so seldom alone that they couldn't be completely open. There were always fans hovering around, groupies, other musicians, journalists, all the hangers-on feeding off the famous rock star. Chrissie and Jagger fought constantly because of it. They were forced to suppress their feelings because they were living in a fishbowl, and the rare moments they were alone the antagonisms had grown so powerful that they exploded, and they'd scream at one another, punch and kick, trying to cause physical pain to relieve the emotional bottleneck. Sometimes, they didn't even know why they were fighting: The Christmas before, they woke in the middle of the night, after a party, and began hitting each other without a word between them.

Most painful, for Chrissie, was the change she could see in Jagger over only a few months, a change in both his personality and his public figure. The Stones' first Paris concert, at the Olympia Theater in October, made her very much aware of how swiftly Jagger was changing into something she couldn't recognize, and it upset her enormously. Chrissie and Shirley were taken to Paris after long arguments with Jagger. He still insisted that the women be kept secret, and stay home, but Charlie had told him that he and Shirley had been married and Jagger fell back to petulant logic: "You won't like being there and you'll just get in our way." Chrissie and Shirley came to attention in front of him, threw their arms forward in salute, and shouted: "*Heil,* Jagger!" And Jagger relented.

They watched the Stones performing from backstage of the Olympia, Jagger primping for an audience that was mostly young French boys, Jagger attracting more boys than girls to his performances. And suddenly, in the middle of a hard rock

172

version of a Chuck Berry song, Jagger threw himself on one knee in front of Keith, as if in sexual supplication to Keith or to his guitar. The boys in the audience went wild at that bit of high camp. Shirley and Chrissie turned to one another. *How awful,* Chrissie thought, *how contrived. Mick's act is getting contrived.* She sensed that Shirley felt the same for both turned away, embarrassed.

But the audience was charged up by Jagger's act. When the curtain fell after the final encore, hundreds of boys and girls stampeded toward the stage. When the gendarmes held them back, the boys tore up seats and smashed windows. Scores were arrested, but many others evaded the police and raced down the boulevard, tearing down posters, breaking windows, and slashing the fronts of newspaper kiosks. At a café near the theater, the boys overturned tables and threw customers out to the pavement.

"I get a strange feeling on stage," Jagger told an interviewer a short time after the Paris riot. "I feel all this energy coming from an audience. They need something from life and they are trying to get it from us. I often want to smash the microphone up or something because I don't feel the same person on stage as I am normally. I entice the audience, of course I do. I do it every way I can think of. Of course what I'm doing is a sexual thing. I dance, and all dancing is a replacement for sex. Even very formal ‘dancing. My dancing is pretty basic sexually. What really upsets people is that I'm a man and not a woman. I don't do anything more than a lot of girl dancers. But they're accepted because it's a man's world. What I do is very much the same as a girl's strip-tease dance, I suppose. I take off my jacket and sometimes I loosen my shirt. But I don't stand in front of a mirror practicing how to be sexy, you know."

Chrissie was amused by that last line, for Jagger had started practicing certain movements in front of the mirror, miming for the mirror when he didn't think she was watching. But she did notice and frequently teased him about it. Jagger was furious at her teasing. He didn't like being called a rock star, a poseur off the stage, he insisted that his stage act and his private life were distinctly separate, two different worlds. *But it's all blurring on him, really,* Chrissie thought one night, weeks after the Paris concert, when she caught Jagger in front of the mirror, and her teasing resulted in another violent argument. *It's all blurring, he's beginning to have a stage personality now, apart from his normal personality . . . In the beginning when I first knew him his stage act was part of his normal self and was honest and real . . . Now it's getting contrived, he's becoming a star.*

Other changes that Chrissie saw in Jagger annoyed her, and frightened her. Particularly his use of cannabis. Bob Dylan had introduced the Beatles to pot when they went to America for the first time, in February 1964, and by the end of that year use of cannabis had become fashionable in London's hip underground culture. Jagger was against pot. "You are never to smoke that stuff or to take pills or anything like that," he told Chrissie again and again. She promised she would stay away from all drugs, and she was very pleased that he was still able to remain above the fantasy illusion that fame brings, that he didn't sink into it and lose his head as so many pop stars were doing. That's what cannabis was to Chrissie—part of the pop world's loss of reality.

One evening she went to the Scotch, a pub in which Andrew was throwing a party for everyone in his office. Someone offered her a toke of cannabis. She refused.

"That's one thing that Mick taught me, never to take drugs," Chrissie said. "And I won't because Mick doesn't."

They all laughed at her. "My God," one of them said, "Mick was in the office this afternoon, smoking and stoned out of his head."

Chrissie smoked pot for the first time. She argued with Jagger, angered at his deception, but soon she began to smoke with him regularly, at home. But she was upset and worried about his smoking, which was further evidence that he was beginning to evolve into someone she could no longer understand.

Carol McDonald was beginning to feel that every time she'd meet the Rolling Stones her instinctive reaction would be: "I just can't believe it." But she really couldn't believe what she was seeing, she kept telling herself, there were no other words to express her reaction. She was backstage in a theater in North London with Goldie and the Gingerbreads, in March 1965, ten months after meeting the Stones for the first time in New York. Now the Stones were headliners in their own right, topping the bill of a British theater tour which included Goldie's band, the Hollies, and three other groups. Carol and the other women in the band hadn't liked the idea of touring with the Stones, would rather not have to put with their greasiness and with Jagger's boorish apeman conduct. But when the Stones came into the theater on opening night Carol's mouth fell open; when she recovered from her suprise she turned to Goldie and asked: "What the hell is this?" Jagger and the Stones were wearing suits—tweed, most of them—their hair was shining as if they had soaked under the shower for days, they wore clean shirts and narrow ties. Dressed to the nines, like respectable public school boys attending a class dance.

"Damn it, when you were in the States you were so filthy, what the hell was going on?" Carol asked Jagger. "You guys look outasite now."

Jagger laughed. "That's what we wanted you Americans to think, that we were dirty and raunchy," he said. "That was our image over there. If those dumb American birds dig that kind of shit, why shouldn't we do it?"

"Well, they sure dug it, the dirtier the better."

"Right, the dirtier we were the more chicks dug it," Jagger

said. "Dumb American birds digging dirty rock stars. That's what they wanted and that's what we gave them."

"And that's where you make your money," Carol said, angry at his attitude toward American women.

"It sure is. What the fuck, we're giving those stupid birds what they want so why shouldn't they pay for it?"

Carol laughed and turned to chat with one of the other Stones. *What can I say,* she thought, *it's the truth.*

During that tour, several things about the Stones surprised Carol—particularly Jagger's control over newspaper photographers, and her strong and recurring feeling that Brian was being destroyed.

One night after a show in the Midlands all the boys—Jagger, Graham Nash of the Hollies, and the other members of the bands—sauntered into the women's dressing room, as they usually did, waiting for the fans to disperse before driving back to their hotels. The Gingerbreads wore blond wigs during their act, and Jagger put one of them on his head and started dancing about. Graham Nash did the same, and he and Jagger began dancing together, pretending to be a pair of outrageous transvestites. Newsmen were there with their cameras and began taking pictures, thrilled that Jagger was putting on such a sordid show for their readers. When Jagger tired of the act and tossed the wig on a dressing table, the photographers turned to leave with their pictures.

"Wait a minute," Jagger shouted. "Wait just a minute."

The photographers returned. "What's up?" one of them asked.

"Gimme those pictures," Jagger ordered. "That was just some private fun, and you can't print those pictures."

Jagger removed the film from each camera and exposed it, and there was barely a murmur of protest from the newsmen; they knew that if they didn't obey they'd never be permitted in Jagger's presence again.

Brian was usually very quiet during that tour, and Carol wondered what was troubling him and began to watch him rather closely whenever she could. In a short time she began to bring into conscious thought the feeling that had been tugging at her: *Brian acts like he's dying, like he's already dead. He's like a shell, like a void.*

Carol had a strong feeling that Brian was being pushed out of the group, that he had a lot to do with the band's success but was being underestimated. *That can ruin somebody, that can kill your insides.* She felt that Brian had a lot on his mind, that he was feeling an extraordinary amount of pain but couldn't talk about it. *He's not really happy with the whole thing,* she thought, *he should be flying high because of the Stones' success but he's so unhappy. I think he feels himself being pushed out.*

An important part of Brian's unhappiness, Carol felt, was that Jagger was being treated as the leader of the band: *Mick Jagger and the Rolling Stones. He's getting most of the interviews, most of the pictures in the papers, most of everything. He's the one who's jumping around and doing everything. And Brian can't deal with it. Some people can deal with that, and others can't if they know they've done most of the work to build the band. Why doesn't Mick give Brian any of the credit? It won't hinder Mick any, he's already on his way. Why doesn't he understand Brian can't handle what's happening?*

And yet, Carol felt there was a strong bond between Jagger and Brian, almost a love. *They get along like they're nuts for each other. Brian's hiding what he's feeling, and Mick's not getting the vibrations. It's like Brian's not strong enough to split from the group, he's being held in there by something strange, and it's killing him.*

Brian wanted to quit. He'd been talking about it for several months. "But I can't," he told a few friends. "I don't want to spend the rest of my life being called an ex-Rolling Stone." There had been joy for Brian a few months before: The Stones were giving the Beatles a fight in the charts, Jagger had been somewhat out of the public view, and Brian was being called upon to give the interviews. But the joy had turned to desolation as Jagger returned to his many roles—giving the interviews again, getting his photo in the papers, directing the band's career, becoming almost a co-manager with Eric ever since Andrew decided to give up his role in day-to-day management in order to concentrate on producing the Stones' recordings. Brian was jealous of Jagger, he admitted it occasionally, but the jealousy was more than Brian's paranoia. There was enough reality fueling Brian's envy to permit even casual friends such as Carol McDonald to understand what was happening. And one of the things that disturbed Brian the most was the Jagger/Richard songwriting monopoly. Brian was writing songs, so was Bill Wyman, but Jagger and Keith ignored them. Bill was almost beginning to sound like Brian, telling friends:

"I've written some songs, but it's very difficult writing anything for the Stones. Mick and Keith are doing it, and there's no opportunity for anyone else. Mick, Keith, and Andrew have this big tight thing with their publishing company, and that's it. Nobody ever talks about it. For somebody else to write anything, or even try, it's like a closed shop."

Brian was glad when he heard about Bill saying that; it demonstrated that his complaints were justified.

One night during a tour of England a few months before the tour with Goldie and the Gingerbreads, Brian was unable to contain his anger any longer and he began accusing Jagger of wanting to be the leader when they had agreed there would be no leader, they'd always be equals. They were driving back in their van to London from a suburban date with Ian Stewart, who had left the Stones before they signed up with Eric Easton and was now the group's road manager, behind the wheel. "Stop the van, Stu," one of the band shouted. "Pull over here." Brian was told he had been a pain in the ass for months, that he could walk home as far as anyone was concerned, and he was thrown out. At 5 a.m. he called Cleo Sylvester. "The boys ordered me out of the van, I have no place to go," he said. "Can I come round?" He showed up about an hour later, having walked several miles. Cleo's mother cooked him breakfast, and he sat with Cleo at the kitchen table, talking in brief spurts about his unhappiness, his feeling he was no longer really a Stone because they didn't want him in the group, that he was trapped because he couldn't leave and they wouldn't fire him while they still had so many worlds to conquer.

Cleo nodded, not saying much except to try and comfort him during the pauses, but thinking: *It's so sad because they're really the most successful band in Britain. Brian is idolized by millions of people all over the world and he's so terribly empty and alone.*

Brian felt hollow, most of all, because he didn't like the direction in which the Stones' music was moving, the direction that the songs of Jagger and Keith were taking them. Away from the black roots and into a more commercial pop sound, Jagger out front becoming a rock star and making the blues into white pop music. Brian spent a great amount of time listening to the tapes the Stones had made at the IBC studios in 1963, the tapes that Eric had bought back when he became their manager. Five tracks: "Diddley Daddy," "Road-runner," "Bright Lights, Big City," "I Want To Be Loved," and "Honey What's Wrong." Five tracks that were more gutsy and honest than anything they'd released officially, tracks they laid down without knowing anything about studio techniques, with only the IBC staff engineer, Glyn Johns, to guide them. That was the kind of music Brian wanted to play, the solid rhythm and blues with the primitive ballsiness of the Delta. Everyone in the band felt those five tracks were far superior to the commercial releases. Even Jagger, whose voice was more prominent in these songs because they were recorded before Andrew came along as producer and decided to mix down Jagger's voice. But now Jagger and Andrew were dominating the Stones, and their primary goal seemed, to Brian, to be a sound that would make the band rich and famous, and the hell with the quality of the music. Certainly, Brian admitted, he wanted wealth and fame as much as anyone—he could almost taste it—especially that delicious taste of becoming so big he could tell everyone who had stood in the way of the Stones, "Go fuck yourself." But he'd rather not sacrifice the music for that, he told friends: "What's the difference if we make a million quid a year as the most popular band in the world, or a half million as the second most popular?" He'd rather not be forced to pollute the blues as the Beatles had done, simply to become as popular as the Beatles. Why, even John was complaining to Brian about the compromises the Beatles had been forced to make, complaining that he sometimes felt like a whore, flat on his back, a million customers tearing out pieces of his mind—which was more important than his body—and Brian was anguished that Jagger was pushing the Stones in the same direction and there was nothing Brian or anyone else could do about it.

He couldn't leave the Stones because there was nowhere else for him to go, no other band around that could give him at least the occasional burst of satisfaction he got from the Stones. No one in the band suggested he leave, certainly not Jagger. They all recognized Brian's unique contribution to the Stones. On the several dozen songs so far released, and the dozens more on tape for future release, Brian was everywhere at once—playing harp, acoustic and electric guitars, dulcimer, mellotron, organ, and anything else that happened to be lying

180

around the studio that would build up the texture of the music. His role in the band was broader and more comprehensive than anyone. While Jagger provided the vocal flash and sexual excitement, Keith the kinetic energy as the band lead, Bill and Charlie the steady blasting rhythms that keep the machine cranking at high pitch, Brian used all his instruments to build ringing harmonics around the tighter rhythmic drive of the others. Brian, sounding the secondary notes behind and above and around the primary notes of the band, emphasizing the natural harmonics of those primary notes, gave the Stones the sound of an R & B symphony orchestra. Brian put the Stones ahead of every other pop group around, even the Beatles, musically.

And Brian knew it, which is why he hurt so deeply. Brian knew that his guitar on "The Last Time," which they recorded at the beginning of 1965, fulfilled the function of both rhythm guitar, chugging along behind the melody, and a subliminal keyboard filling in the spaces between the notes of the others. And his mouth harp on "Money" and "Come On," recorded a year earlier, is a pervasive sound that's both reedy and hoarse, and is always a part of the overall texture rather than an attempt to step out like a blues (or jazz) virtuoso and make a personal "statement" that often detracts from the whole.

Jagger had even gotten over his pique at the accident which befell "Play with Fire," because Brian's musicianship turned a soppy song into what the rock critics called "a minor pop masterpiece." The song, a Jagger/Richard composition released in February 1965 as the "B" side of "The Last Time," had been recorded in two versions. Jagger and Andrew decided that the heavy rock version, called "Mess With Fire," was the one to be released. Chrissie, who was still working for Andrew at the time, was told to send the master of "Mess With Fire" to the studio. By error she sent the slower take, and by the time the error was discovered the rock version had vanished. It was too late to search for it, or to re-record it, so "Play with Fire" was released instead. And even Jagger was pleased at the good response from the critics and the public. The song, although burdened with lyrics only a step above the adolescent (boy warns girl to behave because she's not playing games with the weak dolts of her upper-class background but actually playing with fire . . . all the Jaggers who were raised in London's slums), the song turned out to be a musically sensitive cross between an Elizabethan ballad and a modern Thames-side funeral dirge, primarily because of Brian's tapestry-weaving with the mellotron, which describes endless arabesques built on the basic melody.

Without Brian the Stones might possibly collapse; certainly, they'd lose their momentum at this critical stage of their career. Jagger often spoke of the band's great need for Brian, and he asked friends to bolster his confidence whenever he talked about quitting. But at the same time Jagger occasionally remarked: "You're on Brian's side," creating sides to be on.

To their friends and families, it seemed as if Jagger and Chrissie were always splitting up. The hardest part of all the splits, to Chrissie, was that every time she left him no one would believe her—almost as if they were saying she was incomplete without Jagger, not a whole person, that Chrissie wasn't someone who could survive without her man. And that hurt. No one on the outside could understand why Chrissie would even consider leaving Jagger . . . all that glamour of the pop world . . . the leading symbol of his times . . . what the hell is there to make you unhappy?

Only when other women caused the split did friends believe they understood. But they didn't, really. Chrissie seldom worried about Jagger going out with other women, and the few times it happened he always came back. There was an American girl whom Chrissie knew he saw pretty regularly whenever he was in America. They split up because of her—she had come to London, and Jagger went off to see her and didn't return—so Chrissie went off with singer P. J. Probey, who had always come on strong to her. And Jagger appeared broken, furious, unable to understand her perfidy. He came into the Rolling Stones office the afternoon there was an item in the papers that Chrissie and P J. were flying to America together, wearing dark glasses to hide his eyes because he had to do an interview and didn't want the journalist to know he'd been crying. When the interview ended Jagger took off his glasses, stretched out on the couch, and began to cry. He couldn't control himself. Shirley Arnold, incredulous because Jagger had always appeared to have such marvelous control—she had never even considered the possibility that a man like Jagger could cry—tried to comfort him but nothing she said or did had any effect. And then Chrissie rang the office. She hadn't really gone, she had planted the newspaper story to make Jagger jealous—after all, she had learned a lot about manipulating the press from Jagger and Andrew. They talked for a while, and Chrissie agreed she would give up P. J. if Jagger promised not to see the American girl anymore. He promised, except that she was in his flat, the flat he shared with Chrissie until she had the *gall* to go off with P. J., and he'd need some time to get her out. Chrissie insisted: Right now, the girl goes. On Chrissie's demand, Jagger called her at the Bryanston Mews flat. Chrissie knew him well enough to be certain he'd hesitate for days, screwing up his courage, before ringing the girl, and Chrissie listened in on the extension as Jagger ordered her to pack her things and go to a hotel, the little affair was over.

When Chrissie and Jagger were settled into Bryanston Mews again, Jagger tried to explain why he had left: "You wouldn't even make me a cup of coffee." Chrissie smiled. That was his way of saying she had an ego of her own, she was proud and strong and damn well wouldn't make him coffee since he didn't want a wife or even a wife figure. Let him make his own bloody coffee, take care of his own flat. Except that now everything had changed, Jagger was saying he did want her to act like his wife, he did want a domesticated scene. She decided to try it, to live with him and cook for him—although she couldn't cook at all. For about a month she was on her best behavior, the good little suburban woman taking care of her man, permitting him to do whatever he felt like doing. And Jagger hated it, Chrissie knew; that wasn't what he wanted at all—what he really wanted was a strong woman who would feed his masochistic streak and keep his head in some sort of level place, maintain some reality in his life while everyone on the outside was making him into a pop deity. But Jagger didn't tell her he'd been wrong about his own needs; instead, he began to find fault with everything she did. *Anything I do is wrong*, she thought as she waited for Jagger to come home one evening, *Mick's just being generally bloody-minded, just disagreeing with everything on principle, being bloody awful.* When he came in and made some nasty comment, Chrissie burst. She leaped at him and began hitting him in the face, and a huge ring that he'd given her cut into his face, lacerating his cheeks and leaving scars that were visible for a long time afterward. Jagger went mad—that's how Chrissie thought of the way he leaped back, screaming in pain, tearing around the flat, and finally racing out into the street.

When Chrissie calmed down she called a girl friend and told her what had happened, what she had done to Jagger's face. While they were talking Jagger returned, took the phone out of her hand, put it down, and said: "I'm sorry." Chrissie stared at him for a long moment. And began slashing at him again. "Is this some kind of awful sick joke?" she demanded. "How can you be sorry when I hit *you*?" She couldn't understand how he could be so insensitive to her shame at her own behavior, and she was so furious that she raged through the apartment, trying to break things, almost tearing the curtains down from the windows.

Like all their other brawls, this one was settled, and they picked up their relationship again. Such as it was. From the end of 1964 and through the next sixteen months they didn't see too much of each other because the Rolling Stones were almost always on tour. The United States several times, Europe, Australia, up and down the British Isles . . . In their attempt to become the most popular rock band in the world, the Stones toured even more than the Beatles, more than any other English group. Chrissie went along on some of the tours, at the beginning, but after a while the traveling, the bitchiness of the groupies, the clawing of people who wanted to suck some of the riches the Stones were generating, the violent arguments with Jagger, became too much, and Chrissie remained home. She didn't mind, especially after Jagger told her that he now decided he wanted to marry her after all. They would get a much grander flat, fix it up properly, and after he returned from their third American tour of 1965, in October, they'd be married.

By now Jagger was considered the most modish young man in London, sought after by the younger members of the aristocracy: Gossip columnists were reporting that Jagger was a friend of Princess Margaret, reporting the parties he attended and those at which his absence was felt. Journalists described him as the voice of today, a today person, symptomatic of our society. Cecil Beaton painted a portrait of Jagger in oils and said Jagger reminded him of "somebody who has sprung out of the woods," animalistic, natural man—the portrait made Jagger appear almost as a vampire—and Beaton added that Jagger also appeared to him as the Nijinsky of today, or even a Renaissance angel. Back in August, Jagger was the best man at David Bailey's wedding. Bailey, Beaton, Princess Margaret, the Ormsby-Gores, and others in whose circle Jagger was beginning to move, were people of consequence. Suddenly, a great number of citizens who had always thought of Jagger as a filthy lout began to feel that he, too, was someone of consequence.

"It's all a joke," Jagger told Chrissie about the society column items linking him to the aristocracy. "Silly newspaper stuff about silly, meaningless people." They were invited to Victoria Ormsby-Gore's coming-out ball, and Jagger took Chrissie shopping and bought her several dresses. One of the outfits was a silver dress with matching silver shoes and handbag, and Chrissie decided she would wear it even though she thought it dreadful—Jagger seemed to like it, so she would wear it. She got dressed, and when Jagger came to pick her up he said: "You look awful." Chrissie agreed. She rummaged through her closet and pulled out an inexpensive dress—two quid from Biba's—and asked: "Should I wear this?" Jagger said it was smashing, and off they went in a limousine. From the moment they walked into the ball they were troubled with the giggles: "Michael Jagger and Miss Christine Shrimpton," the butler announced, and Jagger and Chrissie could barely stop giggling even as they were introduced to Sir David and Lady Ormsby-Gore. Jagger and Chrissie were seated at a table next to Princess Margaret and her party, and Jagger was invited over. Chrissie sat alone, furious that she hadn't been asked to Margaret's table. When Jagger returned after a little while Chrissie said she was leaving and Jagger laughed; he followed her out, still giggling over the absurdity of it all . . . Michael Philip Jagger, son of a schoolteacher, a threat to decent society, had become fashionable.

The invitations continued to come . . . the twenty-first birthday party for Guinness heir Tara Browne, at the family castle in Ireland, and they were stoned out of their heads the entire weekend. They attended as many of the parties as they could, Jagger slowly fitting into that social scene, beginning to enjoy it, growing especially close to some of the Ormsby-Gore children. Jane Ormsby-Gore would even feel that Jagger wrote "Lady Jane" (*"My sweet Lady Jane/When I see you again/ Your servant am I/And will humbly remain"*) for her; Jagger's publicity machine led the press to believe the song was based on a letter written by Henry VIII to Jane Seymour telling her he "got rid of" Anne Boleyn and was free to marry her. Jagger made Chrissie feel he had written it for *her*.

The Stones were up in Ireland, a brief tour in early September, and Chrissie remained in London to get their new flat set up—a grand furnished flat in Harley House, Marylebone Road, that they were going to live in after they got married. But when Jagger returned from Ireland he told her he'd changed his mind again, he didn't want to be married. "I expect we'll marry some day, everybody seems to in the end. But I don't think I want to marry until I'm ready to have children, and I'm not ready for that yet. I don't want to break up with you, you're a stabilizing influence, and this scene isn't a very stable life." Chrissie was deeply hurt. "I won't live with you, then, if you won't marry me." She left and went home to talk to her mother, who advised her to accept the relationship on Jagger's terms, to go live with him.

Jagger would later tell an interviewer he didn't intend to marry anyone at the moment, "And yet, I like to have a regular bird. I would like to be strong enough not to need one sometimes because it can be a right drag."

Chrissie soon accepted the fact that Jagger wouldn't marry her, and she was able to dismiss all ideas of marriage and children for now. And for a while her life with Mick Jagger, pop star, actually improved—friends and acquaintances came to understand she didn't particularly care for the London scene that the Stones and the Beatles had created, that she had no intention of becoming a pop star, and the pressures on her eased up. For a little while. Until she began sensing further changes in Jagger, in subtle ways at first. They had always had a maid, Maria, a Portuguese who tidied up Jagger's old flat a couple of days a week. Now she was coming every day to the flat in Harley House, and one day Jagger suggested to Maria that she come up the back stairs. Chrissie was appalled. *I guess he's getting a little bit into the scene of having a servant, but he shouldn't treat her like that. I hope it's a joke.*

Within months, Chrissie was feeling that Jagger's life style had turned into one of artificiality, surface grandeur, flashiness, a pop star's interpretation of the aristocratic life. *He's into that scene and I can't take it*, she thought when she no longer could deny even to herself that Jagger had changed. *He's left me completely behind. He's rich now and he's playing it for all it's worth. The money is too much; what he's doing with the money is abhorrent to me.*

Jagger was quite wealthy by now, the end of 1965. Allen Klein had seen to that. And Eric Easton was dumped by the Stones.

Klein was an American businessman with an unsavory reputation in London. He was usually described as a hustler without ethics, and almost everyone he dealt with virtually hated him—except the entertainers he had made wealthy. As an accountant for a music publishing company in New York City, Klein discovered that record companies were holding back royalty payments and in other ways cheating publishers and recording artists. So he approached several artists and said: "Look, if I can find you money they aren't telling you about will you give me a percentage and let me handle your financial affairs?" Few pop stars could turn down unexpected monies, and enough of them hired Klein to audit record company books that by the early Sixties he was handling several of the more important entertainers in America. On one trip to

London Klein met Mickey Most, who produced and managed several rock groups, including the Animals. Most hired him as business manager and asked him to negotiate recording contracts for Most's groups. Brash, tough-talking and enormously intelligent, Klein upset British record company executives with his very direct style—"a New York hustler," they sniffed—but most of all because he muscled out of the businessmen contracts far superior to anything that any entertainer had ever received, in Britain or America, winning enormous advances against royalties for Most's groups.

Most raved to Andrew and Jagger about Klein's magical touch, as did several pop stars who had recently hired Klein. In the spring of 1965 Andrew signed Klein as his personal financial manager and, when Eric Easton's management contract with the Stones expired shortly after, it wasn't renewed.

"Sorry, Eric, we want Allen Klein to handle our affairs from now on," Jagger said in firing him.

"How can you go with Klein, knowing his reputation?" Eric asked.

"I don't care about his reputation, man, he's great, we need him."

Eric believed he knew why he was released: "They're afraid they won't last, they're worried about what's going to happen the next month, the next twelve months. Jagger is foolishly going for the big advance Klein can bludgeon out of Decca and he's ignoring the longer term royalties that are much more important to him. Mick thinks he's a smart businessman, LSE and all that. He'll learn."

Klein met with Sir Edward Lewis, chairman of Decca, and when the negotiations were completed Jagger—and the other Stones—were wealthy. Up to July 31 the Stones had earned royalties from London Records in America of $236,000 and about $375,000 from Decca. Klein, in renegotiating the contract, got the Stones an advance of $2,500,000 for English and world rights, and $4,500,000 for the United States and Canada. It was probably the largest single recording contract ever written, and Jagger was so thrilled that he had the Stones' office announce in August that Klein was co-manager with Andrew. That wasn't quite accurate. Klein never had a management contract with the Stones; he was Andrew's manager, and since Andrew was the Stones' producer, manager, and partner, Klein took over the Stones' affairs at the same time. But Jagger evidently didn't care about little inaccuracies. He seemed so enthusiastic about Klein's ability to make his artists wealthy that he encouraged everyone he met to hire Klein.

He also asked Klein to help him with his personal affairs—Jagger apparently felt Chrissie was still pressuring him to marry her, and he told Klein he didn't know how to handle her. Klein said: "I'll take care of it for you. I'll be the heavy. I'll tell her it's not in your interest to get married, it'll be bad for your image."

Chrissie abhorred everything that Klein's money represented. It appeared to be changing Jagger even more jarringly now, and the relief she felt in those first few months after coming to understand he would probably never marry her, the relief of being able to accept it, vanished now as Jagger's entire being seemed to be radically changing. Only eight or nine months before, in April, 1965, Chrissie went with them on their third American tour. She remembered getting into the taxi at Kennedy airport and hearing an excited radio announcer cry out: "Mick Jagger and Chrissie Shrimpton have just landed and they're on the way to their midtown hotel." *That's really insane*, Chrissie thought, turning to watch Jagger's reaction. Jagger seemed almost blasé, he was so cool about it, not impressed at all, able to smile at it and handle it. He appeared to be able to cope with the fame and adulation, on that tour, he wasn't taken in by it, he was still the level-headed Jagger she had met three years before. But in Berlin in

September, Jagger sang "Satisfaction" and added a brief but ugly routine to his act that provoked a riot.

The song had been recorded by the Stones in a Los Angeles studio during the last tour, and released in late summer. It was one of the few songs written by Jagger that caught the mood of the times—almost the way so many of Dylan's songs did—and it became one of the group's biggest hits. *"I can't get no/Satisfaction . . . When I'm driving in my car/And that man comes on the radio/And he's tellin' me more and more about some useless information/Supposed to fire my imagination/I can't get no . . ."* Wherever pop was heard, the kids and young adults knew what Jagger was saying: the authoritarians of the world—educators, clergy, politicians, parents—had built a society that denied our sexuality, our freedom, trapped us in the Protestant work ethic, trying to make us machines for the technocratic society. The kids related to it; they were as fed up with it all as the narrator of the song. And Jagger understood that "Satisfaction" had touched a chord among millions—he told interviewers it was his favorite song—but in Berlin the song created something ugly in those kids. Just before he went on stage someone suggested to Jagger that it would be hysterically funny if he goose-stepped during the instrumental break. Jagger gave it a try, but when he slid into his routine he carried it several steps beyond comedy—prancing around, goose-stepping, throwing out his arm in the Nazi salute—leaving you with the feeling that that could actually be a young campy Hitler up there. The audience had been going berserk anyway, and Jagger's routine drove them wild. Young boys—Jagger was still attracting more boys than girls—rushed the stage, trying to reach Jagger, and the police beat them back with truncheons. When the concert ended, and the doors were opened, some of the boys remained in the theater, tearing out seats and smashing windows, while others ran outside and overturned scores of cars and vandalized every train leaving the city.

Yet Jagger was more than simply a rock singer contriving an act to stimulate his audience. What his performance in Paris, where he fell to one knee, and in Berlin suggested was that Jagger was becoming an extraordinary actor, one who makes no distinction between man and performance, who projects an intense and comprehensive stage presence that represents something larger than life. The audience is sucked out of its humdrum reality and into another, greater reality taking place on stage. It is this quality which gives theater its magic. And Jagger, in developing this quality, was beginning to transcend blues and rock, was becoming part of the mainstream of theater. Chrissie was feeling upset that Jagger's act was becoming "contrived," yet all the greatest performers have been contrived in their ability to project a magical quality when they're before an audience, creating a super-reality: Chaplin, Callas, El Cordobès, Nureyev, Marceau, all who possess that electric-shock stage capacity have a trunkful of private information about what to do when they take that stage. Jagger had a trunkful of his own, and the first bit of information he dredged from it was that rock amplification is so high that the singer—the performer of the band—must be so huge that he can match the sound; Jagger couldn't shout above the amplifiers, so he became an actor and a mime. However, all the information about judgment and good taste was left buried in his trunk: Berlin was a prelude to dead butterflies and vulgarized Shelley in Hyde Park and, ultimately, a performance in California in which a spectator was killed.

Chrissie couldn't understand what was happening to Jagger's mind. They were smoking a great amount of grass whenever they were together, and she thought perhaps the cannabis was having these strange effects on him. But she didn't think that was possible—he was acting druggy, yet carried so much further than grass-created reactions, more than the usual interior dialogues, the warped time/space. There were flashes of deep terrors, moments of exquisite joy in Jagger. It was as if his mind had gradually detached itself from this dark room filled with overstuffed pillows and loud music, slipping through a narrow opening in a door to another room, a room filled with wonders. She couldn't make sense of what he was saying on those occasions, didn't know what he was talking about, and it frightened her. She believed she was getting very paranoid—Jagger told her so, again and again. *But I don't know what paranoid means,' really ... he keeps telling me I'm paranoid but how do you only imagine that something crazy is going on when the craziness is so real ... and the reality is so bad that maybe I am getting paranoid?*

She became very emotional about not being able to understand Jagger, very worked up, shouting at him, demanding to know what was going on, why he was saying things she couldn't make sense out of. And it looked to her as though he couldn't take her questions, her assaults on his mind, but simply collapsed within himself, slipping through that door again. She thought: *That's so unlike him, he's not fighting back.* And she thought: *He was always able to take as good as he got but now he's not fighting back against anything I throw at him.* Except to call her paranoid. "Paranoia" was the fashionable word on the drug scene; it was so hip to talk about people who were paranoid, or to be paranoid yourself on occasion. But Chrissie didn't care how unhip she was, she just didn't want to be paranoid, couldn't stand having her head wrenched around by the man she loved.

One night several friends from America—musicians and studio engineers Jagger had met on his tours—came over to the flat and they all smoked a large amount of pot. Chrissie began to hear weird frightening noises at the back of her skull, to feel monstrous things crawling over her. *I'm freaking out,* she thought, and when she looked up to see whether the horrible things happening to her were happening to anyone else in the room, she suddenly felt such an intense heat that she could see the others' faces melting—Jagger and his friends, their faces were slowly melting away. She broke down and cried, began screaming. She was certain the Americans had given her LSD, that she was going out of her mind on her very first dose of acid. Jagger seemed to think so, too, and began shouting about it.

But the guests hadn't given her acid, and they convinced Jagger of it, she recalls. Jagger warned her never to take acid, demanded that she promise she would stay away from LSD. Chrissie promised. It was several weeks before she discovered that Jagger had been taking acid all the while, that on those occasions he had acted so strangely he was tripping on LSD. *That's why I couldn't understand him. That's why he seems so different, like some other person entirely. He's changed so much.* And she thought: *He's progressed so much . . . moved so far ahead of me . . . I can't keep up with him anymore. It all frightens me, it really does . . . the drugs and the unreality of his world . . . the weird things his money is doing to him . . . he's grooving on being a famous pop star, rich and famous . . . that whole dreadful scene. It's making me feel so insecure.*

Her feelings of insecurity, she knew, were in part because Jagger was always calling her "neurotic" and criticizing her, because she was downing a lot of tranquilizer to help her function. "You're freaking out all the time," he said. "You're neurotic, just neurotic." He wrote a song about her—Chrissie felt certain it was about her—"19th Nervous Breakdown": *"On our first trip I tried so hard to rearrange your mind / But after a while I realized you were disarranging mine / You better stop, look around / Here it comes . . . your nineteenth nervous breakdown."* The song didn't help much, of course: *He's always putting me down,* she thought, when she first heard it.

Jagger had a nervous breakdown himself in the United

States, in June 1966, some months after Chrissie learned he had been taking acid. His collapse came several weeks before the start of another American concert tour. He had been working very hard with the Stones, rehearsing for the tour and recording in the studio. The press agents quoted doctors as saying he had been ordered to rest for two weeks because he was "suffering from nervous exhaustion," but in London the hip gossips jumped to the conclusion that it was probably drugs. So many pop stars were into drugs, into acid—musicians, writers, photographers, designers, all the hip people playing with drugs because it was trendy—and rationalizing that they were expanding their minds, reaching another, greater consciousness, when the eventual reality for many was the reaching toward a mind-death. Brian, for example. He had leaped at the chance to experiment with acid, enthralled by its reputed benefits as a mind-expander, and he used it whenever he could score. Brian felt certain there was music locked in his head, trying to escape, incredible music that no one had ever heard before. He heard it, under acid's influence, music that was unable to break free because of the cultural shackles that imprison our minds. Acid would shatter the chains, would open the mind and bring forth that music of the gods. And when it failed to happen, for Brian, he used more acid, and pills, anything he could shove into himself that he hoped would unlock the mind-vault where that music was hidden.

Chrissie worried about Jagger and his use of acid, worried that it would hurt him. She knew it was hurting their relationship, but she understood that Jagger's attitude toward her stemmed from something more basic than drugs. By the time he returned from the American tour and settled into the flat at Harley House again, she was beginning to feel very strongly that Jagger no longer loved her. She knew it, there could be no doubt about it, but she didn't know why. *I think he dislikes being involved with me as much as he is . . . that it's a drag to be with me . . . but he doesn't know how to break it off . . . he doesn't know how to tell me his feelings have changed . . . he can't face up to it directly.* She knew their relationship was over, that she had to get out of his life, but she didn't know where to go. She had become so dependent on him in the five years they were together that she was afraid to leave. She thought: *I have to go, the situation is unbearable. But the idea of going is unbearable. I want to go, but how does one start a life over again? I haven't been on a bus in three years. I don't know how to support myself or keep myself at all. Where can I go? I'm in this goldfish bowl, and the outside world is so alien to me.* She began struggling with it in July, when Jagger returned from the United States, and it wasn't until December that she found the solution. It was the only logical solution, to Chrissie, something thought out at length and not just a hysterical decision: *I'm going to kill myself. At last I've found a solution.*

Jagger had begun seeing a lot of Marianne Faithfull by this time, keeping his meetings with her secret from Chrissie although most of his friends believed that he was becoming enthralled by Marianne—by her soft femininity, her intellect, so stimulating to a young man who had read only James Bond in the past but was now reading poetry and going to art galleries and opening up to aspects of his culture he had always ignored. And he acted as if he were impressed by her upper-class background—the daughter of a baroness and a university don. Marianne was the "groovy chick" he apparently needed to complete himself. He would later tell friends he had spent three years trying to change Chrissie—to make her over into a woman who would cook for him—and when she did change he didn't like it. What he had wanted all along was a groovy chick.

Marianne had gone on a concert tour after "As Tears Go

By." She was excited about her entry into that very strange pop world, despite her disdain of pimply-faced rock stars. (On the bus, traveling from theater to theater, she would haughtily ignore the other entertainers by reading *Pride and Prejudice.*) She told herself she had done it for John Dunbar, who was abroad for the summer; only later could she admit she had made the record and accepted Andrew's offer of a tour because she had to prove she was beautiful and talented. And she learned to manipulate an audience, to work accompanied only by a guitarist and win over audiences accustomed to amplified rock bands, even though she had a weak and childlike voice. She couldn't wait for John to return so she could surprise him—she was the latest woman pop star, of all things. But when John returned, he demanded she give it up. Marianne refused, and they split up for a time.

Several rock performers, like Gene Pitney, wanted Marianne to live with them, but she turned down all offers, persuaded John to accept her career, and moved in with him. She continued touring, and John followed her around the country for almost a year, from one dismal theater to the next, continually asking her to give up this silly pop career. In Wigan, after a concert, John asked her to marry him. She agreed—they'd be married in Cambridge the following week because there were no theater dates scheduled—but she would not retire from the entertainment business. Not so soon, just as it was getting started. It felt so good to be envied and admired. As a performer. As a woman. Dylan admired her, Bob Dylan, who in a way had really started it all, the questioning of faceless authority—John and his intellectual radical friends admitted they owed a debt to Dylan. John had just started the first underground bookshop and art gallery in London. Youthful intellectuals who were creating the underground gathered there to talk about America's Beat poets, the coming revolution that would destroy decadent Western society, gathered to discuss the more effective means of radicalizing British youth. It would take them all several years to understand the futility of their high hopes, to realize that the underground had no philosophy, no morality, no humor, or style, and would collapse of its own deadening weight, coming to an end at the latest boutique and the pusher selling dreams by the ounce, or the pill. But this was 1965, and the builders of the underground just knew they were the future. John Dunbar was in at the start of it all, and it was so exciting, so stimulating—so intellectual—for a convent girl who had been so completely isolated from such sexual and political subversion. And now here was Dylan, the mysterious Dylan, the man who all the young radicals said was the prophet of the revolution—and he was admiring her, Marianne Faithfull.

Dylan had come to London in May 1965 with Joan Baez. Marianne met him after a concert at the Royal Albert Hall, and Dylan asked her to join him later in his hotel room. She went, of course, one doesn't turn down Bob Dylan. Bob seemed to be speeding, and she later remembered thinking: *He's like everyone is when they're speeding, the vacant look, the eyes, the gasping, the long moments in the bathroom working at maintaining the speed-edge.* "I'm gonna write a poem for ya," Dylan said, and she was very flattered, the song-poet of the revolution writing a poem for her. She couldn't fathom what he was all about, whether he was shyly, or slyly, about to put the make on her, and she said: "Oh, are you?" And Dylan, in that interviewer style that draws people out, firing questions at her, got Marianne talking about herself, her background, her dreams of minstrel boys, her hopes . . . Dylan scribbled in his notebook as she spoke, apparently creating one of his poems as she rambled on, and she was feeling so comfortable with this man who didn't behave like an idol that she revealed: "I'm getting married next week." Dylan stopped writing, put his notebook down on the floor beside his chair, and seemed to suddenly grow very tall and menacing. "That's the stupidest thing you'll ever do in your life, if you get married," he said. "Who is this guy who's gonna ruin your life?" Marianne said he was a student at Cambridge. "Fuckin' students," Dylan shouted, "assholes who're afraid to face life," and he speeded off into a vicious condemnation of students, telling Marianne how he despised them, that they were too stupid to understand they'd be better off leaving school and going to Mexico for four years, bum along the road for four years, stand on their heads—anything would be better than having your mind destroyed by knowledge, which was nothing but lies designed to cut you off from reality. And Marianne thought of a line from Voltaire: *History is the lie commonly agreed upon.*

Later when she talked about her hour with Dylan, she sounded almost disappointed that he hadn't asked her to bed, but she was also up so very high over her encounter with the man whose words, whose music had drilled into the minds of millions of the young: "Dylan has thrown out a form of expression that's done a job on our psyches," Marianne said. "The subconscious need for Dylan, the psychic quality of Dylan, is so much greater than what Jagger is doing, what Lennon and McCartney are doing, Dylan's so far ahead of Jagger because Mick is basically a rock-and-roll singer, and Dylan is never basically anything: He's always changing and shifting, like a chameleon, and whatever the uncried feeling of everybody is at the time, Dylan cries it out. Like everybody is getting busted, and Dylan has just come out with 'Subterranean Homesick Blues'—it's on his new album—'jump down a manhole' and 'man in a trench coat, badge out . . .' Every line of Dylan captures what everyone wants to say and just can't express. He reflects the moment in a much more vital way than the Stones are ever able to do."

Marianne married John in the Cambridge Register Office in May. A month later she married him in church and within days announced that she was pregnant. She later told herself she married John only because she was having a baby, but she really needed the security she felt with John and the intellectual stimulation of the underground movement. She was beginning to actually dread leaving John and his friends—smoking grass and mapping out the revolution—just to go off to a club to perform . . . at $5,000 a week. Andrew, the Stones, hit records, and pop glamor were not her reality, were often a drag. John, the underground, the avant-garde writers and painters they knew, that was her reality. For a while. But as her career intruded, as her popularity increased, the promoters kept her working, and she hardly ever saw her husband. People who were making money out of Marianne kept John away in case he "retired" her completely. Marianne, sucked into the scene, permitted it to dominate her life—at one time she was settled into a flat with a secretary-companion—and her relationship with John deteriorated even after Nicholas was born in November. He wouldn't take her career seriously, he wanted her to be a mother, and he didn't want his wife to earn more than he. They were separated in October 1966, two months before Chrissie decided that the only way out of her predicament with Jagger was to commit suicide.

Michael Cooper unwittingly brought Marianne and Jagger together. Cooper, a young, hip Londoner, had begun working as a photographer for *Vogue* in 1962. He was a Stones fan from the very beginning—the Marquee and the Eel Pye Island and other clubs—and when the band cut its first album Jagger went up to *Vogue* to have his photo taken by David Bailey. Michael knew Keith's girl friend, had met Keith, and now that he met Jagger something clicked between them. Slowly, Michael was drawn into their circle until he became the Stones' unofficial photographer and close friend—he was one of the few outsiders they would trust in the early days. They drank together a great deal—Michael, Jagger, Keith, and Brian. "We were lushes," Michael would later say. Around the time Marianne left John, and Jagger was trying to break it off with Chrissie, Michael was working with Roman Polanski, promoting his film *Repulsion*. He had arranged a special screening of the film in the Ship Hotel, Bath, and asked his friends to come down—Marianne, Jagger, Keith, all of the modish young who were revamping London's social scene. He was especially interested that Marianne attend the screening: *I want to ball her*, he thought. *I have to make it with Marianne.* When Marianne arrived in a big limousine Michael took her in tow, chatting her up—he was going to get her into bed with him before the day was out. They walked into Polanski's suite. Jagger was already there. He saw Marianne come into the room, everyone turned to her—Marianne always commanded a fierce, flame-like leap of attention from other people—and he walked to her, took her hand, and said "Hello," very subdued, thoughtful. Marianne smiled in a strange way, and Michael was struck by the look that passed between them. He thought: *Instant buzz. They're staring at each other like there's a kind of charge between them, a high energy charge. There go my plans for that bird.*

Chrissie swallowed a bottle full of pills and lay down on her bed, the bed she had shared with Jagger, waiting for death. It was mid-December 1966, and she thought about the Christmas she would miss, all the Christmasses that would come, and go, without her.

She regained consciousness a few days later, in a nursing home. She assumed Jagger had found her, had saved her life, but she didn't ask. He came to see her in the nursing home, but she didn't ask if he'd found her. She knew only one thing: *Now that I've come around, I haven't died, I know I'm on my own. I can make it now, on my own.* And later, after being released from the nursing home, she marveled at something she'd just come to realize: *Mick completely broke me in the end but until he did I was always stronger than he.*

Several months later Jagger rang Chrissie at her new flat in Knightsbridge and asked her to come over. She had seen him a few times before then, he'd ring and ask her to visit, and they'd get very drunk—so drunk she seldom remembered what happened except that he wanted to make love to her. She was very pleased and flattered that he still wanted that physical contact but she would often think: *I find it all so very strange, because I guess I'm basically a very straight person . . . and I can't understand why he wants me . . . I think it's really a complete ego thing with Mick, it's like he just has to get his way with everyone . . . and I'm just one of the many now, instead of being the one . . . which I was before. I don't like it. He's using me.* She had begun to feel that strongly—that he was using her—a few weeks before, when he visited her flat. He seemed, to Chrissie, all flash and ego. They had run out of cigarettes, and Jagger said he needed some cigarettes pretty badly. "There's a pub open on the corner," Chrissie said. "Go down and get some." And Jagger said: "I can't go down there. You go." He handed her a pound note, and Chrissie started down the stairs. At the bottom she stopped and thought: *Fuck, he has no humility, he's all flash, he's horrible.* She continued on for the cigarettes and when she returned Jagger was lying in her bed. *What cheek!* Chrissie thought, but before she could say anything Jagger took the cigarettes and said: "Keep the change." Now, in his flat, she decided it was the last time she'd see Jagger, intimately, and she decided to make him feel a little uncomfortable, give him a little of what he'd been giving her. Marianne was living with Jagger by then, and he was growing nervous that Chrissie wouldn't leave because Marianne was coming home from the theater soon—she was in Chekhov's *Three Sisters.* Jagger was darting about, demanding

202

that Chrissie leave, almost begging her to leave. Marianne walked in. She was composed when she realized Chrissie was there, very much the lady, and she and Chrissie got into a discussion about Chekhov. Jagger was growing more and more agitated, and Chrissie smiled when she thought: *He's afraid of what Marianne's going to say.* She finally asked Jagger to call her a cab, and he leaped to the phone as if it were an instrument of reprieve.

BOOK FIVE

EIGHT IN THE evening. Marianne, wrapped in a tawny-colored fur rug, is stretched out on a couch in the enormous drawing room in Redlands, the mansion that Keith had bought some months before. Marianne had taken a bath after tramping through the woods all day and running along the beach with Jagger and their friends. She didn't want to get back into her dirty jeans and blouse so she wrapped herself in the rug, enjoying the sensual feel of the skin against her body. Jagger was at Marianne's feet, Keith and Michael Cooper in overstuffed chairs. They're all watching television with the sound turned off and a Who album on the turntable. When you're stoned, as they had been since early morning, there is no better way to watch television: The supercharged beat roaring out of the amplifiers, and the visual flashes, the electronic scan, the million tiny dots that create a television picture . . . the rock sound and the visuals help keep that high-edge on, so deliciously. They had been dropping acid all day, smoking hash, and it was such a gas to come down slowly with the help of the electronic light show from the TV, gliding off from a trip that had started a short time after sun-up, more than twelve hours before.

Henry Schneiderman, a sinister American, or Canadian—he had so many passports no one was certain of his origin—was the first to hear the knocking on the front door. A heavy rapping against the thick oak. "Shall I get the door?" he asked designer Clifford Baldwin (not his real name) as the caller became more insistent in his rapping. Baldwin lifted his eyes from the TV screen, where an American gangster was trying to prolong his inevitable death at the hands of the police by hiding in an amusement park; the flashing lights of the carroussel, speeded up by the film editor, increased the visual assault on their senses. He smiled at the question, in an acid daydream, and said: "Don't bother. Gentlemen ring up first. Must be a tradesman."

When Keith realized someone was trying to come into his house, he went to the door. A small, thickset man in a trench coat stood there and behind him were more than a dozen police officers, several of them women. The man at the door, Chief Inspector Gordon Dineley, held a piece of paper in front of Keith.

"Are you the owner and occupier of these premises?" he asked.

"I live here," Keith said.

"Are you the owner?"

"What? The owner? Yeah, I own it all, the whole bloomin' house and the land down to the beach."

"Here, then. Read this," the Chief Inspector demanded.

"What, what?" Keith asked. "Read what?"

"I'll read it then," and Keith could barely understand his words: ". . . search warrant, dated today, Sunday, twelfth day of February, 1967 . . . suspicion of possessing drugs . . . violation of Drugs Act, 1964 . . . suspicion of permitting premises to be used for the purpose of smoking cannabis . . . violation of Section Five . . . it shall not be lawful . . ."

205

"What? What?" Keith kept asking. He turned, floated through the foyer and to the drawing room, followed by a battalion of police. "Look, there's lots of little ladies and gentlemen outside, they're coming in," Keith announced to his guests. "They have this funny piece of paper, all sorts of legal rubbish."

"We're being raided," Michael said, giggling at the absurdity of all those police officers standing there, gawking at this very beautiful blonde woman stretched out on the couch, wearing only a fur rug. He walked over to Marianne. "We either play it sort of trippy, have some fun with it, or we're all going to freak out."

Marianne smiled, the most seductive stage smile she could command, and let the rug slip a little so that a part of her thighs and a hint of her breasts were exposed. Playing it trippy. And the policemen either turned their heads away in embarrassment or shoved the embarrassed out of the way to get further into the room, to obtain a better view. Jagger laughed, and Marianne believed he felt the way she did: What a decadent scene these coppers are seeing, a half-naked blonde, joss sticks burning all around and filling the air with a sticky sweet aroma, a Moroccan servant in a caftan waiting on them . . . the utter decadence of it all must be amazing them.

"Please shut off the gramophone," the Inspector asked Keith.

"No way. I'll lower the sound, that's all," Keith said.

But someone had beaten him to it. The Who album was replaced by another, and when Keith heard the record some jester had placed on the turntable he slid onto a thick Moroccan cushion. Michael thought: *He's giggling like one of the insane in a Fellini film.* From the speakers came Bob Dylan's laughing, exuberant voice: *"Well they'll stone you when you're tryin' to be so good . . . Everybody must get stoned . . ."*

Dylan's surrealistic songs growled and whined through Redlands for the next hour. Warning of geeks who try to steal your mind and your freedom. Warning against the hypocrisy of men and women such as these, the police, the enforcers of society's straightjacket. As he stood by the French doors, Michael thought: *The whole scene is daft. These straight middle-class people with their jaws hanging open, trying to cop a peek at Marianne's body. The fuzz are as confused by this scene as we are.* Michael had wandered over to the far end of the room, trying to look inconspicuous. He hoped the police wouldn't notice him. And wished he could risk getting his camera, take photos of this farce being acted out in front of him.

Keith was standing in front of a policewoman. Her foot was on the edge of the cushion on which he'd sat to recover from his giggles. She was trying to get him to understand what she was saying, but Keith appeared to Michael unable to focus on her request. Apparently, she was asking for the right to search someone or something. "Would you mind stepping off the Moroccan cushion?" Keith asked. "Because you're ruining the tapestries." The woman said, "Oh, pardon me," and turned to Marianne.

"Please come upstairs with me," she asked. "I must search you."

"I have nothing to search," she said, flashing the rug open again . . . coppers wrenching their necks. The policewoman insisted. Marianne started up the stairs with her, then stopped. "Mick, Mick," she cried, her voice filling the house as if she were projecting it from the stage of the Royal Court, "Mick, help! This dikey woman wants to search me"—another flash of her body under the rug—"What does this bloody lesbian want from me? Where is she going to search me? I have no clothes on"—flash, the rug opens again—and Jagger becomes convulsed, sitting on the floor, laughing hysterically. Marianne turned and danced the rest of the way up the staircase, dancing to Dylan's voice: *"I got a poison headache/But I feel alright . . ."*

Michael had begun moving around, wandering down one corridor and up another in this strange house with little rooms stuck in odd places. *Keep movin' and the fuzz'll leave me alone.* He materialized in the doorway to the drawing room as Marianne shouted from the top of the stairs: "I'm going to be raped by this lady copper!" And Michael thought:

This scene is driving the fuzz out of their skulls. They just can't understand our acid behavior. They don't even know about acid, yet they're tripping themselves . . . they're picking up on the acid vibes coming off us . . . they're sort of stoned themselves, from our high. And from Dylan.

Dylan's voice, from the speakers, angrily spitting out his song: "*. . . He's sure got a lot of gall, / To be so useless and all.*" The police did seem terribly confused by it all, but they tried to go about their business as if this was reality. Said one officer to another: "That strong, sweet smell, that's cannabis." He lifted a tin labeled "Incense" and said, "This could be cannabis, take it." He lifted a pipe that was on the table, sniffed it, and placed it in his pocket. "Cannabis," he said. "All that incense is being burned to hide the smell of cannabis, but it never works, does it?"

Michael now sat on a cushion in the corner of the drawing room, on a different part of his trip. He thought: *God, it's like a Charlie Chaplin movie scene . . . a Chaplin picture . . . these dumb country cops don't know what they're doing . . . all these guys in freaky clothes and this chick in a fur rug showin' her body . . . and Dylan is like in the room with us.* He started to sing with Dylan, softly, so as not to draw attention to himself: "*Inside the museums infinity goes up on trial . . .*" He thought: *I'm going to go up on trial if I don't split from here right soon.* But he couldn't move; the Chaplin film was too intriguing.

Marianne returned down the stairs. "I'm clean," she said . . . a flash of her body beneath the rug . . . and a copper whispered to another: "See her unusual behavior? She's likely

208

under the influence of cannabis." Another officer was holding Jagger's green jacket. "Is this yours?" he asked, and Jagger admitted that it was. The policeman went through the pockets and, from one, pulled out a small chunk of hash. Marianne gaped. Michael covered his eyes and thought: *I've got a lot of stuff in my pockets . . . we've all got enough to hang us.* But the officer, with exaggerated distaste, shoved the hash back into the jacket; he seemed to believe it was a piece of dirt and didn't want to soil his fingers. Michael began laughing and quickly covered his mouth so he wouldn't be heard. But he couldn't hold down the laughter. Several coppers suddenly stopped their rummaging through drawers and stood up straight, almost to attention, deeply offended by Dylan's voice: *"Queen Mary, she's my friend/Yes I believe I'll go see her again . . ."*

Two policemen stood before the chair in which Schneiderman was sitting, asking about the small suitcase beside him. "That's mine," Schneiderman said. "Very good, sir," one of the officers said. "We must search it." The suitcase, which contained several pounds of heroin, cannabis, pills, acid, DMT, every herb and chemical to stab or stroke the mind, was opened gently by the officer, who seemed to expect filthy underclothes or socks to tumble out. What he saw, instead, were dozens of packages, wrapped in aluminum foil. He started to unwrap one. "That's film," Schneiderman said, "I'm a movie maker, and that's unprocessed film. Please don't open it, you'll expose it, and my movie will be lost. A year's work." The officer said, "Oh, certainly, sir," and closed the suitcase. He then searched Schneiderman's pockets and found a tin and an envelope with pieces of hash. "I'm very sorry, sir," he said, "but I must take these for the laboratory."

Another policeman apologetically searched Robert Fraser, an art dealer and obviously a gentleman; through the hubbub, Marianne thought she heard him say to Fraser: "I'm so very sorry, sir, you're obviously a cut above this lot, but we must do this." Fraser was a heroin addict and had twenty-four jacks in an exquisitely crafted antique pillbox. "What is in here?" the officer asked. Fraser replied: "Medicine, for my diabetes. I do have a prescription." The officer closed the box and handed it back to Fraser, then thought better of it. "I'm afraid I must take one of these packets of medicine for tests," he said. "I'm very sorry to trouble you this way, sir." He then searched Clifford Baldwin, found a $125 stick of hash in his pocket, and returned it to him.

Michael had been watching the charade and was stunned by the realization that came over him: *They want the Stones, they want Mick and Keith. They haven't even looked at me, it's as if I don't exist . . . they're not bothering Robert or Clifford or Schneiderman . . . they just want to get the Stones . . . that's their whole thing, get the Stones . . . but they're such bumblers they didn't even know that's hash in Mick's jacket.*

The police were almost ready to leave. They had found four pep pills that Jagger said were his, bought legally in Italy for airsickness and the like, and they had the pipe that had been lying on Keith's table and obviously smelled of dope. And they still hadn't gone near Michael. Half the force were already outside, and Michael was wandering around the zany corridors of Redlands again, when a policeman crashed into him. "And who are you, sir?" the officer asked. "Michael Cooper, I just dropped in to visit." The copper said, "Very good, sir" and left without bothering to search him.

Keith stood at the front door, saying goodbye to his visitors in uniform. They had taken the pep pills, Fraser's jack of heroin, a little bit of hash, but the enormous quantity of dope in the suitcase had been overlooked. The last officer to leave, a detective sergeant, told Keith: "Should laboratory tests prove that dangerous drugs have been used on these premises, and not related to any individual, you will be held responsible."

"I see, they pin it all on me," Keith said.

Jagger rang up one of the lawyers for the Stones and told him about the police raid . . . no arrests, some little evidence taken, the police were total amateurs, real bunglers . . . they took some pep pills that he and Marianne had been given in Italy . . . they're sold over the counter in Italy, all quite legal . . . and he had talked to his doctor in London and the doctor had said it was okay to use them, so that's no problem . . . and Keith didn't really have to know some people in his house were carrying dope, right?

"But Mick, those pills were really mine," Marianne said when he rang off. "I'll take the responsibility for them."

"No, you won't," Jagger said. "We got the pills together, I talked to me doctor about it when we got back . . ."

"But you used all *your* pills . . ."

"They're the same pills, Marianne. Maybe you've been carrying them, maybe they're yours, but they're mine. D'ya understand? Besides, it'll never go that far."

The decision was made: Head off the arrest, buy off the coppers. Keith later talked about it: "What usually happens is that someone gets busted, the papers have it the next day. For a week they held it back to see how much bread they could get off us." And Keith told Michael that they expected everything to be settled quickly and quietly: Someone had a friend who knew bent cops, it would cost them several thousand pounds but the money would guarantee no publicity, no arrests.

But something went wrong: Early in March police announced that a summons had been issued against Jagger, Keith, and Robert Fraser—no mention of Schneiderman or anyone else who had drugs—and that a hearing was set for May 10. One of the Stones' lawyers told Jagger and Keith: "It really seems weird, they really want to do it to you." And Keith: "Unfortunately none of us knew what to do, who to bum the bread to, and so it went via slightly the wrong people and it didn't get up all the way. Mick can tell you how much. It was his bread. Quite a bit of bread. In the States, you know the cops are bent, and if you want to get into it, okay, you can go to them and say, 'How much do you want' and they'll drop it. In England, you can drop fifty grand, and the next week they'll bust you and say, 'Oh, it went into the wrong hands. I'm sorry. It didn't get to the right man.' It's insane."

They began working on their defense. First, try to think it through: How did the police know they'd been doping it up all day? Why were bent police suddenly getting straight? Was there anything behind it all? And suspicions centered on Henry David Schneiderman and the *News of the World*. Jagger told his lawyers he was certain there was a connection between them, that Schneiderman and the newspaper had joined hands to put him on trial for offenses against the Crown.

Precisely one week before the raid, *News of the World* had published an article about the use of drugs by pop stars. There was a two-year-old photo of Jagger above the text, with a caption that said he had been a visitor at a house in Roehamptom that had been leased by the Moody Blues and used for wild drug parties and that Jagger had admitted to investigators that "he had sampled LSD." That statement was repeated within the body of the article, and the story went on to quote the report of investigators for the newspaper:

"He told us: 'I don't go much on it (LSD) now the cats (fans) have taken it up. It'll just get a dirty name. I remember the first time I took it. It was on our first tour with Bo Diddley and Little Richard.'

"During the time we were at Blases club in Kensington, London, Jagger took about six benzedrine tablets. 'I just wouldn't keep awake at places like this if I didn't have them,' he said. . . . Later at Blases, Jagger showed a companion and two girls a small piece of hash (marijuana) and invited them to his flat for 'a smoke.' "

The article outraged Jagger. He insisted he had never talked to *News of the World* investigators, had never even popped an aspirin into his mouth in public. And Marianne cried: "You never have and never will see Mick sitting in a club swigging back pills and saying things like that." What apparently had happened, Jagger and those around the Stones insisted, was that the newspaper's investigators had actually interviewed Brian Jones. Brian had begun to use drugs too much, seemed to be losing himself, and then reappearing, sinking, and then reappearing, and it worried them all, that he appeared to be losing touch with himself, with the world around him—ever since Anita left him for Keith. It was the scandal of the London pop scene, Keith "stealing" Anita.

Anita Pallenberg was first noticed in London in 1965. The first awareness by the Stones social circle of this strangely beautiful blonde was a tea at Lady Harlech's, to which Anita was invited. She was a model then, a very straight sweaters-and-suits woman whose eyes and facial bone structure and long, lean body forced so many to ignore good manners and to stare at her. At Lady Harlech's she was dressed in yellows and golds, she seemed to be reflecting the sun—to be the sun. Anita had become friendly with Lady Harlech's daughter, Jane Ormsby-Gore, with Tara Browne, with the young members of the aristocracy who were almost fawning over Jagger and the Stones as a new kind of aristocracy. She met Brian through them, and in a little while Brian left the woman he'd been living with, and their young son, and moved into a flat with Anita. Soon, Anita's hair was shorter, she was dressing in brilliantly-colored silks, and beginning to look like Brian—he had an almost narcissistic compulsion to remake his women into images of himself.

A weird court scene developed around Brian and Anita. Marianne was still living with her husband at the time and had become friendly with Anita, visited them often in their huge studio in Courtfield Road, and was amazed at their scene: *They're like a king and queen with a whole court, all those upper-class people who are going to be lords and dukes someday, and they're acting like Brian's groupies. They should know better.*

There was something a little evil about it all, some people around them felt: Marianne was there one day when Linda, Brian's former girl friend, came round with their baby and all her family; she stood in the garden, holding the baby up to the window, and Marianne felt she was trying to shame Brian into giving her support for the child. Marianne watched Brian, Anita, several of their friends, looking down into the garden, and she thought: *They're laughing at them, Brian and Anita and their whole court, they're laughing at that girl and her child, to drive them away.* When mother and baby were driven away, Marianne thought: *How awful this is, so cruel and evil. Anita is a very wicked lady, although she's incredible. But almost not human, extra-human. She's done the most amazing things to Brian. She made Brian dress up in a Nazi uniform with his foot on a Jew, a man stereotyped as a Jew, and she's standing behind him, laughing. And Brian couldn't understand why it freaked everyone when the newspapers published it, especially all the promoters, who are Jews. They really freaked at that picture, Anita's picture. She's so terribly wicked.*

Chrissie was still living with Jagger when Anita became part of their circle, and she realized that Anita had developed a very strong influence over the three leading Stones, Jagger, Brian, and Keith. But, she later said: "Anita is very aware of her power but she is very compassionate, whereas a lot of groupies who are around trying to get them are as hard as nails. She's very weird and freaky and strong, but her feelings are genuine, and I think what she feels about Brian is genuine." Chrissie liked Anita very much, felt that she was an amazing woman, that she'd never met anyone like Anita. "Unlike all the other girls who are trying to steal my place I never feel that way about Anita. I never feel I have to be ultra-groovy around her, even though everybody is into this groovy scene and groovy clothes. Anita is into it, but she doesn't make me feel that I'm an outsider because I'm not into that scene. I flew with her to the States a few times, on Stones tours, and I never felt that way about her. I know Mick admires her a great deal. She could be evil, perhaps, because she's very powerful, but what I like about her is that she doesn't use her power in an evil way. But she may be evil to some people, who think in very conventional ways, I guess."

Brian had already been into drugs by the time he met Anita; he was a leader, he was the first Stone to have a big car, the first into flashy clothes, the first to smoke dope and drop acid. The first time Brian took acid he was with Anita, shortly after they began living together. They thought it would be like smoking a joint. They went to bed. "Suddenly," Anita said later, "suddenly we looked around, and all these Hieronymus Bosch things were flashing around." Those were heady days. Acid made it seem that anything was possible; everyone was turning on to acid, the young and the beautiful. Keith began to see what acid was doing to Brian, he saw Brian and Anita flying all over the place, stoned out of their minds, the most incredible visions. Every time Brian was taking trips he would plunge himself into work, making tapes, recording the sounds he was trying to unlock from his mind, and something fantastic seemed to be happening. Keith dropped acid, and he started to live with Brian and Anita, tripping with them, working with Brian.

They drew very close then, and Jagger was practically excluded. Brian and Keith worked out "Ruby Tuesday" together, and Marianne was upset because Jagger was not really a part of it, he was ignored and forced to work off in the engineer's booth, alone. It was an era of great music, for Brian, enormous energy that was captured in their recordings, and he was so electrified by it all, so excited about the possibilities opened up by the acid and dope. He and Keith were the creative forces within the Stones. Marianne, still living with John but close to Brian and Keith, recognized something else about the relationships within the Stones, about the seats of power:

Keith is the interesting person in the group. Whoever Keith gives his loyalties to, that one has the power. Keith is completely devoted to Brian now, and Mick is almost totally left out. He has his domestic scene going with Chrissie, and Brian and Keith are off into other things. Mick is even excluded from their social life, he's not allowed into their clique. They don't think much of Mick, they think he's a little drip, too straight, no personality, he's not an acid head. And the arrogance of Brian is simply amazing, he's a man who acts as if he owns the world. And perhaps he does, in a way. She remembered how Brian and Keith had been so cruel to Jagger several years earlier, around 1964. Jagger had gotten very camp—that period when Andrew Oldham was camping it up—and Brian and Keith immediately went the other way, totally butch . . . and laughing at Jagger, criticizing him for being a queen.

But just before Marianne began living with Jagger, the relationships were beginning to change. Keith and Jagger dropped acid together; Jagger was getting into psychedelics. The acid was destroying his relationship with Chrissie, but Jagger believed that acid was a part of growing, of the process of discovering who you are and what you are, that drugs are as much a part of it as sex, or reading—he said this to friends—that drugs were part of the framework of maturation. Keith and Jagger became very tight friends, dropping acid together, thrown together by their need to write songs for the band. Keith's loyalties shifted to Jagger, and Brian was slowly cut off. Keith saw it this way, in one conversation about Brian: "There was always something between Brian, Mick and myself that didn't quite make it somewhere. It was in Brian, somewhere . . . there was something . . . he still felt alone . . . he was either completely into Mick at the expense of me or he'd be completely in with me, tryin' to work something against Mick. Brian's a very weird cat. He was a little insecure. He wouldn't be able to make it with two other guys at the same time and really get along well."

But it was more complex than Brian's personality, his paranoia. There were subtle little things happening between them all, and some of them centered on Anita. Keith had fallen hard for Anita and desperately wanted her, and Marianne and other friends believed Jagger also was in love with her. But she was with Brian. When she began to perceive what was happening Marianne thought: *Everybody feels that way about Anita. She is someone that everybody wants to follow, that everybody falls in love with.* And the feelings that Anita stirred in Jagger and Keith colored their relationship with Brian. And now that he believed Jagger and Keith had become a team, that they were excluding him from their circle and their music, he started to slowly fall apart.

The week before Christmas 1966—when Chrissie was recovering from her overdose, Jagger and Marianne were exploring and discovering one another, and Brian was feeling that his foundations were crumbling because Keith's friendship had shifted to Jagger—Tara Brown was killed in an auto accident. Tara was young and lovely, one of the few men around whom Brian trusted, felt a deep affinity with, whom Brian could talk to about his problems without being told he was paranoid. And Tara was killed, so senselessly, driving down a hill, losing control of his car . . . and death. It affected Brian deeply, he began to understand how tenuous life really is, and to perceive that the promise held out to them all by acid and hash, by the "groovy" scene they had created, was a lie. That promise was a lie.

"It's just become trendy," he told friends. "Just a ripoff, hip people selling bad dope and thinking they're making a new world. Building a new consciousness, they call it. But it's all bullshit. People are dying. Tara's dead. The whole dream is a lie."

Brian no longer had any illusions about acid and dope, but he didn't stop taking anything he could find that would drug him. He began to use even more drugs now, including STP and DMT, the chemicals that are so much worse because they burn out your brain. And Brian began to burn out. He had a "breakdown" in Switzerland just weeks before the raid at Redlands, and Anita left him in the hospital to go off with Keith. The next weekend Anita and Marianne picked up Brian at the hospital to take him to Tangiers, where they were going to meet Jagger, Keith, Michael Cooper, and several other friends. Marianne and Anita had taken acid the night before and were soaring. They dressed up in brilliant clothes, loaded with red and purple feathers, and looked like a freak show as they helped Brian to the limousine that was taking them to the airport. When they were settled in the back seat Anita said: "Don't you think Brian looks really pale? We must get him into the sun so he'll get as healthy-looking as Keith." And Marianne thought: *Something's happening here. She's beginning to make comparisons between them, and Keith always comes out better.* They gave him some acid—even though he was in the hospital to clean out the drugs, including heroin, which he'd begun to snort and to place on his tongue and rub into his gums. And Brian slid off into an acid-fantasy world. He didn't come out of it for a week, and by then Anita had left him behind in Morocco and returned to London with Keith. She left him for Keith, and that destroyed the last slim thread of friendship between Brian and Keith. He had lost Tara, and now Anita and Keith.

Brian started looking for acceptance, searching for something, someone, anyone . . . and he thought he found it among the heads of London. He needed a crutch very badly. He needed the support of being loved, of being around people who loved him and truly cared about him. But he was weak, and clutching for help, and fell into the hands of parasites who doped him up and stole whatever they could from him. *If Mick gives Brian support, he'll pull through it,* Marianne thought. But Jagger was much too busy, writing songs with Keith for the next album, and the next, dealing with the Stones' financial affairs, discussing possible films for the group, and tours, totally involved in his business interests. And Brian was sliding down the long inclined that had begun with the grooviness of acid and would end in his death at the bottom of his pool.

As Jagger and Marianne talked about the *News of the World* article they agreed that the only logical possibility was that the newspaper's investigators had seen Brian, so wiped out that he would sit in Blases downing Black Bombers and French Blues, whatever the hell pills he's on now, and told their readers it was Jagger. "Either they mistakenly thought they were talking to you because those press people are so straight they wouldn't know the difference," Marianne said, "or they deliberately lied that it was you because they feel Brian isn't a large enough figure, and they'd rather pin it on you. That's like talking to Ringo and saying it was John Lennon."

"Right, right. I'm going to sue the bastards." And Jagger announced the afternoon that the article appeared that he had issued a writ of libel against the *News of the World.*

Now Jagger and Keith had been arrested and could be forced to trial. As they all talked over the raid at Redlands, they grew more certain the *News of the World* had been responsible, that instead of trying to defend the libel action the paper decided to catch Jagger with drugs even if he had to be planted. They sat around the Stones' office, most of them who'd been at Redlands, trying to fit all the pieces together. Especially the role of Henry Schneiderman, who had not been searched by the police and who had been allowed to leave the country. (Jagger's private inquiries had disclosed that Schneiderman had fled.)

"Who is this cat?" Jagger asked. Keith said he had met him in America the year before, just some kind of hanger-on among the bands there. And, very recently, he had turned up in London.

"I know a little about Schneiderman," Michael said. "Strange guy. He's the reason the whole party at Redlands came together, you know." Keith hadn't known, actually. All he remembered was that Clifford Baldwin had said there was some American around with some really good acid, and perhaps they could take it down at Redlands on the weekend, an up trip in the country where they wouldn't have to worry about the narcs from the Chelsea drug squad, who were busting everyone—there were even rumors of frameups and extortion by the police. Keith had agreed to Clifford's plan, had gone off to Munich for a few days, and when he returned he was told the party was on. Schneiderman indeed had outrageous acid from San Francisco. Keith rounded up Jagger and Marianne and a couple of other friends, and on Saturday afternoon they drove down in a convoy of cars, Clifford bringing his Moroccan servant to cook and Schneiderman bringing the acid and dope. "Fuckin' Schneiderman and his dope," Keith said.

"Schneiderman's been in London before, I met him before this," Michael said. "What I understand is, he started off in America, pushing in a small way among other things. And then he got into some other sort of scene. I think he's more than just an informer for the *News of the World*. I think it's more mysterious than that."

"The CIA?" someone asked.

"Well, the way he got out of the country so fast and just disappeared, I'm sure he works for something more than just the *News of the World*. Perhaps the CIA. I certainly have the feeling he's working for the American government."

220

"That's too far fuckin' out—you got any evidence?" Keith said.

"Nothing solid. But I met the guy a few times, and I never liked him. He had a sort of insidious thing about him, I can't quite put my finger on it, sort of the way he had of getting into other people's scenes, taking advantage of people. He took advantage of you, of the Stones. But evidence? Well, there's one funny thing, he had a Canadian passport and an American passport and at least one more from another country. He let me believe he had a dozen of them and was really bending the law all over the world. Another thing about him, he's bisexual, he was living with this friend of mine, bisexuals. I always had the feeling there was something not quite right about the guy. I don't mean the sex trip, but like he was on a James Bond thing, the CIA or something. Seriously."

"The only reason he was there is he had the stuff," Keith said. "Otherwise I would have never put up with him. But there is another possibility." He paused a moment. "Maybe they got hold of someone who works for us, maybe one of the chauffeurs or something. That's how they knew we were going to go down there and trip."

After discussing it for hours, they came to the conclusion that Schneiderman could only have been a *News of the World* plant, that he helped pull the party together for one reason: to give the newspaper proof that Jagger was into drugs so that his libel suit would fail.

The Stones left everything in the hands of their attorneys and flew off on a European tour in mid-March 1967, appearing unconcerned about the date in court to answer to charges of drug possession that awaited their return. They hadn't played Europe for more than a year, and everywhere they went Jagger's sensual mouth, his jerking body, moved the crowds to hysteria. There were riots in almost every city. More than 150 fans were arrested in Vienna after smoke bombs were thrown in a 14,000 seat stadium. The band was forced to flee a concert hall in Orebro, Sweden, when police started beating girls over the head with truncheons, and several thousand fans showed their displeasure by throwing bottles, firecrackers, and chairs. In Warsaw, the first trip into Eastern Europe for the Stones, police used teargas, batons, and water cannon to break up a mob of 3,000 teenagers trying to storm the Palace of Culture; the kids were angry because most of the best tickets to each of two performances had been given to the children of the hierarchy of the Communist Party. Keith actually stopped the band about the third song: "Stop your fuckin' playing, Charlie" . . . and Charlie stopped pounding on his drums. "You fuckin' lot down front, with your fingers in your ears and your diamonds and pearls, get out of your seats and let those people in the back come down here. Get out! Get the fuck out!" Most of the people in the first six rows left their seats and moved to the back of the hall, the real fans dashed forward, and the band got its rock machine moving again.

For Jagger, riots were a minor problem, riots were all part of the act of performing, of charging up his audience. But he was outraged at the indignity he was forced to suffer in many airports in Europe and Britain—Customs officials going through every one of his bags—of all their luggage—in Malmö, Paris, Hamburg, Athens, four times in Heathrow; in Paris, officials searching him at Orly warned him that he had been placed on an International Red List maintained to warn Customs officials of suspected narcotics smugglers. "The bastards were really putting the screws in, all over the fuckin' world," Jagger told an aide when he returned to London after the last date of the tour, April 17. And he told an interviewer of the *Daily Mirror:*

"I see a great deal of danger in the air. Teenagers are not screaming over pop music anymore, they're screaming for much deeper reasons. We're only serving as a means of giving them an outlet. Pop music is just the superficial tissue. When

I'm on that stage I sense that the teenagers are trying to communicate to me, like by telepathy, a message of some urgency. Not about me or our music, but about the world and the way they live. I interpret it as their demonstration against society and its sick attitudes. Teenagers the world over are weary of being pushed around by half-witted politicians who attempt to dominate their way of thinking and set a code for their living. This is a protest against the system. And I see a lot of trouble coming in the dawn."

They went back into the studios to work on their next album, trying to get as much done before May 10, the preliminary court hearing. And before Brian fell completely to pieces. Touring had been very hard on him. He exulted over the fans in Europe, but they tore so much out of him, they wanted so much . . . and the groupies not only wanted to fuck his body, but to fuck his mind, with their dope and their acid, their demands that he beat them, whip them, rip them open . . . It was all twisting his head around . . . Anita gone, Tara gone, Keith gone . . . except Keith was there, in the studio . . . sometimes Anita was there, also . . . and Brian didn't really want to be there, not in that studio with them.

Much of the time he came in stoned, so totally ripped he was unable to lift his guitar. He'd lie on the floor in a corner, out of his skull, his guitar over him like a blanket. Brian was growing more fragile, and Keith began to worry: *He used to be like a little Welsh bull when I first met him, now he's gotten so weak.* Brian never had time to work it out, to think through what was happening to him. The touring, the need to record the new album, the search for affection that drove him to creeps and killers who would shoot formaldehyde into your veins if they could make a profit on it. And Marianne felt that Jagger and Keith were too busy with their writing for the album, with recording, to understand what was happening to Brian. They had an album to do and they could only feel that, as Keith put it, "In the studio, to try and get Brian to play was such a hassle that . . . we started overdubbing, which is a drag because it means the whole band isn't playing."

But Brian's inability to work with them in the studio was more than just the drugs—Brian could make incredibly beautiful music when he was stoned, in the past—more than the disappointments in his personal life. Brian hated the music the Stones were playing now, for this album. *Her Satanic Majesties Request,* it was to be called, a reference to the Queen, Her Britannic Majesty, a title certain to stir a huge controversy throughout the remains of the Empire. Brian loathed the music because he felt it was a deliberate pandering to the taste of a certain part of the public, the dopesters and acid freaks, a deliberate attempt to cash in on the psychedelic craze. The music wasn't Stones music; most of it wasn't even music, but studio electronics. And he may have understood something else about this music, this album. Something that flashed across Marianne's mind when she watched them work in the studio one night: *They're making this album to break up the group, to get Brian out. Mick wants him out because he doesn't want anyone in his way. He got rid of Andrew. And Keith wants him out because of the scandal over Anita.*

On May 9, the day before they were scheduled to appear in the local courthouse for the preliminary hearing on the drug charges, Jagger, Marianne, Michael, and Clifford drove down to Redlands to be with Keith, so they could all go to court together the next morning. They were all quite gay about their problem with the law, expecting a large fine and a slap on the wrist, and joking about it as if it were just another newspaper attack on the Stones. But Marianne was somewhat worried.

"Mick, let me go into court and tell the truth about the pills," she pleaded once more. "They were my pills, and I'll go into the witness box and into prison for them, if I have to, I'll go to jail for my own pills."

"I won't hear of it," Jagger said. "You're not even to be mentioned in court, I've told our lawyers that. I don't want your name brought up in court."

"That's nonsense. I'm not afraid to take the rap for those four little pills. If anybody is going to jail, then we all should go to jail. We'll all go together. I'm not terrified of jail."

"Who's going into the nick?" Jagger asked. "I'm innocent, those pills are legal. And Keith is innocent, by law. They can't prove he knew somebody was smoking hash. Especially since they permitted that bastard Scheiderman to leave the country. Only Robert has a problem, poor Robert with his habit. But no matter what happens, you aren't to be involved in any way, do you hear?"

Marianne thought: *He's so very protective. He thinks I'm too frail a thing to face a drug charge. I am to be spared all of this.* She felt warm inside, because of Jagger's attitude. *It's so charming, that rather light-hearted quality of, "Oh, darling, of course I'll go to court for you, I adore you, I'll do anything for you."* But later that evening, several other thoughts occupied her: *It's all part of the drama, Mick as martyr . . . a far too noble thing to do . . . he will sacrifice himself . . . I have nothing to lose . . . but I'd become a Joan of Arc instead of him . . . his immediate reaction was to protect me, that's real, he's doing it for me . . . but he doesn't mind appearing so noble. . .*

They drove into Chichester early the next morning, using two cars, on Jagger's orders. A chauffeured Rolls was sent ahead, without passengers, its driver ordered to wait at an intersection a half-mile from the West Sussex Quarter Sessions building. "We're going to be followed by journalists, so let's give them the slip." Jagger and his party climbed into Keith's Bentley and started for the courthouse. No journalists were following them. As they pulled into Chichester they met the Rolls, changed cars, and continued on to the courthouse, pulling up to a rear door to avoid the people who had queued up for seats two hours early—this was the most exciting event to happen in Chichester in centuries. Inside, before a packed public gallery, Jagger heard himself officially accused of possessing four amphetamine tablets without authorization, Keith of permitting his home to be used for smoking illegal substances in violation of the Dangerous Drugs Act, Fraser with illegal possession of heroin. They pleaded not guilty, and each was freed on $250 bail for a trial expected the following month.

It was a simple, technical legal process, nothing to change Jagger's view that—except for Fraser and his heroin—he and Keith would beat these absurd charges. But during the luncheon recess, while waiting to hear how much bail would be required, Keith called Brian's flat in London to say they'd be driving up in about an hour. Anita, who was staying with Brian, to pull him out of another period of depression, answered the phone.

"Don't come round," she said. "The police are here."

"The police? What are you talking about?"

"They've found some stuff and have arrested Brian. The Chelsea drug squad. They're still searching for more stuff to lay on Brian."

"The bastards," Keith said. "Ring the lawyers, tell them to get working on it. I'll ring you later."

Keith thought: *The lawyers are right. The coppers are really out to do us, to get the Stones.* He went into the anteroom where Jagger and the others were waiting for court to resume. Marianne looked up and realized immediately that something was dreadfully wrong. "Is it Brian . . . is he? . . ."

"They've busted Brian. We're up here in court waiting to hear if there's going to be bail, and they bust Brian, man," he said, his words cascading over his teeth in anger. "The fuckers have it timed to the minute. We're actually in this fuckin' courtroom, and they're going into Brian's house to do him so the papers can come out with, 'Rolling Stones Keith Richard and Mick Jagger on trial for this, meanwhile Brian Jones has just been found with this'—so they can lay that on: 'Well, they must all be guilty.' "

"Are they really out to get us so bad?"

"Damn right they are," Keith said. "Unbelievable . . . really weird. People think of England as far more tolerant and genteel than America but when they lay this one on us, when they lay it down, they can be just as heavy. They just don't carry guns, that's all."

"They're going to make examples of you, Mick. They really mean this one," Marianne said.

Jagger rose and walked away, to find the lawyers, and Keith sat down in his place, next to Marianne. "I'm worried about Brian," he said. "Brian's weak, he's very fragile, he's not going to be able to hold up under this sort of pressure. If the coppers are really out to do us all, Brian will break. They could destroy him completely."

"Oh, God, yes, just a little shove by the police will send Brian over the edge," Marianne said.

Jagger kept his life as close to normal as possible, while awaiting the trial, recording, seeing friends, going out to the clubs with Marianne—he was, after all, king of the scene as Lennon called him. He and Marianne sat in the Speakeasy one night, watching the truly outrageous performance of Jimi Hendrix and his Experience. Jimi had just become a star in London, the first "real" blues guitarist that Britain ever produced—except that he was born in Seattle, had bounced around New York as a backup musician for years, and had been brought to Britain by Chas Chandler only a few months before. Jimi was the most exciting, dramatic musician heard in Britain in years. Even Eric Clapton, now a guitar super-hero, felt awed by Hendrix' mastery of the instrument. He could run a series of bass guitar notes in one direction and a series of treble notes in the opposite direction—with his teeth—creating a tugging rhythm and a sensual tension; and he heightened the sensuality by lapping and nuzzling his guitar with his lips and tongue, caressing it with his inner thighs, banging it with a series of powerful crotch-thrusts. And at the end of his act, the top of his guitar caught fire. Hendrix became a symbol for the entire decadent London rock scene, the epitomization of raw sensual power, of drugs and drink and dissolution. He was delivering what Jagger had only been hinting at.

As he was finishing up his last set now, Marianne sat with Jagger at a front table, smiling a little as she remembered the first time she'd met Jimi, a few months earlier. Jimi had been playing in a little club in London, during his first weeks in Britain, before he became the rage, and she had gone to see him without Jagger. She'd been introduced to him, and he came on strong to her, almost demanding she spend the night with him. She was so very turned on to him—*playing his guitar with his teeth!*—but she'd been living with Jagger just a few weeks, and their relationship was so passionate and intense that she wouldn't endanger it for a brief scene with Jimi . . . *but this very beautiful spade cat does turn me on so, I want to go with him but I daren't.* She turned him down. And now he'd spotted her at the table and was coming over to join her, and she could feel Jagger's discomfort. Not because Jimi had tried to get her into his bed, she hadn't told Jagger about that, but because Jimi had played for Jagger once, an audition for the production company that Jagger had formed, without Andrew; that relationship was ended and the Stones were going off on their own, with Jagger in charge of the business and management of the band. As Jimi worked his way toward her, through the groupies reaching for him, Marianne thought: *And Mick turned Hendrix down. He had been able to get Jimi, to sign him up with the new production company.*

And he stupidly turned Jimi down. Now I don't think he likes Jimi at all.

Jimi pulled up a chair between Marianne and Jagger, wedging her against the wall. He ignored Jagger. Leaning toward Marianne, his lips against her ear so she could hear him over the music from the stereo system, he said: "Come with me when this place closes down. Leave this place and come with me. You don't want to be with Jagger, he's just a cunt . . ." Marianne said she couldn't possibly leave Jagger, and while listening to Jimi's repeated and urgent demands she kept thinking: *I'd really love to go with him. I'm really tempted.* And she thought: *Mick can't hear what Jimi's saying because of the music. But he knows something's happening, you can't fool him ever, he's not stupid. He picks up on those things. And he's getting very jealous.*

On the way back to their flat later, Marianne told Jagger what Jimi had been saying, how he'd been coming on to her. But she didn't say she'd been tempted, of course. A couple of weeks later Jimi was appearing at the Lyceum, and Marianne insisted Jagger take her. They went, Jagger very uptight during the performance. When the curtains fell and the lights came up for several encores, Marianne said she wanted to go backstage to see Jimi. Jagger was angry, he said he wouldn't go backstage for that cat, and neither would she. Marianne was persistent. And Jagger laid it down: "You'll have to decide who you want, me or Hendrix." They didn't go backstage.

The trial of Michael Philip Jagger, Keith Richards, and Robert Hugh Fraser began before Judge Block on June 27. Jagger and Keith weren't about to be intimidated by the court; they both dressed as if they were attending a press conference with journalists from the music magazines. Jagger wore a pale green double-breasted jacket with white buttons, olive green

229

trousers, a floral shirt, and a black striped tie. Keith was dressed in a navy blue frock coat, black military-style trousers, a lace collar, and maroon and black shoes.

Jagger's trial was called first. Police testified that they found a small phial containing four amphetamine tablets in Jagger's jacket and that he had admitted they were his. "My doctor prescribed them," police said he told them. When a policeman had asked him what they were for, Jagger had said: "To stay awake and work." The defense called Dr. Raymond Dixon Firth, of Knightsbridge, who testified that he had been Jagger's regular physician since July 1965. The doctor testified that sometime before February, Jagger had told him that while he was abroad during a very hectic tour he'd been given some tablets, some kind of Italian pep pill, to help pull him through the enormous pressures. "Is it all right to use them?" Jagger asked. The doctor said that he realized from Jagger's description of the tablets that they were amphetamines, and he told Jagger: "Yes, you may use them in an emergency. But they are not something you should use regularly because they could be dangerous." The doctor testified that so far as he was concerned Jagger was legally in possession of the pills since he, the doctor, told Jagger he could have them. He added that if Jagger did not have the amphetamines, he would have prescribed them. In effect, the doctor said in his testimony he had prescribed those tablets.

Judge Block made short work of Jagger's sole defense: " . . . These remarks cannot be regarded as a prescription," he told the jury. "I therefore direct you that there is no defense to this charge." The jury returned in five minutes and found Jagger guilty of being in unauthorized possession of amphetamines, a crime punishable by a fine and/or imprisonment up to two years. Jagger appeared stunned, his lips set in a harsh line that was no longer sensuous, the lips of a man who'd suddenly aged, as the Judge revoked his bail and remanded him in custody until after Keith's trial. He was hustled into a gray van with Fraser, whose bail was also revoked because of the seriousness of heroin possession, and with several other prisoners on remand. A dozen schoolgirls banged their fists against the closed courtyard gates as Jagger sat in the van. The girls, screaming "We want Mick," tried to climb over the gates. But they couldn't get near Jagger; the van drove him to Lewes Prison, where he was placed in a cell for the night.

Marianne went to visit him that evening, with Michael. As they approached his cell, Jagger leaped from his cot and rushed forward. He began to cry. "You've got to get me out of here, Michael," he said. "I don't think I can make it, behind bars."

"Pull yourself together," Marianne said, a little more harshly than she had intended. But she couldn't help feeling he was indulging in self-pity, and she didn't want to see him like that. "Just try and relax, you'll probably be here only this one night, and after Keith's trial tomorrow you'll all be free."

Jagger continued to cry through the bars. "I didn't do anything," he said.

Michael leaned closer. "I have my camera. Let me get a shot of you behind bars. Give it to the newspapers, and there'll be a tremendous fuss made over it." Jagger wiped his eyes, and Michael shot off a roll of film. It was promptly confiscated by prison officials.

Keith's trial was held the next day. Jagger and Fraser were returned from Lewes Prison to wait below the court for sentencing. They were handcuffed together when they arrived in a police van, and newspaper photographers snapped pictures. They were printed in the papers that evening and the next day and raised a storm, newspapers, lawyers, and several members of Parliament demanding to know whether handcuffs were necessary. "It was, in fact, an outrage which the

Home Secretary should make sure is never repeated," said the *Sunday Express*. Other papers said the authorities seemed to be trying to make a martyr out of Jagger or had simply decided to humiliate him because he was a pop idol.

Keith's basic defense, when he took the witness stand, was that he had no idea anyone was smoking hash in his home and that the raid on Redlands was a plot by the *News of the World* to involve Jagger with drugs and thus defeat his libel suit. The evidence of that was the mysterious Schneiderman, who had been permitted to leave the country. The prosecutor, in questioning police witnesses, devoted much time to "the girl in the fur rug," as Marianne, never identified in court, was called. As she sat in the courtroom next to Allen Klein, who had flown over from New York to help with the defense, Marianne realized that the Crown was trying to make it sound as if some very strange sexual behavior had been taking place at Redlands: a girl in a fur rug, naked beneath, and seven or eight men.

"The only thing they're not bringing up is that damned Mars bar story," Marianne told Klein. The day after the warrants against Jagger and Keith were announced, the hipsters and the gossips of the underground had begun spreading a tale that a wild orgy had taken place in Keith's drawing room, that several of the men were performing cunnilingus on Marianne while she had a candy bar in her vagina. It was absolutely untrue, but the gossips who suck vicarious thrills from their fantasies about pop stars spread the story all over Britain. As she sat listening to the prosecutor questioning Keith about her—the girl in the fur rug—asking Keith: "Did it come as a great surprise to you that she was prepared to go downstairs again into the drawing room still wearing only a rug, where there were about a dozen police officers? You do not think it was because she had been smoking Indian hemp and had got rid of her inhibitions and embarrassment?" Marianne smiled at the absurdity of it all. She thought:

232

It's absurd, but it's quite serious. They're making it sound so decadent, like there was an orgy going on. If Mick hadn't insisted on saying the pep pills were his, if he hadn't protected me, they would never be able to talk about the girl in the fur rug. Had they said it was me from the very beginning, it wouldn't take on all this mysterious evil glamour. The judge will hang them because of it.

She turned to Allen Klein and said: "I want to go into the witness box to set it straight. I've always wanted to do that but Mick wouldn't hear of it."

"I'm afraid it's too late now," Klein said. "They'll never believe you now."

After two days of trial, Keith was convicted by the jury, which deliberated for a little over an hour.

Jagger was quickly brought up to join Keith in the dock for sentencing. Judge Block addressed himself to Keith: "The offense of which you have been properly convicted by the jury carries with it a maximum sentence of as much as ten years . . ." There were cries of, "Oh, no" from the gallery, but Judge Block ignored them and went on: ". . . which is a view of the seriousness of this offense which is taken by Parliament. I sentence you to one year imprisonment and order you to pay five hundred pounds costs."

Jagger was next: "I sentence you to three months and one hundred pounds costs."

Jagger covered his face with his hands and started to cry. He stumbled out of the dock, trying to hide his tears from his friends and the teenage fans in the gallery. He was taken off to Brixton Prison, without handcuffs, for his third night in the lockup. Keith was taken to Wormwood Scrubs.

It was later disclosed that Judge Block imposed the sentences after consulting with three other West Sussex Justices who had listened to the trials: two farmers, one of whom had been a Justice of the Peace since 1939, and a Worthing newsagent; none of them was a lawyer.

233

It seemed to friends that Mick and Keith hadn't really understood, at first, what Marianne and the lawyers were saying when they warned that "they"—the faceless "they" who in some imperceptible way controlled society—were determined to make an example of the Stones. The band, and Jagger particularly, had become symbols of those who live outside the law, who have no respect for society, for work, for the Church. They were bastard offspring of the Devil, threats to the social structure beside whom Jack the Ripper was a simple English eccentric. Jagger was considered a monster corrupting the young, and he became the moral scapegoat for the middle class, the severity of the sentence based not on the offense but on the fact that he most totally summed up the decay of the old values. Jagger was the aristocrat of the new hedonism, sexually free (deviant, most people called it), socially destructive, drugged, and druggy—and he must be punished. The middle class, whose values Jagger had been assaulting for four years, was angered and frightened most of all by his apparent devotion to pure pleasure, and by the fact he'd won enough independence to indulge it. The papers had said he was a dollar millionaire by age twenty-two, and he conceded he was wealthy: "I have enough dollars to last me the rest of my life." He also owned three music publishing companies with Keith, the papers reported, had just sold American rights to their songs for $1 million, spent £150 a month on clothes, owned an Aston Martin, two minis, and a town house on the Thames. And many Englishmen hated him for it. His critics said Jagger was preaching anarchy, despite his wealth, and Jagger's name became a synonym for profligacy and anarchy.

Jagger had himself promoted it—the antidote to the Beatles, in the beginning—in his actions, his songs, and his statements to journalists: According to British press reports over the past few years, Jagger appeared to be calling for a revolution; after putting down their newspapers, most readers could easily fantasize that Jagger wanted to behead the Queen, turn Buckingham Palace into an opium den and Westminster Abbey into a brothel, drop LSD into the water supply, and decree that every English girl lose her virginity by the age of ten or so. "WE'VE DEFEATED THE ADULTS SAYS MICK JAGGER" was the headline in the *Sunday Express* a month before the raid at Redlands. In the article Jagger was quoted in favor of total sexual freedom and talked about the disintegration of the family in Britain. And in other interviews between his arrest and trial he practically demanded that young people "be free and have the right of expression, of thinking and living aloud without any petty restrictions . . ." And though he denied that anyone was advocating they become "drug-takers" or were planning "to tread down their parents," it could certainly sound that way to a reader conditioned to believe Jagger was an anti-Christ Marxist sex and drug fiend.

But after the newspaper stories about the length of their hair, the arrest for urinating against a wall in public, all the little girls and boys who wanted to be violated by the Stones, after those stories sank into the readers' subconscious and broiled there, Jagger's lyrics offended most adults almost continually. The lyrics, quoted in the papers, heard on the BBC (when not being censored), on pirate radio, and on the phonographs of millions of kids, were a constant reminder that Jagger was determined to destroy the foundation of society by corrupting the young. Jagger had finally stopped worrying about the public acceptance of original material, and most of the singles since the end of 1965 were Jagger/Richard compositions, as was at least half the content of the albums. Those lyrics were brutally anti-woman at first—his reactions to the groupies who were reaching out to him on the tours and to the strains of his relationship with Chrissie. They were highly sexual and sexist: man subjugating woman: *"Under my thumb's the girl who once had me down/Under my thumb's the girl who once pushed me around/It's down to me the way she does just what she's told/It's down to me, the change has come, she's under my thumb . . ."* Later, songs of discontent became prominent, songs condemning society and mindless parents: "Satisfaction" and "Mother's Little Helper" among them. And the songs about drugs: *"Connection, I just can't make no connection/But all I want to do, is to get back to you/Everything is going in the wrong direction/The doctor is giving me more injections . . ."* On and on, Jagger's message banging into the heads of British children—messages about freedom, sexuality, dope. And worrying the parents.

And now it became clear that society as represented by Judge Block and the farmers of Chichester, had decided to squash these pests, this blight on the nation. Marianne thought about it a lot, while Jagger was in prison, and she understood that Jagger had carried it all a bit far, that he hadn't correctly gauged "society's" short fuse. "Mick was upsetting the Establishment, and they decided to stop him, now," she told friends after the trial. "You see, our society has evolved to a certain social stage, and they're afraid of where it's going, so society must be kept where it is, and anything that's a threat must be stamped out. It's not so much that they believe in society . . . I don't think that people do *believe* in society any more, or any of its morals, or any of its structures. I think they simply feel they've worked so hard to make it happen they might as well stick to it. And Mick is a threat to it."

She tried to explain some of this to Jagger, when she visited him in Brixton, tried to tell him she felt he would never serve more than a few days of his sentence because the journalists she'd spoken to were so totally on his side that they surely reflected what *intelligent* members of society were feeling. But she didn't think Jagger was able to grasp what she was saying. He only cried. Marianne was distressed at his appearance: his slightly bloodshot eyes, rumpled clothes, and rumpled wig-like hair . . . strange, he was always so careful about his hair, and now it doesn't even look real . . . everything about his appearance smelled of self-pity.

"Pull yourself together," she told him, and he burst into tears and cried through the bars. She lectured him, almost, refusing to permit him to drown in self-pity. She thought of it that way, as she spoke to him very firmly about his need to make the best of it until they could get him out:

I have to be firm with him or he'll drown in self-pity. His crying is a bit of an over-indulgence. I'm sure he really feels like crying . . . it's so hard on him because he is actually innocent . . . I know he can't help crying, he has a great capacity for feeling sorry for himself, like I have, he can see himself wronged very easily, in any situation, and now that he's actually been wronged he's making the most of it.

She sat with him for two hours, finally calming him down. But after she left, Jagger wrote her a letter describing how he felt about the three months' imprisonment he faced. Marianne told Michael Cooper about it later: "Mick is badly shaken, he goes on for three pages, saying he doesn't think he has the strength to put up with prison for three months, he thinks he'll go mad. I hate that in him. We know damn well he won't go mad at all, he'll probably be running the prison in two days."

Michael laughed. "One day," he said. "I give him one more day to get it all together."

"I'm sure you're right," she said. "But we have to be firm with him, we mustn't baby him at all. You know," she continued, "Mick is in there because he thought I was too fragile to go into court, but now he's fragile, and I'm the strong one. In things like this I become the strong one, I can go in there, even though it's so ghastly with the photographers camped outside to see me, and I can be strong and lecture him. 'Pull yourself together, dear, life is what you make it.'

"You must read this letter, it shows how much he loves me and I feel so good about that. He says all he can do is think of me and when he thinks of me he cries. And he asks me to come see him tomorrow, to come see him every day, it's the only thing he lives for, the only bit of happiness in his cell. It goes on and on like that for pages."

By Marianne's next visit, Jagger had been made head of the prison library, and he told her he was writing some songs and poems about prison. One of the songs, he said, is called "We Love You," a thank-you for the fans who were writing letters to the papers and to Parliament, and who had picketed the *News of the World* offices.

She rang Michael that evening to tell him how accurate he'd been. "He went right to the warden and was made librarian," she said. "He got it together in less than two days."

"It doesn't surprise me at all," Michael said. "The thing about Mick is that he's incredibly together, inside. He can cope with almost anything. He's not like normal people. Normal people give you the feeling of togetherness on the outside, but they're really falling apart inside. Mick's just the opposite; he gives an outward appearance of being so untogether, but underneath he's incredibly together, like everything's welded and will never come apart."

"Mick always can make out anywhere; his faculties never desert him," Marianne said. "He's got the best job in the whole prison, so you can see how he makes out. I knew the crying would stop, eventually."

Keith, on entering the 150-year-old Wormwood Scrubs, took one good look around him and, as he later put it: "Man, I wouldn't even want to play here, much less live here." Once inside, warders showed him what his life would be like from now on: They wouldn't give him a belt for his trousers, so that he couldn't hang himself and gave him only a blunt spoon because a knife and fork could be honed into a weapon. His work assignment, he was told, was a shop where prisoners sewed up mailbags for postmen. When he got to his cell other prisoners started dropping pieces of tobacco and cigarette papers to him. Out in the yard that evening, on the mandatory one-hour stroll, several prisoners came up to him and asked: "What do you want, man, acid? Want some hash? We have it here." They spoke without moving their mouths, and Keith was appalled by the idea of dope: "Take acid? In here?" Other prisoners, angered at what had been done to him and Jagger, said: "Bastards. They wanted to get you. They been waiting for you in here for ages." Keith replied: "I ain't gonna be in here very long, baby, don't worry about that." Keith had been told by one prisoner that whenever a Stones record was played on the radio, the guards would say: "That lot has a place for them here, we're going to get them right soon." But that night, when a Stones song was played, every prisoner in the place began to shout: "Hoooooray!" And Keith later said: "They all knew what happened, they were all with us."

In mid-afternoon of his second day in Wormwood, Keith was lying on his bunk when another prisoner suddenly shouted: "You're out, man, you're out. It just came over the news, you got bail." Keith began kicking the door of his cell, screaming: "You let me out, you bastards, I got bail."

Jagger and Keith were granted bail of $17,000 each and released pending appeal of their conviction. Jagger was picked up at Brixton by Keith's chauffeur-driven Bentley, which then went to Wormwood to collect Keith. They drove into London to meet Marianne, and then on to Allen Klein's suite at the Hilton for a conference. As soon as they got comfortable, Marianne began fussing over a jewelry box which had been delivered by a chauffeur. The box contained a secret compartment which she was unable to open, and she asked Allen to help her. When it finally opened, Allen realized it was filled with hashish. He was furious. He tore the box from her lap and threw it out the window, watching as it smashed to the pavement more than twenty stories below. He turned to Marianne: "How goddam stupid can you get?" he demanded.

"The law is unrealistic," Marianne said, standing next to him at the window, peering down at the remains of the jewelry box. "The law must be changed."

"I don't give a shit if it is. I don't want any of you to go to prison," Klein said. "I'm involved, then I'm responsible. It's my job to see that you stay out of prison. And I'm not going to have you blow it for everybody."

Jagger sat in a chair, not interfering. Ignoring them. He was reading an advertisement in the *Evening Standard:*

> The WHO consider Mick Jagger & Keith
> Richard have been treated as scapegoats
> for the drug problem and as a protest
> against the savage sentences imposed on
> them at Chichester yesterday, The WHO
> are issuing today the first of a series
> of Jagger/Richard songs to keep their
> work before the public until they are
> again free to record themselves.

"Peter," he said of Pete Townshend, who had bought the ad, "I'm only happy I don't have to hear your recording down in Brixton."

The next morning, a Saturday, Marianne stumbled out of bed, trying not to disturb Jagger, and ran to fetch the papers that had just been delivered. She opened the *Times* first, running quickly through the story of Jagger's release. As she flipped the pages, a thick black dagger of type over an editorial knifed into her brain:

WHO BREAKS A BUTTERFLY ON A WHEEL?

She dashed back into the bedroom. "This is the most extraordinary thing, Mick. The *Times* criticizing the courts for what they did to you. I thought the papers aren't permitted to do that, it's against the law." Jagger was sitting up in bed now, and Marianne began to read the editorial:

"Mr. Jagger has been sentenced to imprisonment for three months. He is appealing against conviction and sentence, and has been granted bail until the hearing of the appeal later in the year. In the meantime the sentence of imprisonment is bound to be widely discussed by the public. And the circumstances are sufficiently unusual to warrant such discussion in the public interest.

"Mr. Jagger was charged with being in possession of four tablets containing amphetamine sulphate and methyl amphetamine hydrochloride; these tablets had been bought, perfectly legally in Italy, and brought back to this country. They are not a highly dangerous drug, or, in proper dosage, a dangerous drug at all. They are of the benzedrine type, and the Italian manufacturers recommend them both as a stimulant and as a remedy for travel sickness.

"In Britain, it is an offense to possess these drugs without a doctor's prescription. Mr. Jagger's doctor says that he knew and had authorized their use, but he did not give a prescription for them as indeed they had already been purchased. His evidence was not challenged. This was, therefore, an offense of a technical character which before this case drew the point to public attention any honest man might have been liable to commit. If after his visit to the Pope, the Archbishop of Canterbury had bought proprietary air sickness pills on Rome Airport and imported the unused tablets into Britain on his return, he would have risked committing precisely the same offence . . ."

Jagger said the *Times* was going all the way with its editorial.

". . . same offence," Marianne continued. "No one who has

241

ever travelled and brought proprietary drugs abroad can be sure that he has not broken the law.

"Judge Block directed the jury that the approval of a doctor is not a defense in law to the charge of possessing drugs without a prescription, and the jury convicted. Mr. Jagger was not charged with complicity in any other drug offence that occurred in the same house. They were separate cases, and no evidence was produced to suggest that he knew Mr. Fraser had heroin tablets or that the vanishing Mr. Schneiderman had cannabis resin. It is indeed no offence to be in the same building or the same company as people possessing or even using drugs, nor could it reasonably be made an offence. The drugs which Mr. Jagger had in his possession must therefore be treated on their own, as a separate issue from the other drugs that other people may have had in their possession at the same time. It may be difficult for lay opinion to make this distinction clearly, but obviously justice cannot be done if one man is to be punished for a purely contingent association with someone else's offence.

"We have, therefore, a conviction against Mr. Jagger purely on the grounds that he possessed four Italian pep pills, quite legally bought, but not legally imported without a prescription. Four is not a large number. This is not the quantity which a pusher of drugs would have on him, nor even the quantity one would expect in an addict. In any case Mr. Jagger's career is obviously one that does involve great personal strain and exhaustion; his doctor said that he approved the occasional use of these drugs, and it seems likely that similar drugs would have been prescribed if there was a need for them. Millions of similar drugs are prescribed in Britain every year, and for a variety of conditions."

Marianne glanced at Jagger, then continued reading.

"One has to ask, therefore, how it is that this technical offence, divorced as it must be from other people's offences, was thought to deserve the penalty of imprisonment. In the courts at large it is most uncommon for imprisonment to be imposed on first offenders where the drugs are not major drugs of addiction and there is no question of drug traffic. The normal penalty is probation, and the purpose of probation is to encourage the offender to develop his career and to avoid the drug risks in the future. It is surprising therefore that Judge Block should have decided to sentence Mr. Jagger to imprisonment, and particularly surprising as Mr. Jagger's is about as mild a drug case as can ever have been brought before the courts.

"It would be wrong to speculate on the judge's reasons, which we do not know. It is, however, possible to consider the public reaction. There are many people who take a primitive view of the matter, what one might call a pre-legal view of the matter. They consider that Mr. Jagger has 'got what was coming to him.' They resent the anarchic quality of the Rolling Stones performances, dislike their songs, dislike their influence on teenagers, and broadly suspect them of decadence, a word used by Miss Monica Furlong in the *Daily Mail.*

"As a sociological concern, this may be reasonable enough, and at an emotional level, it is very understandable, but it has nothing at all to do with the case. One has to ask a different question: Has Mr. Jagger received the same treatment as he would have received if he had not been a famous figure, with all the criticism his celebrity has aroused? If a promising undergraduate had come back from a summer's visit to Italy with four pep pills in his pocket would it have been thought right to ruin his career by sending him to prison for three months? Would it also have been thought necessary to display him, handcuffed, to the public? There are cases in which a single figure becomes the focus of public concern about some aspects of public morality. The Stephen Ward case, with its dubious evidence and questionable verdict, was one of them, and that verdict killed Stephen Ward. There are elements of the same emotions in the reactions to this case. If we are going to make any case a symbol of the conflict between the sound traditional values of Britain and the new hedonism, then we must be sure that the sound traditional values include those of tolerance and equity. It should be the particular quality of British justice to ensure that Mr. Jagger is treated exactly the same as anyone else, no better and no worse. There must remain a suspicion in this case that Mr. Jagger received a more severe sentence than would have been thought proper for any purely anonymous young man."

Jagger said that everyone was going to have second thoughts, that he was going to win his appeal, and he expressed surprise that the *Times* would risk contempt of court.

"The Establishment is going to stop dead in its tracks," Marianne said. "Butterfly crucified on a wheel, whatever they call it . . . they're so right. To carry on further and make a big thing of it will make the drug situation worse . . ."

Jagger said he was going to call his mother because she had been worrying.

The *Times* editorial was quite extraordinary. By questioning the working of justice while the case was still before the courts, still to be heard on appeal, the *Times* could have been accused of contempt of court. But William Rees-Mogg, the paper's editor, felt so strongly that Jagger had been unfairly treated that he wrote the editorial himself instead of assigning it to a leader writer as is normally done. All the newspapers started to comment on the case the day after the *Times* editorial appeared: The *Sunday Express* condemning Jagger's sentence as "monstrously out of proportion to the offence he committed"; the *Sunday Times* criticizing the "strong sour smell of ignorance" that hung over the courtroom; The *Observer* concerned that "for many hundreds of thousands of youngsters . . . it was like a drumhead court-martial on the battlefield where the war of generations is conducted . . . Far from discouraging others, the case has produced two martyrs." The writers and their editors carried on the debate in articles, editorials, and the letters columns, united in ignoring previous court rulings that inhibited them from discussing criminal cases until the last possible appeal had been decided. It wasn't until eight days after the *Times* editorial that the Attorney General, Sir Elwyn Jones, in response to a question from a member of Parliament, ruled:

"Under the existing law, the press is free to comment responsibly on the verdicts and sentences of criminal courts, even where an appeal is pending. In my opinion, this freedom is a valuable safeguard, and it should not be curtailed."

Jagger, who had thought of becoming a journalist before he became interested in economics, closely followed all the gossip and jokes among newspaper men about which editor would be taken in handcuffs to which prison, and Marianne recalls that he was overjoyed that the arguments continued to rage for weeks. Lawyers and friends told him that the public debate improved his chances of winning an appeal. And Marianne felt there was something else behind Jagger's interest; as she listened to him discussing the controversy she thought: *It's taking on a Joan of Arc quality, and he digs it. He took the rap to protect me, but he sure digs that it's being made into a big issue.*

The *News of the World,* in the meantime, explained its position in its first issue after the trial. "A Monstrous Charge" the editors headlined a page one editorial. The paper said there is "not a shred of evidence to support" Keith's testimony that it had hired Schneiderman to plant dope in his house to avoid paying libel damages to Jagger. At the trial a policeman had admitted receiving information from the paper that a drug party was being held at Redlands, and the editorial said that its editors had indeed passed that information to the police. "It was our plain duty to do so." In a story on the inside, the editors explained that a reader had telephoned the offices on Saturday with information about the drug party and had come in later that night with further details. He asked the editors to pass it along to police, which was done. The paper denied it had ever heard Schneiderman's name until after the raid took place and insisted there was no evidence to substantiate the charges that the paper had planted Redlands. Later, Keith started telling friends he suspected one of the chauffeurs or another Stones employee of being the informer.

The appeal in the case of the Crown v. Michael Philip Jagger and Keith Richards was heard before the Lord Chief Justice's Court on the last day in July. Keith's case was heard first, but he was not present; he was forced to sit alone in another room because he had the chicken pox. After two hours of argument by defense and crown, Lord Parker handed down the decision. It was clear the girl in the fur skin rug, by now identified in the press as Marianne, troubled him the most. All the evidence did not prove she was taking drugs in any form—"One was left with the evidence that was extremely prejudicial, her undress." Perhaps Judge Block had been correct in admitting evidence about the semi-nude woman, the court said, but he should have warned the jury that there actually was not enough evidence in her behavior to prove she'd been smoking hash. Keith's conviction was quashed.

Turning to Jagger, the court ruled that it was impossible to rule that Dr. Dixon Firth's oral permission to Jagger to use the pep pills could be considered a prescription, and therefore the conviction should stand. However, since the drugs Jagger possessed were not heroin, not hard drugs of any kind, but rather common amphetamines; and since the "evidence of the doctor was the strongest mitigation there could be," then Judge Block's proper sentence was a conditional discharge: If Jagger stayed out of trouble for a full year his conviction would be stricken from the record, but if he committed another offense he would be sentenced for the new one as well as this one. In substituting a conditional discharge for the three month sentence, the Lord Chief Justice addressed Jagger:

"I think it right to say that when one is dealing with somebody who has greater responsibilities, as you have—because you are, whether you like it or not, an idol of a large number of young in this country—being in that position you have very grave responsibilities, and if you do come to be punished it is only natural that those responsibilities should carry a higher penalty."

Jagger didn't agree with that at all. In a press conference at the offices of Granada Television, after changing from his neat jacket and tie into brightly colored silks, Jagger tried to answer a question on his responsibility to his fans: "That's very difficult," he said. "One doesn't ask for responsibilities. They have been thrust upon me. I simply ask for my private life to be left alone. My responsibility is only to myself." And he told Marianne that night, back at Cheyne Walk: "I'm not going to be put in that bullshit position, of being the leader. I don't want anybody to think I'm the leader of anything."

The pilot of the helicopter lifted off from his base and, as he'd been commanded, once airborne he tore open a sealed envelope with his destination orders: He was to take his distinguished passenger, Michael Philip Jagger, accompanied by Marianne Faithfull, directly to the country estate of Sir John Ruggles-Brise, Lord Lieutenant of Essex. Jagger had agreed to a TV confrontation with the Establishment which Marianne was saying had stopped dead in its tracks because it had looked foolish in its persecution of a pop star. But Jagger had insisted he be interviewed in the open air rather than a television studio—apparently to emphasize the several nights of freedom he had lost during his trial—and TV executives had persuaded Sir John to let them invade his estate with about thirty technicians, two vans, and four huge cameras. The members of the Establishment who had agreed to participate in this newest form of Royal Variety Show included Lord Stow Hill, former Home Secretary and Attorney General, the Bishop of Woolwich, the Jesuit priest Father Thomas Corbishley, and William Rees-Moog, the editor of the *Times*. These guests arrived in limousines whose drivers had also been given sealed envelopes. The American Air Force stopped all flights from its base near Sir John's estate, to prevent shattering the hush required for such an historic occasion.

When the cameras began zooming in on the show that had been billed as a debate and as a special press conference, Jagger was so loaded up with tranquillizers that he couldn't participate much in his defense of his generation, and a newspaper critic said he fell back on the usual pat answers he'd always used with interviewers he didn't trust as they led him very gently into a discussion as to whether society was corrupt and decadent. It appeared to one critic as "a lost scene from Lewis Carroll." To Chrissie Shrimpton, sitting in her flat in London, watching the bustle devoted to this man she'd lived with for five years, it was more than fantasy.

He's been taken over by them, she thought as the production ended and she snapped off the telly. *They're treating him like a king, he's got to be a king now. How can he be anything else? He must believe it now.*

Just weeks before he'd gone into the studio to begin work on the new album, *Her Satanic Majesties*, at the end of the previous year, 1966, Jagger had been led into a discussion of art and communication by Midge McKenzie, who was interviewing him for an American magazine. They sat in his offices in Mayfair, drinking tea that had been brought to them by an aide, and Midge tried to sum up McLuhan: "He says

Brian leaves court in May 1968 after hearing on drug charge that he insisted was a frameup (Syndication International).

Linda Lawrence arrives from New York with Brian's son, carried by a friend, for Brian's funeral (Syndication International).

Suki (R) leaves parish church after Brian's funeral, with Canon Hugh Hopkins, Brian's parents and his sister (Syndication International).

Jagger's mansion, formerly Oliver Cromwell's headquarters (Pictorial Press Ltd).

Keith, Anita and their son Marlon, on the French Riviera in 1971.

Jagger and Marianne leave court after their appearance on drug charges in June 1970 (Syndication International).

Bianca, wearing her white
St. Laurent wedding outfit,
marries Jagger in St. Tropez, May 1971, backed by
witnesses Roger Vadim and
Nathalie Delon and, cen-
ter, Jagger's parents (Syndication International).

Bianca and Jagger—whose
gesture tells the photog-
rapher off—on the canals of
Venice (Keystone).

Bianca, holding five-month-old daughter Jade, joins Jagger in the boat he's hired for a cruise around Bora Bora, in the S. Pacific (Syndication International).

Jagger, with nail polish for the occasion, pulls David Bowie and a friend closer (Pictorial Press).

Jagger performing in Los Angeles at benefit for Managua earthquake victims (Lynn Goldsmith).

Bianca, in multicolored wig, modeling for charity (Syndication International).

Jagger in full drag costume.

that everything is connected, you can't remove any one element, you can't say this has nothing to do with that . . ."

"No, but you have to try, we have to do that as far as I'm concerned," Jagger said.

"You mean you believe in discipline in art, not this sort of thing of saying, 'Well, I had this thought . . . that's what I thought, and that's art, and that's it?' "

"You gotta communicate. I believe in communication of ideas," Jagger said. "If no one else can understand it's no bloody good at all, except insofar as you're explaining more of yourself by working it out. If you paint a picture and put it up in the galleries it's supposed to be communit . . . commun-i-cative—I have trouble with that word—or if I make a record I have to be commun-i-cative." Warming up to it now: "People've got to understand what you're on about, and I've been a bit frightened of people not understanding what I feel. Or if I'm trying to say something—I don't always try to say something, sometimes I'm just laughing—but if I am trying to say something I'd much rather have them understand something of what I'm saying, and that's very sort of low culture form of art.

"But if you've got something really important to say," Jagger went on, "it should be understood . . . and not only by a small minority of so-called hippies. It should be understood by everyone if you've got a good enough idea. And if you can't get it across to everybody then you're not as good as the artist who can . . ."

And then he went into the studio, trying to get as much work done on the album as possible while waiting to learn whether he'd have to stand trial because of the raid at Redlands, and then preparing his defense. As he joined Keith to write the songs for the new album, and pulled the group together to record it, he must have forgotten what he said to Midge about communication. Jagger had been living under a cloud: the accusations, public and private, that he and Keith

249

weren't able to write songs as beautiful and effective as those of Lennon and McCartney, nor as significant as Dylan's. Dylan, in fact, had remarked to Keith: "I could have written 'Satisfaction' but you cats could never have written 'Tambourine Man.'" Jagger seemed hurt by that, and as they were writing they started to feel even more pressure, "artistic" pressure, Keith later said. *Sergeant Pepper* was released in April, and it stunned the industry; it wasn't simply a collection of songs but a "concept" that many called art, and that the hipsters knew was druggy music, music drenched in drugs, created by men tripping for an audience that was drenched in drugs. And Jagger told a writer: "The music that's being done now—not only *Pepper's*—has been influenced by drugs, LSD, pot. That's damned obvious. A lot of freaky people are playing a lot of freaky music without LSD, but the drug has had an influence on the music. Take 'A Day in the Life': nothing in there is specifically about drugs, yet it's all about drugs."

Jagger had always seemed to be competing with the Beatles, those Liverpudlians who had taken over *his* town, London; through the years he was always good for a gratuitous remark criticizing the Beatles' style, their music, their MBEs from the Queen. Well . . . if the Beatles can get away with art, with freaky music . . . then sure as hell the Stones can. What they began laying down in the studio was a strange sort of music for the Stones: psychedelic music, arty and artificial music; Jagger's attempt at exploration and experimentation, for which he and the Stones lacked the talent, and lacked a George Martin as producer to make it work. Jagger insisted that this album was a reflection of the times, the age of psychedelia, of chemical mind-expanders, "of flowers and beads and stars on yer face," as he told one interviewer. Marianne never told him she thought the album was being made to force Brian out of the group, nor did any of them seem aware that the age of psychedelia was destroying Brian.

Jagger had told Midge McKenzie that he'd been reading a lot of poetry. "It's all rubbish when it's written, but I just got loads and loads of poetry books and go through them at random. They give me great ideas, sort of new ideas of saying things," he said. "You obviously have to learn from other people, you can't completely come up with things all the time. I like Shelley very much, that kind of poetry. Not only that kind, but that style, very romantic . . . very weird dreams he had, which are more like acid dreams . . . like Chaucer, bawdy, direct, nothing flowery about him." He had begun to read enormous amounts of poetry since living with Marianne, including the Tao classic, *The Secret of the Golden Flower.* He was reading Allen Ginsberg and all the New York and San Francisco poets, America's Beat poets; Kenneth Anger was running around turning everyone on to Aleister Crowley; and the so-called San Francisco sound of the Jefferson Airplane—cool music and songs that told you, between the lines, of chemical journeys—seemed about to turn rock into art. And Jagger, obviously aware of all the energy swirling around him seems to have attempted to produce "art" in the new album. He couldn't be expected to understand that every artist has a secret—passion—even though that was the secret of Jagger's enormous talent as a performer. But as an artist—a writer—Jagger shows no understanding that art refines truth, that the artist must passionately refine truth out of his own life, out of his passion, out of his ability to die, in a way, and make himself born again—and to do it with such clarity that his truth has never before been quite that visible.

Their Satanic Majesties Request—the title was changed at the insistence of Decca, which was not about to help the Stones insult the Queen—is the most dreadful collection of songs the band had ever released; Jagger, reaching for artistic creation, turned his back on his roots and fell on his face. The Stones had been masters at recreating the old material on which rock and R & B is based; they were able to actually

251

improve on the originals, modernizing as they interpreted. They had always understood that the raunch sexuality of rock, the ballsiness of the beat, with all the emotions it evokes and sensations it arouses, makes palpable youth's yearning for freedom, makes them feel they are breaking free of the restrictions of authority. *Satanic Majesties* comes on as art, and it fails because it's a dehydration and castration of rock's ballsiness. Keith quickly realized how much this album had cut the band off from its roots and tried to explain how they'd fallen into the trap of psychedelia:

"People would say, 'What you playin' that old shit for?' Which really screwed me up because that's all I can play. So we heard what the people were saying and we sort of laid back and listened to what they were doin' in 'Frisco. And we were diggin' what we were hearin' for what it was. But that other thing in you is saying, 'Yeah, but where's Chuck Berry? What's he doing?' So we laid down the album, and it doesn't connect back. It's got to follow through, it's got to connect."

Jagger sits in the office of Les Perrin, the Stones publicist, talking about the group's plans and promoting *Satanic Majesties*. And talking about Brian. Brian had been convicted of possession of cannabis a few months before, in October 1967, after pleading guilty before Inner London Sessions chairman Reginald Ethelbert Seaton. He had been held overnight in Wormwood Scrubs and then freed on bail, pending appeal, after the judge sentenced him to nine months. In November, Brian's sentence was set aside by the Court of Appeals, partly on medical advice. The court substituted a £1,000 fine, three years probation, and the requirement that Brian place himself in the care of a physician appointed by the court. And now, during Christmas week, Jagger talks to several writers about his plans for an enormous world tour.

"There's a tour coming up, there are obvious difficulties, one of them is with Brian, who can't leave the country. But there is a tour of South America, filming for the Rolling Stones in the jungles and lostnesses of South America, the ancient tombs of the very well-known tribes of Indians, things like that . . . gonna get a film done of this tour by somebody very groovy, I mean someone along the power of Godard but only different. A film of the whole tour, so we're gonna go into the jungle and live with some Indians . . . which is a gas. We're gonna fly into the jungle with the Brazilian Air Force, they're gonna sort of parachute us into the jungle, and we're going to live with the Indians for as long as we can stand it, then they're gonna pick us up . . .

"From South America we go to North America . . . this is all sort of bullshit hypothetical, we haven't signed the contracts . . . in other words, we haven't got the bread. But Madison Square Garden and then ten dates, ending up in Los Angeles. From there to Honolulu, and from there into the midst of unsolved Asia, to the yellow men of Japan, the inscrutable Oriental . . . all the time being filmed, of course. We do a few shows in Tokyo, eat a lot of Japanese food, screw a lot of Japanese chicks, all being filmed of course. Except Brian, again, can't get into Tokyo because he's a druggy . . ."

Jagger never did live out that particular fantasy, because of Brian's drug problems. Two days after his prison sentence was lifted by the court, Brian collapsed in his London flat. A friend called the police, and Brian was rushed by ambulance to St. George's hospital. He walked out within an hour. His doctor told reporters there was no cause for alarm, Brian was simply suffering from overwork and strain. Those around Brian knew better: The night he collapsed he had gone to an underground club with Mariella Novotny, a super-groupie to rock stars and movie actors who had been deported from America after conviction as a member of a high-class call-girl ring. Brian had climbed on the stage to play with the resident rock group at the club. He was flying out of his skull, on acid and coke, and he started to play the string bass. With his boots. Jumping on it and kicking it, until it splintered. Brian never noticed. He plucked at the air where the bass once stood, fingering strings that only he could see and hearing music that no one else heard. Everyone cheered; Brian was "doing his thing," and it was urgently vital for everyone to do their thing, even if it is psychotic. He passed out and was hospitalized several hours later.

Around the Rolling Stones office, the employees were very concerned about Brian. Especially after one of them read the manuscript of a book by two French handwriting experts who had analyzed the script of famous personalities without knowing their identities. The analysis of Brian's handwriting was frightening. The employee who read it told the others in the office: "Brian better be careful. They say he's going to have one year in his life, a year coming up very soon, in which he'll go through an enormous crisis. He'll be so heavily into drugs that either he will die during that year, or he'll get it together —but it'll take a lot of effort for Brian to pull through it, and the graphologists say Brian doesn't have the strength to make it, the chances are he's not going to make it."

Something appeared to be driving Brian to live up to the life—the contrived image of the life—of a Rolling Stone. What Jagger and Keith wrote about, Brian did, out in public. He was destroying himself, almost deliberately. He was even into heroin now, Marianne knew, although she didn't think he was cooking it yet . . . but she thought of Charlie Parker, and Billie Holliday, two of Brian's idols, and she knew he was as self-destructive as they had been. It was almost as if he wanted to die their deaths.

Jagger wasn't seeing too much of Brian now. Brian had cut himself off from so many, had alienated them by becoming a pain in the ass, a whiner always looking for sympathy. Besides, Jagger and Marianne were busy getting their new house together, a Georgian town house in Cheyne Walk, on the banks of the Thames, that Jagger had just bought. It was a very wealthy neighborhood, supertax country, and a curious meeting ground of old and new money and old and new aristocracy. London's young and rich stockbrokers, property developers, doctors with private patients, pop stars, pulp writers, and peers lived in Cheyne Walk. Jagger needs a physically attractive, even enchanting world, and the house in Cheyne Walk was meant to fill that need. Marianne understood that her role—her assignment, almost—was to turn the house into a world of enchantment for him. Christopher Gibbs was hired to decorate it, but Marianne was the supervisor—shopping day after day, selecting the huge old bed, high and soft and dripping with history, that they'd sleep in, for antiques and tapestries and Oriental rugs that Jagger loved and with which he filled up the drawing room, the dining room, all the major rooms of the house, including the nursery for Marianne's son, Nicholas.

Marianne sometimes became embarrassed by the way he would flaunt her upper-class background, his proper English lady who was now the mistress of his enchanted town house. She would often find herself thinking: *It's like he's saying, "Look what I've got. A baroness."* She had found, in a very exclusive antique shop in Mayfair, an enormous seventeenth-century chandelier of uncut crystal. She bought it for the drawing room, paying $15,000. When it was hung, Jagger would point it out to friends and exclaim: "My God, six thousand quid for a fuckin' light . . . ain't it marvelous?" And Marianne, although embarrassed, could smile because she sensed how thrilled he was that she could spend a fortune for a chandelier, and yet before her he had never known a thing about antiquities of any kind.

He was still just a young boy, she felt. Although he was twenty-four and a millionaire, one of the world's most famous personalities, Marianne felt he was still a child in many ways, full of high youthful spirits, a boy who was fun to be with, who was witty and alive and always laughing and larking about. She thought: *It's so marvelous, he takes such great pleasure in being young and famous and rich.* The house, and their life together, was like an island that Jagger wanted to keep as private as possible, almost as if he were trying to build battlements against the intrusion of fame. She thought about it often, lying in bed late in the morning while Jagger played with Nicholas in the garden: *He likes his house and he likes to have it to himself, just him and me and Nicholas, and the cats. He doesn't give dinner parties, we don't entertain too often, because he's afraid he'll appear to be showing off. Except for that silly chandelier, he really hates to show off.*

Marianne didn't mind the seclusion, around the house, for they went out almost every night, making the London scene: the Ad Lib, the Speakeasy, all those little discos and private clubs that the fashionable people of the pop world and the young aristocrats made sparkle with their presence. And, later, they'd all end up in someone's house to put on a buzz with coke and hash, or to drop acid. Marianne didn't object to the way Jagger used Cheyne Walk as an escape because she understood, as Chrissie had before her, that it was absolutely necessary to him: *He genuinely wants a quiet life because he packs so much into his public life.*

And yet, Jagger was so restless, he was still so full of that energy that made it impossible for him to sit still for very long, that he could never stay in one place for too great a period of time. They'd wake late, some mornings, have breakfast brought to them in bed, and Jagger would suddenly leap up and announce: "We're goin' down to Keith's for a while." They'd pack a few things and drive down to Redlands, with Nicholas, and spend the night there with Keith and Anita. By the following morning Jagger had the itch to move again, and they'd dash over to stay with Charlie and Shirley in their 700-year-old house in Sussex, or visit some other friend. A few days later, they'd return to Cheyne Walk. And Marianne would smile at his restlessness because she knew the reason for it. She thought: *The only time he's ever really satisfied is when he's working, when he's on stage or in the studio. That's when he gets the most excitement and the most satisfaction out of his life. Those other periods, when he's not working, those are the down periods. That's when he must have things quiet so he can charge up for the next high, and it's also when the restlessness comes because he can't wait for the next high.* He appeared to genuinely enjoy the domesticity of their life, and Marianne felt it helped him become less flashy in his private personality. *Our relationship is doing something marvelous to us,* she thought after living in Cheyne Walk for several months. *It has taken away all the bullshit poses between us, making us real people together.*

His need to be constantly on the move led him to buy an Elizabethan manor called Stargroves, outside Newbury, forty green acres bounded by wooded hills on all sides. Oliver Cromwell had stayed in Stargroves after the second battle of Newbury in 1644, and immediatley after buying the manor Jagger set in motion a renovation program to repair the decay of centuries and restore it to its original condition. "It's gonna take two years to do the job, and it'll cost me a bundle, but I want Stargroves to look the way Cromwell saw it," Jagger told Marianne as he discussed his plans for rebuilding Stargroves. Marianne smiled. "If old Cromwell's ghost is floating around here," she said, "he's going to giggle at the idea of you, the enemy of English society, that drug and sex fiend named Jagger, being responsible for the preservation of his old mansion."

Jagger's exuberance was infectious, and Marianne was swept up by it. But there were some annoyances, even in the very beginning. Jagger insisted that the Cheyne Walk house be spotless, that Marianne run the house properly, supervising the help in all the procedures necessary to keep a large house from overwhelming its occupants. Marianne felt he expected her to be a proper English lady, demanded that she have that special grace that aristocratic Englishwomen have, always capable of dealing with the help and tradesmen, and with guests. And she sometimes became annoyed, and thought: *That's a very bourgeois aspect of him that his fans don't ever see. His fans don't know that he wants his wife or his woman—"Me old lady" he calls me, and he really digs the posh English accent on his old lady—they don't know he wants me to always be there, faithful to him and his needs. The public just see his wildness. They don't see this very bourgeois part of him.*

She didn't mind it, usually. Jagger was very good to her, and he seemed to adore Nicholas, to love the idea of being a father with a two-year-old son. And Jagger could never stop telling her how much he loved her. He had asked her to marry him, when they started living together, but she had refused. "I'm too frightened of such a binding relationship after my marriage to John turned into such a disaster," she told Jagger. "I was too young when I got married and I'm still frightened of it all." But he kept after her, asked her to divorce John and marry him. She refused. He constantly told her how much he loved her, saying it so often that it was becoming embarrassing for her. Marianne confided to a friend: "When somebody keeps saying over and over again, 'I love you,' the only thing you can do is say, 'I love you, too.' I defy any woman to say to someone at her feet, 'Don't do that.' Though it's awful in a way, it's marvelous too. But it is getting to be a bit much."

Marianne had a strange affinity with Keith. They had been lovers, briefly, for a short period before she and Jagger began living together, and Keith reminded her very strongly of the minstrel boy, dressed in velvets and sitting in the window of a castle, fingering his mandolin, who had played a vivid role in her dreams when she was a child. Recently, Keith had started to wear makeup, kohl to heighten the eyes, sometimes even a trace of lipstick. He never looked campy with makeup; the

258

feminine touch paradoxically made him seem even more masculine; the makeup intensified the unmistakable grace and elegance that Keith possessed. Marianne loved the look, so much so that she suggested Jagger also wear makeup. She applied the kohl, the first time, and when she was done she felt he looked a bit faggy—that he couldn't quite carry it off the way Keith did, which didn't surprise her because she didn't know any other man who could—but Jagger was wild about the sensual feel and look of the makeup, Marianne thought. He began using it whenever they went out. Jagger had been very meticulous in his dress, since giving up the blue jeans and workshirt poorboy look a couple of years before; he would carefully select and change his outfits several times a day. And it flashed on Marianne now: *He has to live up to Keith, he has to look as good as Keith; if not better.* She thought it charming, the clothing and the makeup: Jagger continuing to break down walls, to give the finger to straight English society. But it was also annoying because he insisted that she dress up in the evening, even if no one was coming over—*and no one ever does.* He insisted that they sit to supper dressed in the latest underground and pop world fashions. And as they ate, alone, Marianne thought:

He's trying to live up to Keith and he wants me to live up to Anita. She always excels herself in her dress when we go out together, and Mick wants me to compete with her. Anita's probably not like Mick demands I be, certainly not at home. She probably wears jeans around the house. I'll be damned if I'm going to tart myself up all the time.

But she did follow Jagger's wishes, unable to argue with him about them; she dressed as he demanded, took care of the house and supervised the servants, played the proper English lady. She thought it all a joke, and she wished Jagger could see how foolish it was. But she understood certain things about his personality: *Mick doesn't understand that it's a joke because he never looks honestly at things he doesn't want to see.*

If there's a bill to pay and he doesn't want to pay it he won't, and he's like that with everything. He sidesteps things that are unpleasant, even the most minor things.

That is a typical Leo trait, she knew, but there was something else behind it all, she realized one day when she stopped to think about it: *Mick thinks of himself first. Not always, a lot of times he doesn't. But, basically, Mick's selfish. Maybe not selfish, exactly, but just self-centered. That's understandable, certainly, because of all the attention he gets and can command, the pop star. He'd have to be a saint not to be self-centered under these conditions, he'd have to be working against it and wearing hairshirts. And only a saint can do that.*

The LSE, which Jagger had attended for two years before leaving to become a full-time Stone, had long been the center of student radicalism in England—little knots of young men and women from the middle and upper classes, supported by their parents or government grants, arguing over the best route toward the destruction and rebuilding of the economic system that had given them special privileges: Marx? Lenin? Trotsky? Castro? Jagger had seldom taken part in these revolutionary daydream/discussions, and he never really talked seriously about the defects in capitalistic society, the class system, politics and political philosophy, until the role of "spokesman" was thrust upon him by his fans and by the adults who hated and feared him. The fans quite seriously believed that the Stones, the Beatles, and Dylan were spearheading a movement that would revolutionize all those elements of society that were abhorrent to the young. The adults just as seriously felt that Jagger was leading the country, the entire Western world, into anarchy and purgatory. Now, after his three nights in a prison cell, Jagger began to talk about certain changes that he said he believed must take place in society before man could get beyond the illusion of freedom and become really and totally free.

He'd been bitter, at first, about the way he'd been treated by English justice: "They've made me a target for their hang-ups," he said. "I don't know why people like to take it out on other people so much. They're really hung up on revenge, you know that? You get hung-up people of all kinds—hung-up coppers, hung-up garagemen, hung-up magistrates. They really *have* to take it out on someone. It's not just the jealousy, sexual or financial or whatever, of the ordinary so-called re-spectable person—they have all these *fantasies*, these mad bogeys, and they fix them onto me. It's like bein' a voodoo doll for a whole fuckin' society, everyone sticking pins in. Happy so long as someone gets hurt, anyone."

But Jagger isn't the moron that the newspapers—and his own publicity machine—made the British believe he was. He's intelligent and perceptive about the society around him, and he began to talk to Marianne about his own prison experience, about the kids being hassled and arrested by police—not only for drugs, but for anything that could be pinned on them so long as they wore their hair long and dressed un-conventionally. Marianne said he started to think about poli-tics, the one force in society that could bring change and that was stifling every attempt at change.

In an interview with Jack Bentley, of the *Sunday Mirror,* the discussion turned from religion—"It seems to me that the majority of believers have belief without understanding," Jagger said—to politics. And Jagger told Bentley:

"The Commandments say, 'Thou shalt not kill,' and half the world is in training to annihilate the other half. Nobody would get me in uniform and off to Aden to kill a lot of people I've never met and have nothing against anyway.

"I know people say they're against wars and yet they go on fighting them. Millions of marvelous young men are killed, and in five minutes everybody seems to have forgotten all about it. War stems from power-mad politicians and patriots . . . Politicians? What a dead loss they are . . . There shouldn't be any Prime Minister at all.

"Anarchy is the only slight glimmer of hope. Not the popular conception of it—men in black cloaks lurking around with hidden bombs, but a freedom of every man being personally responsible for himself.

"There should be no such thing as private property. Anybody should be able to go where he likes and do what he likes. Politics, like the legal system, is dominated by old men. Old men who are also bugged by religion. And the law—the law's outdated and doesn't cater enough for individual cases."

Then came Paris, in May 1968: Young French students, Jagger's contemporaries, in their second-hand Army fatigues, overturning cars on the Boulevard St. Germain, battling the gendarmes, storming the barricades—almost like the French Revolution all over again, Jagger said—but this time the kids were lashing out at the technocratic society threatening to overwhelm them. And the year before, the American riots, the burning of the ghettoes in Watts, Detroit, Newark, all the ghettoes of the world seemed about to be set to the torch in sympathy with the American burnings. And in April, the month before Paris, fresh riots in America after the assassination of Martin Luther King. Jagger talked to Marianne, and anyone who would listen, about the riots, the changing political climate throughout the world. Marianne felt he had started from a Democratic Socialist base but had quickly become very anarchist. He said he was so totally excited by the riots. By the "Burn, baby, burn" shouts of the blacks in America. She thought: *He's so very anarchistic now, he feels the system is rotten and should be torn down.*

He talked to Marianne on a very wild level about his concept of revolution, reflecting the slogans of the period, the slogans of young revolutionaries.

"Let's drop acid in all the drinking water in the country," he once said to her. "Let's freak them all out. What we need most of all is somebody to burn down London." And he said: "Out of the ashes of America, a new America will rise. But they shouldn't burn their ghettoes, their own homes. They should go out and burn the white areas."

"I don't agree with that," Marianne said. "If you lived in the damnation of the ghetto you'd want to burn that down first."

"Sure, sure, that's valid. But why don't they go and burn down Washington, D.C.?" Jagger said. "Burn down the cause of their misery, Washington and the white areas . . ."

Jagger appeared so very excited about the American riots, the riots in Paris. He said he was certain they were interconnected in some way, that a chain of events had been set in motion, a chain of reactions against mind-killing authority. Even in Prague, behind the so-called Iron Curtain, the kids were beginning to question the wisdom of their elders. Word was filtering out that the Russian Armies might move in because the Czechs were getting too much freedom, and Czech kids were beginning to hope they could change their society. It's all happening in conjunction, Jagger told Marianne, like some master plan that would evict all those one-dimensional mindless men from the seats of power and replace them with *real* people, people of compassion.

He wanted to get out there, help the revolution along, he said. His first opportunity came with the American Embassy demonstration, thousands of English kids marching on that modern building in Grosvenor Square, that building with the enormous bronze eagle dominating the façade, the symbol of American domination of Britain and Western Europe, of the world. They were demonstrating against Vietnam, against NATO, against the brinkmanship-weapons mentality that propelled the world's politicians into playing with a master game plan that uses the kids as pawns. Jagger marched with the kids, almost as the leader of the demonstration. Even though he had denied being responsible for his fans' lives.

It was, for the most part, a peaceful demonstration, even though some of the kids assaulted police lines and tried to break into the Embassy. Jagger's arms were linked with the arms of a young man on one side and a young woman on the other, as they marched around and around the square. The sounds of the kids banging empty pitkins,* the picket signs, flags and the bright flowing clothes some of them wore, and the thump of marching feet—almost a military sound, those thumping feet, almost a military parade—none of this seemed to have anything to do with revolution, but seemed to be, rather, a fanfare arranged in Jagger's personal honor. Jagger didn't believe he was anyone special, out here on the streets, marching to the drums of revolution, he later told Marianne. He didn't want these kids to think he was special, but they so obviously did. As did the newspapermen who took his photos and demanded interviews. It was all so depressing for him, he told her when he returned to his $125,000 house in Cheyne Walk, after the demonstration. And he said:

"What's most disappointing about it all is that none of it is really interconnected. I used to think it was all connected and that I could throw myself completely into the cause and really help connect them up. I figured to connect them would be easy, I could see people trying to connect it all—America, Paris, all of it—and they couldn't do it. So I decided to connect them. But now I realize that all these things that are sparking off would never have happened had they been contrived. It can only be this spontaneous thing that just happens to young people. I can't connect them. It wouldn't work."

He began to write a song about his discovery. He sat for hours out in the little recording studio he'd built in the garden behind the town house, strumming his guitar, working out a

* Tin containers which hold about eight pints.

melody to go with the lyric that expressed his disappointment:

*"Everywhere I hear the sound of marchin' chargin' feet, oh
boy
'Cause summer's here, and the time is right for fighting
in the street, oh boy.
But what can a poor boy do
Except to sing for a rock-and-roll band . . ."*

Perhaps revolution was out, for Jagger, but there were other possibilities for influencing his times: Establishment politics. When he and Marianne were still living in Marylebone Road, Allen Ginsberg had phoned one night and said he was coming by with a friend, a member of Parliament, Tom Driberg. A greying and very distinguished-looking Labor Party member representing Barking, in Essex, Driberg was one of two MPs who had signed an ad that appeared in the *Times* while Jagger and Keith were awaiting their appeal hearing. The ad, paid for by George Harrison and also signed by the other Beatles, Graham Greene, R. D. Laing, Kenneth Tynan, several doctors, and one minister, recommended the legalization of marijuana. It got Driberg into trouble with his constituents, as did his questions in Commons about the handcuffs Jagger had been forced to wear. But his stand on a number of issues of obvious appeal to Jagger made the pop star appear very open to the politician. They sat talking for hours that night, Driberg mostly listening to Jagger and Allen talk about their lives, their sex interests, about recordings and music and poetry.

After Jagger bought the house in Cheyne Walk he'd call Driberg occasionally, invite him over to dinner or just to talk—about politics. Jagger appeared to Driberg to be extremely interested in the workings of Parliament, of government and, like most young people Driberg had met, he was very impatient about the slow movement of government, the dreadful way government had of being years behind the people's wishes. He felt that Jagger was extraordinarily intelligent, had a quick grasp of the complexities of politics and government. During one conversation Driberg said:

"Why don't you try politics, Mick?"

Marianne was a little surprised. She felt that Driberg was perhaps pushing Jagger into politics, although Driberg was very consciously avoiding that: *I must not interfere in Mick's life; if I entice him into a political career before he is absolutely ready for it, then the complete devotion that politics requires would get in the way of Mick's current life.* They talked about it for hours, Jagger almost interviewing Driberg but seeming to shy away from asking his advice.

Jagger asked where in politics a man with anarchistic feelings would fit.

"The Labor Party, of course," Driberg said. He laughed: "Not because it's my party, but because I believe the Labor Party is the only hope of achieving something like socialism in this country."

Was Driberg saying that socialism is a saner option than pure anarchy? Jagger asked.

"Yes. And Labor is the only hope," Driberg said. "This is a very conservative country, and Labor is a very conservative party. But it has an enormous mass base in the trade unions and the organized working class. It's the only hope for England. It's not happening yet but in a few years, with the strikes, things boiling up out of labor's dissatisfaction, we will be approaching a revolutionary situation. I know that's the view of some of the Trotskyites, that it is all breaking up and loosening up. And the Labor Party is where a young man should be when it happens."

"But what are the chances of a real revolution?" Driberg recalls Jagger asking. "Not necessarily fighting in the streets, but a revolutionary change is what I mean."

"The Trotskyites may be right, it may be starting at this

moment," Driberg said. He was a little surprised he said it because he actually felt that any real change would take a hundred years or more to come about. And he thought: *One begins to share that revolutionary hope when one is in the company of someone like Mick. He's such a very dynamic person, so intent on helping to change things, that one gets carried along with him.*

He came away from his conversations with Jagger feeling that Jagger could be a large benefit to the political climate. He thought: *Mick's intelligent enough to know that pure anarchy won't work yet, not for centuries to come, and at the same time he feels that tremendously widespread disillusion with political parties, which I can sympathize with to some extent. And if Mick becomes active, becomes a militant of the Left and attaches himself to the Left Wing of the Labor Party, he will have a tremendous influence on young people because they are the most disillusioned and hostile of all.*

Jagger didn't seem able to make up his mind, Driberg felt, seemed unable to decide whether he actually wanted to become involved in politics and take a positive step toward it. Jagger had never said, during these conversations, "Do you think I ought to join the local Labor organization and stand for the local council first?" If he had, Driberg would have encouraged him. But they chatted on the fringes of it, and Jagger never came down to the central point—what does a poor boy do?

Often, after Driberg left, Jagger talked to Marianne about his hopes of changing the system he found abhorrent. He was quite explicit at first: "I'm going to enter politics." But after a few months the idea seemed almost absurd to Jagger, and Marianne thought she understood what was troubling him, and later expressed it this way:

"He was too rich. Just the fact that he had made it, that he had pulled himself out of the middle class and had fame, a house in Cheyne Walk, and a Bentley, excluded him from becoming a leader of youth. That's what he wanted to be, a leader of youth. But he felt guilty about the position and wealth he had attained. Had he stayed at LSE he might possibly have become a leader. But he thought the only way people would believe his motives were honest was if he were in the same straits as they were; that the street people wouldn't identify with him unless he were living as they were. He thought his potential constituency would snicker, 'Well, he's all right, he's laughing all the way to the bank, isn't he?' Power was very tempting to Jagger. He would have loved to have been a student radical leader because, he said, they had so much more power than someone who simply wrote and sang songs about dissatisfaction. He thought the song-writing was inferior to the protests and demonstrations."

Marianne tried to tell him that the songs had sparked so much within the radical movement. He said he knew he'd written some songs that people could identify with, but that wasn't enough. "What's the music they listen to, compared to the ideas they have at night?" Jagger said. "People just think how nice it is to listen to a Stones song after a hard day at work, but the song doesn't have much to do with the people of action, the people who're doing things." He said that even "Satisfaction," which caught the discontented mood of the young, the feeling of being fed up with authority, didn't have as much effect as he had hoped it would have. "As great as it is to make people think, it would be greater to make them move," he told Marianne. And he said he was disappointed that in Britain Dylan's "Subterranean Homesick Blues" had a larger effect on the young than "Satisfaction."

Marianne became pregnant in June 1968. "It was one of those silly accidents," she told friends. "I forgot to take my pill. But we're going to have the baby, we want the baby. Mick is out of his mind at the idea of being a father." And Jagger was telling friends: "It's real groovy, it's such a gas. Marianne says she wants a girl, but it doesn't matter to me this time out because I want at least three more. Want to have a lot of little kiddies runnin' around the house."

When the pregnancy became public knowledge a few months later, Jagger gave several interviews and said there were no plans for marriage: "Can't see it happening. We just don't believe in it." Marianne concurred when she was interviewed: "Why should we marry? We've got along fine together so far. The baby is not going to change the way we feel about each other."

The public and the press set up a clamor, of course, and Jagger decided to go on the David Frost television show and get his views across. "Getting married's really nice, as long as you don't get divorced afterward," Jagger said. "It's very important that you shouldn't get married if you think that you could get divorced. If you want to get married and you consecrate your union to God, you can't break it, not even with God. You just have to carry on. I think marriage is really groovy."

"Why did you decide against it?" Frost asked.

"Ah, well, the lady that I am with is already married, so it's a bit difficult. I could be a bigamist, I suppose."

"Yes, that would be a bad idea."

"Wouldn't be such a good idea, would it? But I don't really want to get married, particularly."

"Because you're not sure it would last?"

"No, I don't feel that I really need it. But if I were with a woman that really needed it, well, that's another matter. But I'm not with that kind of woman."

Later, Mrs. Mary Whitehouse, chairman of the British Viewers' and Listeners' Association and the head of the Clean Up Television Committee, came on to debate with Jagger. "The fact of the matter . . . is that if you're a Christian or a person with faith and you have your marriage in church, and you make that vow, when difficulties come you have this basic thing you have accepted,ʻyou find your way through the difficulties. And even if you don't get married in a church, you have this legal thing."

"Your church accepts divorce, and may even accept abortion—am I right or wrong?" Jagger said. "I can't see how you can talk about this bond which is inseparable, when the Christian Church itself accepts divorce. You really can't, you can't say that. Either you're married and you don't get divorced, and that's it, or you don't bother and you can't come along with some compromise Christian opinion on marriage."

Brian was on the witness stand once more, charged with possession of hashish, being tried on this lovely September afternoon by the same judge who had sentenced him to nine months in prison a year earlier. He had been arrested for the second time in May and insisted he'd either been framed or arrested in error. On the afternoon of May 21, 1968, four months before this trial, Les Perrin, the Stones' publicist, had received a call from a friend on one of the newspapers warning him that Brian was about to be arrested. Les immediately called Brian at his flat in Royal Avenue House, King's Road, and told him of the tip. Brian said:

"I've just come from the country. There's nothing here for them to find."

"Brian, this is serious," Les insisted. "It's real. If you have anything there at all get rid of it."

"I swear there's nothing here for them to find," Brian said.

A short time later Detective Sergeant Robin Constable and two other policemen, armed with a search warrant, climbed into the flat through an open window after Brian had ignored their knocks for about ten minutes. Constable was searching Brian's bedroom when another police officer shouted for him to come into the drawing room. The cop held a ball of blue wool and said he'd found "it" in a drawer. No one mentioned

270

dope, but Brian understood immediately. "Oh, no, this can't happen again, just when we're getting on our feet," he said. Asked if the wool was his, Brian said: "Why do you have to pick on me? I've been working all day and night, and now this has to happen." Brian still hadn't been shown the evidence, and the prosecutor was now trying to prove at the trial that Brian's remarks demonstrated he was *knowingly* in possession of drugs, a foreknowledge which the law requires for conviction. Actually, Brian was reacting out of street smarts: He believed strongly he was being framed by the police because he was certain he had not brought any dope into his house. Only later, at the police station, did the cops show him a chunk of hashish and charge him with possession.

Brian was using a large quantity of dope at the time—acid, speed, coke, heroin—but only in friends' flats. He would not carry it around, wouldn't have any in his house in any way, because he was certain he'd be arrested. There was ugly rumors around about the Chelsea drug squad, which had made many raids in the district and arrested pop stars and faceless, anonymous kids; street rumors that certain London cops were planting dope and extorting money from the wealthy, but if the victim was poor or had a sufficiently well-known name that could bring publicity to the arresting officer, there was no way he could buy himself out of it. The names of corrupt policemen never hit the newspapers, of course, but the kids on the street knew who they were. And Brian was not holding, although he continued to use any drug that was offered him. Between his arrest and the trial, he started using even more dope, shooting up heroin now.

Jagger and Keith had called the band into the studio to work on their next album, *Beggar's Banquet*, and Brian would arrive in the studio, always late, and either nod out in the corner or sit on a hard folding chair, his guitar in his lap, and cry into the microphone. Sometimes Jagger and Keith tried to get him to settle down, tried to get music out of him; usually he was told to go off into another room, that he was no use to the band, no use to himself. Occasionally, when he came in feeling fine and ready to play, he would still be ordered into the next room. An American musician, brought in to help flesh out the Stones sound, to fill some of the void left by Brian's inability to play, saw Brian curled up in the corner one night, his guitar over him, crying softly. The other Stones were ignoring him. And the musician thought: *I don't know what their scenes are, what the relationships are between these cats, but it sure ain't pretty.*

Marianne was in the studio several nights and she felt dreadful about Brian's condition. She thought: *I'm sick of this whole thing that Mick is doing to Brian. He doesn't see, he doesn't understand, that Brian desperately needs help. Mick is still back a couple of years ago, competing with Brian for leadership of the group, and he doesn't realize that Brian needs someone to bolster him, to support his crumbling foundations. They're all too busy to see what's happening to Brian. That he's dying of neglect.*

Marianne knew that an important part of Brian's race toward self-destruction was his feeling that he'd been frozen out of all efforts at writing songs for the band. Jagger and Keith both insisted that he never came to them with songs, never asked if he could write with them, that "he's so up-tight" as Keith put it that he never really let them know he wanted some of his songs recorded. But Marianne knew it was somewhat more complex than that. After *Beggar's Banquet* was completed, Bill Wyman described the subtle way he'd also been frozen out. He'd felt it was impossible to write for the Stones because of the tight relationship between Jagger, Keith, and Andrew and their publishing companies. After Andrew had been dropped and Jagger and Keith produced *Satanic Majesties* themselves, things opened up a bit—but just a bit. Bill said:

"When we were doing *Satanic Majesties* I had this song and

I played it for Keith, and he said it was great, so we used it. There was another one I wrote as well, which we did a backing track for, but never finished, so we just released that other track. The next time we went to record, it was six months later and we were starting a new album. Mick was ringing me up before we did *Beggar's Banquet,* asking if I had any more songs, and I said I had a couple. He said, 'I spoke to Brian, and he's got one as well.' So I thought, that's great, they're giving us the opportunity, it isn't like a closed shop any more. So we got them ready, Brian had his and I had mine. Then you come into the studio the first night and Keith says, 'I've got a song,' so all right, let's do it. And then Mick's got one. The next day they've got two more. The day after that each has another one ready. You go on like that, still waiting to record yours when they run out. But, ah, they don't run out. Before you looked around, there was an album done. So it really was a closed shop again."

Bill didn't seem terribly upset as he talked about it, but Brian was weaker. He grew depressed by it—the closed shop, the little room in which they forced him to play, alone—and he either never bothered showing up when a studio session was called or he'd arrive completely wiped out from drugs. Brian had barely played any music at all for *Satanic Majesties,* and this album, *Beggar's Banquet,* doesn't have a note by Brian; Keith overdubbed three other guitars and also brought in Nicky Hopkins on piano and several other musicians to fill in for Brian.

Brian is on the stand now, answering a question about the hashish that police claimed they found in the ball of wool. "I never had a ball of wool in my life," he swore. "I don't darn socks. I don't have a girl friend who darns socks." And he adds that he doesn't have the faintest idea where the hash came from. The defense brings out, under questioning of Detective Sergeant Constable, that Brian had been in the flat only eighteen days—he was using it until the new home he had just

273

bought, Cotchford Farm, was renovated. The previous occupant, Constable testified, was Joanna Pettet, the actress; she had told police the wool might have been hers, but she had no knowledge of the cannabis resin found inside it.

Just before the judge's charge to the jury, Jagger and Keith walked into the public gallery. They walked casually toward the front, toward the group of fluttering schoolgirls who'd been watching every moment of the trial, and sat down among them. Judge Seaton charged the jury: The case against Brian is completely circumstantial, there is no evidence that Brian was using the hash that had been found in his flat; and the judge seemed to agree with the defense contention that Brian had had enough time to dispose of the dope, flush it down the toilet, perhaps, in the ten minutes before police got inside. It sounded so very close to a directed verdict of acquittal that Brian permitted himself a smile for the first time all day, and Jagger larked it up a bit for the gallery while the jury deliberated. No one seemed worried about the verdict. The jury returned after forty-five minutes. "We have reached a verdict, your Honor," the foreman said. "We find the defendant guilty."

Jagger, Keith, the schoolgirls, all actually gasped; they couldn't help themselves because the verdict was a total surprise. Suki Potier, Brian's girl friend—her once-long blonde hair cut short so that she, too, almost looked like Brian—Suki cried loudly. Brian slumped to the seat in the dock, hiding his face in his hands. And his chauffeur remarked:

"The one time in his life Brian tells the truth, the poor bastard gets done for it."

Chairman Seaton wasn't about to commit the excesses of Judge Block in his sentencing of Jagger and Keith; Seaton told Brian: "Mr. Jones, you have been found guilty. I am going to treat you as I would any other young man before this court"—a quick look passed between Jagger and Keith: Was the judge saying he could ignore the fact that Brian was one of those filthy Rolling Stones?—and Seaton went on: "I am going to fine you according to your means. Fifty pounds, and one hundred guineas court costs. You will have one week to get up the money. Your probation will not be changed. But you really must watch your step and keep clear of the stuff."

As everyone rushed outside, to be on the steps to congratulate Brian, reporters talked about how clearly contemptuous of the jury's verdict Judge Seaton had been. "He practically called them assholes," one journalist remarked. Brian strolled out with Suki on his arm, helped her into his chauffeured Rolls, and was quickly driven away. Jagger and Keith climbed into the back seat of Keith's Bentley, enormously pleased that Brian got off, anxious to get back to the studio to complete the mixing on the new album. "We're very happy that Brian did not have to go to jail," Jagger told reporters. And meant it.

Privately, Keith was worried about Brian. "They really roughed him up, man," he said. "Brian isn't a cat that can stand that kind of shit, and they're really going for him like when hound dogs smell blood. 'There's one that'll break if we keep on.' And they'll keep busting him and busting him. Like they did to Lenny Bruce, the same tactics, break him down. Maybe with Mick and me they feel, well, 'they're just old lads.' Especially after that butterfly on the wheel story. But Brian is different, they know he'll break."

The doctors said there were some complications with Marianne's pregnancy. She needed a complete rest, preferably away from the excitement and temptations of the London scene. Jagger rented a mansion near Galway, Ireland, at $260 a week. He was anxious to get away, not only for Marianne's health, for their baby, but because he had to get out of London to prepare himself for a film. Donald Cammell, an old friend, had persuaded Jagger to play a reclusive rock star in a film to be called *Performance*, had persuaded James Fox to play a gangster on the run, and had induced Warner Bros. to put up the money. The money men at Warner's had read the script rather carelessly and had assumed that it would be some kind of rock film starring Mick Jagger, rock superstar, perhaps a more adult version of one of the Beatles films. Cammell had some other ideas, however.

So did Jagger. He had been hired to be Mick Jagger, Donald had said, not to *act* but to be Jagger. But when he read the script he realized that Turner, the musician he would play, bore no relationship to Mick Jagger. He worried about Turner, uncertain how to handle the role. Then, suddenly, it fell into place: Marianne told him: "This character must be a combination of Brian and Keith. Mix up and combine Brian with all his torturedness, all his paranoia and his coked-up movements, and Keith with his torturedness but his *cool,* and put them together to make this character. You simply can't play yourself because that'll be a disaster."

They worked on the character together, putting together bits and pieces from Brian and Keith. Marianne was an actress; she had important roles in two films—although both were disasters, and she later regretted doing them—she'd played in *The Three Sisters* at the Royal Court and had played Ophelia. And she taught Jagger how to move, how to feel the character he was going to become: Brian, primarily, self-destructive and paranoid Brian, into junk, appearing almost anxious to die.

They had been shooting for several days before Jagger arrived on the set for his first morning as a film actor. Donald Cammell had wanted to rehearse thoroughly in the house in Lowndes Square that he had rented to be used as Jagger's seedy mansion, but Jagger was away in Ireland with Marianne. The opening scenes were shot without him. It didn't matter very much because Donald wasn't at all certain where the film would be headed, once they got into it. He knew his script would have to be rewritten because he was more interested in forcing Jagger, as rock star, and Jimmy Fox, as gangster, into confrontations that each would face as if they were actually being lived out, and evolving a film from their natural reactions. Donald and his co-director, Nick Roeg, were shooting the film in continuity, to build the story line directly out of the conflict between Jagger and Jimmy.

The morning Jagger arrived and word swept through the sixty-five actors and technicians working in the house—"Jagger is here"—an adverse reaction that had already set in among the grips, sparks, and other mechanics of the production began to be voiced. As one of them said, over and over again: "Fuck him. Who the devil does this Mickey Jagger think he is? He's not an actor, he doesn't known a damn about movies." Mike Malloy, head cameraman on the film and the liaison between the creative staff and the technicians, was certain there would be trouble. Then Jagger came in, quiet and almost humble: the way he carried himself he seemed to Malloy to be saying that he had never acted before, didn't even know whether it was necessary to act, and that he was there to learn. He listened closely as Donald and Nick told him how they conceived his opening scene—the rock star at his musical instruments behind a screen telling the gangster there is no room for him in this house—and Jagger rehearsed it for a while with Jimmy, working very hard at it. The scene was shot a half-dozen times—none of the bad takes was Jagger's fault—and Jagger never balked at repeating his lines, his movements, never complained about the monotony of film work. And the technicians began to grow respectful of him from that first day.

He won them, finally, with his complete professionalism. He always knew his lines, always seemed to know what was expected of him, and he never became a prima donna. The talk about this bloody pop star pretending to be a film actor ended in the first week. Mike Malloy instructed one of the grips to hammer "termites"—small battens of wood—into various spots on the floor of the drawing room. Jagger saw the man at work and asked Mike: "Why's that guy hammerin' little bits of wood in the floor?" Mike explained: "Nick Roeg's getting into some very complicated shots and you're going to have a lot of moves to make. The wood's like marks so you can feel them with your toes and you won't have to look for chalk marks or anything like that." Jagger said: "I don't need those fuckin' things." Mike shrugged and ordered the grips to tear them out. Jagger went through the scene, never misstepping; he seemed to have the ability to visualize every move he must make. After that, no grip was ever heard to criticize him.

Jimmy Fox was playing a very *macho* gangster running away from hoodlums who are out to kill him. His masculinity is clearly defined from the beginning: "I feel like a *man*," he says in an early scene, "I'm normal." The line was very real for Fox. He had almost become an East End gangster for this film, totally identifying with the hoodlums of London. To prepare for the role he had cut his long hair and taken a flat in the East End, worked out in a gym three days a week, and hung around with gangsters. He began to walk like them, talk like them, think like them. He once came into the offices of David Cammell, Donald's brother, who was producer of the film, and behaved so much like a gangster that he frightened the secretaries in the office. A couple of days later David Cammell received a call from Johnny Shannon, an East Ender who'd been hired to train Fox as a gangster and was so good that he was given the role of the gangster boss in the film. Shannon said: "Listen, I don't want to speak out of turn but the boy"—Jimmy—"I'm a bit worried about the boy because I've introduced him to all the lads and he gets on well, but he's going to be in a real bother if he's not careful." And Shannon implied that Jimmy was getting so good in this gangster role that the boys might ask him to go on a heist with them.

But now, in the rock star's mansion, the film gangster becomes disoriented because sexual identities are blurred. Jagger wears makeup and flowing robes. One of the girls living in the house, a very young French girl, has short hair and very small breasts, and in one scene there is a moment when it's impossible to be certain of her gender. And the very masculine gangster must dye his hair and change his appearance so that he can get out of the country before his killers find him. His sexual identity begins to blur.

In one scene Jagger's secretary, Anita Pallenberg, holds up a mirror against Fox's body so that one of her breasts is superimposed on his chest, and she forces him to look at his own face against her body. The sexual derangement she is suggesting frightens him, and he slowly comes apart. He hallucinates, because of the drugs he's been fed. He sees the gang members in their headquarters, listening to Jagger who is dressed as the syndicate boss, dictating a memo in the form of a song that mocks their way of life. The gang respond to a suggestion in the song by stripping off their clothes and revealing the homosexuality that underlies the hoodlum's masculine bravado.

At this point, halfway through the film, Donald wasn't certain where the story line was headed. He knew only that he had to keep everyone on edge, make them feel insecure and filled with tension. For the dual identity that was beginning to develop in the film—Jimmy now assuming some of Jagger's doped-up rock star characteristics and Jagger beginning to feel like a campy gangster—was so obviously its soul. And the sparks that were flying between rock star and gangster, forced and nurtured, would bring the film to its only possible climax. But it was hard on the actors, difficult for everyone on the set.

"Nobody knows what's happening," Mike Malloy told Cammell's secretary one night after he'd been filming for twelve hours. "Donald is rewriting the script every night, depending on what happens between Mick and Jimmy in front of the cameras during the day, and what he thinks Mick is about to do next. Donald's going off on all sorts of tangents and trying to relay the tangents to the actors, and it's hard to get his thoughts across. The actors are freaking out. Mick and Jimmy.''

"Jagger's picking up on Donald's ideas," Annabelle said. "He's throwing a lot of ideas back at Donald. But it's very hard on Jimmy, he's the one who's suffering at this incredible change of identity he's being forced through. Donald's making him so uptight."

Donald was playing on Jimmy's fears and insecurities, to achieve a special kind of realism. And people on the set say that Jimmy had much insecurity at the time. He seemed to them genuinely prudish, in a hoodlum sort of way: worried about the nude scenes, the drugs, makeup, and wigs, he appeared as uncomfortable as any East End gangster would be if suddenly confronted with drugs and bisexuality. And Jimmy's father, Robin, who was his agent as well, unwittingly contributed to Jimmy's growing insecurity. Jimmy's father had begun to warn him that the film wasn't a proper vehicle for him, that he shouldn't be wearing wigs and makeup and be getting transformed into a bisexual. Robin Fox was also ill with cancer—he would die of it after the film—and Jimmy appeared extremely upset about his father's health.

All of this was communicated to Jagger, of course, and he was beginning to appear tense and insecure as the film came within two weeks of completion. But Jimmy was only one element in Jagger's own confusion. More important was Anita, who had been Brian's girl friend and now was Keith's. People on the set believed Keith was extremely concerned that Anita would get too close to Jagger, making this film with him, and were certain Jagger was aware of it. There was an element of both Brian and Keith in Jagger's film character, the two men who had so strongly attracted Anita. Marianne, who visited the set once and who knew there had been a scene in which Jagger makes love to both Anita and the young French girl and actually fucked them—the scene was cut from the final version of the film—later said: "I didn't say anything about Mick fucking Anita at the time of the film because I knew the only way for it to work was for him to really appeal to her. He was Brian and Keith in one, and that's the only time he hit with her. Because he was a combination of the two men she cared about."

When the film ended, after fourteen weeks of shooting—the two men, evil gangster and bisexual pop star, having merged into one—Mike Malloy told Donald: "This is going to be one of the all-time greats." But Warner Bros. didn't see it that way and refused to release *Performance* because it was felt to be too sordid. Donald and Nick flew out to Hollywood but couldn't get to see anyone at Warner's. Rumors flew around that the president of the company had either ordered the film burned, or had personally buried it in a big hole in a lot on Sunset Boulevard. The film would not be released for two years.

Marianne spent much of her time in Ireland with Nicholas, several pets, and two servants while Jagger was working on the film. The child forming inside her—already completely formed, perhaps, with her fate sealed by her genes . . . it would be a girl, Marianne was certain of that, and they would call her Carena—the child was becoming a weight, physically, and on her moods. Marianne was snorting coke regularly now, an attempt to lift her from the abyss. She thought of it that way: She was facing an abyss into which she might soon plunge. And she tried to understand why she felt so morbid. Jagger? Yes, definitely. She thought about it and then tried to phrase it, to get it out into the open because she could never discuss with Jagger any of her real fears and problems. She thought: *In England you can't talk about your personal life, even with your lover. That just isn't done. You don't mention the unpleasant, it simply isn't mentioned. Mick doesn't like to be faced by the unpleasant. Great taboos everywhere.* And then she thought: *Oh, stop it, Marianne. You're just as much to blame as Mick. You hold things back, repress them, you won't talk about them.*

Marianne later said: "I've always tried to keep separate images of my real self and my professional self, keep them in separate compartments. But Mick wasn't able to separate his image from himself, and he put it on me, too. It's not so much that I was confused about who I was, what's real and what isn't, because I wasn't. But Mick was becoming confused about my image and myself. When I was with John I was able to keep my work identity separate from my own real identity. With Mick I couldn't do that, and it was becoming such a strain. That's part of the reason I started using coke, and Mick's conception of his image was making that a bad scene, too. When you are on cocaine and the person you are with isn't on it, there's a barrier between you because you act wild and he's acting sort of virtuous. And it pissed me off, when Mick did that. It's all wrapped up in his image, he says he has an excessive power and emotion and if he takes coke or something like that it makes it too much for him to bear. But mostly he doesn't like it because he thinks it spoils his skin and his good figure. He's very conscious of his physique, being well-made and beautiful."

She recalled the time she asked him why he had started to wear tightly-cut white pants on stage, and Jagger had said: "It makes me look like I have a perpetual hard-on. That's what the little kids want, and that's what I'm givin' them."

"His damn image," she later said. "The way the whole bust at Redlands turned out was part of his not being able to separate his image from his real self. I can see that now. Taking the rap for me was a noble gesture but he didn't think he would get three months. If he had been in Brixton for three months that would have taken the nobleness too far. But as it worked out he could be noble. I know it started out that he really did want to protect me, but he could be noble and suffer and be martyred and have marvelous photos taken of him handcuffed. He got the full exposure out of it that he always likes to get, and I didn't think he knew any longer where his image ended and the real Mick Jagger began.''

While in Ireland exploring her feelings about Jagger, she thought:

There's a bit of self-destructiveness in me. As in Brian. That's why I can identify with Brian, much more than Mick can, because I know what it's like to be self-destructive. That's why I'm using coke . . . but also to dull the pain. Mick always seems to be saying I should be good, but I don't want to be good. Yet I can see how childish it is, not wanting to be good. That's also a bit of the Rolling Stones rubbing off on me, their image. Mick has drawn me into it very heavily . . . actually, I let myself be drawn into it. At first I didn't mind, but now it's becoming painful.

Living with Mick has eaten up my own apartness. He's tried to copy me. I am an actress. I managed to force myself to become an actress, and I can't do something without Mick doing it, so he had to do Performance. *He's trying to become me, in a way, so that I will merge with him and not be someone apart. He's doing that to me . . . stealing my apartness.*

Marianne was trying to define the reason for her depression over the past few weeks, after the surge of joy she'd felt at becoming pregnant and deciding to have Jagger's baby. She still found life with Jagger enormously exciting, but something was missing.

"It was exciting, with Mick," she later said, "but more mentally because it became a very non-sexual relationship. And since we didn't want to break it up we had to cast about for other things to take the place of the very passionate sexual thing we had in the beginning. The sexual thing had to be sublimated to something else. For Mick, it was his work, he was doing his best work in this period, those were his most productive years.

"And besides his work, he had all his other aesthetic pursuits with me. Which was very nice and very important to him and his music; he got turned on by his aesthetic things with me and would then work in the studio till eight in the morning. The things he got into, they were great. I mean, there are no other girls who can say . . ." She smiled, then threw her head back so that her blonde hair flew out behind her, and laughed. "On the nights he was at home he would be reading M. R. James and say, 'You must listen to this story' and he'd read me a ghost story in bed. We'd be in that very lovely old bed together, I'd be reading and he'd be reading. It was very much that kind of thing, you know, we didn't leap into bed to make love, it became that very nice intimacy you get when you've been married a long time and you know your partner doesn't expect much of you and neither of you is too demanding. That was very nice, I liked that very much, the camaraderie, the easy-understanding thing.

"But there were long periods of boredom, or I wouldn't have begun taking drugs as I did. You take an awful lot of cocaine in your life if life isn't very satisfactory; or if it is too satisfactory. There has been a dissatisfaction in my life that has to be filled somehow, and it's being filled with coke. A relationship doesn't ever work if a woman is not satisfied. Especially if you are secretive about it, as we are. We never talked about it. I was pretending everything was all right, and to some degree the strain of the pretense got me into coke.

"Mick can stay out in his studio in the garden until six or eight in the morning; he has his friends, the other musicians. He was working very hard and very productively with Keith, but I'd be in the house alone, or with Anita. Both of us very bored. For Mick, the wish to work was very strong, he was learning to play the guitar—Eric was helping him learn—and he was getting better at it. What we created together is a situation where he could get totally immersed in his work, and the things that he needed were so secure that he didn't have to look around to see if they were still there. But people can get too sure of themselves. I made his life damn cushy and very comfortable. Too cushy and comfortable. But that's what I wanted to do."

Marianne suffered a miscarriage weeks after *Performance* was completed. She had been warned in her sixth month that she might have difficulty holding the baby to term, and she took to her bed, criticizing herself for not caring for herself properly after Nicholas was born: She'd returned to touring as quickly as she could, Marianne the pop star, riding trains and sleeping in a different hotel room every night, terrified to get out before the audience, not sleeping or eating properly. She was going to be as cautious as possible now that she'd been warned: no more drugs, no more alcohol, staying away from the disco scene. Desperately wanting Jagger's baby.

She lost it a month later, and it devastated her. Jagger tried to help pull her out of her depression. She found him to be the perfect deeply-concerned lover: He dropped everything he was doing, promotion for the new album which had just been completed, his plans for an entertainment extravaganza for BBC television, to be called the Rolling Stones Rock & Roll Circus; he permitted all the work to slide and sat with her in the hospital, holding her hand, both crying as they embraced. *He's so very tender,* Marianne thought, as he stayed with her in the hospital through practically her every moment awake. And she continued to feel the tenderness and compassion in him after she returned to Cheyne Walk. But Jagger appeared to pull himself together very quickly from the shock of the miscarriage, submerging himself in his work, getting back to all the projects he had stewing, including plans to tour again.

The Stones had not toured Britain or America in more than two years, had not worked in Europe for eighteen months, and Jagger was anxious to get in front of audiences again. There was the problem of Brian—"He's a druggy." But, according to people in the Stones' office, Jagger and Keith had decided to tell Brian they wanted to tour; since Brian couldn't get into certain countries because of his arrest record, then he'd have to be left behind and a replacement found at least for the tour. They would do that soon—tell him they would tour without him—but it could hold off for a while.

Marianne was somewhat offended that Jagger seemed able to snap back so quickly from the disappointment of losing a child, by plunging into his work. She knew men could do that, but women can't; the woman who has it physically happen to her after carrying the child for so many months can't snap back simply by busying herself with work. She was a little hurt, and angry at herself for being hurt, and thought Jagger understood what she was feeling. He grew even more tender, more solicitous.

"He lets me have anything I want, in the way of material things," she told a friend one day. "I'll ring the office and ask him to bring back, oh, say some lingerie, and he does. He's doing things like coming back at least two or three times a week from Sloane Square with roses. Out-of-season roses. He's always done that. Whenever he's felt he's been ignoring me too much by working all the time, he would turn up with roses. He'd compensate with a jewel or something. But I always lose all my jewelry. Even if he covered me in diamonds—which would look stupid because the only thing that suits me is pearls—I would lose all the diamonds or leave them lying around, because I always do that. And it makes Mick so furious."

Several weeks after her miscarriage Marianne sat in front of her obstetrician's desk following a complete physical checkup. She asked:

"Why did I lose the baby, doctor?"

He stared at her for a long moment. He reached across the desk, took her right arm at the wrist, and turned it slowly and dramatically until the inside of her elbow was face up, the veins showing faintly beneath the almost translucent skin. Marianne felt as if someone had slapped her across the face. She thought:

My God, he thinks I'm a junkie. He's just like the Archbishop of Canterbury, condemning me from the pulpit for being pregnant and not married. This whole fuckin' society has that image of me, the fallen woman who loves orgies and junk. Well, if they all think I'm a junkie, that's what I'll be, damn it. I don't give a damn any more. That's my image, I may as well be like that.

"Street Fighting Man," Jagger's song of disappointment that the "revolution" had left him behind, had been released on July 26, 1968. It immediately created a storm. Members of the radical movement who thought they were building toward a revolution believed Jagger had written them an anthem with which to storm Buckingham Palace. So did some newspaper columnists, who informed readers that Jagger was at it again, trying to rip down society and destroy traditional values. The BBC didn't play the single as often as its popularity would normally have required. And in America, where it was released in September, the song was banned by many radio stations because, as one broadcasting executive said: "It would incite further riots here." Jagger took the pragmatic view, as he usually does. "I'm rather pleased they've banned it, as long as it's still in the shops," he told interviewers. "The last time they banned one of our records in America it sold a million."

The single had been released prematurely. "Street Fighting Man" was part of the *Beggar's Banquet* album, which had been completed months before and was held up by Decca in Britain and London Records in America because it was felt the jacket art work was offensive: a photo of a lavatory wall studded with graffiti. Jagger refused to let the album be released without the jacket he and Keith had selected, and Decca refused to distribute it with that jacket. It was a standoff for months. Keith said: "It's like Decca saying, we don't give a shit, man, if your album never gets out." Faced with the prospect of the songs aging before they were released, worried that the public had received no new album from the Stones since the vapid *Satanic Majesties*, the band gave in, and the album was released in December with a plain tawny cover. And Keith said: "We copped out, but we did it for money so it was all right."

With *Beggar's Banquet* the Stones turned away from the disastrous "head" music of their previous album and got back to their black American roots, the thunderously loud, driving sensual music aimed at those millions of young to whom rock is the language of an out-of-focus revolution. It is probably the finest album they've done to this point, an album that demonstrates what rock is all about. Not the studio electronics of *Majesties* but hard-driving, rampaging, maniacal rock, and blues songs with sinewy melodies, and country blues that illustrate the Stones ability to absorb and transform earlier styles. It was the kind of music Brian should have loved, especially the explicitly lewd and sadistic "Stray Cat Blues," which could have been about Brian's fantasies six years ago: A fifteen-year-old girl climbs the stairs to find the Stones, and Jagger sings: *"Oh, yeah, you're a strange stray cat/Bet your mama don't know you bite like that/I bet she never saw you scratch my back . . ."* But Brian is no longer a Rolling Stone.

One song, the opening cut of the album, stands out above all the rest. "Sympathy for the Devil." It would, in the near future, play a large role in the public face of Mick Jagger. The song is derived from a book that Marianne had found, *The Master and Margarita*, by the Russian novelist Mikhail Bulgakov. When she finished reading it, late at night and lonely while Jagger was making music in the garden studio with his friends, she insisted he read it. Jagger started on it immediately, near dawn, and Marianne thought: *That's one of my jobs, to turn him onto things he wouldn't normally be aware of. And I like that, it makes for a very strong relationship after the passion thing dies down.* She had not yet become pregnant, had not begun to question that relationship.

Jagger was overwhelmed by the novel. Satan and his retinue come to Moscow in the 1930s, to survey the effects of the Russian Revolution. Satan calls himself by assorted names and says, "Permit me to introduce myself," then turns Moscow on its ear. Police become fools, poets grow ignorant, atheists learn there is a God, saints are sinners, the Devil is God, and everyone seems to go mad. The novel, in which Satan "wills forever evil, yet does forever good," is a vast allegory of the struggles between the powers of evil and the powers of light. And when he laid down the novel Jagger walked to his studio and wrote: *"Please allow me to introduce myself, I'm a man of wealth and taste/I was around when Jesus Christ had His moment of doubt and faith/I made damn sure that Pilate washed his hands and sealed his fate . . ."* In the song Jagger retains the skepticism about revolution that he has in "Street Fighting Man": Satan makes it clear that those in power are the enemy; the righteous and powerless are vilified until they attain power for themselves; they then imitate those they've overthrown; and the process is repeated through all of history. "Just call me Lucifer 'cause I'm in need of some restraint."

They are back in Cheyne Walk, and Jagger is growing restless again. Marianne is still surprised at his energy: He continues to bound around like a teenager, although he is twenty-five, and Marianne had always felt that when he reached that age he would begin to slow down. But there was no sign of a slowdown, not yet.

"I gotta get away from London for a while," he told her. "Why don't we take a holiday with Keith and Anita?"

"I'd love it," Marianne said. She felt a lot stronger now, and a few weeks in the sun might lift her out of the black mood brought on by the loss of their daughter.

"What about Majorca?" Jagger asked. "Great place for a holiday. Went there with my parents when I was a kid."

"Oh, Mick. Everybody in England goes to Majorca. That's silly."

"Where to, then?" Jagger asked, trying not to look crushed, Marianne felt.

"South America," Marianne said. "I'd love to go to Rio."

"Fantastic. Ring Keith and tell him we're going."

Jagger announced it to the press, of course. But this time it was Keith who gave the journalists good copy. When asked why they had chosen South America for a holiday Keith said: "We've become very interested in magic and we're very serious about this trip. We're hoping to see this magician who practices both white and black magic. He has a very long and difficult name which we can't pronounce. We call him 'Banana' for short." Keith's little joke, and the song, "Sympathy for the Devil," produced a rash of stories about the Stones getting involved in black magic. And all the weirdos began to come out of their closets and look to Jagger as a Lucifer who would tear the world apart and create an even more chaotic sort of revolution.

They left for Brazil by ship on December 18, 1968—Jagger, Marianne, Nicholas, Keith, and Anita. Anita had just learned she was pregnant, and Marianne suspected they were taking the slowest possible way across the Atlantic because Keith didn't want Anita to have an abortion. When they arrived they spent some time on a ranch the size of Belgium, owned by a wealthy Brazilian cattleman who was a friend of one of Jagger's financial advisers. After a week at the ranch Jagger felt hemmed in again and he took Marianne and Nicholas to a grand hotel in Rio. One day Jagger was walking on the beach and met a group of young Brazilians who said they owned a hut on the beach about 1,000 miles north, closer to the Equator. It was near the village of Recife, they said, and Jagger could use it for as long as he liked. He promptly flew to Recife with Marianne and Nicholas, located the hut in an isolated area of the beach, and settled in.

Marianne eased herself into a hammock every morning, and Jagger would take Nicholas along the beach to hunt for sand crabs, exotic shells, and coral, and to meet the native children, Jagger in cut-down jeans and no shirt, Nicholas wearing only an undershirt. He wasn't diaper-trained yet, and Jagger patiently worked with him, teaching him to urinate, showing him how grown men did it. And Marianne thought: *That's such a fantastic relationship for a grown man and a little boy. Except Mick is not quite a grown man in many ways, he's still a boy with high spirits. It's as if Nicholas is being taught to pee by another boy.* Marianne was happier than she'd been in several years because Jagger seemed to completely forget his public image. Marianne felt he had become a husband, a warm and open human being who stopped thinking for a while about his public and his fame. He became, to Marianne, more of a husband than her actual husband had ever been. She was content; she felt they were becoming, out here away from fans and the demands of his business, like an elderly married couple. She enjoyed that, she needed that. And she knew that one of the strongest bonds in their relationship was Nicholas' love for Jagger. *He gets on better with Mick than anyone else,* she thought, *including his own father.*

One late afternoon, a couple of days after moving into the hut, Marianne, Nicholas, and Jagger were walking along the beach. They had walked a long distance from their shack, and now off in the distance they could see a group of black Brazilians, several score of them. They were sitting on the sand, playing drums, and it sounded like the voodoo beat Jagger had heard played for the tourists in New Orleans. As they approached the group, that voodoo beat growing louder and more frantic, one of the Brazilians suddenly stood up and pointed their way. The music stopped. The Brazilians rushed along the sand toward Jagger, then suddenly stopped short before him. "They seem frightened of us," Marianne said. "Yeh, yer right," Jagger said. "Wonder what's freakin' them?" The tall coffee-colored man who seemed to be their leader, or priest, stepped closer to Jagger, peering into his eyes. He reached his hand out and touched Jagger's cheek, and then pinched it. Jagger let out a short squeal, and they all rushed forward now, jabbering in Portuguese, pinching Jagger and Marianne, playfully, happily, no longer frightened. "It's as if they thought for a moment we were some kind of gods," Marianne said. "And now they're no longer awed because they can see we're ordinary people." As they were returning to their hut later, Jagger said: "You know, these people have a lot of voodoo and black saint and shrines—sort of a combination of African voodoo and the Catholic Church. Very weird. Why did they make a fuss over us?"

The next day Jagger walked into Recife. He stopped in a shop selling religious articles because he wanted to buy some beads for Marianne. The clerks and customers were staring at him in a peculiar way, appearing somewhat awed, as the people on the beach had yesterday. He walked over to a table stacked with plates that had a portrait of Christ painted on each. The portraits all looked like Jagger, now that he was darkened from the sun; dark, almost black skin, slightly flattened nose with flaring nostrils, very full sensual lips, and a small beard. (Jagger had grown a beard in Brazil.) Everywhere in the shop this Christ/Jagger face was displayed—large portraits on the walls, crucifixes, vases and plates, wooden statues. Jagger turned quickly and walked out of the shop.

Marianne started using heroin after they returned from Brazil. Not too much at first, not injecting it, because she was terrified of needles. She started on junk early one morning, waiting for Jagger to return from the studio; he had brought the Stones together, without Brian, to record a new album so they'd have one timed for release during their next American tour, planned for the following autumn. A girl friend who was on heroin and was also lonely because her man was out playing music until dawn, came to stay with Marianne and introduced her to the drug.

She began to shoot it into her arm within a few weeks. She'd never had an injection in her life and she couldn't get up the courage to stick the needle in. But there were a number of "friends" around only too willing to help—junkies who can't stand being hooked alone—and her connection, who knew Jagger's lady could afford to pay well over the market price for heroin. They shot her up.

Marianne would sit and talk to her girl friend, both of them in a narcotic haze, waiting for their men to return from their gigs. She would try to explain—for her own benefit, primarily—why she was shooting four jacks a day of pure heroin.

"It's all Mick's fault. I knew I could no longer separate my public and private identity, because of Mick," she said. "There's been a strain that I just can't endure any longer. That's why I've turned to junk."

"You shouldn't blame Mick," her friend said. "This thing about identity is in your head."

"No, it isn't, it's something very real," she said. "Mick has taken away my own identity and mixed it with his. But it's more than that. It's the failure of any kind of sex life. I was using a lot of coke because of that, and now I'm using junk, because I need something to take the place of a relationship that isn't working."

Her girl friend seemed to be nodding, and Marianne hurried on, trying not to lose her attention because she was desperate for someone to talk to. "I know I'm just looking for somebody to blame because no addict wants to blame himself so I'm blaming it on Mick. In many ways he let me down. Not me, but as a woman. He failed me, and shooting heroin is my revenge."

Another time, she said: "When I say Mick was responsible for the heroin I mean that things had become too intense and difficult so that I couldn't handle it without erecting some kind of wall. The wall I erected is made of heroin, and you can't penetrate that. But it isn't only Mick. It was what the doctor had done to me, and some family things and my mum, things from way back in my childhood. And the media, making me seem so corrupt. It was all of those strains. None of them helped, and adding the strain of Mick doesn't help it at all."

Jagger didn't know about her heroin habit, in the beginning. At least, Marianne didn't think he knew, but she couldn't be certain. *If he's aware of it he certainly doesn't want to know about it,* she thought. *He doesn't want to know anything that's unpleasant, it might upset his equilibrium.* There were a number of junkies around them, fellow-musicians, some of their women, friends, and Jagger never talked about it. *That's sort of a forbidden pleasure, real drugs. But he never said it was forbidden. We never said anything like that to each other. That's one of the faults of our relationship. You can't mention things like drugs.*

Jagger was working hard on the next album, which had a tentative title of *Let it Bleed*, from one of the songs they'd recorded: *"She said, 'My breasts they will always be open, baby / You can rest your weary head right on me. / And there will always be a space in my parking lot / When you need a little coke and sympathy."* When Marianne heard that chorus from the song, the first time, she smiled at the use of "parking lot" to mean vagina; it came from one of those games she and Jagger played, bouncing phrases off one another. And she wondered if the "coke and sympathy" was a reference to her drug use. But she wouldn't ask Jagger, of course. He was so excited about the album, talking about it whenever Marianne could sit still to listen. One afternoon Marianne placed a Robert Johnson recording on the turntable and Jagger sat there. "You know, Robert Johnson was one of the first pure blues men I got turned on to," he said. "Keith, too. And Eric. Poor Johnson. Got killed when he was still in his twenties."

"Why don't you do one?" Marianne said.

"Do what?"

"A Robert Johnson song. You're always talking about Johnson. So do one of his songs."

Jagger leaped to the turntable and lifted the needle from one cut to the next. He stopped when "Love in Vain" came on, listening carefully to it. "That's my favorite Johnson," he said. "We're gonna record that one." He seemed thrilled at Marianne's suggestion: Johnson had been an idol for so many fine white guitarists, and Jagger told her he'd never thought of doing one of Johnson's songs before.

Soon after, Marianne thought: *Our relationship is beginning to crack now. Mick doesn't realize it, he's too much into his work and he won't see it for a while. But I know it . . . that incredibly great thing we had together is beginning to shatter.*

Brian was staying at Redlands, Keith's mansion, until his own home was renovated, and Jagger and Keith went down there one evening. To tell him that he was being replaced because the band had to tour again and he could never get a visa for America because of his drug record. Brian sat alone, at the kitchen table, when they were shown in by Suki. He was motionless; his body had that inert, frozen look of animals who are frightened and hope to hide themselves by feigning death. Seconds passed. "Brian?" Suki said. "Mick and Keith are here to see you." Brian rose, pushed his golden hair back

295

from his eyes, tried to smile. He looked at Jagger and it crossed his mind that he still loved him, despite what they'd been through in the past seven years. And he smiled.

The conversation, pieced together from friends—Marianne, Alex, Stones employees—who heard slightly differing versions of it, and from an interview Keith gave, went like this:

Keith and Jagger said they had come to talk about the American tour, that they had to get out and tour again.

"You know I can't go, I can't leave the country, and I can't possibly go on the road again right now," Brian said.

They said they understood how he felt, and Brian said: "I'm out. I was dealt out a long time ago."

He would have to be replaced, he was told, because they couldn't travel as a four-man band. And Brian said: "Yes, I know, it's all right. I haven't been a Stone for years, I don't feel part of it any more, haven't felt a part of it for a long time."

Then the next step, they told him, was to determine how to break the news to their fans. Brian said he didn't care, he knew it wouldn't sound too nice if he said he'd been pushed out, so why not just say he quit. "Make up a reason," he said.

They discussed telling the public that Brian had quit because of a disagreement over the music, that they no longer saw eye to eye on the Stones music, and Brian said: "Yes, anything. Say anything, and I'll back you up."

"Because we've got to know. We've got to get someone to take your place because we're starting to think about getting it together for another tour. We've got itchy feet and we've got Mick Taylor lined up."

"Right then. I'm out. Good luck."

They said they would come and see him in a couple of weeks to see how he felt.

An exchange of embarrassed handshakes, and they left. Brian returned to the kitchen, now quite dark, and cried.

And Marianne cried, when Jagger told her about it. She was

sick and tired of it, of what he'd done to Brian . . . and she thought of the knife fight, a couple of weeks after Brian had been fired, that fight in which Brian tried to kill Jagger and then jumped into Keith's moat, to kill himself . . . and had been saved by Jagger. She knew Brian was going to die very soon; there was no doubt in her mind he would die. She thought: *I can feel it. He's been destroyed. And Mick doesn't know it, can't face it.*

Marianne was playing at the Royal Court in Edward Bond's *Early Morning*, a strange play in which Marianne was a lesbian Florence Nightingale, and Queen Victoria makes a pass at her. The play closed after one night. A friend of Jagger, one of those older men with whom he was in contact for business reasons, was backstage with Marianne when Jagger came to pick her up. The three of them got into Jagger's Rolls to go back to Cheyne Walk for some drinks and conversation. Halfway there Marianne suddenly shouted: "Oh, my God, I've forgotten the joints. Mick, go back to the theater. Quickly." Jagger turned the car around and sped back to the Royal Court.

"Where did you leave the fuckin' things?" he demanded.

"On the dressing-room table."

"Oh, shit, no," he shouted, "right where the fuckin' cleaning lady'll find 'em and turn 'em over to the coppers."

Marianne stumbled out of the car and rushed to the stage door, to recover the dope. Jagger sat behind the wheel of the car, furious: "She's so fuckin' careless. She's goin' to get us busted. The coppers are going to have a right high time throwing me back in Brixton."

The same friend went round to see them one night at the end of May, concerned over reports he'd read in the morning papers that Jagger and Marianne had been arrested on drug charges. When he entered the house in Cheyne Walk Marianne was sitting on a sofa in the ground floor living room, apparently oblivious to the coke she had spilled all over the table in front of her. Jagger didn't seem to notice the cocaine because he appeared to be in such a rage, a full twenty-four hours after their arrest. "That fuckin' Detective Sergeant Constable and two of his coppers from the Chelsea drug squad!" the friend recalls him shouting. Jagger seemed so incredibly furious that his visitor thought he was looking for something to smash. "That bloody Constable took me over to the other end of this room, and one of the other coppers went upstairs. And Constable said, 'Oh, you don't have to worry about this, Mick'—that little bastard calling me Mick, who the fuck does he think he is?—and I asked him what did he mean that I had no worries, of course I'm worried about police in me house. And that bloody Constable said, 'Well, a thousand quid, and we'll forget all about it.' I almost punched him, the bastard. And then the copper came down from upstairs with a big chunk of cannabis he said he found in a spare bedroom. That's a fuckin' room we never used in our lives, we've had it closed off since we moved in here, so I knew damn well he'd planted the stuff. I told him, 'I've never seen that stuff before and we never use that room anyway, so the whole thing's a bloody lie.' "

Marianne, busy scraping up the spilled cocaine so that Jagger wouldn't notice and turn his anger on her, began to laugh. Marianne later said: "I had two jacks of heroin on me which I quickly swallowed when the coppers came in. But they did plant Mick and they did demand a thousand pounds to forget it."

Mick continued recounting his arrest: "They know I have a lot of money and could buy me way out of it, but I'd be damned if I'd let them rob me like that. I told them to fuck off, they weren't getting a shilling out of me. 'Fuck off, you dirty crook,' I told him, and he kept asking for money and I kept telling him to fuck off, so he took me and Marianne in and arrested us."

Months later Jagger charged at his hearing that he had been asked to pay a thousand pounds for the police officer "to keep his mouth shut" and had, on the advice of his lawyers, begun to play along with Constable. But Constable broke off negotiations, Jagger charged. Constable denied the accusation. Jagger was convicted and fined $500. Marianne was acquitted. Constable later sued for libel, but nothing came of it. Police authorities investigated Jagger's charge, and police found the policeman innocent. But he was later quietly shifted out of the Chelsea drug squad and given another assignment.

SIX BRIEF COMMENTS

Brian's father, Louis: "We were now within three weeks before he died. Typical of Brian, we had a call in the early hours of the morning, full of bubbling enthusiasm about the beauties of his new house, the loveliness of the particular spirit of summer we were having at that time. He said, 'Come down in the morning' and we said that was easier said than done, it was a Tuesday and we couldn't come down in the morning. We did, in fact, go down the following weekend and spent the weekend with him. An intensively happy weekend with him, the happiest and closest weekend we had spent with him since he was a child. It was the last time we ever saw him."

Pete Townshend: "A lot of people on the day he died rang round and said, 'What have you got to say about it?' I got the first one about ten o'clock in the morning, from Pete Cole of the *Daily Express,* and I didn't really think about what I was saying. It was the first I heard of Brian's death. And it seemed just normal, you know—well, Brian Jones has died, rock singer's death, good newspaper copy, he had to go and like he was dead already kind of thing. So I just said, 'Oh, it's a normal day for Brian, he died every day, you know.' And he said, 'Thank you very much' and put down the phone, and I thought, 'Fuckin' hell.' Then I got a call from the Rolling Stones publicity man, Les Perrin, saying 'This is terrible, it's dreadful what you said about Brian,' so on and so on. And I got all upset about it and to back up my words I wrote this song, 'A Normal Day For Brian, The Man Who Died Every Day.' "

Keith Richard: "Some very weird things happened that night Brian died . . . there were people there that suddenly disappeared. We were at a session that night and we didn't expect Brian to come along. He'd officially left the band. And someone called us up at midnight and said, 'Brian's dead.' Well, what the fuck's going on? We had these chauffeurs working for us and we tried to find out . . . some of them had a weird hold over Brian. There were a lot of chicks there, and there was a whole thing going on, they were having a party. I don't know, man, I just don't know what happened to Brian that night. There was no one there that'd want to murder him. Someone didn't take care of him. And they should have done because he had someone there who was supposed to take care of him. Everyone knew what Brian was like, especially at a party. Maybe he did just go in for a swim and have an asthma attack. We were completely shocked. I got straight into it and wanted to know who was there and couldn't find out. The only cat I could ask was the one I think who got rid of everybody and did the whole disappearing trick so when the cops arrived, it was just an accident. Maybe it was. Maybe the cat just wanted to get everyone out of the way so it wasn't all names involved, et cetera. Maybe he did the right thing, but I don't know. I don't even know who was there that night, and finding out is impossible. It's the same feeling with who killed Kennedy. You can't get to the bottom of it."

Michael Philip Jagger: "Yeah, it was a shock when Brian died. I suppose it was the kind of feeling that if anyone was going to die, Brian was going to die. You always had the feeling Brian wouldn't live that long. He just lived his life very fast. He kind of was like a butterfly . . . Oh, we were very close at one point. And then the myth explodes . . . I didn't really understand quite what Brian wanted to do, really, in terms of his songs. He kept a lot of things to himself like that. He never played me a song he'd written so it was quite hard to know what he really wanted to do. If he'd written—I think he wrote some songs—but he was very shy and found it rather hard to lay it down to us, 'This is a song that goes like . . .' And because he didn't try to bring it out, it wasn't a question of forcefully sort of stifling him."

Charlie Watts: "It was different a few years ago. We were a pack then, when Brian was alive, a family in a way. But sometimes now I'm not sure I even know the others."

Brian Jones, his own epitaph: "Please don't judge me too harshly."

BOOK SIX

MADISON SQUARE GARDEN, New York, November 27, 1969. The first night of the Rolling Stones American tour. Not actually the opening gig—they had played the West Coast and across the country most of the month; the tour is coming to an end with two dates here in New York and then two others further south on the Atlantic Coast. But New York is where it all begins. The rest out there was just a rehearsal for New York. This is still Jagger's city, where the New Society people had come on to him with such fawning abandon five years before. Now the rehearsals in all those other cities are behind them, the singer and the band have their show timed to perfection. "I hate spontaneity," says Jagger, the image of raw spontaneous power. And if any audience is going to be shown what the King of the Scene can deliver, it's going to be the New York audience.

The Garden is studded with celebrities and semi-celebrities: a slightly drunk Janis Joplin, Jimi Hendrix, Leonard Cohen, Viva, Woody Allen, Warhol and his pack of high camp undergrounders come to adore the Highest Camp of them all. They've all come to see Jagger, for Jagger is always the focus. He—the Stones—hasn't performed here in more than three years, and the anticipation over this event is so delicious. "And now, the Rolling Stones, the greatest rock-and-roll band in the world!!!" Out leaps Jagger, appearing gaunt in a black jersey, black mariachi pants with gold buttons down the sides, a wide jeweled belt around his waist, and a red-white-and-blue Uncle Sam hat perched mischievously on his head. "Hi, y'aaaal!" he howls in a Dixie-rag voice, rolling his eyes like Eddie Cantor, dancing from one end of the stage to the other in his moccasins as the band plugs in behind him. And the 20,000 kids and several hundred celebrities erupt. Almost immediately, the band launches into "Jumpin' Jack Flash," Jagger's—the Image's—new biographical song: *I was born in a crossfire hurricane/And I howled at my Ma in the drivin' rain/But it's all right now . . . /I'm Jumpin' Jack Flash . . .* " The lyric sounds like a parody of Dylan, and Jagger is stretching out the syllables and howling the words like the old Dylan, but few seem to notice the imitation as the band drives it on, the surging, powerful roar of jet planes that lifts you out of your seat.

A few oldies now, a Berry song, then "Live With Me." Jagger drops to his knees during the song, wedging the microphone between his thighs, an electronic phallus . . . *"Doncha think there's a place for you, in between the sheets"* . . . bringing the girls and the boys to their feet. They try to rush the stage, the guards holding them back, gently handling them, like fathers trying to calm their hysterical children, holding back a Children's Crusade. Jagger pours it on now, singing "Stray Cat Blues"—the frightened fifteen-year-old girl who's come up the stairs: *"I bet your Mama don't know you scratch like that. I bet she never saw you scratch my back"* —and there's no mistaking where his back is at, why she's screaming and biting and scratching. But now Jagger changes the girl's age, making her thirteen—there are thousands of thirteen-year-olds out there in front of him. They're going wild, there's probably not a dry seat in the house, for this is what rock is all about—orgasm.

It's getting intense, the pressure is building, the kids still trying to reach the stage. And Jagger, manipulating, ever in control, pulls it back, easing the pressure. Two low stools are placed center stage. Keith is handed an acoustic guitar, and Jagger says into the mike, softly, oh so softly: "We're gonna sit for a minute or two." They play a couple of slow blues, the audience calming down, listening to the music of the Delta.

Enough of that. Some real sex and violence and murder now. "Midnight Rambler." The band starts off rather showy, an R & B number, and Jagger's voice is almost indistinct, part of the band's instruments. Then an instrumental break, Jagger on harmonica—he's become an accomplished harp player. Chugging along behind him, the band is pulsating, chugging faster and faster, like a train rolling through the night or a rapist thrusting to a climax/crescendo over his victim's screams, building the tension higher and higher. Until you feel something must snap. Suddenly, the band slows, almost comes to a stop, Keith fingering his guitar as if tuning it, Charlie simply brushing the drums. The audience, which has never heard this song before, begins to applaud as if glad the tension has been released. And then Charlie pounds on his drum, a beat of violence, loud and clear . . . and another, and another . . . emphasizing Jagger's crotch thrusts at the audience. And now Jagger sings, and the lyric becomes clear, Jagger singing menacingly, each word sharp, distinct, a threat of rape: *"Did you hear about the midnight rambler?"* Jagger drops to one knee, and the audience sees it now—his wide jeweled belt is in his hand, raised high over his head . . . and then slap! . . . whipping the stage to emphasize each rape thrust: *"Talkin' 'bout the midnight rambler"* . . . Slap! goes the belt against the stage . . . *"You heard about the Boston*

304

Strangler" . . . and he whips the stage again . . . *"Honey, it's not one of those"* . . . Slap! against the stage . . . *"I'm called the hit-and-run raper, in anger"* . . . Slap! . . . It's a bit of theater from Marat/Sade; Jagger seems almost to be trying to exorcise the evil within himself by projecting it onto the audience, as ancient man bottled up his violent, aggressive tendencies by projecting them outward and creating mythical beasts that lived in the forest and devoured virgins and youths. But this is a live audience onto which Jagger is projecting the dragons within himself—an audience of innocents, of thirteen-year-old virgins who haven't become stray cats, children wearing blinders of innocence, innocently feeding on Jagger/Dionysius, wishing to be raped by him and then to devour him. And the Garden fills with waves of evil, *their* dragons, the dragons Jagger has forced them to absorb from him with his repetitive evocative phrases of sadism and rape. When the song ends, finally, the audience is shaken; Jagger has touched something deep, their fantasies and fears and destructive inclinations, he's brought them to the surface.

As the band prepares for the next song, a young woman in the front row, who'd been prim and a little reserved at first, is now standing on her chair and screaming at Jagger: "Paint it black, you devil," and Jagger is preparing to become Lucifer: *"Please allow me to introduce myself . . ."* he sings, as the band rips into "Sympathy for the Devil." Jagger has become the hermaphrodite gangster Satan, pulling further now on the audience's interior dragons—and playing for the cameras that have been set up in the Garden to film the remainder of the tour and a free concert on the West Coast next week. He's working so hard to pull out those subterranean devils, and the audience surges forward toward the stage, servants to rock's black mass priest.

A woman in her mid-thirties turns to her husband and shouts over the crowd's frenzy: "How are we going to get Teri out of here when it happens?" Her husband looks at her blankly for a moment. His daughter and her girl friend, both thirteen, are sitting down below, in the tenth row. But there are no longer any rows; the once orderly pattern of rows upon rows of chairs has vanished because everyone down on the main floor of the Garden has crushed forward to reach Jagger. It suddenly occurred to the husband: *They're like lemmings,* and his wife's anxiety became very real to him: *It's going to explode. Mick doesn't realize he's opening a door . . . death's door . . . he doesn't seem to know there's only one death to get you out of the world and so many doors to get you there. You open one of them, and you must step through . . . And Mick's opening them all.*

Jagger appears to sense it, finally, as the song ends and the house explodes. He stands at the stage apron, occasionally jumping back as someone tries to seize his ankle, tries to *touch* Lucifer, then shouts into the mike: "I can't see anyone. Let's see how beautiful you are. You can see us, but we can't see you. Let's see how beautiful you are."

The house lights come on, and the kids are able to see one another now, and the fear and tension and violence vanish as Lucifer lights up the forest filled with dragons, transforming them into little children once more. "This next song is when you were little children," Jagger says. He knows precisely what he is doing: "This is from before you let your hair grow long." He's in control again; the dragons have vanished. The Stones slam into their second Chuck Berry song, "Little Queenie," a Fifties teenage song for dancing, and the kids dance, finally dissipating all that evil energy they had soaked up from him.

It had been so well-rehearsed over the past month. The Stones had done this set, with minor changes, dozens of times before now. But tonight, in the Garden, it had been so close. Jagger had come so very near to losing complete control, he had stepped to the edge of a madness and had almost become Dionysius, celebrated by women who elevated him to a temporary sexual kingship and then ripped him apart at the end of his reign to make room for the next Dionysius.

The Stones hadn't toured America in more than three years, and Jagger, an actor and performer most of all, desperately needed to go out on the road again, to feel that coke-rush of playing on stage and manipulating so many thousands to his will. And America was so attractive for that. There was money in America, of course: Touring had become so profoundly attractive because of the fantastic success of English groups—Cream and Led Zeppelin and even obvious frauds like Blind Faith, playing in huge auditoriums across America and bringing home millions of dollars. But there was another attraction in America. There was revolution and anarchy in America, violence and racial war—the only place in the world where "Street Fighting Man" could still be an anthem. And there was a need to reaffirm that the Stones were still supreme. They were bigger than the Beatles now, the Beatles were breaking up, had not toured since 1966, and would never tour again, John Lennon had said. It seemed, too, that Dylan would never tour again. The Stones were alone, at the top of the mountain. And Jagger, once caught in the middle between Keith as punk and Brian as timeless, ethereal beauty, now found the stage his own.

Yet, many on the tour with the Stones sensed something else in Jagger, something radically different about him from the moment he set foot in Los Angeles almost two months before, to rehearse for the tour. In the past, even when Marianne was feeling that he could no longer keep a firm grip on his own identity, Jagger never acted as if he had permitted himself to be smothered by the public Mick Jagger. He seemed to use the public image as a cloak, a protective device enabling him to sidestep problems by pretending to be an egotistical superstar. He had always been able to switch it off and on. But it was very noticeable to those who worked for Jagger that Los Angeles seemed to do something to him. David Sandison, employed by Les Perrin and sent on the tour to handle public relations, became aware of the transformation in Jagger within days after their arrival in Los Angeles.

"He's stopped being casual about everything, as he always was, and now he's becoming Mick Jagger all the time," David said. "He's never relaxing for a second. It's really becoming like, 'I'm Mick Jagger, head of the Rolling Stones, and don't forget it.' Before, there was room for Michael Philip Jagger. But no longer."

Los Angeles. There are few prostitutes available in this city because if you can't score almost everywhere in town, no prostitute in the world would ever accept your trade. Hollywood "starlets" have been replaced by West Coast groupies, the weirdest, most beautiful women in the world, anxious to accommodate any pleasure or perversion. It was rumored that the Stones rushed out to Sunset Strip to make a vital purchase—a collection of whips and thirteen cases of Tutti Frutti douches. Los Angeles, where America's arrogant consumption has been developed into a religion of materialism: You haven't made it if you don't snort your coke with hundred-dollar bills in the back seat of your Rolls. For Jagger and the Stones, everything and anything was made available. Within hours of their arrival on a Friday night, driven in limousines from the airport to two mansions in the Hollywood Hills that would be their base while in America, more dope was laid on them by dealers who wanted their business than they could use on a dozen tours. The dealers destroyed their potential trade by being over-generous with their free samples. Half the kitchen in the house that Jagger, Keith and several others were using as their home, was filled with Acapulco Gold bushes—not marijuana leaves but the entire bushes; groupies were assigned to strip the leaves, dry them out, and roll joints, and in a couple of days a table was piled high with joints, and the groupies continued to roll. There was a birthday party for Bill, October 24, his twenty-eighth birthday. The groupies baked a half-dozen cakes filled with hash, five-pound cakes that were almost pure hash.

When they had come to America on earlier tours all the world was also made available for them, but Jagger had always been able to stand aside objectively and giggle at the absurdity of it all: Mick Jagger, a kid from a London suburb, being treated as a king, or a god—damned foolishness. Now, however, it appeared to those close to the Stones that Jagger accepted it all as his rightful due, a tithe from his subjects, a tax paid the king to assure the king's affection and good will. Los Angeles had stopped dead for him, Mick Jagger; he was the focus of all the perverted energy in that sprawling town. And he played the role as if it were a part of reality. A group of them would go down to the Whiskey to see Chuck Berry—Jagger, Keith, Glyn Johns, several others—and, of course, the owners would clear the way for a special table. Patrons were shoved out so the table could be fit in for the best view of the stage, and the best place for Jagger to be viewed by everyone else in the club. The frenzy, to make room for Jagger's party, made it appear to David Sandison that they were stabbing other customers and carting their bodies out the back door. Jagger sat down, and almost immediately there was a procession of ultra-cool West Coast ladies, slinking past his table and suddenly exclaiming, "Ooooh, is that Mick?" and coming over to chat, hoping he'd take one or more of them home with him. And you could almost see what it was doing to his ego, Sandison felt; Jagger walks around London and gets glances, but here in Los Angeles, in this room and all over town, anything that had been happening before his arrival suddenly stopped and was now focused on Jagger. This hadn't happened to him for a long time because he'd been out of circulation—his only previous trips to Los Angeles in years had been to come in and record quietly, and then slip out of town again.

"This is a sheer, one hundred percent, 'You can fuck me any time you want to,'" Sandison commented the next day. "The whole town, guys and chicks, laying dead at his feet. It must be awfully hard to resist that and keep from getting sucked in."

Jagger appeared to be sucked in by Los Angeles' madness, with gossip columnists like Joyce Haber in the *Los Angeles Times* and Rona Barrett on television every night, reporting on Jagger's movements as if he were royalty.

There seemed, on Jagger's part, to be no deviation from the role: Mick Jagger, king, superstar, Lucifer. And something unusual was happening now. Some in the Stones' entourage said the role was starting to get in the way of his decision-making; Jagger appeared to be making decisions that would fit the role rather than make alternative decisions that would be more beneficial to the Stones. He seemed to be losing his grip on the business end of it, partially because he was so deeply involved in getting the band into the studio every night for rehearsals. Keith appeared to them to be coasting, and it was all up to Jagger to get the band functioning again. The tour was very important, Jagger had said. The Stones had gone through a laid-back period, absorbed in drug arrests and the problems with Brian and the failure of the *Satanic Majesties* album. It was urgent that they show America, and the world, that they were the best band in existence. If they could get back on top again, in the States, then they'd be set for the next two or three years. Jagger had indicated that films could become a tangential career, for the time when he was too old to perform any more, but he now seemed very disillusioned with movie-making. *Ned Kelly* was a critical and commercial flop and *Performance* was still being held up by the idiots at Warner's. So it had come down to getting back on the road again. Mick Jagger and the Rolling Stones.

"He has to play the role now, because he's head of a corporation," Sandison said. "If he loosens up in the role for one moment, then his concentration slips. So he has to be Mick Jagger, because he is the Man.

Jagger had hired Ronnie Schneider, Allen Klein's twenty-seven-year-old nephew, to produce this tour. The Stones' relationship with Klein was ending, and some around the Stones believed that Jagger was using Ronnie to give Klein the finger. Jagger had always been very astute, he knew that there were many ways for a band to be robbed in this business, for sticky-fingered people to skim money off the top because of the enormous cash flow. He said he couldn't fight the system and evidently believed the best way to protect the Stones was to hire people who would steal only a minimal amount. Ronnie was hired because Jagger wanted a cheaper version of Allen Klein, he told friends, and because he didn't think Ronnie would steal. Ronnie's job was primarily desk work, sorting out the best offers from promoters clamoring to handle the Stones in their cities, muscling huge guarantees (60 percent of the gross against a guaranteed minimum for each concert), and making certain to demand in the contracts a number of ego-gratifying items such as the size and furnishing of the Stones' dressing room, specific types of food to be catered for each show, the brands of wine, liquor and beer the boys demanded. Ronnie was working hard to prove his worth; he was indeed a smaller version of Allen Klein and tried to use some of the techniques he'd learned in working several years for his uncle.

The word got around the entertainment industry that Ronnie had stolen the Stones from his uncle, and Jagger chuckled at this; it was a nice story, but not true, for Klein still had control and Ronnie was in effect his uncle's road manager. But Jagger didn't bother correcting the falsehood. Jagger was angry at Klein and was preparing a lawsuit against him that would ultimately be settled to the satisfaction of both, after mutual name-calling. Jagger had introduced Klein and John Lennon, had persuaded Lennon to hire Klein as his financial manager. Klein was then brought in to straighten out the Beatles' organization, which was being bled by industry scavengers, and Klein and others thought Jagger was jealous because Klein was devoting so much energy to the Beatles and not enough to the Stones. Jagger had hired Prince Rupert Lowenstein as his personal financial advisor more than a year before. Rupert's role was as a watchdog over Allen Klein and to help Jagger put together his own corporation for the day that Klein's contract ran out. The corporation would be Rolling Stones Records, its goal to give the Stones more creative freedom, to make it possible for them to keep for themselves a larger share of recording income, and to get them out of the murderous 97 percent tax bracket. But Prince Rupert had had no experience in the record industry so Jagger was constructing the corporation himself, using his own intuition. He'd been working on it for over a year, and all of the business problems had taken an incredible amount of energy for him.

Now, as Los Angeles flowed over him and seemed to make him into the public-image Mick Jagger even in his private life, Jagger pulled back from all business problems, permitting Schneider and the Stones tour crew to handle everything as he plunged deeper into the role of superstar. He didn't seem to give a damn at some of the things being done in his name. There were published complaints of the Stones' arrogance and greed—prices at the first concert, the Los Angeles Forum on November 8, were set at an inflationary $7.50—and when the complaints reached Jagger he told his staff to announce publicly that prices were set by the Forum's owners. Actually, Jagger and the Stones staff set the prices. And Bill Graham, one of the more respected promoters in rock, was so angered that he told a reporter: "Mick Jagger may be great as a performer, but he's an egotistical creep as a person."

Graham had reason to be angry. He had been treated badly by the Stones. Ronnie Schneider, acting for Jagger, of course, had been extraordinarily rude to Graham. Schneider's office was the dining room of a DuPont family house above Sunset

Strip, which was also the home during this tour of Charlie Watts, Shirley, and their baby, Serafina. Each day Schneider would be making deals on the phone while Charlie and Shirley tried to maintain a sane family unit despite the insanity around them. Ronnie's voice would echo through the house, as he wheeled and dealed over the phone: "You tell that cocksucker to come up with the advance or he'll be dead. DEAD! . . . Yeah? . . . So what else is new?"

Ronnie lumbered into the living room one evening, after slamming the phone down on someone, and shouted to Charlie:

"Oh, these pathetic bastards. I'll screw 'em, screw 'em all. Remember when Bill Graham came down, full of bluster, telling us he'd do the whole tour, as a favor? Listen to this, Charlie, you'll get a kick out of it. There's Graham, telling me what a bigshot he is, how he built the Fillmore, how he's booked this group, that group, so I sit and wait for him to finish, then I say, 'Well, Bill, that sounds pretty good, but what did you ever do *big?*' He almost fell on the floor."

Charlie cringed. He knew that Graham had built a Fillmore on each coast and had demanded only one thing of his sound and lighting crews, his stage men, and the bands he booked into his theaters: the very best they could deliver. And Graham got it; the Fillmores were just about the only theaters where live rock sounded like live rock.

"All these people, what are they here for?" Charlie says after Ronnie races back to the dining room to take another call. And Shirley says: "I finally figured why I want to go home. It's because I'm tired of being in a house where everyone is a job, and no one talks anything but numbers. 'Twenty thousand, sixty-five percent, dollars, seats.' And there are too many people who talk nicely to you and then don't say goodbye when they leave. Have you noticed that, Charlie?"

313

Jerry Garcia of the Grateful Dead came over to Jagger's mansion one evening to make a suggestion: Why don't the Stones give a free concert up in San Francisco when the tour is completed? Jagger went for the idea immediately, Garcia said. Perhaps Jagger's reaction was because it would be such a *groovy* ending to the film being made of the tour, Mick Jagger and the Stones performing in front of . . . half a million? a million? . . . maybe the biggest rock audience in history. He ordered Sam Cutler, the tour manager, and everyone else on the staff to begin working on the free concert. And what about security? someone asked. Garcia said he'd get the Hell's Angels, they'd been cooled out by the San Francisco bands, had been hired as security guards at a number of concerts without any trouble, and someone else recalled that the English Hell's Angels had done a perfect job providing security at the Hyde Park concert back in July. The Hell's Angels it would be.

"Take care of everything," Jagger ordered Cutler and several others. "I want it ready for the first weekend after Florida." That would be December 6.

While they were still in Los Angeles, one of the road crew went to see a play that a freak community-theater group in the area had just put on the boards. He came in the next morning, a little shaken, and described his evening at the theater:

"It's a fantasy about a rock-n-roll star who wants to be a martyr. He wants to get killed while performing, at the height of his career, and become a cult figure. Some kind of new Jesus. The last scene, a very brief scene, he's up on stage with his band—up to then there have been no names of any kind, the actors just going, 'Hey, man, how are you?'—shit like that. No names. So he's playin' with his band, in this last scene, and somebody rushes up and stabs him . . . and he dies on stage. And over the loudspeaker, like voices from the band's audience, people are shouting, 'They killed Mick . . . they got

Mick . . .' It was like the ultimate commitment, getting killed on stage."

"God," one of the Stones' employees said, "don't tell Mick, don't let Mick know about it.'

Jagger did learn of it a couple of days later. "He's freaking over it," the word went around the Stones office.

There had been a number of telegrams coming into Stones headquarters. They were for Jagger, from London, telegrams from a woman telling him how much she loved him, how terribly she missed him, please hurry back when the tour is over. Each of them was signed "Fuzzy-Wuzzy."

By the time the third one had arrived, David Sandison was wondering why Marianne was signing that strange name to her love-telegrams. He asked Jagger's secretary about it. She stared at him for a moment, rolling her eyes upward as if to implore God to rescue her from someone so naïve.

"Okay, then who the hell is she?" David asked.

"Fuzzy Wuzzy, don't you get it?" She ran her fingers along her hair. "Get it? Hair."

"Marsha? Of course, Marsha."

It crossed David's mind that Jagger had seemed to love Marianne so deeply. One night, many months before, Marianne had come into the studio while they were working on a song for the new album. She appeared wasted, so terribly strung out on drugs, and had finally fallen asleep in the control room. Just before dawn, when the band had begun to run out of energy, Jagger called an end to the session and came into the control booth. Marianne was sleeping in a chair. He stood over her, looking at her with so much compassion, such a feeling of tenderness, that David thought: *That's so nice, to feel like that.* Then Jagger started to shake her gently. "Come on, little lady," he said, "let's go home." He lifted her into his arms and carried her to the car.

315

Midway through the tour, on the way to Madison Square Garden and, ultimately, the free concert in San Francisco, Jagger learned that Marianne had run away with an Italian millionaire. He spent hours trying to locate her, in London, in Rome.

Marianne was bored, and very lonely, while he was on tour in America. And angry at Jagger for leaving her now, in her mother's cottage in Berkshire. She couldn't stop thinking about Carena, the baby she had lost, about the heroin habit she'd kicked before flying off to Australia and trying to kill herself. Now she was afraid she needed the heroin again, and blamed Jagger for that panicky feeling. *I'm slipping into the abyss, and Mick isn't here to help me. He couldn't help me even if he were here.* She thought again about her relationship with Jagger: *I like him. But I don't think I was ever in love with him at all. I don't think I've ever been in love with anyone. I think the nearest I've come is with Mick, but I've never really been in love with him.* It had taken her a long time to come to that realization, and it hurt now because the years with Jagger had been good years. She thought: *There were bad times, of course, but that's the price you must pay for some really good times.*

She remembered some of the bad times, alone now in the country and Jagger over in America. He often didn't come home, working in the studio on the new album. And working on some other things: She knew there were groupies in the studio, and Jagger fucked them, there, but it didn't matter so much because he always came home to her. Except, he was staying away so often. And she'd spent a lot of time alone, crying. That terribly dreadful night just a few months before, when Tom Driberg stopped in for a visit at Cheyne Walk. Marianne was expecting a few people over for dinner, one of the rare times that friends outside of a small circle of band members and their women were being entertained by Jagger and Marianne. Jagger had promised to be home early. And while Driberg was there, Jagger had called and said he was working in the studio on a few songs and couldn't make it until very late; go ahead with the dinner without him. Marianne hung up and ran up the stairs, sobbing. She came down again in a few moments and asked Driberg to stay to dinner, as her escort. He was flattered, but he explained he had a political dinner he couldn't possibly miss. Marianne said she understood, then asked:

"Will you please go down to the pub and buy me a few bottles of wine? I have no money."

And she thought: *But there were good times. They were very good in their supreme affection and comfortableness . . . I had a sort of peaceful happiness for so many of those years.* But she knew it couldn't possibly be good, now, if she felt she was slipping over the edge. Like Brian had. She thought about Brian, and how alone he'd been when he died, and how she had almost died out there in Australia because she believed she was Brian. *I was dead, really, for eight days,* she thought. *I didn't come alive again until that dream about Brian.* While in a coma, in the Australian hospital, she had dreamed that she was dead, walking along on what seemed to be enormous puffs of clouds. Brian was in the distance, extending his hand to her. She hurried to Brian, stretching out her hand, anxious to join him wherever it was that death was taking them. But as she grew close, almost close enough to touch him, to grip that slim, weak hand again, Brian pulled away from her. "Go back, Marianne, go back," he told her. He looked at her as if he knew, as only the dead can know, that she was not one of them. And he cried: "You can't come with me. Go back." He stepped back and vanished over the edge of the clouds, the edge of her dream. Marianne woke from her coma then. She knew she wasn't dead, would not die.

Jagger sat at her bedside, in a chair, gripping the hand she had held out to Brian. Marianne smiled weakly at him, and he cried. "Don't worry, love," Marianne whispered. "Wild horses couldn't drag me away."

As her strength returned, Jagger went out on location every day to film *Ned Kelly*. He visited her as often as he could, bringing presents, talking about his disappointment with film-making. With the boring routine. And never telling her about how he'd almost been killed, when an old-fashioned pistol blew back on him in one scene in which Ned Kelly was shooting at a copper. The wound took sixteen stitches, and Jagger told Marianne the dressing was just part of his costume.

Marianne had been permitted to sit in the garden of Mount St. Michael Hospital in Ryde, outside Sydney. The winter sunshine made it good to be alive, and Marianne sat on a brilliant tartan blanket, wrapped in a mufler and several sweaters, thinking about Jagger as she so often did. And she began to realize, there in Australia, a few months before Jagger left her behind in England to go on tour, that she was no longer able to distinguish between being Mick Jagger's girl friend and being Marianne Faithfull. She had once been aware that Jagger was mixing up the real Marianne with the image he'd created for her, but she was certain back then that she had them completely separated in her own mind. Now, however, she felt they'd been merged. *That's one of the reasons I took the overdose, I didn't know who I was,* she thought.

They had returned to London on September 12, two months after she tried to kill herself, and went straight to Cheyne Walk. She was feeling so much better now, physically. But in great distress because Jagger was preparing for the tour, and she dreaded being left alone. He seemed to recognize it and he tried to draw her into the plans, make her a part of the preparations. He called her from the office one day. "Marianne, please run over to the Antique Market and get me some clothes for the tour," he said. She asked what he thought he'd like to wear and Jagger said: "You pick it out." And she thought it was strange that he didn't tell her precisely what he wanted her to buy because he'd always been so careful about his dress. A month after their return from Australia, the Stones flew to Los Angeles for the American tour, and Marianne went to stay with her mother, who'd been caring for Nicholas. She felt so alone, and thought often about her discovery that she hadn't really been in love with Jagger. The realization stunned her, it was too much for her to handle alone; and she thought about the daugher she had lost, and about the son, Marlon, born to Keith and Anita in August, while Marianne was still in a coma.

She started ringing up friends, looking for some cocaine. She hadn't touched any drug since her suicide attempt, but now she needed coke, needed it so badly. No one she could reach had a supply of coke. However, to relieve her loneliness, one of her friends suggested she ring up Mario Schifano, who was known as a painter, a film director, and was a wealthy Roman. Marianne had met him several times before and she'd been attracted to him. Mario represented the best of the charming, intellectual life she had known with John Dunbar. She reached him, and he said he'd come up for the weekend.

Within a few days she packed her clothing and, taking Nicholas, flew off to Rome with Mario. She felt very sad about leaving Jagger and Cheyne Walk, but also quite exhilarated. She had seldom been able to make a firm decision of her own, she had always permitted events to flow around her and sweep her along, but now she had decided for herself—she was leaving Jagger for Mario.

When Jagger learned about it, during the tour, he became terribly upset, according to Stones' employees. Marianne's act seemed to have wounded him, to have wounded his vanity; he was Mick Jagger, the world was his, every groupie and every dealer and every aristocrat in the world was fawning on him —and his woman had run away. With an Eye-talian, no less.

He got Mario's phone number in Rome and rang Marianne, demanding, then pleading, that she come back. He cried over the phone, each time he called, and Marianne felt it somewhat despicable of him: He wasn't being manly, he was being as self-indulgent as when he was in Brixton Prison. She knew that he was probably much more capable of deep feelings than she had given him credit for, more sensitive than she had once believed, but she felt that every time he did have deep feelings he would indulge himself, break down and cry. And she despised that trait in him, now that she had some distance between them. She told him their relationship was over, that she wasn't ever returning to England. Later, she said it publicly, telling journalists that Mario was her one true love, "my Prince Charming." It got headlines, of course: Mick Jagger, sex symbol, had lost his lady friend to another man.

Jagger appeared determined to give that free concert in San Francisco. Free concerts had started there—the Grateful Dead, Jefferson Airplane, all the Northern California groups that had turned that city into a freak's paradise, giving free concerts in the parks and on the streets until the Haight-Ashbury became as commercialized as Coney Island. And there had been Woodstock: three days of music and good times in upstate New York, perhaps as many as half a million kids creating such a beautiful feeling of love and peace and music that the record industry and the advertising men started calling them "The Woodstock Nation" in order to sell them more goods they didn't really need. A film had been made of Woodstock, scheduled for release in spring 1970, and Jagger told his people he was eager for a film of the Stones tour to be made and released before *Woodstock*. Beat them into the theaters. Without this free concert there would be no Rolling Stones film; negotiations with one film-maker had fallen through at the last moment, and Jagger had asked the Maysles brothers, Albert and David, to shoot some film as a form of audition. The Maysles, who are New York film-makers, weren't brought into it until near the end of the tour; the first footage they shot was at Madison Square Garden. Jagger saw the rushes, and Stone Promotions, the company set up by the band to produce the American tour, contracted with the Maysles to do a feature-length film. But the several dates remaining in New York, Boston, and Florida wouldn't be enough for a film, so the free concert became an absolute necessity. And a very vital climax to the film—perhaps as many as a million kids, the largest audience ever assembled . . . gathering to see Mick Jagger. The real reason for the concert was to get a film: Jagger was guaranteed, said a representative of the Maysles, that the film would be rush-processed for a March 15 release date, beating *Woodstock* by a full month.

After the last concert date of the tour, at the West Palm Beach Pop Festival in Florida, the Stones went into a studio in Muscle Shoals, Alabama, to lay down some tapes for a new album. In San Francisco, Jagger's aides were having difficulty finding a site for the free concert. Originally, the plan had been to hold it in Golden Gate Park on Saturday, December 6, but the city refused to issue a permit. Jagger was on the phone constantly, demanding that a site be found, that the concert must be held no matter what sort of legal problems popped up. "We'll hold it in the fuckin' streets if we have to, but we're gonna have a concert," he told aides. "Mick wants . . ." was a phrase heard often around the Stones, and when Jagger wants, his aides see that he gets.

Wednesday morning, only a few days before the concert must be held, and miraculously a site became available. The director of the Sears Point Raceway, an auto race strip outside the city, offered his grounds free of charge. It was immediately accepted. Chip Monck, who had built the stage and special lighting effects for the Stones tour, ordered his crew to begin moving tons of equipment out to the site. Jagger was called and told he would have his concert. And then trouble started: revenge on the Stones organization, meaning Jagger. Stone Promotions had savaged promoters wherever they had played, demanding what was considered by some promoters to be excessive dollar guarantees and percentages of the gate, making it impossible for some of them to make a profit of any kind; some claimed they were forced to promote the Stones concert at a loss. Concert Associates had produced the Los Angeles concert, and the firm's executives felt they had been victimized by the Stones. Concert Associates is owned by a large holding company called Filmways. And Filmways also owns the Sears Point Raceway, where Chip Monck and his people were slaving away to construct the stage and get light towers built.

On Thursday afternoon, Jagger's people got a taste of their own viciousness: Filmways summoned them to a meeting and laid down certain conditions for the use of their raceway—the Stones must place $100,000 in escrow to pay for possible damage to the track and must either give Filmways exclusive distribution rights to the film of the tour, or pay a flat $100,000 fee. Stones management, which had charged all the traffic would bear when they held the monopoly, now began to scream it was being robbed. And none of them could see the delightful irony in the situation.

The concert must go on, Jaggar decreed from Alabama. Melvin Belli, the West's most flamboyant and effective trial lawyer, came in to help the Stones sort out things. The free concert—love and peace and good vibrations for the kids—was starting to be seen for what it was: corporate strategy, big business, all those sleazy elements of Western society that the underground and the "Woodstock Nation" said it despised, and for which the Stones had once seemed to offer a revolutionary antidote. While legal maneuvering was still going on Friday morning, another track, a stock car oval called Alta-

322

mont, was offered free by Dick Carter, its operator. Carter had heard about the Stones' problems with Filmways—local disc jockeys broadcast minute-by-minute accounts and quoted Keith as saying, "We'll hold it in a bloody parking lot if we have to"—and he had called Ronnie Schneider to offer his track.

It was now twenty hours before concert time, and the Stones sent out an announcement: The free concert will go on, at Altamont, fifteen miles east of Berkeley. Chip Monck and his crew, now aided by the Grateful Dead communal family, tore down the stage and carted all the equipment out to Altamont, racing the clock. No one in the Stones organization, not Jagger, nor Ronnie, nor tour director Sam Cutler, seemed to be deterred by the fact that Woodstock had been planned for months, that you can't lure hundreds of thousands of kids to a festival site and have it ready in twenty hours, unless you consider those kids to be no more than film extras who don't require toilet facilities, water, and food stands. Outside the Jagger circle more level heads were appalled at what was taking place, Bill Graham commenting, "They can't do it, they should call it off or it'll explode in their faces." But Graham and others were ignored as the incredibly arrogant Stones machine raced to create an instant Woodstock for the film. "Mick wants . . ." It was as if everyone believed the earth would open if "Mick wants"—that there was nothing that couldn't be done if Mick Jagger, leader of the Rolling Stones, commanded it. There was a compulsiveness to the event, a compulsiveness on the part of the Stones' organization, and from the audience that began to stream out of town and toward Altamont the moment the new site was announced. Jagger had said the concert *must* take place, and no one dared question the command. Jagger had said hiring the Hell's Angels sounded like a good idea, and no one dared point out that California Hell's Angels are a different breed from London Hell's Angels. It seemed to some observers, in fact, that the

Angels had not been hired for protection, but to heighten the feeling of evil and violence that Jagger/Lucifer was going to portray from the stage.

It's Saturday morning now, an hour into Saturday. About 2,000 people in sleeping bags and blankets are camped in front of the stage that Chip and his crew are still hammering together. Altamont, the enormous meadow in front of the track, looks like a science fiction movie by Fellini. Spindly light towers slowly growing toward the sky, generators for the work crews pounding and roaring and spewing out monoxide fumes. Helicopters for the elite—Jagger, journalists, wealthy hippies who have left their San Francisco mansions to get a spot next to the stage—clatter overhead. Circus tents for the workers dot the area. Campfires burn everywhere, and in the eerie light of the fires you can see people spilling down into this valley that is really California desert, dry and cold and almost barren. The crowd had begun to form so early because radio announcers at the site were describing the long lines of cars that had already begun to clog the highways, were announcing the groups that had been selected by Jagger to appear with him, including Jefferson Airplane, San Francisco's own superband. No broadcaster said, because none of them knew it yet, that Jagger had not wanted the Airplane at his free concert because they had outplayed the Stones in Florida a few nights earlier; Jagger had finally relented, but he ordered the Airplane to perform its set early in the day and ordered his aides to make certain there were at least three acts between them and the Stones. He wasn't going to get upstaged again.

Jagger and Keith arrive at the site around 2 a.m., after flying to San Francisco a few hours before. They clamber out of their helicopter, wave to the crowd, and split up: Keith wanders off somewhere, and Jagger strolls around near the stage. One girl gives him her long yellow scarf to protect his throat from the December cold, another plants a kiss on his cheek and runs off crying at her audacity. Jagger strides around like a prince out of a fairy tale, dressed in red velvet cape and red velvet cap slung over the side of his head. A radio interviewer asks if he's seen all the preparations being made and Jagger says: "Yeah, man, it's great." He seemed to be so obviously enjoying it, swimming in it: he had ordered a free concert, and here was the free concert, shaping up. Lights suddenly come on, for the television cameras, and Jagger answers a few more questions. Then a huge joint is passed up to him but before accepting it he commanded: "Turn off the lights and cameras." He was obeyed, and he took a hit from the joint and passed it on. After an hour he climbed into his helicopter and was flown back to San Francisco.

Keith has decided to spend the night here. He wanders around for a while. "I'm just hanging out, feeling the vibes. It's great," he says to one reporter. "Everywhere I go it's a gas. People sitting around their fires, really cool, getting high. Just absolutely beautiful." He apparently is spared what other observers see. Michael Lydon, covering the Stones tour for *Ramparts* magazine, could see the beauties of the people sharing food and dope, the friendliness of people offering their campfires to keep warm by. But he sees another side of it.

One young woman tells him: "It's going to be a very heavy day because the sun, Venus, Mercury, and some other planet are all in Sagittarius, and the moon's on the Libra-Scorpio cusp." Others conscious of the stars have the same feeling, and they communicate to any who will listen: "It's weird," says one. "They consulted the astrologers before setting the dates for Woodstock, but they couldn't have consulted an astrologer for today. Anyone can see that with the moon in Scorpio it's going to be an *awful* day to do this concert. There's

325

a strong possibility of violence and chaos, and any astrologer could have told them. Oh well, maybe the Stones know something I don't know."

Lydon comes across another woman who presents him with a grotesque doll that had been made, she said, by her dead husband: "He lives in the doll, I know it. He sees everything." And the Jesus freaks are out in force, passing out leaflets warning that the Stones are in collusion with the forces of Lucifer—chaos, anarchy, and revolution—and that Lucifer is planning a catastrophe that will destroy their souls unto eternity.

It's 7 a.m., and the Hell's Angels rent-a-cops permit the mob at the top of the hill to enter the valley where the stage has been set up. They come rushing and whooping down the hill, flinging themselves as close as possible to the stage. The Woodstock Generation, Western Division—a so-called community that believes it is the social and aesthetic center of the age. They have deluded themselves into thinking they've made a fundamental break from the "old" society, helped by drugs, sex, and rock music. They have an illusion of superiority, believing that by hating their parents, hating anyone who doesn't agree with them, they have been given a special insight into the universe. They're too arrogant to understand they are the mirror image of all they condemn in their parents and in all authority—frozen and lifeless in their delusion that they're a special breed because they listen to groovy music, smoke-eat-shoot dope, grow their hair long, and don't worry about spreading venereal disease because penicillin is available free at any street clinic. The kids assembled here, kids of the hip culture, don't realize they're blind, believe they have superior vision. And that superior vision creates other illusions: that festivals, "tribal gatherings," are revolutionary; that Mick Jagger is leading them to revolution; that Altamont will be instant revolution, as Woodstock was. This is not true of all of them, to be sure. Many of the hundreds of thousands

326

assembled here have come simply for the music. But those who are blind with illusion and dope seem to be in psychic control, and they cannot perceive that Jagger is no revolutionary but a millionaire businessman, a superstar now caught up in his own myth, trapped by his own creation.

It's 10 a.m., and as many as 100,000 have arrived now, the fields filled with these kids who abandoned their cars eight and ten miles back because the roads were clogged. It's so beautiful to see them coming over the rise of a hill in the sun-haze that has settled over this near-desert. Pure poetic beauty, a film-maker's beauty. And the Maysles crew is getting it on film. Simply beautiful. But now the bad acid, the hash and pills and coke and peyote, are starting to take effect, and the psychic distress that had only been glimpsed in the night begins to manifest itself more clearly. The weirdos are starting to send out their psychotic waves. With daylight, they can be seen: acid heads whose faces are like masks hiding brains that have been burned out by too many acid flashes and visions; speed freaks with hollow eyes and gaps in their teeth; fourteen-year-olds who look thirty and will die at twenty, gulping pills and washing them down with gallons of red wine. And the dealers, hundreds of them wandering through the crowd, hawking every imaginable form of dope ever created. Most of the acid is bad, laced with speed, and an occasional kid on a bad trip, screaming and writhing against his interior demons, sets off a chain of them.

And the violence begins, long before the Hell's Angels make their presence felt. This crowd is waiting for Jagger, for that evil Lucifer, that man and his band who have contracted with Satan, and the ugliness that had infected a few now spreads like pus over thousands. Fights break out, over dope, food, water, on the long lines in front of the few toilets, kids assembled for love and music smashing one another in hatred.

The ever-amazing intensity of the psychedelics grips them, warping enough of the 300,000 who have arrived by noon to infect even those who are smoking only grass. A fog rolls in, the sun vanishes, and the beauty of the morning has been transformed into the monstrous garden of earthly delights: psychedelic California Bosch. A feeling of paranoia hangs over the crowd. They see the fights, the weirdos, the freakouts. Many of them have heard rumors and reports about the millionaire lawyers and businessmen fighting over the site for this free concert. Many begin to feel they are perhaps being used as film extras for the enrichment of Mick Jagger and company, for they can see the TV and movie cameras in action. Jagger may be ripping them off, the freaks and weirdos are sending out bad vibrations, the stars have decreed disaster. And the buzzing demonic acid is intensifying the need for Lucifer, in the guise of Mick Jagger.

Some in the crowd demand that everyone be drawn into the feeling of evilness. Including the Angels. At mid-morning the radical dopesters from Berkeley started passing out thousands of tabs of acid to the Hell's Angels. Most of the acid was cut with speed. The tabs were passed to the Angels down at the stage and at their bus thirty yards uphill. The Angels had been instructed that their job was to guard the stage to the death, and were given $500 worth of beer in payment. Sam Cutler, the Cockney-accented tour manager for the Stones, was overheard answering an Angel's question on how rough to be in handling the crowd: "We don't give a fuck. Just keep those people away." The Angels were gulping acid, gulping reds, washing it all down with enormous amounts of wine and the beer provided by the Stones. And now, primed on dope, sucked into the audience's own paranoia, the Angels reverted to *their* public image. The violence that had been sweeping through the crowd since early morning began to take on a different focus.

Santana, the lead band of the day, begins setting up, two

hours behind schedule. A young man with long straight blond hair tries to pass through a knot of Angels, to get closer to the stage. An Angel sitting on the edge of the stage kicks the man in the face; several other Angels punch him to the ground. Jagger's movie crews come closer to film the action. They aren't disturbed; they have several Angels as bodyguards. But a free-lance photographer taking pictures of another Angel assault nearby, Angels smashing a couple of naked people to the ground with pool cues, is himself attacked and requires thirteen stitches in his scalp. Santana has begun playing, and through their set—interrupted several times by Angels leaping across the stage to beat someone—the violence swept all around the band. When he got down from the stage Carlos Santana told reporters:

"There was bad vibes from the beginning. The fights started because the Hell's Angels pushed people around. It all happened so fast, it just went right on before us, and we didn't know what was going on. There were lots of people just fuckin' freaked out. During our set I could see a guy from the stage who had a knife and just wanted to stab somebody, I mean, he really wanted a fight. There were kids being stabbed and heads cracking the whole time."

The Jefferson Airplane was the second group on stage. Early in the afternoon, hours before the Stones would appear, as Jagger had ordered. From the opening notes of the first song it was clear the Angels had commandeered the stage; dozens of them up there playing out their special roles in this insane, spaced-out, and hellish tribal gathering. Marty Balin is about to begin his vocals on "We Can Be Together," and a young, muscular black man, shirtless, leaps onto the stage. Several Angels beat him with pool cues, lift him and throw him down into the crowd. He staggers around, spitting blood and trying to stay on his feet, but several other Angels reach him and start beating him again. Marty leaps off the stage. A path is opened for him, as the Airplane continues to play, and he rushes to the Angels beating the kid. He seizes an Angel by the arm and shouts: "Stop hitting that kid." An Angel smashes him in the face, knocking him to the ground. Someone in the crowd asked why he'd done that, since the Airplane had performed at benefits for the Angels, and he replied: "Because he was disrespectful to a fellow Angel. Nobody gets away with that."

The Angels were now in control, and there wasn't a thing anyone could do to head off the ultimate climax. Paul Kantner took the mike and demanded to know what the hell the Angels thought they were doing, slugging a member of his band, and an Angel on stage seized the mike to shut him up. "What the fuck is going down?" Grace Slick asked from her microphone. A fight almost broke out between Paul and the Angel but several people stepped between them, and Grace began to sing. They got through the song, shakily, and Marty returned to the stage as other fights were breaking out between Angels and the audience.

"People, people," Grace cries, still not completely aware that all control over this festival has been lost, "why do we have to fight? Everybody please cool it so we can get on with the fun."

Jagger's helicopter set down inside the Speedway stadium at this point. As he climbed out of the helicopter with Mick Taylor and a retinue, a couple of Hell's Angels clearing a path through the crowd for them, a freak rushed up to Jagger. "I hate you, I hate you," he screamed, then punched Jagger in the face. Jagger was shaken, and he was quickly hustled off to the trailer that was the Stones' dressing room.

Inside the trailer, packed tight with the band, their aides, and guards, Keith was told that Marty Balin had been knocked unconscious by a Hell's Angel, and he began to understand what was happening to the crowd out there. He thought: They're getting out of hand. It's just going to get worse, obviously it's not going to get better. Nothing's going to cool them out once they start. What a bummer! What can you do? Just sit tight. Word kept filtering into the trailer about the chaos out front, the beatings and stabbings and freak-outs. Jagger later insisted that he'd never been told anything about it; he later lashed out at all the other musicians for not coming down from the stage and telling him how frightful it was out there, how dangerous. But he and the Stones were getting reports about the violence from the moment Balin was slugged through the next couple of hours in what had become a Hell's Angels festival. "But what can you do?" Keith said. "Just sit tight." No one would dare suggest an alternative to Jagger; the free concert had to go on.

The Flying Burrito Brothers took the stage after the Airplane stopped playing and raced to a helicopter to get away as quickly as possible. With its soft country music, everything calmed down for a little while. Jagger came out of his trailer during this set, surrounded by a half-dozen burly Angels. He slipped behind the stage, then walked up the steps and strolled around at the back of the stage to see what was going on out front. Total calm. Surely the reports of violence were exaggerated. He didn't tour the medical tent, where doctors were sewing up split scalps, walking with the kids on bum trips, shooting thorazine into dozens who had freaked out.

The Angels rampaged again when the next group, Crosby, Stills, Nash and Young, began to play. Their pool cues flailing at anyone who got in the way, the Angels charged into the crowd again and again. At the end of their act several stretchers were passed into the audience and bodies were placed on them, and handed across the stage to the medical tent.

And now the Stones, the primary reason everyone had assembled here. But the Stones don't come out. They're tuning up, the press corps is told, it will take a little time for them to get their instruments tuned. But there was no tuning up inside the trailer. The Stones always delay after their warmup acts have finished, giving the audience time to work itself up in anticipation, to make them forget how much the earlier groups had moved them. But something else was also happening, in the trailer: Jagger is waiting for it to get dark, so that the banks of spotlights would have the most dramatic effect possible. Theater, for the crowd that will freak over the grand entrance. And, most of all, for the cameras, those cameras that had been shooting all the violence throughout the day. Darkness was needed to capture those satanic majesties properly, to capture Jagger's stunning makeup and costume in a swirl of colored lights. Never mind that it was growing colder outside, and the crowd getting uglier.

Many of the men and women with press credentials, and others of the elite permitted in the backstage area, knew what was happening here: Jagger, and the Stones, were wrapping themselves ever more in an enormous ego bubble. "The gigantic and insatiable ego of a Mick Jagger," one of them says into his tape recorder, as so many of them were to say in similar words. As the crowd waited, one of the Hell's Angels security guard came out of the Stones trailer and told a journalist: "Jagger's so vain with the whole scene. We kept telling him, 'Hey, you know what? You got a half-million fuckin' people out there that made you what you are, and here you are, stalling!' The man says, 'Well, my makeup looks better at night.' " To some of the journalists, it seems that Jagger has become a prisoner of his own image, an image that makes the music secondary to the need to be a rock demigod; "He no longer knows when he is just Mick Jagger, or when he is the Mick Jagger of the media and his own fantasies," one writer said as the wait for Jagger stretched into an hour, and beyond. The kids wait. And, for some, the wait becomes too much. One young man sitting in front of the stage begins twitching in an acid-vision seizure: "We are all going to die, we are all going

332

to die. Right here. We've been tricked!'' Friends carry him to the medical tent for tranquillizer, if someone has time to shoot him up. Dozens of people lay injured in the medical area, some with skull fractures, some on bad trips—there had been so many bad trips that the doctors ran out of thorazine even though they didn't start using it until late in the day—but despite the battlefield look in the tent, it was practically dark inside: The Stones representatives refused to turn on the backstage lights so the medics could tend to the sick and injured. No lights until the Stones took the stage; to have lights on before then would rob them of their entrance impact, so the injured would have to wait along with everyone else.

It is dark now, almost an hour and a half since the last band has left the stage. The lights come on, and the crowd surges toward the stage until the first hundred feet of ground are packed so densely that it's difficult to breathe. The Angels, crew, and cameramen seem to have multiplied on stage, and the wooden floor sags in the center. The Angels continue to attack anyone who displeases them, smashing skulls with their pool cues.

In the trailer, the Stones and everyone around them are tense, and very nervous, but it breaks when Cutler sticks his head in the door and says: "Time to go on." Security men, including Angels, surround them. The band is escorted in a tight cordon to a tent a few yards away, directly behind the stage. Now Keith, Bill, and Mick Taylor tune up, while Angels punch at faces that peek through holes in the canvas. Ten minutes, and they're ready. The Angels form a wedge, almost lifting the band up the four steps to the stage. Jagger halts for a moment behind stacks of amplifiers. He begins jumping, a taut spring limbering up, appearing to a journalist to retreat into himself, to focus all his strength on tapping his emotions. He looks behind him and into the sky, which is dark now. A few stars are visible even through the marijuana haze hanging over the meadow. Jagger bounces into the lights, and a group of Angels escort him to the mike; it seems to some in the crowd that Jagger is endorsing all their violence and brutality. The stars, which he probably can no longer see, appear to be mocking him as the band leaps into "Jumpin' Jack Flash" on Keith's signal. Jagger's orange and black satin cape glows wickedly under the lights, and he launches his dance. Haltingly, at first; between 100 and 200 people are on stage, and Jagger has no room to dance. He waves his arms at the onstage mob—"Gimme some room"—and then stops his song. "Move back, woncha?" he asks. The Angels step back a few paces, shoving other people back. As Jagger watches, it crosses his mind that something is wrong:

This crowd is weird, he later told a friend he was thinking. *They're not shutting up the way they usually do when I start, they're pushing and shoving. This is very strange, this audience. Something's off balance. There's no control.*

Jagger gets back into the song, forced to perform in a small pocket at center stage. For one very brief moment, Jagger and the band seize control of the mob: *"Cause it's all right, now, in fact it's a gas, I'm Jumpin' Jack Flash . . ."* Four Angels flash from behind the amps, one of them almost vaulting over Charlie's head, rush past Jagger to the edge of the stage, and leap into the crowd. That brief moment of performer getting control is gone. The crowd makes way, screaming in panic, and the Angels smash someone who has offended them. The fight is over quickly, and the band plays on, hesitant now; they've lost the flash. More Angels crowd the stage, wandering among the performers, almost colliding with Jagger as he dances and sings. The band stops.

"Fellows, fellows, move back, woncha, fellows?" Jagger says again. His touch of sarcasm is effective, the Angels give him some room. The Stones begin to play "Carol" and as he waited to begin his vocal, Jagger told his friend he was

334

thinking: *The stage is too fuckin' low. None of us feels any security up here at all. We're down too low, too close to the people, and there are too many people surrounding the stage.* Through the song, the Angels continue to beat people at random. Perhaps not so randomly: Many in the audience nearest the stage are demanding to be made victims, young men and women, some of them stripping nude despite the cold, climb onto the stage only to be thrown off and beaten on the ground below. They raise themselves, hair and faces matted with blood, and climb up again. To be beaten again. They seem to be trying to devour the creature they've elevated to fame . . . Jagger/Dionysius . . . but are themselves devoured. Collaborating in the violence.

The one song, that brilliant exploration of evil set to hard, stinging, vicious music, summing up all that this crowd fantasizes on Jagger, is played next: "Sympathy for the Devil." Jagger as Lucifer. As he begins to sing a nude girl, large and grotesque in the blue and red lights, climbs on one of the small amps standing in front of the stage. She is trying to reach Jagger. Five Angels pounce on her. Jagger breaks off in mid-verse and says, calmly: "Something always happens when we get into this number . . ." He picks up the verse again: *"I killed the czar and his ministers . . . Anastasia screamed in vain . . ."* The Angels are trying to pry the girl loose from the amp she's gripping, attempting to push her back into the audience, and Jagger shouts, sarcastically now: "Fellows, I'm sure it doesn't take *all* of you to take care of this," his voice sounding high camp. "Surely one of you can handle her." The crowd cheers his put-down of the Angels. Good thinking: One Angel can certainly beat up a girl. Four of the Angels back off, and the one remaining lifts his pool cue and smashes it over her head; she falls into the audience, and the Angel leaps after her, continuing to beat her.

Angels on stage are angered at Jagger's sarcasm. One, standing only three feet from him, dances in place to the music as Jagger vamps at the mike, casting his eyes left at Jagger, eyes filled with hatred and contempt. You can almost hear the thought behind the searing doped-up eyes: "I'd love to kill this faggot bastard." Sonny Barger, leader of the Angels, glares into Jagger's back, thinking:

Jagger's in some kind of panic. We got five guys trying to keep that chick off stage without hurting her, and people in the audience are trying to put her up on stage, and Jagger gets on this big trip about not needing five guys to handle one girl. So one guy handles it, and a little bit more violence for you, Mr. Mick Jagger. We're just doin' what one of your managers asked us to do, getting people off the speakers in front of the stage. You cunt, Jagger, you're using us as dupes . . . we're the biggest suckers for that idiot I ever did see.

"Sympathy for the Devil" is going badly but Jagger sings on, trying to regain control by invoking Lucifer over these children of violence. And then, suddenly, Jagger stops. Although Jagger later denied seeing a gun, Mick Taylor recalled that Jagger turned away from the mike, panic in his eyes and shouted:

"Fuck, man! There's somebody out there . . . there's a cat pointing a gun at us."

The band stops. Keith has seen the gun. An Angel who sees its glinting steel in the lights, a gun pointing directly at Jagger, drops to the stage to get out of the line of fire. Jagger stands there, his hand over his mouth, appearing terrified, gazing to the left of stage where the gun had flashed. Then he retreats from the microphone, back toward the equipment. Mick Taylor stands in place, his mouth open, appearing numbed. He had seen it, a black man in a green suit, leaping about. *I think he was waving a gun around,* Taylor thought . . . and then the man vanished, chased into the crowd by a pack of Angels.

The man with the gun is Meredith Hunter, an eighteen-year-old black man who has come to the concert with his pretty, white, blonde girl friend and has angered the Angels, perhaps because his girl is white. They had been standing near the stage, up against one of the amps, when a fat Hell's Angel who had been ordered to keep people away from the amps, leaned over and yanked Meredith's hair. Pulling it and laughing at Meredith's surprise and pain. Meredith pulled loose and gave the Angel a very mean look. The Angel punched him in the mouth and leaped from the stage to beat him further. Meredith tried to run away, and several other Angels grabbed him, began beating him as he continued to push through the crowd, Angels hanging on his back. One Angel pulled out a knife, the crowd fell back as the blade glinted in the light, and he plunged it into Meredith's back. Meredith didn't go down. He turned, a gun in his hand, holding it in the air. His girl friend screamed: "Don't shoot anyone." A Hell's Angel grabbed the gun from him, and another stabbed him in the back again. He pulled the knife out and smashed it into Meredith's temple. Meredith stumbled to his knees, then rose and began running, the blood streaming down the side of his head. He fell to his knees again, and the Angel with the knife stabbed him repeatedly; the fat Angel, who had started it all, grabbed Meredith's shoulders and started kicking him in the face, four or five times. Meredith fell into the sand, on his face. Another Angel kicked him in the side, and Meredith rolled over. "I wasn't going to shoot you," he said. An Angel demanded: "Why did you have a gun?" He didn't give Meredith time to answer; he lifted a trash pail and smashed Meredith over the head with it, then kicked the pail away, and five or six Angels smashed their boots into his head and body. When they were done, the fat Angel stood on Meredith's head for about a minute, then walked away.

No one in the crowd tried to interfere. Hundreds of them stood there, watching Meredith being killed, crying and gasping at what they were witnessing. And now that the Angels had stopped smashing Meredith's body, the crowd slowly

337

came closer. "Don't touch him," the Angel with the knife said. "He's going to die anyway so let him die, don't come near him." The Angels stood over Meredith for several minutes, not permitting anyone near the body. Several young men came over and tried to comfort Meredith, and the Angels walked away. A couple of people turned Meredith over on his face, ripped off his jacket and shirt, and began to rub off the blood so that they could see the wounds. There was a large hole at his spine, another on his side, and a hole in his temple that seemed to go in at least an inch. One man picked up his arms, and another his legs. "We got to get him to the stage for help, because he's going to die. We have maybe fifteen minutes." The small crowd around Meredith began shouting to Jagger to stop playing.

Twenty-five feet away, Jagger recovered and leaped to the mike. The audience directly out front of the stage and flowing up the hill for a quarter-mile—it was peaceful up the hill; all the violence was focused around the stage—the audience started to boo Jagger because they didn't know why he had stopped singing and fled to the rear of the stage.

"Brothers and sisters, come on now!" Jagger shouted. "That means everybody just cool out! We can cool out, everybody! Everybody be cool now, come on!" Keith is staring out at the Angels who swarmed all over Meredith, picking a few notes on his guitar as if to start playing again, but Jagger turns to the side of the stage, attracted by the commotion, but unable to see, because of the crowd, that Meredith is being stabbed to death. And he shouts:

"How are we doin' over there? Everybody all right? Can we still collect ourselves? I don't know what happened, I couldn't see, I hope you're all right. Are you all right? Okay, let's just give ourselves another half-minute before we get our breath back. Everyone just cool down. Is there anyone there who's hurt? Okay, I think we're cool, we can groove. We always have

338

something very funny happen when we start that," he repeated.

Jagger seems very fragile, begging his audience not to riot. Always, he was able to bring them to the edge of riot and then pull them back, with his art, his performer's magic. Now, he seems a small, frail, and very vulnerable little boy in Halloween costume, stripped of his sensual aura, vulnerable to a sudden knife thrust, a bullet, a pool cue to shatter his skull. He appears to know it, and he looks frightened.

Keith signals, and the band starts the song again, lacking conviction. Jagger doesn't have his usual drive, his voice weak and his dancing leaden. He leans over to his left as he sings, trying to hear the people shouting at him to stop playing, that someone out there is dying. But he can't hear them clearly and he continues to sing. Someone tries to climb onstage, to tell Jagger about the knifing, but Angels throw him back into the audience. Jagger stops again. "Why are we fighting?" he demands. "Why are we fighting? We don't want to fight at all . . . we gotta stop right now. You know, if we can't there's no point . . ."

Fights continue to break out in front of the stage. There is a long silence at the mike. Jagger has totally lost control and he must know it now, but he doesn't seem to know what to do about it. Keith steps forward to the edge of the stage, pointing a finger at the Angels beating someone, and shouts:

"Either those cats cool it, man, or we don't play . . ."

But the Angels don't cool it. More beatings directly in front of the stage, and a long silence from the rock stars who are witnessing it. Long pause. Then Jagger takes the mike again, his voice almost a sob: "If he doesn't stop it, man . . ."

Keith shouts out: "Keep it cool! Hey, if you don't cool it you ain't gonna hear no music!"

An Angel grabs the mike from Keith and shouts at him: "Fuck you!"

Word has finally reached the stage that someone has been seriously hurt. Sam Cutler steps forward and takes the mike. His voice is hoarse, flat with fear: "This is an important announcement. Someone has been hurt, and a doctor is leaving the stage right now. That's him with his arm raised, he's got a green jacket on. Will you please let him through. Someone has been badly hurt."

Jagger shouts: "We need a doctor here, now! Look, can you let the doctor get through please. We're tryin' to get to someone who's hurt."

The doctor walks through the crowd, his arm upraised. Men and women standing around Meredith Hunter also have their arms raised, waving bloody hands at Jagger to show him how serious it is. Hunter was carried into the medical tent by the doctor, Robert Hiatt, a resident at the San Francisco Public Health Hospital. It was obvious to Hiatt and other doctors that Meredith could not live; there was no equipment on the scene to help him, and no helicopter to get him to the hospital. He died within moments. The doctors were furious. "The people in charge of this concert are morally irresponsible," one of them said. The medical men had been promised telephone communications and a helicopter for any serious emergency, but none of it was ever given them.

Altamont has ended. The crowd calmed down, and the Stones played several more songs. Jagger finished up his performance with "Street Fighting Man," a rather insensitive selection for a crowd that had seen so much carnage in eight hours. At the end of that song Jagger shouted: "We're gonna kiss you goodbye," and he slowly left the stage, throwing kisses, waving campy fluttering hands, batting his eyes. Waves of sound smashed over the stage as the crowd cheered and saluted with closed fists upraised. As Jagger left the stage, surrounded by Hell's Angels, one writer turned to a friend and said: "It's a giant fascist rally, and Jagger is playing Adolf Hitler."

An enormous negative reaction swept the West Coast over the next several days. Altamont had been touted as another Woodstock, another gathering of the tribe to demonstrate to adult authoritarians that kids can live together in peace and harmonious vibrations. And one man was murdered, two others killed in their sleeping bags by a hit-and-run driver, and another man on a bad trip was drowned when he jumped into a canal. What went wrong? The newspapers, radio, and television tried to answer the question for days. At first, the Hell's Angels were blamed. Later, as more information on the scene at Altamont started flowing in, there were second thoughts. David Crosby, whose group played through the violence during the afternoon, told interviewers:

"The Rolling Stones are still a little bit in 1965. They didn't really know that security isn't a part of anybody's concert anymore . . . We didn't need the Angels. I'm not downgrading the Angels, because it's not healthy and because they only did what they were expected to do. The Stones don't know about Angels. To them an Angel is something in between Peter Fonda and Dennis Hopper. That's not real. But I don't think the Angels were the major mistake. They were just the obvious mistake. I think the major mistake was taking what was essentially a party and turning it into an ego game and a star trip. An ego trip of, 'Look how many of us there are,' and a star trip of the Rolling Stones, who are on a star trip and who qualify in my book as snobs. I've talked with them many times and I think they're snobs. I'm sure they don't understand what they did Saturday. I think they have an exaggerated view of their own importance. I think they're on a grotesque ego trip. I think they are on negative trips, essentially, especially the two leaders."

And Bill Graham: "I ask you what right you had, Mr. Jagger, in going through with this free festival? And you couldn't tell me you didn't know the way it would have come off. What right did you have to leave the way you did, thanking everybody for a wonderful time, and the Angels for helping out? What did he leave behind throughout the country? Every gig he was late. Every fucking gig he made the promoter and the people bleed. What right does this god have to descend on this country this way? It will give me great pleasure to tell the country that Mick Jagger is not God, Jr. But you know what is a great tragedy to me? That cunt is a great entertainer."

The Stones returned to London after the disaster at Altamont and performed two concerts, one at the Savile on December 14 and the other at the Lyceum a week later. Jagger continued to call Marianne in Rome, asking her to return. She refused, and he stopped calling. She returned to England for Christmas, with Mario and Nicholas, and went to stay with her mother. She was worried that Jagger would show up and create a scene with Mario. The day after Christmas Jagger called. "I'm down at Keith's," he said. "I'd like to drive up and wish you a Merry Christmas. I have a present for you." Marianne said it was silly for him to drive a couple hundred miles to give her a present, but Jagger insisted. She told him to come. When she hung up the phone she thought: *I've been stupid. Mick and Mario may as well meet, and then Mick will go away and it will all be cool.*

Jagger arrived at about ten that night and gave Marianne her present: a small silver box filled with cocaine. *That bastard,* she thought as she kissed him and thanked him, *knowing me, he had to bring coke.* She snorted some and was feeling exquisitely high, so pleased to see Jagger. She knew she could never have left him had he not been away, on tour, and she had refused to go near him because she knew his presence was so strong, he had so much vitality, that other men would look pale next to him. Almost immediately, Mario started to pale in her eyes. Marianne's mother had gone to bed. Jagger and Mario started arguing over Marianne, and as she listened she thought: *The minute Mick walked in the door I knew he had come with the intention of wiping the floor with Mario.* And she thought: *I believed I was in love with Mario, but on the other hand there is a lot between Mick and me, and we know each other and each other's faults.* The two men argued, then lapsed into long periods of staring at each other, and Marianne felt them mentally tugging at her and pushing at each other. Then they began arguing again, Mario being very intensely and passionately Italian, waving his arms around, and Jagger shouting: "Okay, let's go outside and fight." And Marianne thought:

Neither of them intends to leave. And that creates an interesting problem. There's only one bed left. Well, fuck it! Let the best man win. I'm going to bed. Whichever one I wake up with that's the one I'll stay with.

She took a couple of sleeping pills and went off to bed. In the morning, when she woke, Jagger was sleeping beside her, and it all seemed so natural, so perfectly normal. Mario had slept on the couch and left early, before anyone got up; he must have been mortally offended. When Jagger woke he stalked around the house, somewhat arrogant: "Wop in your bed, girl?" he said to Marianne. "What are you thinking about, an Eye-talian?" Marianne laughed. They caught the next plane to London and returned to Cheyne Walk.

In her own mind, however, Marianne had not really returned to Jagger. She was still very dissatisfied; Jagger was constantly busy with his recording and his career. He was putting the finishing touches on Rolling Stones Records; involved in the suit against Allen Klein; working closely with Prince Rupert on plans for the Stones to move to Europe in order to cut down their tax debt to the British government; and recording every night for the next album. Marianne was sure that Jagger knew she was unhappy, for she was getting very paranoiac and emotional: She would call up the office several times a day, crying that Nicholas had vanished, and Jagger would have to calm her down; a few moments later she'd call back and say Nicholas was fine, he'd just gone round the corner to see his playmates. Jagger appeared to be getting very annoyed by it. Whenever she'd call he'd say, "Oh, no, not again . . ." and began avoiding her calls. Their friends, and Jagger's employees, knew that Marianne was becoming too emotional for Jagger, she was beginning to open up, emotionally, no longer able to hold it in. She wasn't being *cool* and the one thing Jagger needed was everything to be cool around him, they felt, because he was under a great deal of pressure with the business dealings.

Jagger and Marianne never talked about Mario, directly. Marianne knew the lack of communication was as much her fault as it was his. *This head in the sand business, I'm as much to blame as Mick is, I'd rather not talk about it.* But one night Jagger started shouting at her, about her dissatisfaction, and about her leaving Cheyne Walk; not the affair with Mario, but her audacity at walking out on him. He worked himself into such a fury that he seemed about to attack her, to beat her. Marianne threw herself on the floor, cowering, knowing that a total defenselessness would stop him. Jagger looked down at her and said: "I can't beat you up, girl, you look as though the floor's swallowing you up." He lifted her to her feet, gently, and said: "Come listen to this song I've written for you." And Marianne thought: *He's changing his tactics, he's trying to seduce me.*

He put a reel of tape on the tape deck, turned it on, and Marianne began to cry when she heard his voice: *"Graceless lady, you know who I am. You know I can't let you slide through my hands. Wild horses couldn't drag me away. Wild, wild horses couldn't drag me away . . ."* Australia. The hospital room and the first words she said when coming out of the coma: *He's fucking my mind completely with this song,* she

344

thought, *it's such a high emotional plane of love,* and she fell into his arms, sobbing almost hysterically.

Their relationship was all right after that, Marianne felt, but she knew it couldn't last because the self-destructiveness in her, flamed by Jagger's apparent need to be the public Mick Jagger even in his personal life, made it unbearable for her. She started using heroin again, and she was certain Jagger knew it although he never talked about it. In May 1970, he told her that they would be moving to France. For tax reasons. But Marianne thought there was something more compelling: *He knows I'm a very obvious way for the London coppers to stick a drug charge on him, I'm a marvelous opportunity for them to keep busting Mick because I do have drugs on me all the time.* She told Jagger: "I will not move to France. If this is what we're doing to each other—if we have to go to fuckin' France to be all right together—then let's split up." She left that evening.

Janice Kenner, a tall, vivacious blonde from California, was vacationing in England, visiting the Stones' recording engineer and occasional producer, Glyn Johns, and his wife and baby. The Stones were recording the new album, *Sticky Fingers*, in a studio at the edge of London, and Glyn was co-producing it with Jagger and Keith. Just before it was time for her to return to California, Janice told Glyn she'd love to stay in England for a while if she could get a job. Glyn said he'd ask around the studio that night. Next day he told her Jagger could use some help in the house in Cheyne Walk and added: "But Mick said he'd have to see the person first." And Janice thought: *Oh, my God, how bizarre!*

They went to the premiere of *Ned Kelly* a couple of nights later, June 24, 1970, which Jagger didn't attend because he was working in the studio. Janice sat through the film, watching Jagger up on the screen, larger than life, and said to

Glyn: "My God, you mean after this movie I have to go meet this man, he has to look at me to see if I qualify to work for him?"

When the film ended they drove out to the studio, and Janice went into the control room. After a time Jagger, Keith and the other Stones entered the control room, and Janice thought how small they all looked. Jagger didn't know who she was or why she was there, and he ignored her, sitting in a chair opposite her and listening to the playback of the tapes they had just mixed. Eventually he must have figured out that Janice was his prospective employee, smiled slyly, and leaped to his feet. He strode to her, standing directly in front of where she was sitting, and thrust his crotch in her face, she remembers. He started to dance to "Bitch," the song being played, slowly moving his hips in front of her. Janice didn't know what to do; she looked to the right, to the left, down at the floor, then finally stared straight ahead at his undulating crotch. She thought: *He either expects me to leave or to grab his balls, and I'm not about to do either.* Midway through the song Jagger said:

"Do you dance?"

"Yeah, I dance," Janice said.

"Wanna dance?"

Janice didn't move for a moment. She thought: *Oh, fuck, he's going to make me dance, he's really playing the game. He's going to make me get up in front of all these strangers and dance with him, the best dancer I've ever seen. Fuck it, I'll dance.* She rose and danced with him, and everyone seemed to relax; she had passed some kind of test. Joints were broken out, every one was friendly, listening to the tapes, smoking and drinking. Jagger and the band recorded some other tracks for the album, working until 7 a.m. Before they quit Jagger came into the control room again.

"So you want a job?" he asked Janice.

"Yes I do. I don't want to go back to America just yet."

346

"What can you do?"

"Anything," Janice said.

"Can you cook?"

"Sure, I'm a really terrific cook."

"Oh." He turned and left.

Janice went back to the studio with Glyn several times, but Jagger never said anything further about the job and she assumed she hadn't been hired. The third time she was there, when the recording session again broke up at dawn, Glyn asked if anyone would give Janice a lift into London.

"Yeah, I will," Jagger said.

Janice was a little upset. She thought: *Oh, no, I've been with him in a room full of people and now I'm going to be in a car with him alone.*

They got into Jagger's old white Bentley. He started the ignition, then turned to her and said: "Well, where do you like to wake up, in the country or in the city?"

Janice fidgeted for a moment. She thought: *What a pretentious bastard! He knows I'm supposed to meet friends in London and he assumes I'll drop all my plans to go with him.* She turned to Jagger and said: "The country." And she thought: *I may as well, it's not every day this is going to happen to me.*

They drove down to Stargroves, and on the way Jagger explained that they'd be forced to stay in a small cottage next to the house because restoration work hadn't yet been completed, and Janice envisioned a small shack with dirt floor. The cottage was a three-bedroom house, complete with manservant. They lived there for three days and when they were driving back to London, Janice smiled as something crossed her mind: *All those jokes about the chick with a Jagger fantasy, fucking guys and saying not as good as Jagger, and then finally getting to fuck Jagger and saying, not as good as Jagger—well, that's bullshit. He's fantastic, he's had a lot of experience at it.*

Janice was hired, but Jagger insisted on making one thing clear: "If I give you the job we won't be lovers, you'll be around to maybe cook once in a while and live in, and get the cleaning lady to do a right proper job. She comes in every day." Janice said that was fine, and Jagger told her she'd have the floor above his bedroom, a two-room suite with a bathroom. She moved in several days later, and Jagger showed her around the house. Many of Marianne's clothes were still hanging in the bedroom closet. "I'm gonna send them to her," he said. But he didn't get around to it for many months.

After a couple of weeks in the house Janice realized she was growing very protective of Jagger, and fond of him. They weren't lovers, just an occasional night together, but they sat around and talked a great deal, and she understood something: *He doesn't have that many friends, it's difficult for a Mick Jagger to have friends because he can never be sure who's a friend and who's sucking off him. He needs a friend more than he needs a lover.*

Eventually, however, Catherine came along—introduced to Jagger by Eric Clapton—and she moved in, a replacement for Marianne in a way. Catherine is a Californian, outstandingly beautiful but Janice didn't think she was especially sophisticated. Catherine is a super-groupie, the elite of the groupies: Instead of flying on her own to meet a superstar, the superstars send her plane tickets so that she won't forget to come to them. Jagger impressed on Catherine the fact that she was living in a grand house, had a lot of money to spend on it, and must learn to be a real English lady, Janice recalls. But Catherine seemed to have no idea how to be a lady: She took to flicking her cigarette ashes on the floor because there was someone around to clean them up, Janice felt. Catherine appeared to be trying to play the role Jagger was forcing on her, telling Janice it was all so romantic to be Mick Jagger's lady and how madly in love she was with him. And Janice thought: *Mick's not in love with you, he's just interested in fucking you*

348

and having a good time. He's fucking around with your head, and you're going to be terribly hurt when you wake up. Jagger's games made Janice angry, and she tried to warn Catherine about it, gently. Catherine refused to permit reality to get in the way of romantic dreams, Janice felt, and the two women started getting into arguments over it. Janice later said: "Mick knew it and loved it. He played it up and instigated arguments between us. I remember thinking: 'The guy is fantasizing that we're fighting over him.' "

The Stones were going off on tour again—a month in Europe through September and part of October. Catherine appeared furious because she was being left behind, and even Janice was being taken along, a last minute assignment to help Anita take care of her baby because Shirley Arnold had sprained her ankle and couldn't go. They were up in Jagger's bedroom, packing his clothes for the tour. Catherine sat on the bed crying that she was being left behind, and Jagger seemed to be feeling sorry for her. He leaned over and stroked her hair very lightly. "Let's go downstairs to the other bedroom," he said. Turning to Janice: "Finish packing this shit." They left the room, and Janice sat on the bed, lit up a huge joint, and thought: *He's giving her a farewell fuck.* She sat there a long while, smoking, getting too stoned to finish packing. And she thought: *I'm really glad he took her downstairs because it'll make her feel a lot better; she's done nothing but cry for days.*

Suddenly, Jagger came rushing back into the bedroom, shouting: "I don't understand her," followed by a tall, willowy, and very exotic woman, a friend who had dropped in to visit. She also shouts: "I don't understand." Catherine rushes in, screaming: "I hate you, I hate you." And Janice, stoned, sits there thinking: *It's like a fucking movie comedy.* When everyone quiets down, and the woman goes home, and Jagger leaves the room for a moment, Catherine explains what the commotion was all about:

"We're in bed, fucking," she tells Janice, "when in walks this bitch and makes some remark, and Mick invites her to get in bed with us. I guess I just got hysterical and I started screaming and kicking Mick and scratching. My last night in bed with Mick, and he wants another chick to join us."

Jagger met Bianca Perez Moreno de Macias, a dusky, exotically beautiful Nicaraguan, at a party given for the Stones after their concert at the Olympia, in Paris. A friend of Jagger introduced them and, according to the most romantic version that later got back to the London gossips, he warned Jagger: "Listen, dance with her, but remember she's spending the night with me." Jagger said of course, danced with Bianca for hours, and then she suddenly left. Alone. A short time later Jagger also left alone. And met Bianca somewhere, a rendezvous arranged while they were dancing.

The next stops on the tour were Vienna, for a one-nighter, and then Rome. Janice had heard that Jagger had met someone in Paris, a woman he'd really fallen for. A couple of hours before the concert in Rome, he told Janice: "I want you to take one of the limousines out to the airport and meet a lady coming in from Paris. Her name's Bianca."

"Fuck, I shine your shoes for you," Janice said, "but I don't want to pick up your French whores for you."

"You have to pick her up. I described you to her, and she'll be looking for you. Go get her. And take her back to the hotel, I've booked a room for her."

"Her own room?" Janice asked.

"Yeah, her own room. Now go get her."

Janice thought that was very strange, Mick Jagger's chick getting her own room. She went to pick up Bianca and was immediately fascinated by her: *She's so beautiful and sophisticated.* Janice is very curious about her and begins to ask questions on the ride back to London, but Bianca won't reveal too much. Janice thought: *I'd like to know how she did it and what she does to survive.* Bianca started to open up, just a little bit, almost an official biography that she'd memorized, everything she had done since flying off to Paris seven years before. Then she said she was twenty-one, and Janice thought: *Impossible, lady. You've filled me in on seven years of your life and you couldn't possibly have started at the ripe old age of fourteen.* Later, Janice saw Bianca's passport—age, twenty-six—but Bianca continued to insist she was twenty-one. She had a habit of saying, "In nine years, when I'm thirty . . ." and Janice and Jagger would laugh.

Bianca is the daughter of a none-too-wealthy businessman in Nicaragua. Her parents are separated, and her mother, Dora Macias, operates a small refreshment stand in Managua. When Bianca graduated from high school at eighteen she flew off to Paris to study political science at the Sorbonne. She returned home after two years and was offered a job on the Nicaraguan foreign office staff. She turned it down. Within weeks she was back in Paris, living in a $7.50-a-week room. Once, when she was short of funds, she took a job as a hostess at the Paris Meat Fair, greeting businessmen and directing them to the exhibits. She then got a job on the staff of the Nicaraguan Ambassador, began moving in international circles, and became a big hit at Embassy parties because of her striking looks and her fluency in several languages. She went to work for a record company run by Eddie Barclay, the Stones' European representative, was Michael Caine's girl friend for a while, and was rumored to be engaged to Barclay when she met Jagger.

Photographers started to follow Bianca and Jagger everywhere they went, and Janice recalls that he got very upset over it. One night in a hotel in Frankfurt, Jagger's bodyguard smashed a photographer's camera while Jagger and Bianca scurried over a wall to escape. Jagger loved it, Janice felt— climbing a wall with his lady was so romantic.

Janice wondered whether Jagger was aware of the intrigue among the women on the tour, intrigue and schemes that she found so funny. She described it to a friend when she returned to London:

"It was almost hysterical when Bianca came on the tour," she said, "because suddenly Mick had a woman, and the pressure is off the other women—they can stop worrying that Mick is going to bring in a lot of chicks that will threaten their men. All those women are so paranoid because they're the Rolling Stones' old ladies, and that's a very insecure position to be in. And I wasn't a threat, I was the employee that all the women could come and talk to. They would come and tell me how much they didn't like the other women. But when they were together they loved each other and would rush off and leave me out. I thought, what a weird life to have all that money and clothes and dope, and the ego thing, but to be that paranoid."

"How did Anita and Bianca get along?" Janice was asked. "I mean, Anita is like the queen there, she's got such a hold on the men."

"Anita didn't really seem to like Bianca at first," Janice said. "She would say, 'Bianca darling, I haven't opened my trunk yet. Can I borrow something to wear?' Bianca seemed so paranoid about blowing it with Keith's lady that she'd say, 'Yes, darling, of course.' Anita would borrow a suede dress with mink trim and leave it on the floor, in a pile. She was careless with clothes. And she didn't open her trunk for a week after Bianca showed up. She just kept borrowing things. She would say, 'How nice to have Bianca, I didn't have to bother packing.' And I'd be hysterical. Anita and Bianca would be very friendly and then wouldn't speak to each other and would hate each other behind the other's back."

When the tour ended, Bianca accompanied the Stones to

London. Stargroves was ready now, and Jagger, Bianca, and the entourage moved down to the country. Bianca and Jagger had a suite of their own in the house.

They were all down at Stargroves the first week in November when Jagger got a phone call telling him he was a father: Marsha Hunt had given birth to a girl. Jagger seemed excited; he laughed into the phone, smiled broadly when he hung it up, then walked out of the room. He didn't say anything; Marsha's pregnancy was supposed to be a secret, although all the gossips in London knew about it.

Jagger was shopping in a market in the King's Road a few months later and bumped into Chrissie Shrimpton. They chatted a bit, and Chrissie said that she had just had a baby.

"I've got one, too," Jagger said. "Marsha won't let me see her. She's a very funny lady."

Weeks later Marsha gave several interviews—she was appearing in *Catch My Soul* *—and talked openly about the baby, whom she'd named Karis. She said when she was discharged from the hospital and went home with her baby to her flat in St. John's Wood, the baby's father—she refused to name him—was waiting for them with his chauffeur and housekeeper. They spent the afternoon celebrating. He left after a couple of hours.

"We had a child on purpose," Marsha said. "He said he wanted a child, and I said I wanted one as well. So we had a baby together, and now he is no longer involved with us. At first I thought he was a person I cared for a lot, but I found out afterward I didn't really know him at all. I mean, when people said he was no good I didn't believe them because I saw

* A rock version of *Othello* and dreadful. T.S.

353

goodness in him, and I do forgive him because I don't think he understands what he's doing.

"The sad thing about our relationship was the attitude he assumed after the child was born. I think I loved somebody who never existed. It is sad that we are not friends now. Maybe he feels some sort of intimidation . . .

"When Karis was born," she went on, "the father felt a great deal of confusion which I didn't have time for, so I told him to go and solve his own mental and emotional problems and that *I* would take care of *my* child."

In July 1973, Marsha's attorneys moved in Marylebone Magistrate's Court to have Jagger named as the father of her child. At the request of Jagger's attorney, the court ordered blood tests to be taken and adjourned the hearing. A spokesman for Jagger, who was in Italy, said: "This allegation is not admitted. There are discussions between the parties about the merits of these allegations."

The Stones are on the road again, a quick tour of Britain, March 1971. It's their first British tour in almost five years, and it's being billed as their farewell to Britain. Then off to the villas which they've rented or bought in the South of France, within a short driving distance of one another. The Stones' publicity office passes the word that they've been helped in their move to France by merchant bankers Leopold Joseph and French financial lawyer Maître Michard-Pelessier—better see the Stones now, fans, or you may never see them again.

Jagger is almost dressing like a Frenchman on this tour: He wears a brushed grey suede maxicoat, a tight, ribbed sweater, and a blue printed cap perched on the back of his head as he boards the plane to Glasgow, one of a dozen concerts. Bianca is with him. She plays gin rummy during the tour and speaks to

Jagger in French much of the time. A journalist travelling with them observed that her face seems to give nothing away; it told him she's been there, she's seen it all, and she isn't about to tip you off to what she is thinking; it's a gambler's face, except for the blinding smile she frequently gives. But behind the mysterious eyes he sensed a small fleck of fright hiding, as if she knew her defenses might be penetrated at any moment. But not on this tour. She doesn't react when Jagger, discussing how insipid rock has become, says: "But rock-'n'-roll's not over. I don't like to see one thing end until I see another beginning. Like when you break up with a woman. D'y'know what I mean?"

If Bianca knew, she didn't signal it in front of the journalists and other strangers. She is one of them now, a Rolling Stone, just as Anita became a complete Rolling Stone after she started to live with Brian. "Bianca's a groovy chick," Keith later said. "We all dig her."

Bianca doesn't react, either, when a groupie makes it through the guards and into the dressing room at the Roundhouse, London, the final date of the tour. "Excuse me," she says to Bianca, "but didn't I see you with Osibisa in their dressing room last week?" Some of those crowded into the dressing room have heard her and they watch, stunned: This groupie is asking Bianca, Mick Jagger's woman, whether she is a groupie for this new band. "What is Osibisa?" Bianca asks. "Oh, wow, there's someone with your exact vibrations around," the groupie says. "I mean, like a twin sister. Someone who is walking around with your face." The groupie is ushered out, quickly.

They all moved off to France the following month, five Stones, assorted wives and girl friends, babies, secretaries, chauffeurs. A band of gypsies fleeing confiscatory taxes and fear of drug arrests. Jagger didn't place his two houses for sale, didn't even lease them. He would be returning to London three months out of every year—or whatever time span the British tax laws permit someone who claims foreign residency. But the papers were quite upset, and headlines made it appear that Jagger, who had once been condemned from one end of the country to the next, was a good lad whose heart should remain in his native land. "I can't see why they're making such a big thing of me coming to France," Jagger said soon after settling in his villa on the Riviera. "I never said I was leaving England for good. Why don't they leave me alone?"

A month after crossing the Channel, Jagger called his mother. He was going to marry Bianca, he said, on May 13, in St. Tropez. He told her he wanted his parents to come, of course. And had booked a suite for them at the hotel he and Bianca would be staying in. Eva Jagger cried. She had wanted him to marry Chrissie, wanted him to marry Marianne. He was finally getting married, would perhaps settle down, no more drug arrests, no more scandal, perhaps he'd even give her a grandchild. She had never met Bianca, didn't know much more than she'd read, but if her son had chosen her then she must be a superb girl.

Jagger told his mother she was to tell no one about the wedding. It must be kept a secret because he didn't want it turned into a circus.

The Great Mick Jagger Wedding Circus began a few days later. Jagger had invited about seventy friends on the London pop and young aristocracy scene to the wedding. A chartered jet would fly them to St. Tropez on Wednesday evening, May 12, and they would all be his guests at the Hôtel Byblos. He called his press agent, employees in the Rolling Stones office, spreading the glad tidings. And demanding secrecy. Reporters and photographers were rushing to St. Tropez before Eva Jagger had a chance to shop for a new hat, in Dartford, and take the train to London for a new dress. The writers scavenged around for stories to cable back to their editors, and one of them came up with a choice item: Jagger had taken four weeks of instruction in Catholicism, to prepare for his marriage. Abbé Lucien Baud, pastor of the fisherman's chapel of St. Anne, perched on a hill overlooking a sweep of the French Riviera and the Mediterranean, told journalists: "It's not a question of his becoming a Roman Catholic, just an understanding of our faith. He is a very serious, intelligent man. He is an Anglican, of course, and I don't think a practicing one. He has a great sense of religion, that boy. He really has a feeling for it."

Wedding Day. And it appeared the wedding might not come off as planned. There was, to start, a problem over the wedding contract. Under French law, a couple must sign one of two marriage contracts: Either joint ownership of all property and earnings, or a total separation of all worldly goods. Bianca demanded the former, Jagger the latter. There were some heated discussions between them, assorted officials, aides, attorneys, before Bianca agreed to sign the contract Jagger demanded. In the meantime, down in the St. Tropez council chamber, where they would be married in a civil ceremony before the church wedding, Mayor Marius Estezan stood beneath a portrait of President Pompidou, beaming merrily. Scores of fans filled his chamber, plus reporters and cameramen from around the world. Interviewing the mayor and taking his photo while they waited to witness the most publicized secret wedding in history.

An aide phoned Jagger in his hotel suite to warn him of the crush he should expect when he arrived. "If there's going to be all that crowd, I'm not going to get married," Jagger said. "I am not a goldfish bowl and I am not the King of France." When Jagger's words were flashed to the room Ray Connolly of the London *Evening Standard* almost laughed: "If he'd wanted a quiet wedding, why on earth did he tell the world so far in advance?"

Les Perrin, Jagger's press agent, informed the mayor that Jagger refused to attend the wedding unless the chamber was cleared. The mayor removed his tricolor sash and said: "We are now twenty minutes late. If Mr. Jagger is not here in ten minutes I shall leave, and there will be no ceremony."

Perrin asked a French-speaking English journalist to appeal to Police Commissioner Jean-Pierre Haramboure to clear the chamber. "Monsieur, you are in France," the police chief explained, "and it is the law that the ceremony is held in public." Perrin winced. The journalist was asked to appeal again to the mayor: "Ask him to give Mick another fifteen minutes and tell him the delay isn't meant as a discourtesy." Replied the mayor: *"D'accord.* But you must tell him if he is going to let everyone in the world know he is getting married, it is no use blaming me if the town hall is full." Connolly smiled at the theft of his line.

Les phoned Jagger: "You've got to come down and face it, Mick, you've got to."

The wedding party started to arrive shortly. Jagger's parents came first, looking pale and nervous at their first taste of the insanity of fame. Roger Vadim and Nathalie Delon, who were to be the witnesses, struggled through the crowd. Followed by Keith. "I've had four fights just to get here," he said and threw an ashtray on the marriage table.

Les asked the police chief to please move the photographers to the center of the room so there would be at least a little dignity in the ceremony. He refused. "The floor is weak, and if they stand there we shall all go through," he explained.

Jagger and Bianca finally arrived, fifty minutes late. Bianca was trembling and appeared very frightened, and the fear seemed to soften her insolently beautiful face and her mouth, which usually appears so cruel that it heightens the aura of mystery about her. She wore a white midi suit by Saint-Laurent, cut so deeply to her waist that there was almost a hint of her nipples, and a white picture hat ringed with roses. It was not possible to tell she was in her fourth month of pregnancy. When Jagger and Bianca stepped into the room, photographers' flashbulbs blinding them and the din of reporters' shouts almost deafening them, they turned back again.

"I'm not going on," Jagger said. "I'm not going through with this."

Press agents and other aides persuaded him to get married, fast, get it over with. Jagger relented. He asked the photographers to take their final pictures and leave him in peace. They took their photos, but refused to leave. Fist fights broke out among the newsmen, jockeying for the best position to witness the wedding, and the floor felt as if it would collapse them all into the basement. The police chief insisted he could not eject anyone, under French law. Jagger muttered a few "Fucks" and marched up to the marriage desk, Bianca clutching his hand, sobbing. They went through the brief ceremony and signed the register to make it legal. Mick Jagger was married.

It was far from over, however. The Catholic ceremony in the little church up the hill was next. And the violence that Jagger evoked from the stage flared up now; French photographers who were angry that Jagger wouldn't pose with his bride for the rest of the afternoon, and several teenage "radicals" upset at French press reports that the wedding would cost about $50,000, kicked at and smashed the sides of Jagger's Bentley as it pulled away from the town hall. A Jagger aide who objected was smashed over the head by a French photographer.

At the church, an hour behind schedule, Abbé Baud was uneasy at the reports he'd heard of the scene at the council chamber, but he insisted that all would be calm in his church. The guests, carefully screened, were let into the church, and the doors were locked. Jagger drove up with Bianca, walked through a crowd and up the steps, and couldn't get inside. He knocked repeatedly on the door, but no one would open it. "Les, dammit, Les, let me in!" Jagger shouted while a mob at his back demanded autographs. An aide eventually lifted the beam sealing the door, peeked out, and swung it wide. Jagger, angry, took his place at the altar rail. The organist played Bianca's requests—which included a medley of themes from *Love Story*. Lord Lichfield, appearing aristocratically splendid in a white suit and blue shirt and looking out of place among the weird fashions on most of the guests, led Bianca down the aisle. Abbé Baud was visibly upset at breasts showing through see-through tops and other parts of the anatomy being displayed by the demands of fashion, but he plunged ahead with the ceremony. In his sermon, he told Jagger:

"You have told me you believe that youth seeks happiness and a certain ideal and faith. I think you are seeking it too, and I hope it arrives today with your marriage."

Then he smiled and added: "But when you are a personality like Mick Jagger it is too much to hope for privacy for your marriage."

That evening, in a small and shabby theater next to the Café des Arts in St. Tropez, the guests assembled to celebrate Jagger's wedding. Among them were Ringo Starr, Paul McCartney and his wife, several Ormsby-Gores, and Joe and Eva Jagger. Bianca had changed into a new outfit: an old skirt, two blouses—one over the other—and a sequined turban. Ossie Clark had come to the wedding with a dress he'd designed especially for this party, but Bianca couldn't get into it because her breasts were so swollen from her pregnancy. Bianca also wore her wedding present, a $10,000 diamond bracelet.

Jagger had ordered the press excluded, but several reporters and photographers managed to get into the reception. A local band opened the show while the guests ate and drank—more than $1,000 was spent on caviar alone—and the music went on all night as about 200 guests danced and got drunk and stoned. Jagger was up on stage, performing with a batch of musicians, ten hours after he'd been married. But Bianca slipped away early. So did Joe and Eva Jagger, who had spent the evening searching for a quiet place to give the couple their wedding present. Eva Jagger still clutched the present when she left to go back to the hotel. "I hope my other son doesn't become a superstar," she told a reporter.

John Morris, an American who has been promoting concerts in Britain and on the Continent, pulls up to Jagger's villa in France a couple of days after Jagger's twenty-eighth birthday. Jagger has asked John to come over to France and help him plan a tour of America in 1972, a year away. Sitting in the front yard, they begin to talk about the Rainbow, which John has just reopened in London. The Rainbow's capacity is 2,800 customers, John tells him, and Jagger says:

"I'd much rather play a three-thousand-seat house on the next American tour than ten or twenty thousand. Places like the Forum or the Garden are really too big to get something cooking between the band and the audience."

"It can be done, if you want it," John said. "Every city in America has a theater that size. Old theaters, with fantastic acoustics, like the Fillmore East."

"Yeah, I know, but the big problem is whether the band will have the energy to tour for nine months. That's what it'll take to satisfy the ticket demand. And we wouldn't be able to get visas for that long anyway."

"Closed circuit TV," John said.

"Yeah, I've thought of that," Jagger said. "Bill Graham sent me a letter suggesting we play the Fillmore East for thirty days, with closed circuit TV or film for the rest of the country. But I'd rather have as much live audience as possible."

The talked about it for hours, trying to figure out how it could be done. "You've got to help me with it," Jagger said. "I want to do small places and get back in touch with the audience on that level, like in the old days before we got so big and the economics of it got out of hand.''

Bianca had vanished. Seven months pregnant, and she had lost herself somewhere in Paris, and Jagger couldn't find her. The Stones had been working extraordinarily long, hard hours, trying to get together a double album for release in time for the 1972 American tour. They had been recording through most of the summer in a studio Keith built in the basement of his villa outside the small town of Villefranche. Jagger would fly up to Paris to be with Bianca, fly back to get in a couple of days recording, then return to her. This time he'd flown down to work with Keith on a couple of songs, telling Bianca he'd be gone only two days. But the songwriting and recording stretched out to four days, and five. One night, Morris recalls, Jagger phoned Bianca to say he'd need another day or two. But he couldn't reach her where she'd been staying, and none of her friends knew where she was. He returned to Paris and took a suite in L'Hôtel. John Morris went with him, and they sat up until dawn talking about the American tour between Jagger's phone calls, searching for Bianca.

Bianca gave birth to a daughter on October 21, 1971, in Paris. They named her Jade. Jagger threw a small champagne party for close friends. He remained in Paris for several weeks; Bianca didn't have to insist on it because Jagger was so overwhelmed with his child that he wouldn't think of leaving. He told Keith to lay down whatever tracks were needed to fill out the album, he'd be down in several weeks to record his vocal tracks.

"I'm a fantastic dad!" Jagger shouted when someone asked him what kind of a father he was going to be. "Jade's a fantastic kid, a lovely baby, very sweet and good-tempered. Most babies seem to cry all the time, but mine doesn't. Every time I look at her she's just gurgling and smiling away to herself. I've always been a good father, and this kid makes it easy to be that way."

Jagger and John Morris are drinking beer in a suite in the Continental Hyatt House, Hollywood, in January 1972, still trying to work out a tour that could be held in small theaters. Peter Rudge, who had promoted several tours for The Who, sat on a window sill, looking out at Sunset Strip; John had been busy with the Rainbow and had asked Jagger to bring Peter in as co-producer because John couldn't handle it alone. And Peter suddenly said:

"No matter how small or large a hall you play, you have to have security. What about security?"

Jagger was silent for a moment. "Yeah, I'm really scared about this tour," he said. "We must have perfect security. America is getting even heavier now, and people are into a lot of coke at concerts." Jagger asked if they had read what just happened to Jethro Tull, in Denver. The audience was coked up and threw bottles at the band. Jagger had been in Los Angeles with Keith a short time before, working on the final mix for the new album, *Exile on Main Street*, and had seen how strange a lot of the freaks were getting now that coke had become the fad drug.

"There are some really weird people here in California," Jagger said. "And this tour is going to bring them all out of the woodwork. Anything can happen on this tour, it scares me."

"We have to make sure it doesn't happen," John said.

"If somebody wants to kill me there is no way in the world you can stop him. What can you do about it? How can you subdue him?"

"Very simple," John said. "We can do one of two things. We

can put you in a glass booth. Or you can grow a beard and just sit home and write."

"Yes, but I want to perform," Jagger said. "I must perform."

As the summer tour date came nearer and the plans started firming up, Jagger was overtaken by financial reality. "We have to make a lot of money out of this tour," Jagger said, "to pay off taxes and keep us goin' for a while." John Morris was back in London, trying to salvage the Rainbow, which was failing, and waiting for a call from Jagger to go out to Los Angeles and start putting together all the details of the tour. Instead, he received a call from Prince Rupert, who said that he and Marshall Chess, who had been hired by Jagger to run Rolling Stones Records, had persuaded Jagger that the economics required the Stones to play in America's largest halls. Rupert added that Peter Rudge would be tour manager; John Morris had been dealt out.

A couple of weeks later, Jagger called. He asked about the Rainbow, said he'd like to do a special concert to raise money to keep the Rainbow open. They talked about a half-hour, and it was clear to John that Jagger couldn't bring himself to talk about the way the tour plans had been changed. And John said:

"Look, Mick, stop worrying about how the tour turned out. If you need any help, I'll help. I figure the way it turned out has very little to do with you personally."

"I had to make the decision," Jagger said. "There's nothing I can say about it except there was a lot of pressure, and I hope it works out best this way."

Security is extraordinarily tight on this tour; the entire Stones organization seems to be concentrating most of its energies on protecting Mick Jagger. In each city, police chiefs have been contacted far in advance and have been persuaded to assign more than the normal number of police to maintain security outside the stadium in which the Stones are to perform. Inside the halls are special guards. Each of them has been personally approved by the tour director, Peter Rudge, who tells any journalist who asks: "I've done five tours for The Who and I've never seen one like this. This one's a military campaign. Truly. It's more than rock and roll. It's an event. When I've finished here the only thing I'll be good for is managing political campaigns." The Stones have been assigned two personal bodyguards, both over thirty-five, both veteran guards. One of them must stay with Jagger at all times that he's not in his hotel room.

The precautions didn't appear to be excessive, once the tour began. The night before the first concert, in Vancouver on Saturday, June 3, Rudge sent several members of the tour crew to clubs and coffee houses in Vancouver's equivalent of Greenwich Village. They were told to ask any freaks they met: "Got any Stones tickets?" Much of the time the answer was: "No, man, we don't need any. We're going to crash in." That night, about 2,000 kids almost smashed down a corrugated metal door at the rear of the stadium but were beaten off by police; several bottles thrown from the audience splintered on the stage before the Stones came on; and during Jagger's second song two kids fighting with several ushers ripped up a section of heavy iron railing and threw it toward the stage.

In Seattle, police confiscate a .22-caliber automatic pistol from one kid, knives from several others, as everyone entering the hall is thoroughly searched. In Montreal, a small explosive charge placed under an equipment truck goes off several hours before the road crew is scheduled to unload, destroying the truck and a number of amplifiers; police blame French-Canadian extremists.

The memory of Altamont, almost three years before, is like a shadowy specter riding along with this traveling circus of five Stones and seventy employees, and spooking everyone. Jagger will take few chances, this time around America. He doesn't perform "Sympathy for the Devil," the song he was singing when Meredith Hunter was murdered, and although he denies the killing has anything to do with the deletion of the song, his press agents admit privately that several "volatile songs" have been dropped from the act. Jagger had been asked, before the tour started, whether he wasn't afraid of getting shot by someone in the audience. He answered each interviewer in almost the same words, as if they'd been rehearsed: "It's something I just don't think about. If I thought too much about getting killed I wouldn't even cross a road." Yet friends back in London were saying that Jagger seemed almost paranoiac about being killed and had said: "I'm not game to getting bumped off over there." Now, on the tour, Jagger does appear afraid. In Chicago, as he is singing "Brown Sugar," an object soars toward the stage, flashing briefly in the lights. A writer on the tour notes that Jagger never saw it coming and that as it hits him in the forehead a wince of fear flashed across his face—for the briefest moment time seemed to stand still for him—and then the missile, a small harmless ball, bounced into the audience. In Nashville, firecrackers exploded near the stage, and Jagger leaped away from the microphone, then quickly recovered and began to dance.

There are other fears that seem to possess him on this tour, journalists observed. During the flight to Denver the pilot of the chartered jet announced that there might be turbulence ahead. It was reported that Jagger blanched and rushed for his seat. On another flight, as the plane leaves the runway and begins to nose into the sky, Jagger suddenly cuts short a laugh and jumps into his seat. "This is the most critical part, right here," he says. A writer saw him biting hard on his lower lip. "The power turn. If it's going to happen." He closes his eyes, his face and body tense. And in each city he tells journalists that he doesn't ever think about Altamont.

Jagger's public mask came down briefly in Detroit, as he sat in a late-night restaurant several hours after the show at Cobo Arena. He was teasing about with Chip Monck, threatening to throw a soggy whipped cream concoction in Chip's face but hesitant because Chip's own dessert was poised for throwing. A stranger stopped at their table, directly in front of Jagger. A sudden and almost tragic look of fear was seen in Jagger's eyes as he raised his head to the stranger. The man said he wanted to thank him for the performance, and Jagger's body seemed to relax. When the man walked away, Jagger said to one of his friends at the table:

"Sometimes, you know, I just get very frightened by it all."

As he performs during this tour, Jagger no longer seems to be the wild man of abandon. His act is more studied, there is less frenzy in Jagger, and in his audience, because he is much more cautious now. In the past he would risk coming to the very edge of the stage, to entice the kids into reaching for him, on occasion, someone would reach up and seize his ankle, and Jagger would have to shake himself loose to keep from being pulled into the audience. Now he performs as if there are invisible marks on the stage, mental guides that tell him how close to the audience he can get, to provoke them with his pointing toes and then twist out of reach; and Jagger never misjudges. His dancing, which had always been so wild and frantic, so unstudied, has grown stiffer. His back, chest and abdomen are completely rigid, where once they had been supple. The feeling was of over-rehearsal, of a desire to maintain such total control that some of the flash and brilliance of the 1969 performances had been polished and buffed and polished again so that it's now Jagger interpreting Jagger. "Sometimes the professionalism does detract from the spontaneity," Peter Rudge says to a journalist who comments on the change in Jagger. He adds: "You always become a parody of yourself."

By the time the Stones reach Madison Square Garden in New York, the last dates of the tour, the fifty-one previous performances in a fifty-day period have turned them into such a finely-honed unit that the final performances come off almost slick. Yet, in a strange way, these performances are the best of the entire tour. After two months of solid playing the band, which had often been out of tune and apparently unable to keep together in previous tours, was now tight and randy and bitchy, a steaming beast of a band, filled with the sweat and drive of black ghetto musicians. It no longer mattered that the press had written about the ego trips, about promoters bleeding people dry, about superstars Truman Capote and Princess Lee Radziwill traveling with the Stones; it didn't matter because the Stones came through with outstanding rock. And even a somewhat subdued Jagger, who ignored shouts from the audience to do "Sympathy" and who seemed to be holding back even as he whipped the stage in "Midnight Rambler," pulled and tugged at the audience's emotion. Capote, observing the performance from an edge of the stage, later told Andy Warhol:

"He's one of the most total actors I've ever seen. He has this remarkable ability to be absolutely totally extroverted. Very few people can be entirely, absolutely, altogether extroverted. Just to pull yourself out and go—*Whammm!* He's really an extraordinary actor . . ."

"It's really good to be back," Jagger told a London recording industry acquaintance as he sat with Bianca and a few friends one night in Tramp. "One more day in France and I'd start screamin' like Yoko." The American tour had made the Stones a little less than $2 million before taxes and would help them pay some of the British tax they owed, the corporate umbrella of Rolling Stones Records would cut down their tax liability in the future and make it possible for them to bank a larger share of their earnings, and Jagger was a Londoner again. As much as he'd ever be. He had the mansion in the country, had bought a large house in Ocho Rios, Jamaica—where he had also, the gossips said, bought a half interest in a club that featured black musicians but excluded black patrons—continued to maintain his home in the South of France, and planned to travel often.

He told journalists he had returned to England because: "I don't like the people or the weather in France, and the food's greasy. They're all thieves down there, too. They've had 150 years of living off tourists. All they try to do is steal from you. Never treat you as anything other than passing tourists." Privately, there were more compelling reasons for leaving: French police had kept Jagger and the other Stones under surveillance from the moment they arrived in France. The gendarmes had forced one of the band's suppliers to become an informer and had reportedly sent *agents provocateurs* to help set up some of the Stones for an arrest. The police seemed ready to move; Keith had been cited as a material witness in a narcotics case. It felt like 1967, the year of the big drug raids, so they decided to leave. "They're going to bust Keith and accuse him of being a junkie," Jagger told friends. "We can't stay around in that kind of atmosphere anymore." Keith was permitted to leave after the Stones' lawyers and advisors assured police he would return if he were needed. It was later reported that Keith was convicted of drug possession and banned from France for two years.

Marianne kept bumping into Jagger at parties. She was shooting heroin again, and Jagger talked to her briefly, the first time they met at a party, and Marianne thought: *I'm blocked out of my mind with heroin, and I think Mick is trying to find out if I'm on it again.* Their conversation was brief. Bianca was there, and Marianne was very nervous about her and avoided looking at her. *The poor girl doesn't want to hurt me,* Marianne thought, *but I certainly don't want to make friends with her.* Jagger and Bianca left early.

They met at another party a few nights later, and Jagger was alone. He asked Marianne to leave with him. She felt he was still anxious to know whether she'd been hooked again, and she told him she'd go with him. Jagger took her to a hotel suite and began to caress her and to tell her about his trip to Bangkok the year before, about the brothels in Bangkok that offer the most varied sexual pleasures on earth.

"Did you go to them in Bangkok?" Marianne asked.

"Yeah, I sure did, and I haven't had a good fuck since then," Jagger said. "That's why I want you."

"How *dare* you treat me like a Los Angeles groupie!" Marianne shouted. "How dare you take *me* to a hotel room just to fuck me."

Jagger was persistent. And as they lay in each other's arms hours later, Marianne thought: *It's weird, because we've slipped back into a relationship. I think we'll always be connected, no matter what happens. But I have gotten over him.*

Jagger was somewhat out of public view, resting and living quietly between public appearances, as he'd always done. But his new woman wasn't content, as all the others had been, to sit around the house with him and wonder why he didn't invite friends to dinner or give sumptuous parties. Bianca became the celebrity and darling of London's hip world, appearing in the fashion magazines almost every month, the social and gossip columns, modeling Ossie Clark's creations at benefit fashion shows, her photo all over the newspapers and the glossy magazines. One of the glossiest of which whispered lasciviously:

"She wears no underwear, just tights, and her nipples are shaped like rosebuds."

Jagger reportedly told a friend he was going to call Bianca "Rose Bud" because when she got angry her eyes made her look Oriental.

She can teach Jagger a few things about publicity. Only a few months back in London and she is being hailed as a legend, a woman who is building herself into a myth, "Tomorrow's Garbo," and Bianca appears to revel in it, using the media with as much charm and grace as her husband had done years earlier by pretending to be a brutish East End lout.

Bianca arrives at a *Vogue* studio, very, very late, of course, but photographer Norman Eales doesn't mind because he is so anxious to photograph her. When the lift reaches the studio floor, where a dozen people wait so expectantly and nervously for her, out steps a chauffeur carrying a coffin-sized suitcase and a leather box full of hats. Then shoemaker Manolo, of Zapata, with two dozen pair of shoes with four-inch heels. Followed by hairdresser Ricci Burns, carrying an assortment of wigs and feathers. He is followed by Jay Johnson, one of Warhol's superstars—Andy has been after Bianca to star in one of his films, and Jagger laughs about it all and tells reporters: "When gi*rrr*ls get together there's a lot of talk, but nothing ever gets done." Finally, behind the Warhol superstar, Bianca herself, stepping out of the lift in a $250 green Tommy Nutter suit and carrying her collections of walking sticks, which have become as famous a trademark in some circles as Dietrich's legs. Bianca is a lady. The gossips may call her a super-groupie and giggle over some of the deliciously bitchy tales that have been spread about her. But she is every inch a lady.

Around the same time that Bianca is making her grand

entrance into the fashion studio, Capote is sitting in a New York restuarant with Andy Warhol, describing what he discovered about Bianca when he traveled with the Stones on their last tour.

"She has extraordinary South American chic," Capote says in his high, pre-teen voice. "There's a certain type of thing that some South American women have and if they have it, they have it more than anybody else. I think Bianca has that, although her particular quality is very theatrical. It's what I would really call 'high yellow chic.' "

"What does that mean?" Andy asks.

"It's a certain kind of chic that women who have been raised—not that they themselves are Negro, perhaps—but who've been raised in a culture that has a basic element that's Negro. And somehow they adapt things from Negro culture into Spanish culture, and it turns into something that's totally unique. And I think that's certainly true of Bianca."

And Bianca, appearing a little more confident of her place now, in London where she is being hailed as a mythical beauty, and in the Stone's hierarchy as the Head Stone's rather headstrong and independent lady, is able to confide to an interviewer:

"When I was a child I had a complex. My brother looked European with green eyes and fair skin. I was Indian-looking, I have Indian blood. The dark skin/light skin thing bothered me. But in Europe I have got over that." Several breaths later she adds: "Jade is beautiful and very light-skinned, don't you think? She looks exactly like Mick."

Bianca may not be aware that both Chrissie and Marianne were as strong as Jagger in the early years of their relationship, and then felt themselves becoming smothered by him, absorbed by him. But Bianca seems determined not to let Jagger's concept of his public persona deflect her own needs.

She knows about the groupies and says she gets jealous; but she says she knows Jagger is also jealous and she makes certain to keep his jealousy-edge cutting sharp. Jagger went off to America to record, and the rumors flew back to London that he was having an affair with Carly Simon; Jagger sang backup vocals on Carly's recording, "You're So Vain," and seemed rather hurt when Carly hinted it was written about Warren Beatty rather than Mick Jagger. Bianca was furious, friends said. She flew off to Paris, and the gossips said she was involved with a well-known French actor. Jagger flew to Paris to bring her home. And Carly Simon married James Taylor.

"Bianca told me she's not taking any shit from him," one of their dearest friends says. "If he's going to be naughty, she's going to be twice as naughty. Three times as naughty, as much as it will take to shake him up."

Bianca is, friends say, the kind of strong woman who feeds that masochistic streak in Jagger that Chrissie and Marianne believed was an elemental part of his personality. Bianca fights with him as violently as Chrissie once did, but she carries it a step further: After one explosive domestic battle, Bianca rushed to Jagger's closet and ripped all his expensive silk shirts with her teeth, an act that perhaps wounded him more than Chrissie scarring his face with her ring.

"I don't want to be a rock-and-roll wife. I don't want to be Mick's wife—I want to be myself," she tells interviewers. "If I were him I wouldn't want to be merely Bianca's husband. Perhaps the public thinks of me that way, but to my friends I am a person in my own right. Mick's achievements and his accomplishments are his. Nothing to do with me. I must achieve my own. He's a musician, and I am not. The people who surround the Stones bathe in the reflected light. I refuse to. Since I've had the baby, I feel a change in myself. I feel life is just beginning. I need to concentrate on something. Mick's just starting to notice."

Bianca made certain he'd notice. In late autumn 1972,

while he was in Jamaica with the band, working in a studio on a new album and flying into New York occasionally on business, Bianca said she was growing restless at his absence. One late morning she suddenly decided she was tired of her long hair—that luxuriantly beautiful black hair that Jagger was always telling her he loved so much. She went into her dressing room, took a pair of scissors, and quickly snipped off her hair at the base of the neck. She wasn't satisfied at the way it looked and trimmed it a bit more. It still didn't seem right. She trimmed it shorter, then burst into tears. She rushed to the phone and called her hairdresser.

"Ricci, I just chopped off all my hair!" she cried. "What shall I do?"

"Oh, my Lord, Mick will be furious," Ricci said. "Come down here, right now. Right now!"

Bianca appeared more than an hour later; she'll never leave her bedroom for any reason until she's had her bath, oiled her body, and has her makeup applied to absolute perfection. When she walked through the door of Ricci's salon on the King's Road, all the other customers were forgotten. Ricci took one look at her and dashed into the rear and summoned all the help: "Come look at what Bianca has *done* to herself." They're all in a panic for a time, Ricci stalking around Bianca, muttering that she's ruined everything.

"I can't repair that," Ricci said. "I can't do anything with that."

Bianca seemed about to cry. Several other customers, most of whom knew Bianca at least casually, tried not to laugh.

"I'll have to cut it all off, it's the only hope," Ricci said. "Everybody in London will want short hair when I'm done with you."

A long while later, just as Ricci was completing Bianca's new hair style, Charlie and Shirley Watts walked in; they had come up from the country for a day of shopping and for Shirley's appointment with Ricci. They both stared briefly at

Bianca, who looked so strange but somehow even more exotically stunning than before, and Shirley cried out:

"What's Mick going to say? He always says he likes to wake up in the morning and see your hair flowing on the pillow."

And Charley turned to whisper to a young woman who has worked with the Stones: "You know what it means when a woman cuts her hair? She wants a change."

"Poor Mick," she said. "Marianne cut her hair, and now Bianca."

Another woman said: "Mick doesn't have much worry. When Marianne cut her hair she looked like Brian. Bianca cuts her hair and she looks like Mick. He'll love it."

Weeks later Jagger cut his hair almost as short as Bianca's. And the London gossips chuckled: "It's perfect. Now they look like twins."

Jagger sits around with several friends, talking about how dreadfully Heath has mucked up England, and he kills all further conversation when he says:

"I'm thinking about entering politics, really doing it this time. I'd love to do it. But I haven't got the right wife."